TEAM PERFORMANCE ASSESSMENT
AND MEASUREMENT
Theory, Methods, and Applications

SERIES IN APPLIED PSYCHOLOGY

Edwin A. Fleishman, George Mason University
  Series Editor

Teamwork and the Bottom Line: Groups Make a Difference
Ned Rosen

Patterns of Life History: The Ecology of Human Individuality
Michael D. Mumford, Garnett Stokes, and William A. Owens

Work Motivation
Uwe E. Kleinbeck, Hans-Henning Quast, Henk Thierry, and Hartmut Häcker

Psychology in Organizations: Integrating Science and Practice
Kevin R. Murphy and Frank E. Saal

Human Error: Cause, Prediction, and Reduction
John W. Senders and Neville P. Moray

Contemporary Career Development Issues
Robert F. Morrison and Jerome Adams

*Justice in the Workplace: Approaching Fairness in Human Resource
Management*
Russell Cropanzano

*Personnel Selection and Assessment: Individual and Organization
Perspectives*
Heinz Schuker, James L. Farr, and Mike Smith

Organizational Behavior: The State of the Science
Jerald Greenberg

Police Psychology Into the 21st Century
Martin I. Kurke and Ellen M. Scrivner

*Benchmark Tasks for Job Analysis: A Guide for Functional Job
Analysis (FJA) Scales*
Sidney A. Fine and Maury Getkate

Stress and Human Performance
James E. Driskell and Eduardo Salas

Improving Training Effectiveness in Work Organizations
J. Kevin Ford, Steve W. J. Kozlowski, Kurt Kraiger, Eduardo Salas,
and Mark S. Teachout

Job Feedback: Giving, Seeking, and Using Feedback for Performance Improvement
Manual London

*Team Performance Assessment and Measurement: Theory, Methods,
and Applications*
Michael T. Brannick, Eduardo Salas, and Carolyn Prince

TEAM PERFORMANCE ASSESSMENT AND MEASUREMENT
Theory, Methods, and Applications

Edited by

Michael T. Brannick
University of South Florida

Eduardo Salas
Carolyn Prince
Naval Air Warfare Center, Training Systems Division

LEA LAWRENCE ERLBAUM ASSOCIATES, PUBLISHERS
1997 Mahwah, New Jersey   London

Lawrence Erlbaum Associates, Inc., Publishers
10 Industrial Avenue
Mahwah, New Jersey 07430

Library of Congress Cataloging-in-Publication Data

Team performance assessment and measurement : theory, research, and applications / edited by Michael T. Brannick, Eduardo Salas, Carolyn Prince.
       p.   cm. — (Series in applied psychology)
    Includes bibliographical references (p.) and index.
    ISBN 0-8058-1638-0 (cloth : alk. paper). — ISBN 0-8058-2687-4 (pbk. : alk. Paper)
    1. Work groups—Evaluation.   2. Performance. I. Brannick, Michael T. II. Salas, Eduardo. III. Prince, Carolyn. IV. Series.
    HD66.A85   1997
    658.3'125—dc21   96-46274
                                                 CIP

Books published by Lawrence Erlbaum Associates are printed on acid-free paper, and their bindings are chosen for strength and durability.

Printed in the United States of America
10 9 8 7 6 5 4 3 2 1

Contents

PART IV: APPLICATIONS

Foreword

Edwin A. Fleishman
Series Editor

There is a compelling need for innovative approaches to the solution of many pressing problems involving human relationships in today's society. Such approaches are more likely to be successful when they are based on sound research and applications. This Series in Applied Psychology offers publications that emphasize state-of-the-art research and its application to important issues of human behavior in a variety of societal settings. The objective is to bridge both academic and applied interests.

Despite the reliance of many organizations on teams to accomplish important goals, surprisingly little research has been conducted on the measurement of team process and outcome. Currently, there is a small research base available to guide us in deciding what to measure, how and when to measure it, and how the context of measurement should lead us to choose one or more measures that will be most useful.

The authors of the current volume waste little time wringing hands about such a lack of guidance; instead they set about providing it. There are several different frameworks for measurement developed within the book. One such framework was developed with military teams on ships, but has much broader applicability. Another framework is designed specifically for measuring teams during training. Such frameworks help answer questions about what to measure when considering team performance.

Several chapters illustrate the development of measures for specific teams and purposes. One such measure was designed to evaluate theater technical crews. Other such measures were designed for giving feedback to military teams that are coordinated electronically across geographically isolated simulators, or for providing team members in organizational settings with feedback by and for themselves through survey feedback. Such chapters present a rich source of examples and ideas about how to measure team process and outcome.

The beginning and ending chapters discuss unresolved issues in measurement, and comment on how the context of measurement may influence the choice of measures. Although prescriptions for team performance assessment and measurement are sprinkled throughout the book, the final chapter offers a single set of guidelines intended to help people who are faced with the challenge of devising new measures of team performance.

From a broader perspective, the book focuses on the intersection between the literature on teams and the literature on measurement. Such a focus is relatively rare, perhaps because the literature on teams tends to focus on theoretical developments and interpersonal relations, whereas the literature on measurement tends to focus on individual differences and statistics or other methodological issues. Thus, the book offers a unique contribution to applied psychology by developing the technology of measures of team process and outcome.

Measurement is central to the scientific enterprise. Many scientific breakthroughs have immediately followed the development of new measurement techniques. It is difficult to proceed either with theoretical development or with applications without good measures. Measures are central to such applied activities as team training development and evaluation, the certification of teams competencies, or the evaluation of the effects of selection of team members on team process and team outcome. Thus, this book is a foundation that can help support numerous applied activities by those concerned with team performance.

All of the authors contributing to *Team Performance Assessment and Measurement* are trained as applied psychologists. However, they come from various employment settings, including academic, consulting, and government research and development. Therefore, there is a rich diversity of perspectives evident in the chapters. Such a diversity of perspectives assures that a broad range of measurement approaches is captured in the volume. The diversity of approaches makes the volume valuable to a relatively wide audience.

The volume presents a collection of recent thoughts on measuring team performance by experts currently working with teams in such capacities as training, evaluation, and process consultation. As such, it presents, in one place, much of the current wisdom about the measurement of team performance. The volume should find a home on the bookshelves of many an applied psychologist and others interested in assessing and improving the performance of teams in a variety of settings.

Preface

This book began at a conference on team performance measurement held at the University of South Florida in October 1992. Several of us at the conference felt that a book on team performance measurement would be of interest to a broader audience, and we began looking for authors in diverse disciplines. Some of the chapters in the book follow closely material presented at the conference. Many others, however, report work that was done subsequently or was done by authors not present at the conference. The result is a book rich in diversity of approaches to measurement and contains illustrations of many different teams.

There are both theoretical and practical reasons for the current interest in teams. Psychological research interest in groups and teams has returned and is now a thriving area. Self-managed work groups and semi-autonomous work groups have become increasingly common in industry, so there is an increased interest in team functioning from a practical standpoint. The purpose of this book is to describe recent advances in the measurement of team performance, both process and outcome. Several of the chapters provide recommendations on how, when, and why to measure aspects of teams. In addition to describing what is currently known, the book also discusses what remains to be known and what needs to be done next.

The intended audience for the book is primarily those interested in research about team processes and outcomes. That is, the book is written primarily for researchers and academics. The bulk of the research reported here has applied aims, however, and this means that there is plenty of practical information in the book. For example, there is information about designing simulations, rating forms, and dimensions of team performance useful for feedback to all sorts of teams. In addition, there are examples from several types of teams in hospitals, ship combat information center teams, and theater technical crews. Therefore, the book should be useful to people who want to design measures to evaluate teams.

A volume such as this one cannot be completed without the efforts of many people. We thank the many chapter authors for their efforts and especially for working with us throughout the revision process. We also thank the editorial staff at Lawrence Erlbaum Associates, who have worked with us from the beginning to produce a better book. We are pleased to be a part of the Applied Psychology series.

—Michael T. Brannink
—Eduardo Salas
—Carolyn Prince

I OVERVIEW

1 An Overview of Team Performance Measurement

Michael T. Brannick
University of South Florida

Carolyn Prince
Naval Air Warfare Center, Training Systems Division

INTRODUCTION AND PURPOSE

Teams are a fact of life. From medicine to aviation to the policeman on the beat, from management to modern warfare to the Superbowl clash, teams carry out much of the work (and some of the recreation) in our world. Broad outcome measures of the teams' performance are generally available (e.g., the plane landed safely and on time; the team won six games, lost nine). Individual tasks within the teams may be sufficiently delineated so that individual performance may, to some extent, be evaluated (e.g., the pitcher pitched a no-hitter; the pilot gave a thorough briefing to the crew). Despite the reliance on teams for much that is accomplished in our society, there is still little known about the processes that occur within a team that help account for real differences in outcomes.

There has been considerable research interest in teams in recent years. In aviation, a recognition of the importance of the crews that are responsible for achieving a safe, efficient flight has prompted research into how they function (Wiener, Kanki, & Helmreich, 1993). Military interest in teams other than aviation teams has been responsible for a large-scale research effort in team decision making (Cannon-Bowers, Salas, & Grossman, 1991). There is also a widespread recognition that much of the work accomplished in business and industry is the result of teams (Sundstrom, De Meuse, & Futrell, 1990). As a result, a wide variety of teams have been studied and various approaches to team measurements have been applied.

Definitions

The distinction between groups and teams is often unclear, although the terms *group* and *team* have been used to describe rather different entities. *Group* has been used in a much broader sense than *team* and has been applied to a larger number of social and organizational forms (Hackman, 1990). Group dynamics research, for example, has focused on therapy groups, T-groups, and self-study groups, where the task of each member was to achieve personal goals. Hackman (1990) stated that group is a rather generic label and needs to be differentiated from *work groups* that can be defined by certain criteria. These criteria include differentiated roles and tasks to be performed. We define a team to be two or more people with different tasks who work together adaptively to achieve specified and shared goals. The central feature of teamwork is coordination. Coordination means that there is some kind of adjustment that one or more of the team members makes so that the goal is reached. Teams' functional requirements always include simultaneity, sequencing, or both. Simultaneity means that team members must do something at the same time, such as play different notes in an orchestra. Sequencing means that the output of one team member's task or tasks is the input to another team member's task or tasks, such as a tank commander telling the gunner what kind of shell to load.

Groups often have members whose functions are interchangeable, such as a group whose task is to solve anagrams. Teams generally have distinct functions, such as the surgeon and anesthesiologist in the operating room. However, some teams divide up tasks to suit themselves, and may change the distribution of tasks. For example, in an aircrew, usually only one person will talk on the radio to air traffic control. The person designated to do this may change during flight, however.

Teams usually have a history and a future. Groups are usually brought together for a specific purpose and disbanded when the task is achieved. However, this is not a hard and fast rule, because some teams form briefly for a specific task (e.g., aircrews may form for a single flight), and some groups may last for long periods (e.g., a steering committee for a professional organization). Most of the teams described in this book complete tasks (or task simulations) that serve some function for a host organization rather than tasks designed primarily for psychological inquiry in the laboratory.

Different models of team performance have generally agreed that teams must be considered on three different levels of analysis: individual, team, and organizational. They tend to categorize team functioning as consisting of input considerations (e.g., type of task, equipment, training), throughput (e.g., team processes), and output or team product. Goodman,

Ravlin, and Argote (1986) reviewed the work that had been done on these models and concluded that there was still much to be learned, particularly about the interrelationships among variables. Measurement is the first step in this inquiry. Each chapter presented in this book describes the development and use of a measurement instrument for a particular kind of team or provides a theoretical perspective that suggests specific measures to be developed.

THE ROLE OF MEASUREMENT

Data and Theory

Measurement is central to the evaluation and elaboration of theories. For example, theories of team functioning such as those proposed by Hackman (1983); Gladstein (1984); Nieva, Fleishman, and Reick (1978); and Salas, Dickinson, Converse, and Tannenbaum (1992) cannot be tested without measuring aspects of teams.

Some measurement efforts focus primarily on global team outcomes. An early example was the measurement of bombing accuracy in World War II (e.g., Thorndike, 1949). Some measures focus more on the process of teamwork, that is, on the moment-to-moment behaviors of individuals in teams that must work together — in other words, coordination. Studies focusing on communication content and frequency are examples (e.g., Foushee, 1984; Siegel & Federman, 1973; Williges, Johnston, & Briggs, 1966).

It is often the case that the distinction between process and outcome is not highly emphasized by particular researchers. Researchers tend to measure what seems to be useful to the purpose at hand at the time of the study (see Cannon-Bowers, Tannenbaum, Salas, & Volpe, 1995). Consequently, there are a large number of behaviors grouped into different labels across studies, and it is difficult to define and label a specific set of constructs that should be measured whenever team performance is of interest.

Uses of Measures

There is generally some time and expense involved in measuring performance. One can think of measurement as an investment in which one purchases information to inform a decision or some kind of action. Common decisions and actions can be thought of as forming several classes, including certification, development, and selection.

Although certification is usually in the province of individuals rather than teams, there is increasing emphasis on certifying entire teams, especially where safety is concerned. Nuclear power plants are moving toward certifying operation/control teams in emergency procedures, for example. Airlines are also moving toward certifying pilots in teamwork skills in cooperation with the FAA. The primary approach to certification has been to simulate emergencies in simulators and to evaluate team proficiency. Despite the appeal of observing team behaviors in realistic situations, there are difficulties in such an approach. These difficulties include reliability of measures (both of judges and team performance), time and expense, and the unit of analysis (e.g., if team performance is poor, is it attributable to one or more members?).

Team training is the focus of much basic and applied research in both military and civilian sectors. The major uses of measures of team performance in training are problem diagnosis and skill development. In problem diagnosis, team members or outside experts help pinpoint areas of difficulty in team functioning. In the civilian sector, various team building and other organizational development efforts have been explored for some time. Surveys are one of the most commonly used methods to give feedback on team functioning to both team leaders and members.

For skill development, the cornerstone of productivity and process improvement is feedback. Feedback for teams probably requires both individual-level and team-level feedback for optimal results. However, little empirical research has addressed how to measure performance for team training. Little can be prescribed based on what is currently known about what should be measured, when it should be measured, how it should be measured, and how feedback should be given to team members.

Measures of teamwork could prove useful in selecting team members. From the early days of team research, a common finding is that more cohesive teams seem to perform better than less cohesive teams and that more cohesive teams are more likely to want to continue working together. In addition to the social and emotional aspects of teamwork, part of coordination concerns processes such as monitoring and feedback. Some members may be more willing to correct errors or admit ignorance than others (e.g., Brannick, Prince, Prince, & Salas, 1993). It may be possible to select such appropriately assertive members for teams or perhaps to train them (e.g., Smith, Salas, & Brannick, 1994).

Considerations Related to How to Measure Teamwork

Several considerations seem relevant in deciding how to measure aspects of teams and team functioning. Important considerations include:

- The purpose of measurement.
- The choice of stimuli or assessment situations.
- The attribute(s) and behavior(s) to be measured.
- How to quantify the response(s).
- The time of measurement.
- The expense of measurement.

Purpose.   Perhaps the foremost issue in team performance assessment is that of purpose of measurement. Purposes just described included certification; problem diagnosis; feedback for training; and selection and training evaluation. This last measure is practical for determining the usefulness of various interventions to improve teamwork. Measurement is also valuable for research, for example, to be able to study naturally occurring differences in teams. Purpose is a critical concern. If a measure fails to fulfill the given purpose(s), it will not be useful. It is not immediately obvious that measures collected for one purpose will necessarily serve another. A measurement instrument to provide feedback to team members may not be adequate for providing an evaluation of training value of an intervention. Whether the measure serves its purpose amounts to a consideration of validity as described by Cronbach (1990).

Once the purpose of measurement has been established, the remaining issues must be addressed. However, they are somewhat interdependent, so a particular choice on any one issue may affect choices on the other issues. The remaining issues are thus presented in an order that can be considered arbitrary.

Attributes and Behaviors.   The choice of attributes and behaviors can be thought of as two sides of the same coin. Selecting specific attributes to measure is often one of the most difficult choices to make in measuring teamwork. If team process is the issue, there are many possible attributes to measure. Such attributes can be considered to be behavioral skills (e.g., assertiveness) or to be functions (e.g., monitoring and feedback; task allocation). On the other hand, if a global outcome is of interest, what should be measured is performance relative to a goal set for team success, that is, the reason for the team's existence in the first place

Attributes may help determine what behaviors to examine. For example, if we want to measure assertiveness, we could look for team members correcting others' mistakes. On the other hand, examining behaviors may lead to organizing schemes that are essentially attributes. For example, aircrews decide who will do what task before flying, and they sometimes change tasks during flight. Such behaviors could be organized into a task allocation dimension.

Stimuli.   The choice of stimuli or assessment situation (and the specific events to be embedded in that situation) will have an impact on what behaviors are elicited and thus what attributes are measured. The stimuli in team research used for measurement can range from the actual task situation to questions used to probe team members' recall of team events. The stimuli for team performance measures are often embedded within fairly realistic task simulations, such as flight simulators or nuclear power control room simulators. Just as in test construction, the selection of the measurement stimuli must include considerations of the adequacy of content and concerns of reliability (e.g., do team members have sufficient opportunity to exhibit the behaviors or attributes of interest?).

Quantification.   After the stimuli have been chosen to elicit behaviors relevant to the attributes of interest, actual behaviors have to be examined, and some system for quantifying the behaviors has to be put in place. Quantification includes a range of options such as having observers document performance as it occurs, or as captured on tape, or by having team members complete paper-and-pencil questionnaires about their own performance. In the case of paper-and-pencil measures, the quantification process is usually straightforward. In the case of direct observation, however, judges are generally required. The judges either take notes or complete checklists that are quantified, or else the judges will render directly numerical estimates of attributes. There is a great deal of leeway in providing structure to judges in observing and evaluating behavior in simulations. Measurement instruments can range from relatively specific and objective (e.g., did the pilots contact the tower before takeoff?) to relatively global and subjective (e.g., were the pilots appropriately assertive during the flight?).

Time.   There is some evidence that teams evolve over time (Morgan, Glickman, Woodard, Blaiwes, & Salas, 1986), and that the length of time that they have worked together can have a significant effect on group processes (Foushee, Lauber, Baetge, & Acomb, 1986). If there is an interest in examining the team processes in a particular kind of team, there should be some consideration of how generalizable the results will be to more or less "mature" teams. Not only do teams apparently evolve, but team members are also likely to change. There is evidence that the way novices and experts prioritize available information and utilize it is different. One would expect, then, that at least for a time, both individual members and the team itself are changing. This means that measurements taken at one time in the team's life may not be representative of how they work together at another point.

Expense. The measures can vary in expense. Simple simulations involving work aids or microcomputers can be relatively inexpensive to develop and use. On the other hand, computer-controlled large-scale simulators such as full motion flight simulators and nuclear power control room simulators that simulate emergencies are extremely expensive. Any simulation that requires an expert judge tends to be expensive. Paper-and-pencil measures tend to be less expensive once they have been developed and refined. There may be a tradeoff between the psychometric adequacy of measurement and expense due to the organizational reality of limited resources.

CHALLENGES IN TEAM MEASUREMENT

The chapters in this book paint a fairly complete picture of the state-of-the-art in team performance measurement. However, there are several issues that remain unresolved, even though they are addressed in some of the chapters.

The Unit of Analysis

The first issue is the so-called unit of analysis problem. All of the chapters in this book concern teams. Therefore, the team is logically the focus or unit of analysis for all of the authors. On the other hand, teams do not actually do anything; people do. It seems clear that team research must go beyond the competence of individual members to do their assigned tasks. Thus, task allocation (the assignment of who does what) and changes in task allocation during the task (such as pilots switching who actually flies the aircraft) are clearly elements of team performance beyond individual performance. However, it is not always clear when some activity or behavior belongs properly to the team rather than the individual. Such a distinction is important not only for theoretical reasons, but for practice as well. If we are to design training programs for both individuals and teams, we have to know what contents belong in the individual training, and what contents belong in the team training.

Process Versus Outcome

A second issue concerns outcome versus process in team performance assessment. Teams are valued in large part for their outcomes — whether the team won the basketball tournament, whether the army won the battle, and so forth. However, outcome measures often contain variance attributable to factors other than teamwork. If we look at the distribution of times to complete a sailboat race, for example, part of the variance will be due to the team operating the boat, but part will be due to characteristics of the boat itself. Team process measures may give us a truer picture of team functioning than do outcome measures. Unlike outcome measures, team process measures may shed light on problems encountered by the team and the means to fix them. Our position is that a comprehensive measure of team performance needs to contain elements of both process and outcome.

Process measures of teamwork may focus on more interpersonal, stylistic elements or more task-oriented elements of process. Note that the two factors are highly interdependent. For example, suppose one team member notices that another member has made a mistake that will have important consequences for the team. In a task-oriented scheme, the focus would likely be on how long the mistake went unnoticed, what member provided corrective information, and what use that member originally made of the corrective information in what time period, and so on. A more interpersonal scheme would focus on how the corrective information was given and accepted. The interpersonal part of the process can be thought of as providing the grease that keeps the parts of the team working together smoothly. On the other hand, difficulties in individual member performances can act like sand in creating friction within a team, thus interfering with interpersonal harmony.

The Organization of Teamwork and the Naming of Constructs

A final issue concerns the constructs that form the basis of teamwork. There have been many different measures of team process and outcome over the years. There is as yet no agreed upon set of dimensions, factors, skills, or activities that can explain differences in team functioning. Morgan et al. (1986) suggested that the important team processes could be categorized as communication, cooperation, team spirit, giving suggestions, acceptance of suggestions, coordination, and adaptability. Prince and Salas (1989) identified seven dimensions of team process for aircrews that included communication, leadership, decision making, adaptability, assertiveness, situation awareness, and mission analysis (planning). Helmreich and Foushee (1993) suggested four major group processes, communication and decision behavior, team building, workload management and situation awareness and operational integrity. Most recently, Cannon-Bowers et al. (1995) developed a taxonomy of skills based on constructs such as adaptability, shared situational awareness, and performance monitoring and feedback. There are clear similarities in the proposed process categories, but differences need to be resolved. Experience with team process measurement clearly will contribute to this resolution.

OVERVIEW OF THE BOOK

The book is partitioned into five sections: Overview, Theoretical Developments, Methodological Developments and Issues, Applications, and Reflections. The first section, Overview, is of course, this chapter.

Theoretical Developments

This section contains four different theoretical approaches to team performance measurement. Chapters 2 and 3 have foundations primarily in industrial and organizational psychology. Chapter 2 develops a general model of team performance and links it to measurement. Chapter 3 develops a more specific model focused on team training. Chapter 4 provides a view from cognitive psychology, and chapter 5 provides a view from a human factors standpoint.

In chapter 2, Dickinson and McIntyre develop a model of effective team functioning and explicitly link observed (measured) variables to the model. The model indicates that teamwork requires members who have (a) positive attitudes toward the team, (b) rewards based on team goals, and (c) knowledge of their own tasks and those of other members with whom they interact. Such requirements allow team members to coordinate their activities by monitoring their own performance and that of other members, communicating with other members, and providing feedback and backup assistance when needed.

In chapter 3, Cannon-Bowers and Salas provide an overview of team performance and training. They then develop a framework for conceptualizing team performance measures and show how the framework can guide the development of particular measures. Their position is that measures should include both the individual and team unit of analysis, capture process as well as outcome, describe and diagnose performance, and help to provide knowledge of results to the team for developmental feedback. They explicitly link measurement procedures to process and outcome measures for both individuals and teams.

In the fourth chapter, "Conceptual Development and Empirical Evaluation of Measures of Shared Mental Models as Indicators of Team Effectiveness," Kraiger and Wenzel first describe the notion of the shared mental model. The shared mental model appears to have come from cognitive psychology, and is invoked to account for the kinds of interaction often observed in successful teams. They do not propose to measure shared mental models directly, but rather articulate a theoretical position that embeds shared mental models in a nomological net. The net includes inputs such as environmental, organizational, team, and individual variables, and outputs including team performance and effectiveness. They discuss measurement in terms of processing information, structuring knowledge, common attitudes, and shared expectations. For each domain, they propose specific measurement methods.

In the fifth chapter, Bowers, Braun, and Morgan outline a viewpoint from human factors psychology. They note that one of the most widely studied areas in human capability has been concerned with operator workload. They review the literature on individual workload and task performance, noting that the relationship between workload and individual performance is characterized by a curvilinear function. They describe work in teams as falling into two broad classes: *taskwork* and *teamwork*. Taskwork implies an interaction with tasks, tools, machines, and systems. Teamwork refers to interpersonal interaction that are necessary to accomplish team goals, such as exchanging information and coordinating actions. They propose that team workload consists of demands associated with teamwork. They go on to describe factors that influence team workload, such as coordination, communication, and experience. They then present efforts to measure team workload through several measures derived from surveys of team members.

Methodological Developments and Issues

Each of the five chapters in this section outlines an approach to measuring team performance. The approach differs considerably across the chapters. One of the chapters describes a measure that is intended to provide feedback to a very large number of diverse teams. Two describe techniques designed to give team members functioning in advanced simulators feedback about their performance in scenarios. One describes the development of measures of team decision making in a laboratory context, and one is devoted to team task types and aggregation issues.

The chapters in this section are similar in that they all illustrate ways of devising measurement tools. They differ from one another in numerous ways, including types of teams, the purpose of measurement, the choice of stimuli or assessment situations, the attributes and behaviors to be measured, the quantification of responses, and the time and expense of measurement. Together, they present a very rich set of illustrations that should prove useful both as a template for other applications and as a source of stimulation for future research.

In chapter 6, Hollenbeck et al. summarize results from several studies on team decision making. The authors present a creative method of quantifying what information teams have and how the teams use the information in reaching decisions. Because the simulations used are subject to laboratory control, the authors can not only provide quantitative descriptions of team decision making, but can also compare the teams' actual use of information to the optimal use in a given decision.

In chapter 7, Dwyer et al. describe a general method that can be applied to virtually any behavioral observation task. The basic approach is to determine through task analysis precisely what should be done during the task, and to create a checklist that is used by observers to record the team's behavior. They describe the technique in some detail and present an application in a distributed simulator. They conclude with the strengths and limitations of the technique.

In chapter 8, Hallam and Campbell describe the development of the Team Development Survey (TDS). Unlike most of the measures in the book, the TDS is based on measures from the team members themselves. As it is typically used, team leaders and others who are knowledgeable about the team also complete the survey. The survey measures 18 different constructs, including mission clarity, team coordination, team unity, and material resources. The chapter describes the development of the survey, its psychometric characteristics, and ongoing validation work.

In chapter 9, Mathieu and Day present a rather different survey for assessing team processes. The major thrust concerns generalizability theory and its use to analyze measures of processes both within and between teams. They are able to show where teams in a nuclear power plant differ from one another on measures of such constructs as centralization, formalization, information exchange, and decision making.

In chapter 10, Tesluk, Zaccaro, Marks, and Mathieu discuss two main problems. The first is the type of team task. They discuss tasks that can be described in four different ways: pooled interdependence, sequential interdependence, reciprocal independence, and intensive. These cover the spectrum for team coordination requirements from low to high, that is, pooled interdependent teams need the least coordination and intensive teams need the most. They then develop measurement strategies tailored to the types of teams. The second problem is that of aggregation in data analysis. The aggregation problem occurs when data from team members are aggregated (e.g., averaged) to stand for the team as a whole. They note that four criteria must be met for aggregated scores to be meaningful. The criteria are (a) a theoretical rationale, (b) proper construction of the stimulus (e.g., "My team feels. . ." instead of "I feel. . ."), (c) adequate psychometric characteristics (reliability), and (d) empirical demonstration of within-group agreement. Many of the points in the chapter are illustrated with examples taken from a hospital setting.

Applications

The four chapters in this section provide lessons in developing team performance measures from diverse teams. Each of the chapters shows the development of one or more measures for one or more purposes. Taken together, the chapters show that creating good measures of team performance is difficult but not impossible. This section provides advice to researchers attempting to create their own measures.

In chapter 11, Komaki describes the development of a measure of effectiveness of theater teams. As much as any chapter in the book, this one develops logical criteria for devising a measure of team effectiveness. More specifically, Komaki argues that a good measure of a team's effectiveness should focus on behavior that is complex (both product and process; multiple constituencies), reliably observed, and under the control of the team. She illustrates her points with an actual form used to evaluate theater technical crews.

In chapter 12, Toquam, Macaulay, Westra, Fujita, and Murphy discuss several measures used in the training of nuclear power plant operating teams in Japan. The crews were observed in several different simulations. Toquam et al. were able to show predictable differences in teams, not only in terms of mean functioning across problems, but also differences in variability across problems. The chapter concludes with practical advice on how to measure team performance.

In chapter 13, Prince, Prince, Brannick, and Salas describe several studies of aircrews in simulators. They describe the development of several different types of rating technologies, including checklists, rating guides, and associated training strategies. The chapter includes a series of suggestions in developing team performance measures. The suggestions concern (a) rating techniques, (b) stimulus design, (c) sources of information, (d) constructs to measure, and (e) team training and feedback. A sixth category is reserved for special problems in reliability and validity, such as designing equivalent scenarios, problems with lack of opportunity for observing behaviors and so forth.

In chapter 14, Johnston, Smith-Jentsch, and Cannon-Bowers describe measurement tools for enhancing team decision making. They describe four event-based exercises in combat information centers in Navy ships. Each of the five combat information center team members has specific duties that must be coordinated with other members for effective performance. The performance measures include team and individual outcome measures. The authors show examples of each type of measure and discuss the role of the measures in feedback and team skill development.

Reflections

The final chapter by Baker and Salas serves two purposes. The first purpose is to provide a summary evaluation of the progress in team performance assessment provided in the earlier chapters of this book. The second purpose is to update a set of principles established for measuring teamwork published by Baker and Salas (1992).

REFERENCES

Baker, D. P., & Salas, E. (1992). Principles for measuring teamwork skills. *Human Factors, 34*, 469–475.

Brannick, M. T., Prince, A., Prince, C., & Salas, E. (1993). *Impact of raters and events on team performance measurement.* Paper presented at the eighth annual conference of the Society for Industrial and Organizational Psychology, San Francisco.

Cannon-Bowers, J., Salas, E., & Grossman, J. (1991). *Improving tactical decision making under stress: Research directions and applied implications.* Paper presented at the International Applied Military Psychology Symposium, Stockholm, Sweden.

Cannon-Bowers, J. A., Tannenbaum, S. I., Salas, E., & Volpe, C. E. (1995). Defining team competencies and establishing team training requirements. In R. Guzzo & E. Salas (Eds.), *Team effectiveness and decision making in organizations* (pp. 333–380). San Francisco, CA: Jossey-Bass.

Cronbach, L. J. (1990). *Essentials of psychological testing* (5th ed.). New York: Harper & Row.

Foushee, H. C. (1984) Dyads and triads at 35,000 feet: Factors affecting group process and aircrew performance. *American Psychologist, 39*, 885–893.

Foushee, H., Lauber, J., Baetge, M., & Acomb, D. (1986). *Crew factors in flight operations: III. The operational significance of exposure to short-haul air transport operations* (NASA Technical Memorandum 88322). Sunnyvale CA: National Aeronautics and Space Administration-Ames Research Center.

Gladstein, D. L. (1984). Groups in context: A model of task group effectiveness. *Administrative Science Quarterly, 29*, 499–517.

Goodman, P. S., Ravlin, E. C., & Argote, L. (1986). Current thinking about groups: Setting the stage for new ideas. *Designing effective work groups.* San Francisco: Jossey-Bass.

Hackman, J. R. (1983). *A normative model of work team effectiveness* (Tech. Rep. No. 2). New Haven, CT: Yale University.

Hackman, J. R. (Ed.). (1990). *Groups that work (and those that don't) Creating conditions for effective teamwork.* San Francisco: Jossey-Bass.

Helmreich, R. L., & Foushee, H. C. (1993). Why crew resource management? Empirical and theoretical bases of human factors training in aviation. In E. L. Wiener, B. G. Kanki, & R. L. Helmreich (Eds.), *Cockpit resource management* (pp. 1–45). San Diego, CA: Academic Press.

Morgan, B. B., Glickman, A. S., Woodard, E. A. Blaiwes, A. S., & Salas, E. (1986). *Measurement of team behaviors in a Navy environment* (Tech. Rep. No TR-86-014). Orlando, FL: Naval Training Systems Center.

Nieva, V. F., Fleishman, E. A., & Reick, A. (1978). *Team dimensions: Their identity, their measurement, and their relationships* (Final Tech. Rep. ARI Contract DAHC 19-78 C-001). Washington, DC: Advanced Research Resources Organization.

Prince, C., & Salas, E. (1989). Aircrew performance: coordination and skill development. In D. E. Daniel, E. Salas, & D. M. Kotick (Eds.), *Independent research and independent exploratory development (IR/IED) programs: Annual report for fiscal year 1988* (NTSC Tech. Rep. No. 89-009; pp. 45–48). Orlando, FL: Naval Training Systems Center.

Salas, E., Dickinson, T. L., Converse, S. A., & Tannenbaum, S. I. (1992). Toward an understanding of team performance and training. In R. W. Swezey & E. Salas (Eds.), *Teams: Their training and performance* (pp. 3–29). Norwood, NJ: Ablex.

Siegel, A. I., & Federman, P. J. (1973). Communications content training as an ingredient in effective team performance. *Ergonomics, 16,* 403–416.

Smith, K. A., Salas, E., & Brannick, M. T. (1994, April). Leadership style as a predictor of teamwork behavior. In K. J. Nilan (Chair) *Understanding teams and the nature of teamwork.* Symposium presented at the ninth annual conference of the Society for Industrial and Organizational Psychology, Nashville.

Sundstrom, E., De Meuse, K. P., & Futrell, D. (1990). Work teams: Applications and effectiveness. *American Psychologist, 45,* 120–133.

Thorndike, R. L. (1949). *Personnel selection: Test and measurement techniques.* New York: Wiley.

Wiener, E. L., Kanki, B. G., & Helmreich, R. L. (Eds.). (1993). *Cockpit resource management.* San Diego, CA: Academic Press.

Williges, R. C., Johnston, W. A., & Briggs, G. E. (1966). Role of verbal communication in teamwork. *Journal of Applied Psychology, 50,* 473–478.

II THEORETICAL DEVELOPMENTS

2 A Conceptual Framework for Teamwork Measurement

Terry L. Dickinson
Robert M. McIntyre
Old Dominion University

Successful performance often involves interaction among several individuals who must work as a team. A critical feature of teams is that individuals must coordinate their decisions and activities by sharing information and resources to attain shared goals. Clearly, efforts to improve team performance must focus attention on the performance of individuals. However, individuals are dependent on other team members to provide information and for coordination of activities. Those behaviors of members that engender a sharing of information and a coordination of activities are collectively called teamwork.

A conceptual framework is presented for developing teamwork measures that can be used to ensure effective individual and team performance. As shown in Fig. 2.1, the framework requires that measures be tied to a theory or model of teamwork. An exemplary model is described to illustrate how a model shapes the development of teamwork measures. Examples of teamwork measures are also included to illustrate the construction of teamwork measures.

The framework emphasizes the importance of measurement principles to ensure scientific rigor. Various facets of reliability are considered and their appropriateness is discussed for assessing teamwork measures. Validation issues are also described for developing a base of inferences for interpreting teamwork measures.

Finally, because reliability and validity do not guarantee that the measures will be implemented effectively, the conceptual framework recognizes the person requirements for teamwork measurement. A group (or team) of individuals is ultimately required to observe and rate teamwork.

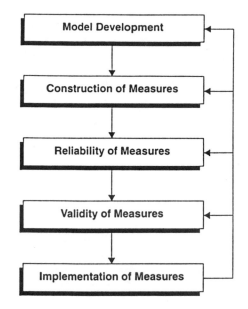

FIG. 2.1.   A framework for developing teamwork measures.

These individuals must be motivated and have the skills necessary to use the measures effectively.

TEAMWORK MODEL

Over the past several decades, much research has been devoted to the investigation of team training and performance (see reviews by Denson, 1981; Dyer, 1984; Nieva, Fleishman, & Rieck, 1978; Salas, Dickinson, Converse, & Tannenbaum, 1992). Despite the abundance of team research, few efforts have been devoted to investigating the components (i.e., attributes) of teamwork, and in particular, to developing measures of those components. With few exceptions, the research has studied the influence of task, individual, and team characteristics on team performance (Salas et al., 1992). Although these "input" variables are important determinants of team performance and must be considered in a comprehensive theory of teams, teamwork components and their measures are needed to explain the mechanisms by which the "input" variables determine team performance.

Based on recent research efforts and previous reviews, we and several colleagues reviewed the teamwork literature (Dickinson et al., 1992). In the review, we identify and define seven core components of teamwork. These components and their relationships are depicted in Fig. 2.2.

INPUT   THROUGHPUT   OUTPUT

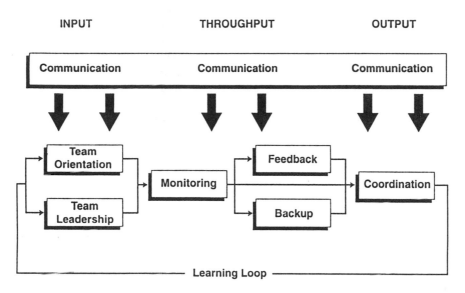

FIG. 2.2. Teamwork model.

Communication is a major component of teamwork processes (Denson, 1981; Dyer, 1984; Glanzer, Glaser, & Klaus, 1956; Nieva et al., 1978; McIntyre et al., 1990; McIntyre, Salas, Morgan, & Glickman, 1989; Morgan, Glickman, Woodard, Blaiwes, & Salas, 1986). Communication involves the active exchange of information between two or more members of the team, as well as an individual team member providing information to others in the appropriate manner. In general, communication is a mechanism that links the other components of teamwork. For example, communication is the important link between monitoring other members' performance and providing feedback about that performance (McIntyre et al., 1989).

A second critical component of teamwork is team orientation. This includes the nature of the attitudes that team members have toward one another, the team task, and their team leadership (Glanzer et al., 1956; Larson & LaFasto, 1989; McIntyre et al., 1990; Morgan et al., 1986; Nieva et al., 1978). It also includes self-awareness as a team member (Dyer, 1984; McIntyre et al., 1989), and group cohesiveness (Nieva et al., 1978).

Team leadership is another critical component of teamwork. This includes the direction and structure provided by formal leaders as well as by other members (Glanzer et al., 1956; Larson & LaFasto, 1989). Team leadership implies that planning and organizing activities have enabled members to respond as a function of the behaviors of others.

Monitoring team performance is a crucial component of teamwork

(Cooper, Shiflett, Korotkin, & Fleishman, 1984; McIntyre et al., 1989, 1990). This component refers to the observation and awareness of activities and performance of other team members. Monitoring implies that team members are competent in their individual tasks and have a substantive understanding of the tasks of other members. Therefore, before a group of individuals can function effectively as a team, the members must have the technical knowledge and skills to perform their own tasks (Cooper et al., 1984; Glanzer et al., 1956; Larson & LaFasto, 1989).

Feedback is a fifth critical component of teamwork (McIntyre et al., 1990; Morgan et al., 1986; Nieva et al., 1978). Teams must adapt and learn from their performance to be successful. This requires the giving, seeking, and receiving of feedback among team members.

Another critical component of teamwork is backup behavior. This component involves actually helping other team members to perform their tasks (McIntyre et al., 1989, 1990; Morgan et al., 1986). Backup behavior implies a degree of task interchangeability among members (Glanzer et al., 1956) and willingness to provide and seek assistance (Denson, 1981; Dyer, 1984; Nieva et al., 1978).

The final component of teamwork is coordination (Denson, 1981; Dyer, 1984; Morgan et al., 1986). Coordination reflects the execution of team activities such that members respond as a function of the behavior of others. Successful coordination implies the effective operation of other components of teamwork (e.g., communication, monitoring, and backup). In this way, the actions of individual members are merged to produce synchronized team performance.

In summary, teamwork requires team members who have positive attitudes toward the team and its task, have been provided adequate direction and support for accomplishing team goals, and know their own tasks and those of other members with whom they interact. These require-ments allow team members to coordinate their activities by monitoring the performance of other members, communicating with them, and providing feedback and backup assistance when needed. As a result, team leaders and members focus their attention and concern on improving *teamwork* rather than on individual success and performance.

CONSTRUCTION OF MEASURES

There are several approaches to the construction of psychological measures (cf. Hase & Goldberg, 1967). The approach we advocate has several assumptions. First, whenever possible, the construction of measures should be based on a theoretical model of the psychological attributes of interest. We determined in our literature review that there was sufficient research and theory to justify the use of a model to guide the construction of measures. In fact, a strong case could be made that the seven teamwork components are generic to all team tasks. Nonetheless, measures often must be developed to delineate the components for a specific team task. This is particularly true for training applications in which team members must learn and be evaluated on the nuances of teamwork. For example, backup behaviors are important because they allow the team to function smoothly, even when some members become overloaded with their individual tasks. However, the specific activities that reflect backup behavior vary with the team task, and they may differ for each team member performing a particular task. Therefore, a measure of backup behavior must have sufficient detail to identify and evaluate the activities of each member that appropriately contribute to this aspect of teamwork.

Second, teamwork measures must be behaviorally oriented in content. Teamwork is seen as behavioral activity by members that serves to explain the influence of organizational, task, individual, and team characteristics on team performance (Salas et al., 1992). That is, teamwork components and their measures focus on what team members do to attain various levels of performance.

An Example: Measures for Anti-Air Warfare Teams

In our recent work (Dickinson et al., 1992), we adapted the critical incidents methodology (Flanagan, 1954) to construct teamwork measures for anti-air warfare (AAW) teams. These are teams that operate in the combat information center of a Navy ship. They are responsible for the protection of the team's own ship as well as other ships that are part of the ship's battlegroup.

The job analysis method of critical incidents (Flanagan, 1954) has gained wide acceptance for developing behaviorally oriented measures. In fact, several investigators have used this methodology to develop measures of teamwork and team performance (Cooper et al., 1984; Glanzer et al., 1956; Larson & LaFasto, 1989; Morgan et al., 1986). Our teamwork measures were developed through an iterative process incorporating both the team-work model and data. Four major stages of development are distinguished to highlight the process.

Stage 1: Critical Incident Workshops

In the first stage, the critical incident method (Flanagan, 1954) is employed to obtain descriptions of occurrences of teamwork from individuals who are experts about the focal teams. A workshop format is employed to collect data. At the beginning of the workshop, the participants are provided with definitions of the seven components of teamwork (e.g., Fig. 2.3). Next, the participants generate effective and ineffective critical incidents of teamwork for each component and each of the team member positions. Several examples of effective and ineffective incidents are described for the participants to clarify the nature of incidents and the task of generating critical incidents.

After an incident is generated, it is analyzed to produce task-oriented, behavioral statements. To accomplish this, the participants are asked to rephrase each of their critical incidents to include the following information: (a) who were the pivotal members involved in the incident; (b) what were the circumstances surrounding the incident (i.e., the background of the incident or situation), what behaviors were involved, and what were the consequences; and (c) how were the behaviors effective (or ineffective), and how did the behaviors positively (or negatively) influence teamwork.

Stage 2: Clarification of Behavioral Statements

In Stage 2, the statements are edited and revised for clarity through a series of workshops involving the investigators and small groups of subject matter experts. In our workshops, this editing process led to the development of detailed decision rules to serve as a rationale for identifying behaviors associated with a particular teamwork component (e.g., Fig. 2.4). The decision rules also identified similarities and distinctions among the teamwork components. We have found that these decision rules can be valuable training aids for individuals who are to observe and measure teamwork (McIntyre, 1995; McIntyre & Dickinson, 1992).

Stage 3: Statement Matching

In this stage, the revised behavioral statements are matched (or retranslated) by experts to the teamwork components (Smith & Kendall, 1963). That is, each statement is judged as to the teamwork component that it illustrates. The decision rules are employed in making these judgments. We have found that statements are typically matched to the component they were originally generated to represent. For example, the preponderance of the AAW statements (86%) were correctly assigned to their component by all experts (Dickinson et al., 1992).

Stage 4: Construction of the Teamwork Measures

In the final stage, teamwork measures are constructed. The behavioral statements, matched successfully to their original teamwork component, provide the content for the measures (see Fig. 2.3 for example statements).

COMPONENTS OF TEAMWORK

TEAM ORIENTATION: refers to the attitudes that team members have toward one another and the team task. It reflects acceptance of team norms, level of group cohesiveness, and importance of team membership.

- assigns high priority to team goals.
- willingly participates in all relevant aspects of the team.

TEAM LEADERSHIP: involves providing direction, structure, and support for other team members. It does not necessarily refer to a single individual with formal authority over others. Team leadership can be shown by several team members.

- explains to other team members exactly what is needed from them during an assignment.
- listens to the concerns of other team members.

COMMUNICATION: involves the exchange of information between two or more team members in the prescribed manner and by using proper terminology. Often the purpose of communication is to clarify or acknowledge the receipt of information.

- verifies information prior to making a report.
- acknowledges and repeats messages to ensure understanding.

MONITORING: refers to observing the activities and performance of other team members. It implies that team members are individually competent and that they may subsequently provide feedback and backup behavior.

- is aware of other team members' performance.
- recognizes when a team member performs correctly.

FEEDBACK: involves the giving, seeking, and receiving of information among team members. Giving feedback refers to providing information regarding other members' performance. Seeking feedback refers to requesting input or guidance regarding performance. Receiving feedback refers to accepting positive and negative information regarding performance.

- responds to other members' requests for performance information.
- accepts time-saving suggestions offered by other team members.

BACKUP BEHAVIOR: involves assisting the performance of other team members. This implies that members have an understanding of other members' tasks. It also implies that team members are willing and able to provide and seek assistance when needed.

- fills in for another member who is unable to perform a task.
- helps another member correct a mistake.

COORDINATION: refers to team members executing their activities in a timely and integrated manner. It implies that the performance of some team members influences the performance of other team members. This may involve an exchange of information that subsequently influences another member's performance.

- passes performance-relevant data to other members in an efficient manner.
- facilitates the performance of other members' jobs.

FIG. 2.3. Definitions and example statements for teamwork components.

BACKUP BEHAVIOR

DEFINITION: involves assisting the performance of other team members. This implies that members have an understanding of other members' tasks. It also implies that members are willing and able to provide assistance and willing to seek assistance when needed.

KEY WORDS: assists, helps, seeks, steps in, takes (e.g., takes over, takes control).

DECISION RULES: Backup behavior is present when a team member is unable to perform duties and another member performs the actions necessary to ensure that the duties are completed. The member may be unable to perform duties because that member is overburdened, incapable, or simply made a mistake.

In order for a member to provide backup, certain things must take place. First, the member must be capable of doing the backup. This means that the member must have the necessary skills and resources (e.g., time) to perform a backup function. Next, the member either had to have monitored the other member's performance prior to providing backup or the other member had to seek assistance.

Backup behavior may involve a physical act or it may be in the form of a verbal statement or decision. Backup can be distinguished from feedback in that backup completes an activity or solves a problem. In contrast, feedback to a member requires or encourages that member to perform another action. For example, the behavior, "The Identification supervisor informs the Air Tracker of blinking symbology on the video without corresponding codes for that symbology." This is feedback, because the Air Tracker must now put codes for the symbology on the video.

FIG. 2.4.   Decision rules for the backup behavior component of teamwork.

We recommend three separate formats for constructing teamwork measures: behavioral observation scale, behavioral summary scale, and behavioral event.

The behavioral observation and behavioral summary scale formats are numerical scales for measuring teamwork, whereas the behavioral event format is a checklist for showing the occurrence of critical events requiring teamwork. The behavioral scale formats generalize beyond the critical incidents, have desirable measurement properties, and have high user acceptability (Borman, 1979; Dickinson, Hassett, & Tannenbaum, 1986; Landy & Farr, 1983; Latham & Wexley, 1981). The behavioral event format is appropriate for structured research or training environments, and relies on an analysis of these environments to determine critical events.

Behavioral Observation Scales.   These scales can be used to rate the occurrence of teamwork by a particular team and its members. Each scale corresponds to one component of teamwork (e.g., Fig. 2.5). A scale contains the definition for a teamwork component and a series of behavioral items reflecting that component. Each item is rated according to its frequency of occurrence on a 5-point scale ranging from 1, (*almost never*) to 5 (*almost always.*). Space is provided at the bottom of each scale to allow comments to summarize the reasoning behind the ratings.

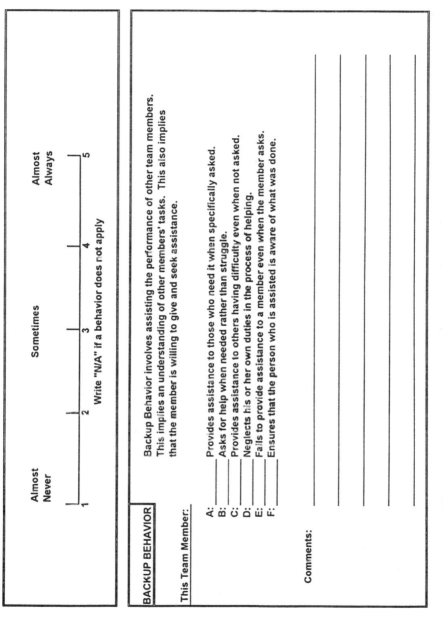

Almost
Never

Sometimes

Almost
Always

1   2   3   4   5

Write "N/A" if a behavior does not apply

BACKUP BEHAVIOR

Backup Behavior involves assisting the performance of other team members. This implies an understanding of other members' tasks. This also implies that the member is willing to give and seek assistance.

This Team Member:

A: _____ Provides assistance to those who need it when specifically asked.
B: _____ Asks for help when needed rather than struggle.
C: _____ Provides assistance to others having difficulty even when not asked.
D: _____ Neglects his or her own duties in the process of helping.
E: _____ Fails to provide assistance to a member even when the member asks.
F: _____ Ensures that the person who is assisted is aware of what was done.

Comments:

FIG. 2.5.   Behavioral observation scale for backup behavior component of teamwork.

27

The behavioral observation scales are constructed from a consideration of the behavioral statements generated from the critical incident work-shops. The items on these scales are generalizations of the behavioral statements. In particular, the items do not refer to interactions between specific team members. It is recognized that teamwork can occur between any of two or more members of the team. In addition, the items show a less specific detail of teamwork behavior compared to the behavioral state-ments. In this way, team members can be evaluated without limitation to a specific instance (i.e., critical incident) of teamwork. For example, the item, "Team members go over procedures with other members after an assign-ment, explaining each step and identifying mistakes," was generalized from statements such as "During slower periods of AAW activity, the tactical action officer informs the electronic weapons specialists of aspects of their performance that could be improved."

Behavioral Summary Scales.   These scales can also be used to rate the degree of teamwork displayed by a particular team and its members. However, the scales do not contain multiple items. They require the observer to rate each component of teamwork only once (e.g., Fig. 2.6). The team's level of skill on each component is rated according to a 5-point scale ranging from 1 (*hardly any skill*) in this component of teamwork to 5 (*complete skill*) in this component of teamwork. It should be noted that the high (5), medium (3), and low (1) points on the scale also are anchored by very broad behavioral statements (i.e., summaries) to help illustrate and define the scale. Space is provided at the bottom of each component scale to allow comments to describe the reasoning behind a rating.

Behavioral Event Format.   This format is designed according to the occurrence of critical events that are opportunities for teamwork. These critical events and the appropriate teamwork behaviors required from each of the team members can be identified by subject matter experts who participate in event analysis workshops similar to the workshops employed to generate the behavioral statements. In an event analysis workshop, the experts identify the critical events in a scenario, describe the teamwork behaviors required by each event, and match these events to the teamwork components. We have found that the behavioral statements obtained from the matching workshop (in Stage 3) are useful illustrative material and an aid to experts for describing the teamwork behaviors associated with the critical events, and for matching the events to the components (McIntyre & Dickinson, 1992).

Clearly, the behavioral event format is specific to the scenario because the critical events and the instances (or lack) of teamwork determine the contents of the format. As this format can provide an abundance of

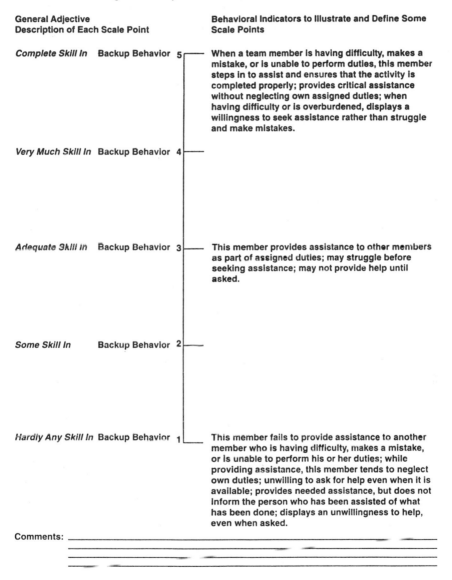

Definition: Backup Behavior involves assisting the performance of other team members. This implies an understanding of other members' tasks. It also implies that the member is willing and able to provide and seek assistance.

General Adjective Description of Each Scale Point

Behavioral Indicators to Illustrate and Define Some Scale Points

Complete Skill In Backup Behavior 5 — When a team member is having difficulty, makes a mistake, or is unable to perform duties, this member steps in to assist and ensures that the activity is completed properly; provides critical assistance without neglecting own assigned duties; when having difficulty or is overburdened, displays a willingness to seek assistance rather than struggle and make mistakes.

Very Much Skill In Backup Behavior 4 —

Adequate Skill In Backup Behavior 3 — This member provides assistance to other members as part of assigned duties; may struggle before seeking assistance; may not provide help until asked.

Some Skill In Backup Behavior 2 —

Hardly Any Skill In Backup Behavior 1 — This member fails to provide assistance to another member who is having difficulty, makes a mistake, or is unable to perform his or her duties; while providing assistance, this member tends to neglect own duties; unwilling to ask for help even when it is available; provides needed assistance, but does not inform the person who has been assisted of what has been done; displays an unwillingness to help, even when asked.

Comments: _____

FIG. 2.6. Behavioral summary scale for backup behavior component of teamwork.

valuable data on its own, it can also be used to collect data for completing behavioral observation or summary scales. That is, the behavioral event format can be used to note and record behaviors that occur during a scenario, and this information can subsequently be used to complete the behavioral observation or summary scales. We have found this two-step process of observation followed by evaluation to be particularly useful (McIntyre, 1995).

As an example behavioral event format, consider a training scenario in which a Navy cruiser has been assigned to escort ships in the Northern Persian Gulf at a time of increasing tensions with Iran. During the scenario, several Iranian F-4 fighter jets make an overflight run at the cruiser and its escorted ships. The AAW team on the cruiser must be alert to the hostile intentions of the F-4 fighter jets and ensure the safety of the cruiser and the escorted ships. Three critical events that could take place for this scenario and a behavioral event format for them are contained in Fig. 2.7.

The first critical event involves the distribution by the tactical action officer (TAO) of a report from the ship's signal exploration space (SESS) and reactions by the tactical information coordinator (TIC) and electronic weapons specialist (EWS). During this critical event, observers would check whether the expected and appropriate teamwork behaviors have occurred, such as the entering of a non-real-time (NRT) radar track. For each critical event in the scenario, there are expected behaviors. However, there are also other teamwork behaviors that may be inappropriate or that may occur subsequently to a critical event but before the occurrence of the next critical event. The observer would record these additional behaviors on the behavioral event format and indicate their teamwork component.

Criteria for comparing the three formats are described in Table 2.1. The goals of team development and evaluation have been broadly defined for comparing the formats. The measures can be employed to provide feedback to teams for developing teamwork skills. Of course, the formats differ in the specificity of the feedback. The behavioral event format is geared to the

TABLE 2.1
Three Formats for Teamwork Measures and Criteria for their Comparison

		Criteria		
Formats	*Goals*	*Ease of Use*	*Training Time*	*Specificity*
BOS	Development Evaluation	Moderate	Moderate	Moderate
BSS	Development Evaluation	High	Moderate	Low
BEF	Development	Low	High	High

Note. BOS = Behavioral observation scales; BSS = Behavioral summary scales; BEF = Behavioral event format.

EVENT 1: SESS reports two sections of aircraft to be probable F-4s. They departed Shiraz heading to the Persian Gulf to provide routine targeting of maritime shipping.

Check if Observed:

    _____ Tactical action officer disseminates the SESS report internally over the command net.
    _____ Tactical information coordinator advises the identification supervisor to enter NRT track.
    _____ Electronic weapons supervisor reports the threat weapon configuration to the tactical action officer.

Teamwork Component
(TO,LD,CM,MO,FB,BU,CO)

LD
FB
CM

Abbreviations: TO = Team orientation, LD = Team leadership, CM = Communication, MO = Monitoring, FB = Feedback, BU = Backup behavior, CO = Coordination

Record Observations:

Indicate Component
(TO,LD,CM,MO,FB,BU,CO)

_____ _____
_____ _____
_____ _____
_____ _____
_____ _____

FIG. 2.7. Behavioral event format for training scenario.

31

specific behaviors that occur in a structured environment. Observers look for particular and appropriate teamwork behaviors and, therefore, it is more likely that this format will be successful for use in developing teamwork skills. However, the behavioral observation and summary formats can also be used for development. For this goal, both require that observations be recorded for feedback to the team to aid development. A strength of these formats is their ability to obtain numerical scores that summarize skills with respect to the teamwork components. Such scores provide the quantitative information necessary to evaluate teamwork with respect to team selection and training as well as the environmental conditions (e.g., high stress) in which teams must perform.

The three formats differ in their ease of use. The behavioral event format requires focused attention on the details of team performance to identify specific instances of teamwork. This requires extensive training time to ensure that observers are fully familiar with critical events, instances of poor teamwork, and ways of recording observations. In contrast, the behavioral observation and summary scales can be used in less structured environments. For use in these environments, less training time is necessary in that observers must only understand the teamwork components and the nature of the items and anchors contained in the scales. Furthermore, in comparison to the behavioral observation scales, the behavioral summary scales are easier to use. The behavioral observation scales require observers to make multiple ratings for each teamwork component, whereas the behavioral summary scales require a single rating for each component.

All of the formats are behaviorally based and emphasize observation. The behavioral event format should be completed as teams are being observed, while the behavioral summary scales, and to some extent the behavioral observation scales, can be completed after observation of the team. The greater the time lapse from observation to completion of the behavioral observation and summary scales, the greater the risk of memory distortions in the ratings. The potential for these distortions emphasizes the need for training in how to make accurate observations. In this regard, a format similar to the behavioral event format should be considered as an accompaniment to the behavioral scales and be employed for recording observations. Of course, for structured situations the behavioral event format itself serves this purpose.

RELIABILITY OF MEASURES

The foundations of psychological measurement theory were established long ago by Charles Spearman and others. During the 1930s and 1940s, the early efforts flowered into many principles of modern measurement theory

(DuBois, 1970). These principles are important in that adherence to them has repeatedly resulted in the development of measures that are useful in understanding psychological attributes.

The fundamental quality of measurement is reliability. A reliable measure orders objects with respect to a common attribute in a consistent manner from one instance of measurement to another. Another useful way of thinking about reliability is a measure's freedom from measurement error. To the extent that a measure is free from measurement error, it is reliable. Because there are several sources of measurement error (e.g., time period of measurement, raters, measure content), there are multiple ways that a measure can be unreliable. Indeed, reliability indexes reflect a measure's freedom from one or more sources of measurement error.

The basic assumption in the use of stability-over-time indexes of reliability is that the attribute being assessed is a stationary characteristic from one time period of measurement to another. Consequently, if objects can be ordered similarly from one time period of measurement to another, there is reliability in measurement in the sense that the measure is free from the time source of measurement error. In situations where a particular attribute is dynamic and cannot be considered inherently stationary over time, other indexes of reliability must be considered.

If a measure depends on the subjective evaluations of raters, interrater measurement error is likely to be a primary source of unreliability. Indexes of interrater reliability reflect consistency between two or more raters who evaluate objects with respect to the same attribute. If the attribute is dynamic, then raters must evaluate the objects during the same time period to obtain an indication of reliability. If the attribute is considered stationary over time periods, then consistency between raters who evaluated the objects at different time periods is a reflection of freedom from rater and time sources of measurement errors.

Internal consistency reliability indexes reflect a measure's freedom from content sampling error. Put another way, they reflect consistency between two or more indicators of the attribute in ordering objects during the same time period. The indicators can be the items of a measure, whose scores are usually summed to define the score of each object with respect to the attribute. If the indicators order the objects similarly, their collective score is considered a reliable measure. However, some indicators may be poor reflections of the attribute, and correlations among the indicators should always be checked for improvements to reliability.

The indexes of reliability differ in their utility for evaluating teamwork measures. Consider the assumption of stability in the teamwork components. In many work environments, people are constantly transferring, retiring, or quitting jobs such that turnover of team members is typical. Furthermore, the work itself may be constantly changing, which requires learning new methods of operation. In such work environments, many team members are always in training and development, and the components of teamwork cannot typically be considered stationary except over short durations of time. Reliability indexes that reflect stability appear to have limited utility for reflecting the reliability of teamwork measures. On the other hand, interrater reliability indexes are usually relevant for evaluating the reliability of teamwork measures. Our three examples of teamwork measures require observers and raters of teamwork behaviors. Whenever a measure depends on subjective evaluations, freedom from rater measurement error must be shown.

VALIDITY OF MEASURES

Validity refers to the inferences that can be made about an attribute from its measures. Both content and construct validity are important. Content validity involves an inference about the adequacy of the procedures used to develop a measure. If the domain of stimuli and responses that define the attribute is judged by experts to be reflected adequately in the measure, the inference of content validity is warranted for that measure. For example, a measure of a teamwork component for AAW teams must be developed from a consideration of the domain of threat situations that could be faced by a team, as well as the responses that could possibly be made by a team. In this way the measure can reflect a teamwork component in any situation with consideration of the actual (or lack of) teamwork displayed by team members. In sum, content validity is an inference that the measure can be used to obtain attribute scores for all relevant situations.

Scientific procedures are available for obtaining adequate coverage of a content domain (e.g., Christal, 1974; Fine & Wiley, 1971; Flanagan, 1954; McCormick, 1976). Collectively, these procedures are called job analysis methods, and they have been evaluated with respect to several criteria that are important for developing teamwork measures (Levine, 1983; Levine, Ash, & Bennett, 1980; Levine, Ash, Hall, & Sistrunk, 1983). First, any method should describe accurately and reliably the important behaviors involved in team performance. This information should encompass all of the various team member positions, as well as a variety of situations, and should include a description of what is done, how it is done, and why it is done. Regarding the general approach to job analysis, a task-oriented method is appropriate for developing measures to have content validity (Lawshe, 1975; Prien, 1977). Such an approach would identify and describe the specific activities or behaviors comprising each of the teamwork components. For example, a behavior within the communication component might be "acknowledges and repeats a message to ensure that the message is understood." Other criteria for a job analysis method include costs of the job analysis instruments, number of informants needed, and amount of time involved in data collection.

Construct validity requires the testing and development of theory with empirical research that uses one or more measures of an attribute. Every attribute has theory associated with it. The theory may range from a rudimentary assertion that the attribute (i.e., construct) is correlated with another attribute, to assertions that the attribute has causal relations with several other attributes. The complexity of the theory is only important in that more complex theories lead to more hypotheses that could be tested with empirical research. The important issue for construct validity is that hypotheses must be tested with empirical research. When a theory is tested in a study that focuses on an attribute, the theory is either confirmed or modified by the results. In either case, the results indicate the inferences that can be made about the attribute based on those measures used in the research.

Construct validity places no restrictions on the amount and kind of empirical research. Indeed, confidence in construct validity grows with the volume and variety of the research that supports the inferences that can be made about the attribute. With respect to teamwork measures, several examples serve to illustrate the variety of issues that could be investigated for construct validity. First, because teamwork is an important determinant of team performance, a component of teamwork should discriminate between better and poorer performing teams. Several teams could be classified by their performance using the opinions of experts (e.g., supervisors, training instructors), and then, team scores on the component could be obtained and compared for differences. The research results should show that teams classified as better performing teams have greater mean scores than poorer performing teams. If these results do not occur, then doubt is cast on the construct validity of the component. Of course, this lack of evidence for construct validity was obtained with a particular measure, and so, the research also suggests that the measure may be a poor indication of the teamwork component. However, if mean differences between greater and lesser effective teams do not occur using several reasonable measures of that component, serious doubt is cast as to the meaningfulness of the component.

Another example builds on the notion that an attribute should have several methods of measurement in order to separate the biases of the method from the substance of the attribute. Consider three methods of obtaining scores for a teamwork component: observer, self-, and supervisor ratings. Hopefully, these methods of measuring would agree in their ordering of teams with respect to the component. If observer and supervisor ratings ordered the teams similarly but self-ratings showed no agreement with them, doubt is cast about whether the self-rating method is appropriate for measuring the teamwork component. For this result, the construct validity of the component would be limited to observer and supervisor ratings. If the three methods showed no agreement among themselves, serious doubt would be cast as to the meaningfulness of the component. Additional research would be needed to find out which (if any) method was appropriate for measuring the teamwork component.

A final example stems from a developmental model of teamwork (Morgan, Salas, & Glickman, 1994), which suggests that the components of teamwork change in their importance over time as the team gains in task proficiency. An hypothesis could be tested that procedural communications are important to master early in training to establish the protocol for teamwork, whereas other components of teamwork, such as backup behaviors, become more important later in training. A field study might be done to evaluate the hypothesis. For example, observers could record the feedback provided to team members during team training. If the results showed that training instructors spent a high percentage of their time during the first week of training informing team members about the proper ways to exchange and receive information, this would lend support to the hypothesis. During subsequent weeks of training, the results should also show a decline in feedback on procedural communications and an increase in feedback concerning other aspects of teamwork.

IMPLEMENTATION OF MEASURES

Although teamwork measures may possess reliability and validity, this does not guarantee that the measures will be used to improve teamwork and team performance. There are several issues that must be addressed in the implementation of teamwork measures.

Acceptability of Measures

Those individuals who use the measures must perceive them to be acceptable (cf. Dickinson, 1993). For training instructors, acceptance requires that the measures are seen as helping and not detracting from the training process. For example, measures that have multiple indicators or that must be completed repeatedly during training could be perceived as impractical for use during team training. Instructors must also perceive the components and their measures to be aids for training teams. The components' names and definitions as well as behavioral examples to illustrate these components should be a reification of the team task. Esoteric names and examples do not provide a nomenclature that instructors can use in guiding the development of team members.

Acceptance of the measures by team members implies additional perceptions. Because team members may be held accountable for their performance, the measures should be perceived by members as providing a fair and accurate assessment of teamwork. Otherwise, members will interfere with the application of the measures or discount results that suggest areas of needed improvement. In some work environments, fairness and accuracy perceptions are critical. For example, Navy gunnery crews are evaluated periodically in operational settings to determine their effectiveness. Each crew is required to undergo a series of simulated firing exercises intended to improve their performance as a team. Feedback is provided to the team by the training instructors upon completion of each exercise. If the feedback provided with the measures is perceived as unfair or inaccurate, the information is likely to be discounted. The team may fail to recognize the need for changes in behavior and may make only superficial changes to beat the system. This approach to training feedback could have dire consequences for performance in actual combat situations.

Acceptance of teamwork measures is enhanced when the measures are based on relevant performance and contain items referring to observable behaviors. Such measures can be described as having high face validity in that what they purport to measure is obvious. Therefore, the use of a content validation strategy in which subject matter experts (e.g., training instructors) generate specific behavioral examples of teamwork components should result in measures with high acceptability. Acceptance should also be enhanced to the extent that the measures are believed by the users to discriminate accurately between effective and ineffective teams.

Teams to Measure Teams

For many teams, a single person cannot collect information on all the instances of teamwork. An instance of teamwork occurs as the result of interactions between two or more members of the team. In the AAW environment, a single observer could be assigned to no more than two team members, because of physical proximity and frequency of interaction. Other observers are needed to measure teamwork interactions for the remaining members. For many teams, it surely takes a group or team of observers to obtain the necessary information to measure all instances of teamwork.

A special form of data collection involves the team itself. Self-reports of teamwork could be obtained with behavioral observation or summary scales. Because team members are always located in the proximity of teamwork, they can provide descriptions of member interactions. Although this mode of data collection is convenient, it has several limitations. Team members probably can only provide retrospective reports of teamwork. A requirement of simultaneous position performance and data collection does not seem feasible for most teams. Thus, self-reports may not describe the temporal nature of teamwork. Another limitation is the developmental maturity of the team (Morgan et al., 1994). In the early stages of team development, many team members may be occupied in learning the taskwork of their positions. Self-reports by these members can provide invalid or biased information about teamwork.

Aggregation Issues

Another issue in the implementation of measures is the aggregation of teamwork information (cf. Roberts, Hulin, & Rousseau, 1978). The teamwork displayed by a particular member as a result of interactions with other team members can be summarized readily. For example, ratings with the behavioral summary scales and observations with the behavioral event format can readily describe a member's amount and quality of backup behavior. However, how is the information about all members aggregated to describe the backup behavior for the team as a whole?

In one sense, the aggregation of observation data is not a problem. A focus solely on the interactions between two or more team members only requires that the teamwork components be described for these members. Clearly, such information is quite useful for identifying problems and improving the teamwork of those members involved in the focal interactions. In the sense, however, that teamwork influences more distal and global measures such as the accuracy and success of the team, the issue of aggregation is important. For example, those AAW teams that display more teamwork would be expected to identify targets with greater speed and accuracy, shoot down more enemy targets, make fewer errors in firing on friendly and neutral targets, and in general, ensure the survival of their ship. To understand the impact that teamwork has on such global measures of team performance, a measure of teamwork must also be available at the global level.

There are two obvious ways to aggregate teamwork information to obtain global measures. First, the data collected by observers of a team can be summed or averaged to reflect the components of teamwork. The ratings obtained with the behavioral observation or summary scales are readily amenable to this manner of aggregation. However, there are several concerns that must be addressed with such "summary" variables. The assignment of observers to team members surely influences the nature of the teamwork information collected. Some observers may be assigned to watch two or more members, whereas other observers may be assigned to individual team members. In this case, the teamwork information collected on individual team members is weighted more heavily in the summing or averaging of all data. Of course, this differential weighing may be appropriate if it can be justified theoretically by the nature of the team and the work required of the team.

The accuracy and reliability of the observers are also concerns in using "summary" variables. Observers who are more accurate and reliable in rating teamwork should have their information weighted most heavily. Unfortunately, observers cannot be distinguished easily in terms of the accuracy and reliability of their ratings. Training may be a better solution to deal with observer differences in accuracy and reliability. If observers are highly trained initially and recalibrated frequently with refresher training (e.g., Hedge, Dickinson, & Bierstedt, 1988), their differences can be reduced to eliminate the need to weight ratings.

The second way to aggregate teamwork information is to capitalize on the fact that a group of observers has to provide this information. The observers can be brought together for a group meeting to pool information and decide on ratings to describe the team as a whole. Indeed, when multiple observers are required for gathering teamwork information, a group decision-making meeting is logically necessary to attain an integrated view of teamwork. A procedure for the meeting might include (a) sharing of observations, (b) generating and posting initial ratings for a teamwork component, (c) discussion of ratings, and (d) repeating the second and third steps until a consensus-like rule is reached for a component rating (e.g., identical ratings by 80% of observers). This procedure would be employed for each of the teamwork components.

Group decision-making meetings have been shown to produce ratings with reliability and accuracy greater than that obtained simply by averaging or summing individual ratings (Dalkey & Brown, 1971; Larreche & Moinpour, 1983; Van de Ven & Delbecq, 1971). A side benefit of the group meeting is that observers themselves must operate as a team, and this should lead to greater acceptance of the measures by the observers (Quade, 1970; Tannenbaum & Dickinson, 1987). Indeed, team training for observers who must participate in group decision-making meetings has been shown to increase the level of teamwork and subsequently to improve rating accuracy (Baker, 1989). We have found the use of group meetings in our own work to be highly effective and frequently mentioned by observers as the most important aspect of the teamwork measurement process (McIntyre, 1995; McIntyre & Dickinson, 1992).

The aggregation of self-report data has special concerns considered in research on organizations (James, 1982; James, Demaree, & Wolf, 1984; Roberts et al., 1978; Rousseau, 1985). Both conceptual and empirical justifications must be made for aggregation. When a variable's data are collected at a lower level (e.g., team members), a conceptual argument must be made that the variable represents higher level phenomena (e.g., teams) to justify aggregation. For the teamwork components, conceptual arguments have not been developed per se, but research and literature reviews consistently suggest that the components distinguish between effective and ineffective teams. Nonetheless, a sophisticated theory of teamwork will need detailed conceptual justifications for aggregation of its variables. This theory will need to distinguish components that are perceptual in nature (e.g., team orientation) and clearly apply to the entire team, from those that reflect specific behavioral activities (e.g., feedback and backup) and may apply only to a subset of team members.

The empirical justification for aggregation involves the use of analysis of variance to show that the higher level phenomena account for significant variation in lower level data (James, 1982). That is, the analysis should show that teams differ, on average, in members' self-reports of teamwork. Another empirical requirement is interrater reliability (James et al., 1984). Entities within each instance of the higher level phenomena should agree regarding their self-reports. Thus, members of each team should agree highly in their ratings of the team components.

CONCLUSIONS

A framework for developing measures of teamwork has been described. The framework relies on a model of seven components to specify the processes that shape teamwork and lead to effective team performance. Example measures reflect that teamwork occurs when there are no problems with communication, orientation, and leadership and when team members are individually competent and understand the relationships of their activities to those of other members. The measures also reflect that team members utilize the processes of monitoring, communication, feedback, and backup to enable the team to perform in an integrated and timely manner.

The framework emphasizes that the development of measures is never finished. The link between measures and theory implies construct validation involving concepts as well as the measures themselves. The appropriateness of theory and the inferences that can be made about measure scores must be continually assessed and expanded. Nonetheless, this does not suggest that measure development must be an academic effort that continues without end and has no practical benefits.

The measures described herein can readily be implemented for the development and evaluation of teams, especially teams in the AAW environment. The measures are behaviorally oriented and have content validity. They were developed using procedures that are highly acceptable to the eventual users of measures. Nonetheless, attention must be paid to the manner of implementation. Regardless of whether the measures are to be used for team development, evaluation or research, observer and rater training are crucial to ensure understanding of the measures and of the procedures for collecting and summarizing teamwork information.

REFERENCES

Baker, T. A. (1989). *The effects of training strategies on assessor behavior and the accuracy of assessment center consensus ratings.* Unpublished doctoral dissertation, Old Dominion University, Norfolk, VA.

Borman, W. C. (1979). Format and training effects on rating accuracy and rating errors. *Journal of Applied Psychology, 64,* 410–421.

Christal, R. E. (1974). *The United States Air Force occupational research project* (AFHRL-TR-73-75). Lackland AFB, TX: Occupational Research Division.

Cooper, M., Shiflett, S., Korotkin, A. L., & Fleishman, E. A. (1984). *Command and control teams: Techniques for assessing team performance* (final report). Wright-Patterson AFB, OH: Logistics and Human Factors Division.

Dalkey, N., & Brown, B. (1971). *Comparison of group judgment techniques with short- range predictions and almanac questions* (R-678-ARPA). Santa Monica, CA: The RAND Corporation.

Denson, R. W. (1981). *Team training: Literature review and annotated bibliography* (AFHRL-TR-80-40, AD-A099). Wright-Patterson AFB, OH: Logistics and Technical Training Division.

Dickinson, T. L. (1993). Attitudes about performance appraisal. In J. L. Farr, M. Smith, & H. Schuler (Eds.), *Issues in selection research* (pp. 141–161). San Francisco: Jossey-Bass.

Dickinson, T. L., Hassett, C. E., & Tannenbaum, S. I. (1986). *Work performance ratings: A meta-analysis of multitrait-multimethod studies* (AFHRL-TP-86-32, AD-A174 759). Brooks AFB, TX: Training Systems Division, Air Force Human Resources Laboratory.

Dickinson, T. L., McIntyre, R. M., Ruggeberg, B. J., Yanushefski, A. M., Hamill, L. S., & Vick, A. L. (1992). *A conceptual framework for developing team process measures of decision-making performance* (final report). Orlando, FL: Naval Training Systems Center.

DuBois, P. H. (1970). *A history of psychological testing.* Boston: Allyn & Bacon.

Dyer, J. C. (1984). Team research and team training: A state-of-the-art review. In F. A. Muckler (Ed.), *Human factors review* (pp. 285–323). Santa Monica, CA: Human Factors Society.

Fine, S. A., & Wiley, W. W. (1971). *An introduction to functional job analysis, methods for manpower analysis* (Monograph No. 4). Kalamazoo, MI: W. E. Upjohn Institute.

Flanagan, J. C. (1954). The critical incident technique. *Psychological Bulletin, 51,* 327–355.

Glanzer, M., Glaser, R., & Klaus, D. J. (1956). *The team performance record: An aid for team analysis and team training* (AD-123 615). Washington, DC: Office of Naval Research, Psychological Science Division.

Hase, H. D., & Goldberg, L. R. (1967). Comparative validity of different strategies of constructing personality inventories. *Psychological Bulletin, 67,* 231–248.

Hedge, J. W., Dickinson, T. L., & Bierstedt, S. A. (1988). *The use of videotape technology to train administrators of walk-through performance testing* (AFHRL-TP-87-71, AD-A195 944). Brooks AFB, TX: Air Force Human Resources Laboratory.

James, L. R. (1982). Aggregation bias in estimates of perceptual agreement. *Journal of Applied Psychology, 67,* 219–229.

James, L. R., Demaree, R. G., & Wolf, G. (1984). Estimating within-group interrater reliability with and without response bias. *Journal of Applied Psychology, 69,* 85–98.

Landy, F. J., & Farr, J. L. (1983). *The measurement of work performance: Method, theory, and applications.* New York: Academic Press.

Larreche, J., & Moinpour, R. (1983). Managerial judgment in marketing: The concept of expertise. *Journal of Marketing Research, 20,* 110–121.

Larson, C. E., & LaFasto, F. M. J. (1989). *Teamwork: What must go right/What can go wrong.* Newbury Park, CA: Sage.

Latham, G. P., & Wexley, K. N. (1981). *Increasing productivity through performance appraisal.* Reading, MA: Addison-Wesley.

Lawshe, C. H. (1975). A quantitative approach to content validity. *Personnel Psychology, 28,* 563–575.

Levine, E. L. (1983). *Everything you always wanted to know about job analysis.* Tampa, FL: Mariner.

Levine, E. L., Ash, R. L., & Bennett, N. (1980). Exploratory comparative study of four job analysis methods. *Journal of Applied Psychology, 65,* 524–535.

Levine, E. L., Ash, R. A., Hall, H., & Sistrunk, F. (1983). Evaluation of job analysis methods by experienced job analysts. *Personnel Psychology, 24,* 519–533.

McCormick, E. J. (1976). Job and task analysis. In M. D. Dunnette (Ed.), *Handbook of industrial and organizational psychology* (pp. 651–696). Chicago: Rand McNally.

McIntyre, R. M. (1995). Teamwork assessment: Some practical considerations. In T. J. L'Heureux (Chair), *Assessing performance in team-based organizations: Advances in research and practice.* Symposium conducted at the annual meeting of the Society for Industrial and Organizational Psychology, Orlando, FL.

McIntyre, R. M., & Dickinson, T. L. (1992). *Systematic assessment of teamwork processes in tactical environments* (final report). Orlando, FL: Naval Training Systems Center.

McIntyre, R. M., Glickman, A. S., Ruggeberg, B. J., Yanushefski, A. M., Llewellyn, J. C., & Salas, E. (1990). *Measures of teamwork effectiveness* (Tech. Rep.). Orlando, FL: Naval Training Systems Center.

McIntyre, R. M., Salas, E., Morgan, B., & Glickman, A. (1989). *Team research in the 80's: Lessons learned* (Tech. Rep.). Orlando, FL: Naval Training Systems Center.

Morgan, B. B., Jr., Glickman, A. S., Woodard, E. A., Blaiwes, A. S., & Salas E. (1986). *Measurement of team behaviors in a Navy environment* (Tech. Rep.). Orlando, FL: Naval Training Systems Center.

Morgan, B. B., Jr., Salas, E., & Glickman, A. S. (1994). An analysis of team evolution and maturation. *The Journal of General Psychology, 120,* 277–291.

Nieva, V. F., Fleishman, E. A., & Rieck, A. (1978). *Team dimensions: Their identity, their measurement and their relationships* (DAHC19-78-C-0001). Washington, DC: Response Analysis Corporation, Advanced Research Resources Organization.

Prien, E. P. (1977). The function of job analysis in content validation. *Personnel Psychology, 30,* 167–175.

Quade, E. S. (1970). *Cost-effectiveness: Some trends in analysis* (P-3529-1). Santa Monica, CA: The RAND Corporation.

Roberts, K. H., Hulin, C. L., & Rousseau, D. M. (1978). *Developing an interdisciplinary science of organizations.* San Francisco: Jossey-Bass.

Rousseau, D. M. (1985). Issues of level in organizational research: Multi-level and cross-level perspectives. *Research in Organizational Behavior, 77,* 1–37.

Salas, E., Dickinson, T. L., Converse, S. A., & Tannenbaum, S. I. (1992). Toward an understanding of team performance and training. In R. W. Swezey & E. Salas (Eds.), *Teams: Their training and performance* (pp. 3–29). Norwood, NJ: Ablex.

Smith, P. C., & Kendall, L. M. (1963). Retranslation of expectations: An approach to the construction of unambiguous anchors for rating scales. *Journal of Applied Psychology, 47,* 149–155.

Tannenbaum, S. I., & Dickinson, T. L. (1987, August). *Estimating SDy: The effectiveness of Delphi and critical incident methodologies.* Paper presented at the annual meeting of the American Psychological Association, New York.

Van de Ven, A., & Delbecq, A. L. (1971). Nominal versus interacting group processes for committee decision-making effectiveness. *Academy of Management Journal, 14,* 203–212.

3 A Framework for Developing Team Performance Measures in Training

Janis A. Cannon-Bowers
Eduardo Salas
Naval Air Warfare Center
Training Systems Division
Orlando, FL

Clearly, the importance of teams in the modern workplace has been firmly established in this volume and elsewhere (e.g., Guzzo & Salas, 1995; Hackman, 1990). Moreover, it is not difficult to understand why the topic of team performance measurement has been gaining interest in recent years. Without accurate, reliable measures of team performance, it is difficult to select or train team members or to manage team performance. Unfortunately, little research exists that provides theoretically based guidance to those interested in assessing team performance. This may be because the challenge of measuring team performance is a formidable one—it presents a complex problem that requires a complex solution. Moreover, because performance measurement information can serve several purposes (e.g., selection, performance appraisal, training), it is likely that multiple approaches to team performance measurement are required. In fact, it has been asserted that the purpose for which measurement data will be used should determine what measurement are made and how measurement data are gathered (Cannon-Bowers et al., 1989).

We focus here on a discussion of team performance measures that are geared specifically toward use in training. We selected this focus because it is one that has been largely overlooked in past writing, yet has significant implications for both team performance measurement and training. Therefore, the purpose of this chapter is to specify the nature of team performance measures that are particularly useful in conducting the type of assessment required in training. First, we review briefly the literature in team performance and training to set the stage for subsequent discussion. Next, we explain why we believe that performance measures employed during training should be considered a special case of the more general class of performance measures, describing those characteristics. Following this, we present a framework for conceptualizing team performance measures (TPMs) in training, and describe how the framework can guide specification of particular measures that serve various purposes in training. Finally, we discuss the implications of this line of thinking for training and performance measurement, and delineate future research and development opportunities.

TEAM PERFORMANCE AND TRAINING

To begin the discussion, it is first necessary to examine more closely the nature of team performance and team training with the purpose being to establish the requirements for performance measures to be used in team training. Our goal here is not to provide a comprehensive review since it is beyond the scope of this chapter; instead we summarize this work (interested readers are encouraged to see Cannon-Bowers, Tannenbaum, Salas, & Volpe, 1995; Salas, Cannon-Bowers, & Johnston, 1997; Salas, Dickinson, Converse, & Tannenbaum, 1992, for more detail).

Teams are often called on to perform complex, stressful, and hazardous tasks in the public and private sectors. In fact, many team tasks have in common the characteristic of being dynamic—requiring team members to harness resources and adapt quickly to changing conditions. Moreover, interdependence among team members means that team performance itself is complex, requiring a delicate balance of input by multiple team members that has consequences both for task success (i.e., in terms of the temporal, sequential, and reciprocal aspects of performance) as well as for the team's well-being (i.e., in terms of social interactions, attitudes, and motivation; Tannenbaum, Beard, & Salas, 1992). For these reasons, the study of team performance presents challenges that are unparalleled when considering individuals working alone.

The implications of this added complexity of team performance for training and measurement are vast. To begin with, team training must address the dynamic aspects of team performance, with emphasis on training such elusive skills as adaptability, flexibility, and implicit coordination (i.e., coordination that occurs in the absence of overt communication; Cannon-Bowers, Salas, & Converse, 1993; Orasanu & Salas, 1993). In addition, teams have a variety of other competency requirements that can be cognitive, behavioral or attitudinal in nature (Salas & Cannon-Bowers, 1997). Table 3.1 provides a synopsis of required team competencies compiled recently by Cannon-Bowers et al. (1995). As is evident from this table, teams require a wide range of knowledge, skills, and attitudes (KSAs)

TABLE 3.1
Team Competencies

Knowledge	Skills	Attitudes
• Cue/strategy associations • Task-specific teammate characteristics • Shared task models • Knowledge of team mission, objectives, norms • Task sequencing • Accurate task models • Accurate problem models • Team role interaction patterns • Understanding team work skills • Knowledge of boundary spanning role • Teammate characteristics	• Adaptability flexibility dynamic reallocation of function compensatory behavior • Shared situational awareness • Mutual performance monitoring and feedback self-correction • Leadership/team management conflict resolution assertiveness • Coordination task integration • Communication • Decision making problem solving metacognition	• Team orientation • Conflictive efficacy • Shared vision • Team cohesion • Interpersonal relations • Mutual trust • Task-specific teamwork attitudes • Collective orientation • Importance of teamwork

Adapted from Cannon-Bowers et al. (1995). Copyright © 1995 Jossey-Bass Inc., Publishers.

in order to meet demanding environmental conditions. Training for these KSAs has been the subject of much recent thinking and research.

According to Salas and Cannon-Bowers (1997), team training can be thought of as being composed of tools, methods, and content that combine to form particular team training strategies. Briefly, the *tools* of team training include: performance measures, team task analysis, task simulations, feedback, and principles of learning; *methods* include: information-based methods (e.g., lectures), demonstration-based methods (e.g., videotapes), and practice-based methods (e.g., role-plays). These tools and methods combine with *content* (i.e., required KSAs) to produce strategies such as guided practice (i.e., practice that incorporates specific feedback), cross-training, team coordination training, team leader training, team building, and the like. Preliminary evidence to support the efficacy of these interventions can be found in Salas, Cannon-Bowers and Johnston (1997) and Volpe, Cannon-Bowers, Salas, and Spector (1996).

One of the commonalties among these team training strategies is that they require performance to be assessed and diagnosed accurately. In fact, many team training situations require *dynamic assessment*—that is, the ability to track, assess, and interpret the moment-to-moment changes that occur in team performance so that appropriate feedback can be devised and/or other remediation implemented. Therefore, a measurement scheme that is specific to the training situation (i.e., in addition to measurement conducted for other purposes) may be in order to support team training.

Given this, we can now turn the discussion more specifically to the requirements for TPMs in training. It is our contention that attention should be given to the challenge of developing TPMs for training that are distinct (in purpose, form, and specificity) from TPMs developed for other purposes. Therefore, the following sections delineate what we believe are the requirements for TPMs in training.

TPMs IN TRAINING

Inherent in virtually all training is the notion of assessment of trainee progress. In some training situations, assessment may be rather informal as is the case when a lecturer searchers the faces of his or her audience for cues that indicate whether they are following the material. Sports coaches observe plays, making note of effective and ineffective performance as a basis to specify feedback. Moving to more formalized situations, instructors in some aviation contexts employ observational checklists as a means to record progress in training (Gregorich & Wilhelm, 1993; Prince & Salas, 1993, in press). In many computer-based instructional systems, trainee progress is assessed (via computer input) so that the system can match the content and format of training material to the trainee's current state of learning; intelligent tutoring systems take this a step further by attempting to infer the student's cognitive state on the basis of his or her responses (see Nichols, Chipman, & Brennan, 1995). Still more involved are modern weapon systems that are beginning to track trainee performance in complex systems down to the key press as a means to record behavior and infer its causes. In all these cases, whether formalized or not, some type of assessment during the training process is taking place; hence the need for performance measures in training.

Although such measures share common characteristics with measures developed for other purposes, performance measures in training are specifically necessary to support the instructional process. At the core of this requirement is the notion that TPMs in training allow for remedial activity. We are defining *remediation* here to refer to the process by which performance deficiencies are used as a basis to design and structure subsequent instruction. This is consistent with Webster's definition, specifically *remedial* is defined as intended to correct or improve one's skill in a specified field. However, the term *remedial* has often been used in the educational literature to refer only to instruction that is geared toward bringing a student from below average performance levels, or as a means to ameliorate unsuccessful instruction. In contrast, we consider remediation to include a variety of activities that move a trainee from a current state to a state where targeted learning (in terms of knowledge, skill and/or attitude) has occurred. Furthermore, we contend that remediation can only be accomplished when accurate assessment of a trainee's current skill/ performance level is accomplished.

Defined as we have here, remediation becomes a central concept in all training. It suggests that the training process is a cycle of providing instruction, assessing learning (and other) outcomes, and then adjusting instruction accordingly (either to repeat or amplify previously presented material, or move onto new material). In order to support this process of remediation, TPMs in training must be useful to: (a) provide the instructor (or instructional system) with information about trainee progress, (b) provide a basis to construct feedback, (c) provide the trainee with knowledge of results, (d) help determine which instructional strategy is appropriate (or trigger a change in strategy if a current one is unsuccessful), and (e) aid in structuring the content of training by indicating when trainees are prepared to move to different or more complex material. For these reasons, we contend that simply measuring performance during team training is not sufficient to ensure its success; rather, particular types of measures are required to support the instructional process. However, despite the volumes written about team training and performance measures, few attempts have been made to focus directly on the nature of TPMs in training.

Figure 3.1 delineates the characteristics of TPMs in training that we believe are paramount to remediation, and hence, the instructional process. Inspection of this figure reveals that TPMs in training must measure team- as well as individual-level performance and address the processes, as well as outcomes of team behavior. By assessing these aspects of performance, TPMs in training are then useful as a means to describe, evaluate and diagnose team performance. On this basis, TPMs in training can support the instructional process by allowing for remediation—specifically, the generation of feedback and instructional strategy selection. Implicit in this

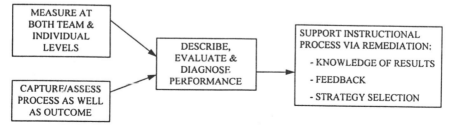

FIG. 3.1. Requirements for TPMs in training.

contention is the fact that: (a) trainee learning is optimized when training is tailored to his or her needs, and (b) the training program itself is improved through the feedback process (i.e., data collected in assessing performance triggers both real-time modification of instructional strategy and potentially longer term improvements to the program. In the following sections we describe the requirements for TPMs in training, and then present a framework that consolidates our thinking in this area.

REQUIREMENTS FOR TPMs IN TRAINING

TPMs Must Consider Multiple Levels of Measurement

A primary issue that must be raised in defining TPMs in training involves the level of measurement or unit of analysis (McIntyre & Salas, 1995); in this case referring to whether measures are taken at the individual and/or team levels. In the simplest sense, we contend that both individual- and team-level measures are crucial for assessing team training and, more importantly, diagnosing team performance. To complicate matters somewhat, however, it may be that the "individual versus team" distinction is overly simplistic. In fact, according to Cannon-Bowers et al. (1995), team competencies (and for our purposes, performance measures) exist at several levels. These include individual competencies (i.e., the knowledge, skills, and attitudes required to fulfill individual job/task requirements); team competencies held at the individual level (i.e., knowledge, skills, and attitudes that are generic with respect to the particular task and/or team involved) and team competencies held at the team level (that are specific to the task and/or team involved). These are important distinctions because they drive what is measured and how it is measured (i.e., at the team or individual level). For example, effective communication skills may be conceptualized as an important teamwork skill, but one that is held at the individual level, and therefore best measured (and trained) at the individual level. On the other hand, collective efficacy (i.e., the team's belief that it can cope with task demands) can be measured meaningfully only at the team level. In this case, it may be that appropriate feedback is best delivered at the team level as well.

The point of this discussion is that careful consideration needs to be given to the nature of the competency being trained so that appropriate measurement can be accomplished (Cannon-Bowers et al., 1995). Perhaps the most important consideration in this regard is the form that remediation is likely to take. Remediation is related to the level of measurement in the sense that when the performance deficiency requires an intervention at the individual level, then it must be assessed at this level. Using the example of communication behavior noted earlier, this would mean that communication behavior would need to be tracked and evaluated at the individual level because remediation is likely to be delivered at this level. However, because the individual's communication behavior also has implications for team performance, it may be desirable to assess it at this level as well, but not as a basis for specific feedback. In fact, measuring an individual-level competency solely at the team level is only effective if it allows for specific remediation of performance deficiencies. To summarize, we contend that the nature of the competency being trained and of the form of remediation associated with training are both important drivers of the level of measurement for TPMs in training.

TPMs Must Address Process as Well as Outcome

Another distinction that can be drawn in TPM development is related to several of the ideas expressed here. Specifically, consistent with Goldstein (1993), we draw a clear distinction between *process* measures and *outcome* measures of training performance. We use the term *process* in a similar vein to Coovert, Cannon-Bowers, and Salas (1990), meaning the collection of activities, strategies, responses, and behaviors employed in task accomplishment. "Outcomes," on the other hand, are defined as their name implies, as the outcome of the various task processes. This process–outcome distinction becomes crucial to TPM in training for several reasons.

First, outcome measures are usually not diagnostic because they do not indicate what might be the underlying causes of performance. As noted earlier, this means that they are often not useful as a means to provide constructive feedback or to tailor training to the trainee's needs. For example, knowing that a team failed to reach its desired productivity gives no indication of why this may be the case, nor how to improve it through subsequent training.

Second, process measures more directly describe the (correct) performance of interest. Consider, for example, a team that achieves acceptable outcomes, but does so through a flawed process (through chance or luck or both). Reinforcing the outcome then reinforces an unwanted process. In cases where the outcome is a "go, no-go" decision (i.e., where the probability of a correct decision is 50% by definition), this can happen quite often. Therefore, in such situations, we advocate the notion that the goal of training should not be to train people to make the right decision (i.e., an outcome); rather it should be to train them to make the decision right (i.e., a process). Another example is when under routine or low workload conditions, one member of the team dominates in arriving at an outcome. Once again, reinforcing the fact that the outcome is correct may actually bolster interaction patterns that are dysfunctional at higher workload levels. Of course, we realize that outcome measures do have an important role in team performance measurement—clearly, if the team achieves incorrect or otherwise unacceptable outcomes, this is crucial in assessing their performance. Our point here is that outcome measures in isolation (i.e., without explanatory processes) are not very useful for training.

It should be noted that we are using the term *outcome* in the broadest sense to include outcomes that may be cognitive, behavioral, or attitudinal in nature. This is in contrast to the "results" category employed by Kirkpatrick (1976) and others that typically is used to refer to organization-level outcomes. Although our definition of outcomes includes these types of measures, it also refers to other, less global aspects of outcome performance.

TPMs in Training Must be Able to Describe, Evaluate, and Diagnose Performance

Thinking about TPMs in training according to (a) whether they are at the team or individual level, and (b) whether they address process or outcome is a necessary first step in generating such measures. In particular, these considerations help to define the specific nature of measures necessary to support the team training process. They are also useful delineations because they enable us to more accurately describe, evaluate and, most importantly, diagnose team performance. In fact, in order to accomplish effective assessment during training, TPMs must be able to achieve these goals simultaneously.

First, the measures must be able to describe behavior accurately. In many complex team tasks, this in itself is an extremely difficult goal to meet. The reason is that team tasks are often characterized by high workload, rapid interaction demands, and high degrees of communication. Moment-to-moment changes in the situation require complex cognitive and behavioral responses on the part of multiple team members, often simultaneously. Therefore, TPMs in training must themselves be dynamic—they must adjust to changing situational characteristics and be sensitive to relatively small deviations in performance.

Moreover, many modern tasks require the manipulation of advanced equipment (i.e., computer keyboards or other input–output devices), for which it may be difficult to record performance in a manner that is meaningful for constructing feedback. Alternatively, many tasks present largely cognitive demands, with little or no obvious (behavioral) indicators as to the trainee's performance at any given time. These factors all complicate the matter of recording team performance, particularly if it is to be accomplished in real-time (which is necessary for many types of training).

Assuming that it is possible to describe team performance accurately and completely, it is then important to evaluate performance. Obviously, by this we mean that observed performance (whether it be cognitive or behavioral) must be assessed as to its appropriateness given the task situation. As has been discussed in much detail (e.g., see Goldstein, 1993), standards may be normative or criterion-based; in either case, it is important to be able to assess team performance in relation to some standard. This matter is complicated somewhat by the fact that measures of skill acquisition (i.e., learning) may not be similar to those indicating task mastery (Schmidt & Bjork, 1992). The implication here is that evaluating performance in training may require measures that are conceptually distinct from those used to evaluate posttraining performance or transfer.

Once performance is evaluated, it is crucial to be able to diagnose the causes of effective and ineffective performance as a basis on which to construct feedback, designate remedial activities, adjust the pace of instruction, and manipulate training content (particularly in terms of content difficulty). Therefore, we argue that perhaps the most important feature of TPMs in training is their diagnosticity—that is, their ability to establish the causes underlying performance—because it drives the training process itself. Hence, the nature of performance deficiencies, and explanation of them, determines the nature and content of feedback required to improve performance, and selection of subsequent instructional strategies.

To conclude this section then, we have argued that TPMs in training must be at once descriptive, evaluative, and diagnostic in nature. It is impossible to overstate the importance of these performance measurement characteristics for training. This is because the ability to construct meaningful remedial activity is dependent largely on how well performance deficiencies are identified and diagnosed. The following section expands this notion further.

TPMs Must Provide a Basis for Remediation

As noted, the overriding purpose of TPMs in training is that they support the instructional process. Specifically, they allow for remediation by providing information about trainee progress to the instructor or instructional system; provide trainees with knowledge of results; provide trainees with feedback that indicates how performance can be improved (often called *process* feedback); drive the selection of subsequent instruction; and aid in structuring the content of training. In the following sections we focus on three of these: providing feedback, providing knowledge of results, and driving subsequent instruction.

Obviously, the role of feedback in training cannot be overestimated (Goldstein, 1993; Jacoby, Mazursky, Troutman, & Kuss, 1984), and due to the limitations here, we do not attempt to review the literature in this area. In summarizing this work, we can conclude that one of the most important features of TPMs in training is that they allow accurate, detailed, comprehensive, and timely feedback to be formulated and delivered to trainees. As feedback is often the primary mechanism by which training is delivered, the success of performance measures in training will depend largely on their ability to support the feedback generation process. There are at least two types of feedback of interest in training: knowledge of results and process-oriented feedback.

The term *knowledge of results* (KOR) has often been used interchangeably with the term *feedback* in past work (e.g., Wexley & Latham, 1981), and others use the term *outcome feedback* to refer to KOR (e.g., Balzer, Doherty, & O'Connor, 1989). We prefer to treat KOR separately from other types of feedback because we contend that it serves a slightly different purpose in training. Namely, KOR is a mechanism to provide trainees with directive information. It alerts trainees to performance problems and helps them to focus their attention in subsequent training. KOR can also help trainees assess their progress toward a specific performance goal (Wexley & Latham, 1981). For these reasons, KOR has both directive and motivational properties (Ilgen, Fisher, & Taylor, 1979). However, KOR is not necessarily informative, that is, it lets trainees know that their performance must change, but not necessarily how to change it; in fact, there is evidence that for some tasks, KOR may actually impede learning (Jacoby et al., 1984). Therefore, more process-oriented feedback is also required.

Process feedback can be defined as feedback that indicates to trainees what to change and how to improve their performance in subsequent trials (Early, Northcraft, Lee, & Lituchy, 1990). Closely related to this is the notion of cognitive feedback (see Balzer et al., 1989), which generally refers to feedback regarding the trainee's decision-making strategy during training. Research into process feedback is much less common than is KOR research. What is available indicates that it is generally more effective in improving performance than simple KOR (e.g., Balzer et al., 1989; Early et al., 1990; Johnson, Perlow, & Piper, 1993). From a team training standpoint, it has been suggested that process feedback is an essential tool for imparting crucial teamwork competencies (e.g., Cannon-Bowers et al., 1995; Salas et al., in press). Once again, this bolsters our conclusion that TPMs in training must support the generation of corrective process feedback.

Beyond the outcome versus process distinction, there are several other aspects of feedback that are pertinent to the current discussion. First, past research generally indicates that to be most effective, feedback must be presented closely in time to the performance situation (Wexley & Latham, 1981). This implies that any measurement system implemented in training must provide performance information (descriptive, evaluative, and diagnostic) quickly so that it can be used as a basis for feedback. Second, past research indicates that feedback must be specific (Goldstein, 1993; Wexley & Latham, 1981), particularly when it is associated with a particular instructional goal. The implication is that a measurement scheme must both identify and capture performance data required to provide specific feedback to the trainee.

A final process to be supported by TPMs in training is selection of an instructional strategy or approach that is appropriate to the trainee's current level of mastery. As noted, training systems almost always depend on some assessment of the trainees' progress as a means to select subsequent training content and delivery mechanism. For example, computer-based instructional systems collect evidence that a trainee has mastered certain material before moving onto new concepts. In addition, human instructors match perceived performance deficiencies to a training strategy (in terms of what material they repeat or highlight, what feedback they deliver, and when they move onto new material) as a natural part of the instructional role. In team performance situations, this means that performance measures must indicate mastery of particular KSAs so that the instructor (or instructional system) can determine the next instructional step. Therefore, TPMs in training must be informative if they are to support strategy selection and development.

To conclude this section, we have maintained that TPMs in training support remediation by serving three related purposes (providing KOR, providing process feedback, and guiding instructional strategy selection). This requirement has several implications for the nature of TPMs in training. First, it highlights the need for diagnosticity in measures. In order to provide a basis for remediation, TPMs in training must indicate the underlying causes of effective and ineffective behavior. Without this ability, it is impossible to tailor remedial activities to the trainee's needs.

A second implication of this section for TPMs in training is more practical in nature; namely the timing of performance recording and interpretation. Unfortunately, the task of simply recording team performance is difficult due to the complexity of many team tasks. However, it is essential to the remedial process that performance is measured closely in time to its occurrence—otherwise it is impossible to provide immediate feedback or make necessary changes to the instructional strategy. In fact, we recommend that TPMs in training be collected and interpreted in "real time," a feat that is not possible in many current situations. Research and development in this area are needed.

A FRAMEWORK FOR MEASURING TEAM PERFORMANCE

Based on the notions presented thus far, we now present a framework for developing TPMs to support assessment in training; it is depicted in Fig. 3.2. Inspection of this figure reveals that we are conceptualizing TPMs in training as differing on two primary dimensions: process versus outcome, and team versus individual. However, these are by no means dichotomous distinctions. For example, on occasion, a particular behavior can be considered a process measure (e.g., when a series of procedures is required to accomplish a task), but in others it is considered to be the outcome measure of a subtask. In fact, a collection of interim outcome measures taken together can be descriptive of a task process or strategy.

As noted earlier, the team versus individual split is also not a straight-forward one. For example, certain teamwork skills may be held at the individual level, making it difficult to decide in which category they fall. The decision rule we find most useful here is whether the performance is measured at the team or individual level. In other words, because teamwork skills held at the individual level are measured at the individual level, we would place them in the "individual" category.

	TEAM	INDIVIDUAL
P R O C E S S	• Shared Task Models • Cue/Strategy Associations • Task Organization • Compensatory Behavior • Collective Efficacy • Dynamic Reallocation of Function • Task Interaction	• Assertiveness • Information Exchange • Task-Specific Role Responsibilities • Procedures for Task Accomplishment • Cue/Strategy Association • Mutual Performance Monitoring • Flexibility
O U T C O M E	• Mission/Goal Accomplishment • Aggregate Latency • Error Propagation • Aggregate Accuracy	• Accuracy • Latency • Errors • Safety • Timeliness • Decision Biases

FIG. 3.2.   Framework for developing TPMs in training.

Further inspection of Fig. 3.2 reveals that the specific categories of criteria—based on the KSAs that we believe require assessment during training—are contained in each quadrant. To arrive at these entries, we reviewed the compilation of team performance KSAs presented by Cannon-Bowers et al. (1995) and assessed each of the potential KSAs in light of whether it: could be measured in training; would serve to describe, evaluate, and/or diagnose performance; or would provide a basis for feedback or strategy selection. To this we added a series of outcome measures that we believe are appropriate to assess in training. The result of this effort is a preliminary list of TPMs that we believe are useful during training. Empirical verification and validation of these TPMs is necessary.

On a more practical level, the next step in making this framework more useful is to establish recommended measurement techniques that are appropriate for each class of KSAs. Therefore, Fig. 3.3 displays the specific TPM techniques that we believe can support team training; these vary as a function of the quadrant in which they fall. In all cases, the success of measurement hinges largely on the ability to not only measure performance, but also to interpret it in light of task demands. Careful, comprehensive team task analysis procedures are required to accomplish this so that models

	TEAM	INDIVIDUAL
P R O C E S S	• Observational Scales • Expert Ratings • Content Analysis • Protocol Analysis	• Decision Analysis • Policy Capturing • Protocol Analysis • Observational Scales
O U T C O M E	• Observational Scales • Expert Ratings • Critical Incidents • Automated Performance Recording	• Automated Performance Recording • Critical Incident • Expert Ratings • Archival Records

FIG. 3.3.   Measurement tools useful to assess TPMs in training.

of effective and ineffective performance can be developed to guide interpretation of observed performance. Because this is beyond our scope here, Fig. 3.3 delineates only the methods that might be useful to measure performance, but not necessarily to interpret it.

To begin with, individual outcome measures are necessary to determine whether team members can demonstrate the requisite team-related KSAs in order to function as an effective team member. Measuring such outcomes can be accomplished via automated performance recording (i.e., recording precisely when required behaviors occur), critical incident-based observational protocols (i.e., that point out to raters or observers what is to be measured and when; see Johnston, Cannon-Bowers, & Smith-Jentsch, 1995; Johnston, Smith-Jentsch, & Cannon-Bowers, this volume), and expert opinion (e.g., in the form of rating scales; see Borman, 1991). Individual process measures indicate the manner in which individual team members accomplish their tasks. Decision analysis (e.g., Klein, Calderwood, & MacGregor, 1989), policy capturing (Hobson & Gibson, 1984), protocol analysis (Bainbridge, 1995), and observational scales (see Borman, 1991) are all methods that can be used for this purpose.

Moving to the team level, team process measures collect information about how the team accomplishes its objectives. To measure team process, observational scales (see Smith-Jentsch, Tannenbaum, & Cannon-Bowers, 1995), expert ratings, communication content analysis (Foushee & Manos, 1981; Kanki, Lozito, & Foushee, 1989), team-level critical incidents (Fowlkes, Lane, Salas, Franz, & Oser, 1994; Morgan, Lassiter, & Salas, 1989), and team-level protocol analysis can be developed. Finally, team outcome measures are necessary to assess the effectiveness of the team (as a whole) in accomplishing its objectives, and can be measured via observational scales, expert rating scales, team-level critical incidents, and automated performance recording.

In a general sense, we would recommend that measures be sampled from all four quadrants in Fig. 3.2 for any team training situation. However, the specific choice of measurement techniques in a particular training situation depends on the nature of the task and KSAs being trained. For example, when performance is highly dynamic, online observational scales may be necessary to capture performance because they are unobtrusive and do not impose additional workload on trainees. Under more static conditions, it may be possible to conduct protocol analyses by asking trainees to "think aloud" while performing. In addition, tasks for which there are high degrees of behavioral discretion on the part of trainees may require expert ratings because more than one solution path might be appropriate; in such cases, constructing specific behavioral checklists may not be possible. Finally, the degree of task interdependence will affect the choice of measures. For example, in highly interdependent tasks, team process measures become paramount; in such cases multiple techniques for assessing team process may be desirable.

CONCLUSIONS

We have attempted to consolidate several lines of thinking in the area of TPM to delineate what we believe are the requirements for TPMs in training. We did so because we believe that it has been a topic that has not received much interest in past work, but is one that has vast implications both for measurement and for training. Perhaps our most important message is that TPMs in training must support the instructional process by providing a basis for remediation. In this regard, we argued that TPMs in training must exist at both the team and individual levels; address process and outcome; describe, evaluate, and diagnose performance; and provide a basis for feedback and instructional strategy selection.

To better organize our thinking in this area, we presented a framework for developing TPMs in training. This framework is intended to be useful as a means to establish the categories of measurement needed in team training, the specific KSAs that might be useful as a basis for assessment, and the measurement techniques and criteria associated with each. At the simplest level, it should be useful to those measuring team performance in training as a means to ensure that important aspects of team performance are being assessed and remediated. Beyond this, we believe that the framework provides a basis to specify hypotheses about the nature of team performance and TPM; as such, we hope it stimulates research in these areas.

We also noted several times in this chapter the difficulty in assessing team performance dynamically (to provide immediate remediation), in part due to the complexity of team performance. Fortunately, advanced technologies are becoming mature enough to address this problem. For example, automated systems are beginning to be developed that can automatically assess a trainee's progress (e.g., see Nichols et al., 1995). Underlying this capability are human performance technologies (i.e., human performance models; theories of skill acquisition, interpretations of observable behavior) and hardware and software technologies (i.e., systems to automatically record performance, "intelligent" interpretation algorithms). Much more research is required in this regard. In addition, conceptual development — using what we have laid out here as a starting point — is necessary so that we can better understand the nature of team competencies and how best to measure them. Only then will optimal applications be possible.

Overall, we hope that what has been put forth here is useful to those who study team training and to those who conduct it. Clearly, there is much work to be done in the team performance area, both in terms of what to measure and how to measure it. We are convinced that this endeavor will be most successful only if the research and practitioner communities work closely together.

REFERENCES

Bainbridge, L. (1995). Verbal protocol analysis. In J. R. Wilson & E. N. Corlett (Eds.), *Evaluation of human work: A practical ergonomics methodology* (pp. 161–179). London: Taylor & Francis.

Balzer, W. K., Doherty, M. E., & O'Connor, R. (1989). Effects of cognitive feedback on performance. *Psychology Bulletin, 106,* 410–433.

Borman, W. C. (1991). Job behavior, performance, and effectiveness. In M. D. Dunette and L. M. Hough (Eds.), *Handbook of industrial and organizational psychology* (pp. 271–326). Palo Alto, CA: Consulting Psychologists Press.

Cannon-Bowers, J. A., Prince, C., Salas, E., Owens, J. M., Morgan, B. B., & Gonos, G. H. (1989). *Determining aircrew coordination training effectiveness.* Paper presented at the 11th annual meeting of the Interservice/Industry Training Systems Conference, Ft. Worth, TX.

Cannon-Bowers, J. A., Salas, E., & Converse, S. A. (1993). Shared mental models in expert team decision making. In N. J. Castellan, Jr. (Ed.), *Current issues in individual and group decision making* (pp. 221–246), Hillsdale, NJ: Lawrence Erlbaum Associates.

Cannon-Bowers, J. A., Tannenbaum, S. I., Salas, E. & Volpe, C. E. (1995). Defining team competencies and establishing team training requirements. In R. Guzzo & E. Salas (Eds.), *Team effectiveness and decision making in organizations* (pp. 333–380). San Francisco, CA: Jossey-Bass.

Coovert, M. D., Cannon-Bowers, J. A., & Salas, E. (1990). *Applying mathematical modeling technology to the study of team training and performance.* Proceedings of the 12th annual Interservice/Industry Training Systems Conference.

Early, C. P., Northcraft, G. B., Lee, C., & Lituchy, T. R. (1990). Impact of process and outcome feedback on the relation of goal setting to task performance. *Academy of Management Journal, 33* (1), 87–105.

Foushee, H. C., & Manos, K. L. (1981). Information transfer within the cockpit: Problems in intra cockpit communications. In C. E. Billings & E. S. Cheaney (Eds.), *Information transfer problems in aviation systems* (NASA TP-1875). Moffett Field, CA: NASA-Ames Research Center.

Fowlkes, J. E., Lane, N. E., Salas, E., Franz, T., & Oser, R. (1994). Improving the measurement of team performance: The TARGETS methodology. *Military Psychology, 6,* 47–63.

Goldstein, I. (1993) *Training in organizations.* Albany, NY: Brooks/Cole.

Gregorich, S. E., & Wilhelm, J. A. (1993). Crew resource management training assessment. In E. L. Wiener, B. G. Kanki, & R. L. Helmreich (Eds.), *Cockpit resource management* (pp. 173–198). San Diego, CA: Academic Press.

Guzzo, R. A., & Salas, E. (1995). *Team effectiveness and decision making in organizations.* San Francisco, CA: Jossey-Bass.

Hackman, J. R. (Ed.). (1990). *Groups that work (and those that don't): Creating conditions for effective teamwork.* San Francisco: Jossey-Bass.

Hobson, C. J., & Gibson, F. W. (1984, March). Capturing supervisor rating policies: A way to improve performance appraisal effectiveness. *Personnel Administrator, 29*(3), 59–68.

Ilgen, D. R., Fisher, C. D., & Taylor, M. S. (1979). Consequences of individual feedback on behavior in organizations. *Journal of Applied Psychology, 64,* 349–371.

Jacoby, J., Mazursky, D., Troutman, T., & Kuss, A. (1984). When feedback is ignored: Disutility of outcome feedback. *Journal of Applied Psychology, 69*(3), 531–545.

Johnson, D. S., Perlow, R., & Piper, K. F. (1993). Differences in team performance as a function of type of feedback: Learning oriented versus performance oriented feedback. *Journal of Applied Psychology, 23,* 303–320.

Johnston, J. H., Cannon-Bowers, J. A., & Smith-Jentsch, K. A. (1995). Event-based performance measurement system for shipboard command teams. *Proceedings of the First International Symposium on Command and Control Research and Technology* (pp. 268–276). Washington, DC: The Center for Advanced Command Concepts and Technology of the National Defense University.

Kanki, B. G., Lozito, S., & Foushee, H. C. (1989). Communication indices of crew coordination. *Aviation, Space, & Environmental Medicine, 60,* 56–60.

Kirkpatrick, D. L. (1976). Evaluation of training. In R. L. Craig (Ed.). *Training and development handbook* (2nd ed.). New York: McGraw-Hill.

Klein, G. A., Calderwood, R., & MacGregor, D. (1989). Critical decision method for eliciting knowledge. *IEEE Systems, Man, and Cybernetics, 19* (3), 462–472.

McIntyre, R. M., & Salas, E. (1995). Measuring and managing for team performance: Emerging principles from complex environments. In R. Guzzo & E. Salas (Eds.), *Team effectiveness and decision making in organizations* (pp. 149–203). San Francisco, CA: Jossey-Bass.

Morgan, B. B., Jr., Lassiter, D. L., & Salas, E. (1989). *Networked simulation application for team training and performance research.* Paper presented at the meeting for Interactive Networked Simulation for Training, Orlando, FL.

Nichols, P. D., Chipman, S. F., & Brennan, R. L. (1995). *Cognitively diagnostic assessment.* Hillsdale, NJ: Lawrence Erlbaum Associates.

Orasanu, J., & Salas, E. (1993). Team decision making in complex environments. In G. Klein, J. Orasanu, R. Calderwood, & C. E. Zsambok (Eds.), *Decision making in action: Models and methods* (pp. 327–345). Norwood, NJ: Ablex.

Prince, C., & Salas, E. (1993). Training and research for teamwork in the military aircrew. In E. L. Wiener, B. G. Kanki, & R. L. Helmreich (Eds.), *Cockpit resource management* (pp. 337–366). Orlando, FL: Academic Press.

Prince, C., & Salas, E. (in press). Team processes and their training in aviation. In D. J. Garland, J. A. Wise, & D. V. Hopkin (Eds.), *Aviation human factors.* Mahwah, NJ: Lawrence Erlbaum Associates.

Salas, E., & Cannon-Bowers, J. A. (1997). Methods, tools, and strategies for team training. In M. A. Quinones & A. Eheenstein (Eds.), *Training for a rapidly changing workplace: Applications of psychological research.* Washington, DC: APA Press.

Salas, E., Cannon-Bowers, J. A., & Johnston, J. H. (1997). How can you turn a team of experts into an expert team?: Emerging training strategies. In C. Zsambok & G. Klein (Eds.), *Naturalistic decision making* (pp. 359–370). Mahwah, NJ: Lawrence Erlbaum Associates.

Salas, E., Dickinson, T. L., Converse, S. A., & Tannenbaum, S. I. (1992). Toward an understanding of team performance and training. In R. Swezey & E. Salas (Eds.), *Teams: Their training and performance* (pp. 3–29). Norwood, NJ: Ablex.

Schmidt, R. A., & Bjork, A. (1992). New conceptualizations of practice: Common principles in three paradigms suggest new concepts for training. *Psychological Science, 3,* 207–217.

Smith-Jentsch, K. A., Tannenbaum, S. I., & Cannon-Bowers, J. A. (1995). Training team leaders briefing skills. In R. J. Stout (Chair), *The science and practice of enhancing teamwork in organizations*. Symposium conducted at the meeting of the American Psychological Association, Toronto, Canada.

Tannenbaum, S. I., Beard, R. L., & Salas, E. (1992). Team building and its influence on team effectiveness: An examination of conceptual and empirical developments. In K. Kelley (Ed.), *Issue, theory, and research in industrial/organizational psychology* (pp. 117–153). Amsterdam: Elsevier.

Volpe, C. E., Cannon-Bowers, J. A., Salas, E., & Spector, P. E. (1994). The impact of cross-training on team functioning. *Human Factors, 38,* 87–100.

Wexley, K. N., & Latham, G. P. (1981). *Developing and training human resources in organizations*. Glenview, IL: Scott, Foresman.

4

Conceptual Development and Empirical Evaluation of Measures of Shared Mental Models as Indicators of Team Effectiveness

Kurt Kraiger
University of Colorado at Denver

Lucy H. Wenzel
Colorado State University

In the last 10 years, there has been a renewed interest by researchers in the topics of teams and team performance. This interest has sprung from two research tracks that have conceptually defined core construct(s) (i.e., specifying what a *team* is), and empirically validated team-related measures and theories, particularly with respect to team behaviors.

Much of this research was characterized by its behavioral focus. For example, preliminary work by Morgan, Glickman, and associates identified a set of core behaviors characteristic of successful teams, regardless of task context (McIntyre, Morgan, Salas, & Glickman, 1988; McIntyre & Salas, 1995; Morgan, Glickman, Woodard, Blaiwes, & Salas, 1986). Among the crucial team behaviors are closed-loop communication, compensatory (backup) behavior, mutual performance monitoring, giving–receiving feedback, adaptability, and coordination (McIntyre & Salas, 1995).

Just as the training field in general has expanded from primarily a behavioral orientation to include a cognitive focus (Kraiger, 1995), so has the study of team performance. For example, whereas Oser, McCallum, Salas, and Morgan (1989) defined teams in terms of representative or typical behaviors, Cannon-Bowers, Salas, and Converse (1993) defined teams not only in behavioral terms, but also emphasized qualities such as cooperative, adaptive interaction toward the pursuit of shared objectives, and clearly defined, differentiated roles and responsibilities. Cannon-Bowers and Salas (1990) introduced the construct of a *shared mental model* to account for the fluid, implicit interaction often observed in successful teams (see Brehmer, 1972; Kleinman & Serfaty, 1989; Orasanu, 1990).

The shared mental model construct has become popular among a number of team researchers (Bettenhausen, 1991; Kleinman & Serfaty, 1989; Klimoski & Mohammed, 1994; Minionis, Zaccaro, & Perez, 1995; Rentsch, Heffner, & Duffy, 1993; Orasanu, 1990; Rouse, Cannon-Bowers, & Salas, 1992). To date, shared mental models have yet to be directly measured, though some researchers have assessed some components of mental models (e.g., Minionis et al., 1995; Rentsch et al., 1993). This lack of immediate progress in measuring shared mental models is to be expected. As we discuss later, a shared mental model is a complex, latent construct and may not be amenable to scaling by a single measure. Rather, at this point in time, it may be more valuable to make inferences about shared mental models by employing multiple measures and testing a priori hypotheses about the relationships among measures and other attributes of the team performance environment. Although this increases the complexity of the measurement process, it makes shared mental models no less valuable as a construct for assessing training needs, designing team-based training, or evaluating training effectiveness.

Thus, our intention here is to stimulate the development of multiple measures of shared mental models by embedding the shared mental model construct within a process framework describing the determinants, outcomes, and measurement implications of the shared mental models. In doing so, we hope to make the following contributions to the emerging literature on team performance measurement: Suggest potentially construct-valid measures of shared mental models; and logically link proposed measures to a conceptual model of the determinants and outcomes of shared mental models.

In doing so, we are also following a construct-oriented approach to the measurement of shared mental models. Kraiger, Ford, and Salas (1993) noted the benefits of a construct-oriented approach to developing new evaluation measures, and also reviewed the requirements of such an approach: The first requirement is to adequately define the construct, both at the theoretical and at the operational level. Considerable attention has already been paid already to defining shared mental models (e.g., Cannon-Bowers & Salas, 1990; Cannon-Bowers et al., 1992; Rouse et al., 1992), and the construct further delineated in this chapter.

The second requirement is to identify a nomological network of multiple concepts, measures, and their interrelationships (Cronbach & Meehl, 1955). A nomological network requires the development and testing of hypotheses about interrelationships between the focal variable and other measures of other similar constructs; specification of the boundary conditions regarding the focal variable (e.g., the conditions under which a measure of shared mental models would and would not account for team performance variance); and specification of relationships between the focal variable and variables exogenous to the network such as determinants and outcomes.

The final requirement is to develop hypotheses about the variable at the operational or measurement level, and then apply empirical observations to these hypotheses. Thus, conceptual hypotheses built into the nomological network must be transformed to operational hypotheses given an understanding of how the measure in question relates to the theoretical construct model. Where appropriate in this chapter, we offer hypotheses that can provide a basis for future research to be conducted to test the validity of the measures we propose.

Our chapter is organized as follows: We first provide an overview of our shared mental model framework. This framework builds on earlier theories of individual and shared mental models; within this framework we propose a number of construct-relevant measures of aspects of shared mental models. Next, we present an overview of the hypothesized determinants and outcomes of shared mental models; these are used to specify hypotheses concerning our proposed measures. Finally, we discuss the implications of this framework for measuring team-shared mental models.

MEASUREMENT OF SHARED MENTAL MODELS

Figure 4.1 shows a preliminary framework for depicting the relationships among the latent construct of a shared mental model, their determinants and outcomes, and potential measures. The construct of shared mental models was drawn from theories of individual mental models used to explicate individual cognitive functioning or understanding. At the individual level, mental models refer to a structure of known elements (e.g., declarative knowledge) and the relationships among those elements (Shavelson, 1974). These structures serve as mechanisms that enable individuals to describe functions and forms of tasks, explain and observe integration of tasks, and anticipate future task requirements (Rouse & Morris, 1986).

As noted earlier, Cannon-Bowers and Salas (1990) proposed extending the concept of individual mental models to the team performance domain, hypothesizing that team performance is a function of the extent to which team members held similarly organized expectations surrounding the task or each other. Shared mental models represent shared knowledge about the team and its objectives, as well as common information about team roles, behavior patterns, and interaction patterns. A shared mental model is an appealing way to characterize the process(es) by which team members share task information and mutual expectations for complementary task behavior. Shared mental models are thought to improve team performance because: they enable team members to form accurate explanations and expectations for a task (Cannon-Bowers et al., 1993; Wickens, 1984) using a common and sophisticated language (Kaplan, 1990), allow members to

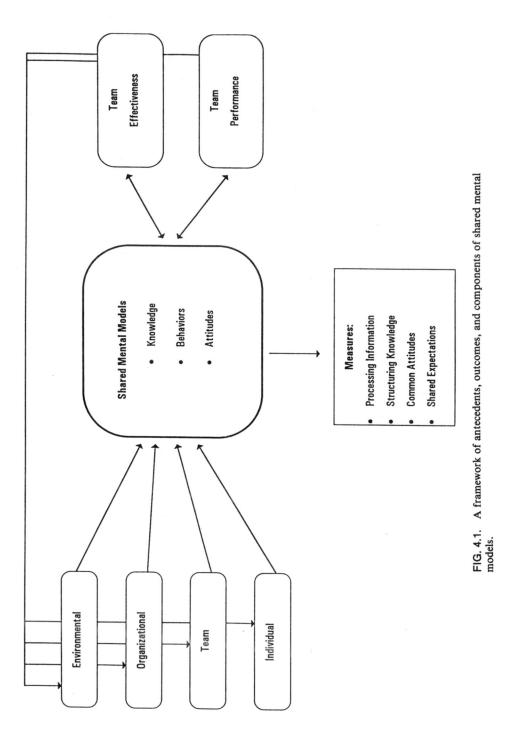

FIG. 4.1. A framework of antecedents, outcomes, and components of shared mental models.

coordinate actions and adapt behavior to task demands (Cannon-Bowers et al., 1993; Lesgold et al., 1989), facilitate information processing (Kaplan, 1990).

Cannon-Bowers et al. (1993) proposed that shared mental models may be characterized by the object or focus of the model: team, task, equipment, or interactions among members. In addition, the knowledge contained in any shared mental model may be described in terms of knowledge type (declarative, structural, procedural, or strategic; see Cannon-Bowers et al., 1993; Jonassen, Beissner, & Yacci, 1993), detail, or function. Model elements may vary from concrete and specific to abstract and general, or may provide information about what the element is, how it works, or why it is needed (Rouse et al., 1992). Thus, an airline cockpit crew may share one mental model for task demands, and another for team attributes. The former model may be very detailed and procedural (how to perform a task), and the latter may principally contain abstract ideas of why it is important to work together as a team.

Proposed Measures

To date, prior taxonomies of shared mental models have emphasized their knowledge elements (e.g., Cannon-Bowers et al., 1993; Rouse et al., 1992), but the framework proposed here takes a broader approach and suggests that shared mental models may be consist of any of three elements: knowledge, behavior, and attitudes. Our proposed measures map these three components. Specifically, our measures are intended to assess: (a) how team members perceive, process, or react to external stimuli, (b) how team members organize or structure task-relevant knowledge (e.g., condition-rules for action), (c) common attitudes or effect for task-relevant behavior, and (d) shared expectations for behavior.

Processing Information.   Teams may share knowledge that is principally declarative (e.g., information about task attributes or equipment limitations), procedural (e.g., information about communication channels or operating procedures), or strategic (e.g., task strategies or interpersonal skills) in nature. Because teams are dynamic and interactive, it may be helpful to focus on how information or knowledge is acted upon, rather than the knowledge per se. Thus, measurement may be at the schema level. Schema theory proposes that knowledge is stored in coherent wholes, or schemas, that represent mental constructs for objects, events, or ideas (Rumelhart & Ortony, 1977). Schemas develop from experience and are comprised of a set of attributes that help individuals recognize an object or event. Furthermore, schemas allow us to predict unknown attributes about events, and to process new information about the object of the schema (Norman, Gentner, & Stevens, 1976).

Rentsch et al. (1993) proposed the notion of a team schema—shared representations about either how teams operate (i.e., a process schema) or how team tasks should be accomplished (i.e., an event schema). Rentsch et al. focused principally on shared perceptions of teams as objects. Using a card sort task, they attempted to assess whether teams could be characterized by the degree to which team members agreed on the common attributes of work teams. Team members were given 100 teamwork adjectives and asked first to sort them into categories of like concepts, then label the concepts, and finally rate the similarity among categories. An underlying assumption of this approach is that the dimensions team members choose to sort attributes reflect stable personal constructs for representing attributes of teams.

A similar methodology could be used to assess team members' collective schema for events. This strategy would be more valuable for assessing procedural or strategic knowledge than declarative knowledge. After defining a scenario or problem to be solved, team members could be given attributes to be sorted that represent situational cues, diagnostic steps, or action steps. Overlap in categories among team members would indicate that team members share common episodic information for accomplishing team tasks. Alternatively, probed protocol analysis (see Means & Gott, 1988) could be used by providing team members with the series of steps necessary to perform a team task. Team members would then be asked questions such as "why would you perform this task?" or "what should other team members be doing as you perform your duties?" Answers could be scored not only for correctness, but for the degree to which they overlap with, or complement, answers of other team members. For example, if there were 10 steps for accomplishing a certain task, it may not be necessary that all team members know all 10 steps, but all steps must be known by at least one team member. Different scoring algorithms could be derived to detect the degree of overlap (the extent to which multiple team members hold the same information) or the degree to which members' knowledge complements each other (the extent to which one member has information that others do not).

Organizing Information.   As noted previously, a critical element of shared mental models is how team members organize or structure knowledge about the task, equipment, team, or member roles (Rouse et al., 1992; Rouse & Morris, 1986). Structural knowledge mediates the translation of declarative knowledge to procedural knowledge, and facilitates the application of procedural knowledge (Jonassen et al., 1993). By determining how team members jointly define interrelationships among key concepts, one may determine whether they hold similar knowledge structures for team-related phenomena.

Structural assessment refers to a systematic process for eliciting, representing, and evaluating knowledge structures. According to Goldsmith and Kraiger (1997), structural assessment consists of four steps: First, a set of concepts is defined that represents core knowledge in a particular domain. For shared mental models in teams, these concepts may be key elements of the task, equipment, team, or roles. Second, individuals' judgments of the similarity or relatedness among concepts determined in the first step are elicited. This step assumes that relatedness judgments represent meaningful distances within members' knowledge structures models. For example, if two team members rate "knowing each other's roles" and "providing backup" as being highly related, it would be assumed that both agree that knowing each other's roles is structurally related to providing backup.

Third, individuals' relatedness judgments are represented by transforming the ratings using a data analysis procedure such as multidimensional scaling or link-weighted networks (e.g., Pathfinder; Schvaneveldt, Durso, & Dearholt, 1989). Pathfinder generates concept maps in which concepts are depicted as nodes and relationships are depicted as links between nodes. These networks represent any team member's organization of the relevant knowledge of task, equipment, team, or roles.

Finally, the representations can be evaluated in order to assign an index of "sharedness" at the team level. One advantage of Pathfinder solutions (over multidimensional scaling or other representation methods) is that Pathfinder solutions can be reliably and validly scored (Goldsmith, Johnson, & Acton, 1991; Goldsmith & Kraiger, 1997). The most common scoring method is to determine the structural similarity between one representation and another representing a target or referent structure. For example, trainees' posttraining solutions may be compared to an expert or trainer's solution (Kraiger, Salas, & Cannon-Bowers, 1995). Similarity is usually represented as the ratio of common links (between representations) to all possible links averaged across all nodes in a concept map.

To date, Pathfinder has been applied only to individual assessment (e.g., Goldsmith et al., 1991; Kraiger et al., 1995) but may be readily adapted for assessing shared knowledge structures among team members. For example, similarity scores can be assessed between each pair of team members, then averaged to compute a team similarity score. Alternatively, members' ratings can first be averaged and then represented and evaluated as a single team measure. In situations where team members must act in complement, individual ratings can first be weighted by the importance of the relationship to individual to team functioning, and these weighted ratings can be averaged and represented.

At the individual level, Pathfinder representations have been found to be valid predictors of classroom performance (e.g., Goldsmith & Johnson, 1990; Goldsmith et al., 1991, Kraiger et al., 1995) as well as posttraining transfer (Kraiger et al., 1995). Thus, extrapolation of the method to the team level may hold promise as well. However, research is needed to compare and evaluate different methods of representing and scoring team-level measures of shared knowledge structures. Given the framework just provided, various methods of representing and scoring knowledge structures can be directly compared by their relationships to other proposed constructs in the framework. For example, weighted and unweighted ratings can both be represented and compared to a measure of team coordination, with the expectation that the weighted ratings will be more highly related.

Shared Attitudes.   In addition to common processing and knowledge structures, attitudes unique to the team context may have a direct impact on the team interaction processes and team effectiveness (Cannon-Bowers, Tannenbaum, Salas, & Volpe, 1995). The several studies that have examined team attitudes have found that beliefs and attitudes are strongly associated with team processes and team performance (e.g., Gregorich, Helmreich, & Wilhelm, 1990; Ruffel-Smith, 1979). Attitudinal components of shared mental models consist of those attributes that enable team members to coordinate information or actions, and function effectively as a team. Prior research on cohesion and team effectiveness has provided mixed results (e.g., Hare, 1962; Stogdill, 1972). However, cohesion seems to be more highly related to team functioning when the team is well trained and is goal oriented. High cohesiveness may also enable team members to be flexible enough to adapt different interactive styles depending on task demands (McIntyre & Salas, 1995). Additionally, balance theory predicts that within-group similarity would facilitate the development of effective shared mental models. Specifically, if two team members liked each other, they would be more likely to hold similar affect towards the knowledge elements constituting a shared mental model (e.g., hold similar goal structures). Because affective states influence information processing (Isen, Shalker, Clark, & Karp, 1978), members would assimilate these knowledge elements in similar ways.

Two attitudes hypothesized to be essential to team effectiveness are a collective orientation (Driskell & Salas, 1992) and collective efficacy (Travillian, Baker, & Cannon-Bowers, 1992). The former refers to the shared capacity to take others' behavior into account during team interactions or a belief in the team approach, whereas the latter refers to the team members' assessment of his or her team's collective ability to perform required tasks. Research by Driskell and Salas (1992) found that collectively oriented teams performed significantly better than individual members, whereas egocentric teams performed no better than did members performing as individuals. Research on collective efficacy also provides evidence of a positive relationship between the attitude and team performance on tasks (Forward & Zander, 1968; Shea & Guzzo, 1987; Travillian et al., 1992). In the studies described here, the attitudes are measured at an individual level and aggregated to assess a team-level construct. To date, these constructs have not been measured in ways that would allow us to conclude they were "shared," nor have they been assessed in a manner consistent with definitions of mental models. One way to assess the degree to which attitudes are shared would be to have team members first complete an assessment of their own perception of the team-level attribute (e.g., team members rate collective efficacy), and then have them rate how they believe others perceive their attitudes. The extent to which team members can accurately predict others' perceptions of their attitudes would provide an index of the extent to which team members share team-oriented attitudes.

Shared Expectations. A fourth aspect of shared mental models to be assessed is members' shared expectations. The behavioral components of shared mental models at the construct level include a number of interrelated team-level skills. First, teams may share scanning or diagnostic activities. For example, in hierarchical decision-making military teams, different team members may scan different aspects of the environment, or seek different cues of a potential problem or threat to the team. Second, team-shared mental models may contain shared expectations for behavioral tendencies of team members. These shared expectations allow team members to provide information in a timely manner, provide backup support as necessary, or coordinate actions to accomplish a team goal.

Cannon-Bowers et al. (1993) argued that these common expectations for task and team behavior are the most critical component of shared mental models. More specifically, members should share expectations for each member's functional responsibility and task contributions, as well as each member's probable response to likely task demands. Shared expectations may be held for behaviors, responsibilities, mentoring activities, or decision making.

There are several ways in which members' shared expectations could be measured. The most direct way is to ask members what other team members are likely to be doing at any point in time. For example, a scenario could be described in which the correct sequence of behaviors is known for each team member. Individual members could be asked to state what they expect another to do at a certain step in the sequence, or they could select a behavior from among several alternatives in a rating task. The "correctness" of the response could be scored by its correspondence to the specified behavior in the sequence.

The problem with this type of measurement is that the proper sequence of behaviors can rarely be known in actual, dynamic situations. Or, the actions of one team member may change expectations for future behaviors of another. Furthermore, it cannot be known whether a team member who can predict another's behavior actually understands why that action was taken, or is simply observant of past behavior.

An alternative format is to adapt methods of process tracing used in cognitive task analysis of individuals. Specifically, Kraiger et al. (1993) recommended the use of probed protocol analysis to assess individuals' understanding of why and how steps contribute to the completion of the task. Applied to a team setting, individual team members may be interviewed individually and be asked to articulate the steps they would take given a particular problem, objective, scenario, and so on. They would also be asked questions such as: "Why perform that step?" "How would you know if the steps were successful?" "What would be the different possible outcomes of that action, and what would be your response to each outcome?" These steps and probes would then be given to other team members. Thus, other team members would not be expected to describe the steps others would take (because the steps are given to them), but to articulate the reasons for the steps, diagnostic information to be gained from each step, cues to determine success or failure of the step, and so forth. Team members who could provide detailed responses to these probes would be more likely to hold accurate expectations for others' behavior in different situations.

DETERMINANTS OF SHARED MENTAL MODELS

In the prior section, we discussed the relationship between the latent construct of a shared mental model and potential measures. As noted previously, one way to establish the construct validity of any measure is to show that it is logically and empirically related to other variables in a meaningful nomological network. Accordingly, in this section, we present proposed determinants of shared mental models, along with hypotheses that logically relate the determinants to the shared mental model construct and its measures. In the next section, we draw linkages between measures of shared mental models and indices of team effectiveness and team performance.

Shared mental models provide team members with a common understanding of task requirements and the coordination activities required for performance (Cannon-Bowers et al., 1993). Variables within and outside of the team affect the development of individual mental models and subsequent shared mental models. As indicated in the model in Fig. 4.1, determinants exist at several levels, including environmental, organizational, team and individual. By understanding the relationships between these determinants and resulting mental models, we can make testable hypotheses that can help validate the measures of the shared mental model construct. Following is an outline of variables at each of these levels that act as antecedents of mental models.

Environmental Antecedents

Organizations and employees do not function in a closed system. The social, political, and economic culture in which we live and work affects our behaviors, cognitions, and attitudes (Triandis, 1988). The broader cultural environment will therefore have an effect on the development of mental models for teamwork and team performance. For example, teams are a hot topic in business today and widely supported by many organizations (Cannon-Bowers, Oser, & Flanagan, 1992; Hackman, 1990; Rosen, 1989). This pro-team climate affects the development of each individual's mental model differently than if the U.S. business environment was unsupportive of teams. Similarly, economic conditions affect the extent to which employees are willing to focus on team needs rather than their own needs (Lawler, 1986), affecting the development of individual and shared mental models. Finally, the degree to which the environment is fundamentally individualistic or collectivistic (Triandis, 1972) may affect the development of mental models for team process and performance. In a highly collectivistic society, it is more likely that team members will share similar views toward teamwork as well as more generalized beliefs, values, and norms (Triandis, 1989). For example, other researchers have suggested that quality circles are more likely to succeed in Japan than the United States because the Japanese culture provides a greater emphasis on collective action and reward (Ouchi, 1981). Environmental variables are predicted to have the strongest effect on affective components of shared mental models:

> H1: Teams formed in environments favorable to collective behavior will be characterized by greater affect among team members and a greater level of collective orientation than teams formed in less favorable environments.

Organizational Antecedents

Organizational-level variables such as organizational culture, reward systems, structural support and training will also affect the structure of team members' mental models regarding their team and general performance.

Culture.   The shared values, beliefs, artifacts, and assumptions of an organization make up its culture (Peters & Waterman, 1982; Schein, 1990). The content of the organizational culture (e.g., conservativism, humanistic values, etc.) will influence the way in which team members interpret their tasks and their interactions with others. The strength of the culture will determine the degree to which the culture content will have an effect on individual behavior, cognitions, and attitudes (Schein, 1990). Because cultures carry information about the meaning of events and the value of certain actions, organizational culture will have the strongest effect on knowledge and affective components of shared mental models.

H2: Presence of strong organizational culture will have a positive effect on teams' shared knowledge structures, regardless of whether shared knowledge structures are measured in terms of the degree of overlap, relatedness, or complement among team members.

H3: Presence of strong organizational culture will have a positive effect on measures of collective orientation and cohesion or affect in teams.
Culture within an organization is carried by artifacts and symbols (Triandis, 1989).

Furthermore, artifacts and symbols are defined from the meaning expressed in the declarative knowledge of the culture. Thus, the extent to which team members share strong, common artifacts and symbols will influence their shared knowledge structures. To the extent that team members accept the same values conveyed by the culture, they will be more accepting of each other.

Reward Systems.   Reward system structure has been found to influence behavior and attitudes in organizations (Lawler, 1990; Weiner, 1980). One of the most important considerations for teams is individual incentive plans versus group incentives (Cascio, 1989). Group incentive plans promote greater teamwork by rewarding team members based on the productivity of the team as a whole. In using group incentive plans, the organization reinforces the importance of group effort. It is assumed that reward systems that favor team output or team processes will positively influence team-oriented mental models.

H4: Team-based reward systems will be positively related to measures of collective orientation and collective efficacy.

These reward systems will encourage interaction among team members and increased perceptions of the saliency of team-related actions. However, in the absence of knowledge about how to perform together to accomplish team goals, team effectiveness may not improve. Therefore, team training is also important.

Training.   Task-related and developmental training are the most proximal organizational determinant of mental models. Several papers have investigated the effectiveness of training for developing a well-defined mental model (see, Cannon-Bowers et al., 1993; Kraiger et al., 1993). Evidence from these studies indicates that task training improves the distinctiveness and clarity of subjects' knowledge structures. It does so by providing team members with shared knowledge (procedural, declarative, and strategic) as well as similar or complimentary behaviors and attitudes.

H5: Training that is team-based will have a positive effect on teams' shared knowledge structures and shared expectations. Teams experiencing team training will show greater similarity among team members in their knowledge structures and will be more likely to anticipate the actions of other team members or interpret the reasons for those actions.

Team-Based Antecedents

Team-level variables will also affect the development of shared mental models. The most important of these include task characteristics, process characteristics, and shared efficacy.

Task Characteristics.   The task itself will predict the form and cohesiveness of mental models held by team members. Tasks may be characterized by their degree of structure or cognitive load. Tasks that are highly structured will promote conformity and produce more closely related mental models. Similarly, abstract tasks will likely lead to broad interpretation and possibly more variation in mental models among team members. This does not mean that teams will perform better on highly structured tasks because of similarity in individual mental models; mental models may also need to be overlapping or complementary to foster effective performance.

H6: Task characteristics will have a direct effect on task-based schema and shared knowledge structures held by team members. Greater task complexity will result in more complex schema and shared knowledge structures (evident by the number of dimensions, number of clusters, or number of contingent goal structures).

Concrete tasks will lead to specific, well-defined knowledge structures at the individual level, and, accordingly, it may be easier for team members to articulate their knowledge. Accordingly, the overlap among knowledge structures would be expected to increase.

Team tasks also differ in complexity, or the degree of cognitive load they place on team members. Cognitive load refers to the sum of demands on the capacity of an individual's working memory (Jih & Reeves, 1992). Cognitive load is additive in that demands may come from the nature of the task (e.g., a well-defined vs. ill-structured problem), the nature of the environment (e.g., face-to-face vs. human–computer interactions), the number of response options, or the availability of feedback. Performing tasks in a team setting increases cognitive load in several ways—task demands increase as members must add coordination activities, the response environment shifts, the number of options may change (team members may make a decision, defer, or share information), and additional sources of feedback become available. Without adequate equipment, training, or leadership, cognitive demands from other task aspects may be so large that cognitive resources for task behaviors may be insufficient. Whenever cognitive load increases during training, learning is imperiled. However, if teams are aware of increasing cognitive load, then they may be more likely to form shared mental models as a strategy for coping with the changes.

H7: Task characteristics that increase cognitive load will result in the distribution of knowledge across members of successful teams; measures of team schema, knowledge of steps, and shared knowledge structures will differentiate between effective and ineffective teams when scored for how well team members complement each other than scored for overlap.

Process Characteristics.   Interdependence of team processes may affect development of mental models both individually and collectively. The extent to which team members rely on each other and must communicate with each other is central to the level of coordination required for effective performance. As the requirement for coordination increases, so does the importance of shared mental models among team members. Members of highly interdependent teams must receive more training, in particular more cross-training to assure development of shared mental models (Burgess, Salas, & Cannon-Bowers, 1993). Teams that routinely interact are more likely to develop shared mental models as a result of consistent communication and feedback.

Shared Efficacy.   Shared efficacy for performance in a team setting may greatly influence the synchronization of team members' mental models.

Shared efficacy in a team setting can be defined as the degree to which the team members agree upon their ability to succeed at a team-related task. The previous success or failure experiences as a team or as individuals may help in formulating their shared mental model for successful coordination and performance. To the extent that teams have had prior success, they may be more likely to develop positive shared mental models. Teams who have had poor, ambiguous, or varied experiences, or who have had unpredictable task success as individuals (and therefore doubt their abilities), will be less likely to develop shared mental models that compliment those of other team members.

H8: Prior success as a team will have a direct effect on affective components of shared mental models; teams with a prior history of success will have higher collective efficacy than teams without prior success.

Individual Antecedents

Individual differences are the most proximal variables to shared mental models and thus may have an important impact in their development. For example, previous research has shown that the development of individual mental models is related to learning styles (Jih & Reeves, 1992), interactivity (Jih & Reeves, 1992), conceptual complexity (Suedfeld & Coren, 1992), and previous team experience (Burgess et al., 1993). Because these variables affect individual development, it is reasonable to conjecture that in a team setting, their heterogeneity or homogeneity may affect the rate at which teams are able to reconcile individual mental models into a collective one:

H9: Teams classified as homogeneous with respect to individual difference variables will be more likely to hold shared mental models characterized by overlap among team members; components of mental models most likely to be shared are structural knowledge and information processing variables.

The individual antecedents most likely to have the greatest effect on shared mental models are personality and motivational variables. Personality has long been studied as a predictor of behavior (Costa & McCrea, 1992; Cropanzano, James, & Citera, 1992; Staw & Ross, 1985; Weiss & Adler, 1984). Recently, links have been established between personality measures and team behavior (George, 1990). This is most clearly seen in the work related to team roles (Fleishman & Zaccaro, 1992; Margerison & McCann, 1989); however, others have investigated specific personality constructs and their relation to team behavior and performance (e.g., George, 1990).

Much of the team personality research has focused on team leader personality and its relation to how leaders interact with other team members (Burgess et al., 1993; Cannon-Bowers et al., 1992; Chidester & Foushee, 1989; Orasanu & Fischer, 1993). Specifically, much work has been done with aircraft cockpit crews. An analysis conducted by Cooper, White, and Lauber (1980, cited in Prince, Chidester, Cannon-Bowers, & Bowers, 1992) examined aircraft accidents between 1968 and 1976 and found many of the causes to be linked to error in cockpit crew communication, decision making, judgment, and leadership. Several studies have since investigated the role of pilot personality and cockpit crew coordination–performance and reported a positive relationship between the two constructs (Chidester & Foushee, 1989; Chidester, Kanki, Foushee, Dickinson, & Bowles, 1990). Specifically, teams have been most effective when the leaders are directive, but communicative, and the team members are open and not afraid to speak up (Chidester & Foushee, 1989; Chidester et al., 1990; Orasanu & Fischer, 1993). These personality traits may influence the leader's and members' mental models of how to interact with team members, thereby affecting performance.

Motivation theory may also provide insight to the development of mental models. For example, according to expectancy theory, for motivation to be present there must be a valued reward (valence), the subject must believe he or she is capable of the effort required to obtain the goal (instrumentality) and the reward must be obtainable with effort (expectancy; Vroom, 1964). If a team member believes any of these is lacking for team performance, it will alter both the individual's mental model as well as the shared mental model, negatively affecting performance.

OUTCOMES OF SHARED MENTAL MODELS

As shown in the Fig. 4.1 the shared mental models are thought to directly affect both team performance and team effectiveness. Team effectiveness refers to any indicator of how well a team accomplishes its assigned tasks, mission objectives, and so on, and team performance refers to any indicators of how the team carries out those tasks. Over-simplifying, team performance refers to process measures, and team effectiveness to outcome measures. Both outcomes are related—the quality of the process will affect the quality of the product and products will influence the direction of future team process. However, in order to develop a nomological network about shared mental models, it is probably helpful to understand the links between mental models and performance measures, as the latter are more proximal to shared mental models than are effectiveness outcomes.

Team Effectiveness Variables. Team effectiveness can be measured in terms of tangible and intangible outcomes; Tannenbaum, Beard, and Salas (1992) described these outcomes in terms of product quantity and quality, time spent, costs, errors and general productivity. The specific product of interest will be dictated primarily by the type of team and its goals. Success in obtaining these outcomes will be affected by the shared mental models of team members.

Team Process Variables. Process variables for teams have been broadly defined along several dimensions: decision making, communication, leadership, coordination, adaptability/flexibility, assertiveness, situational awareness, morale, feedback, and backup behaviors (McIntyre & Salas, 1995). Other process variables have also been suggested as important considerations for team effectiveness. Bettenhausen (1991) included cohesion, commitment, conflict, and goal setting. Fleishman and Zaccaro (1992) further defined team process in terms of various functions: orientation, resource distribution, timing (activity pacing), response coordination, motivational, systems monitoring, and procedure maintenance. Although there is an overlap among these sets of proposed process variables, there is still no consensus as to a definition of team performance variables.

Whichever team performance variables are considered, they are likely to be influenced by shared mental models. The areas in which the greatest impact is expected are decision making and communication. Decision making has long been considered an integral component of many team activities (Dyer, 1984; Hackman, 1990). Orasanu (1990) investigated team decision making in aircraft crews. Her research suggests several stages of decision making: communication to define and understand the problem, solution strategizing, selecting a strategy, and assigning responsibilities to team members for implementing the solution. These steps are influenced by mental models in that each member approaches the task with a model for problem solving and decision making. In addition, the process of decision making will help team members form shared mental models for future decision making. The influence of and influence on shared mental models can be measured at each stage, as outlined by Orasanu (1990).

Team communication has been widely researched and several taxonomies for classifying behaviors associated with communication have been utilized. Altman (1966) used six categories, including ordering/telling, informing, asking, repeating, inferring, and evaluating. Each of these components is critically linked to effective team functioning. The manner in which team members understand their responsibilities in communicating with each other defines their shared mental model for communication. Evidence supports that teams perform more proficiently when their communication is well coordinated with little excess chatter and concise statements of questioning, feedback, and confirmation (McIntyre & Salas, 1995; Willis, Hubert, Burgess, & Travillian, 1992). This suggests that team members share models for the most efficient, effective manner in which to communicate. Their shared mental model for communication facilitates their performance in this area.

The extent to which team members share mental models in these important areas will affect their successful interactions and effectiveness. By investigating the relationship between shared mental models and team process variables we will more fully understand how and why teams are effective.

SUMMARY AND NEXT STEPS

In developing measures of shared mental models, it is important to recognize that though a shared mental model is a multidimensional construct, multiple measures may be necessary to adequately represent the criterion space. By drawing upon a framework such as the one proposed in this chapter, a set of measures may be proposed that capture what is shared among team members. Rather than a single measure of a shared mental model, we believe it is necessary to assess individual components of a shared mental model collectively, or as a set. Different measures may be valuable for different applications. For example, measures of team schema may be helpful for understanding how teams respond to team-oriented training, yet measures of shared expectations may be helpful for analyzing breakdowns in team communication. Thus, not all measures may be necessary, but may depend on the purpose of measurement.

In any practical situation, the selection or weighting of particular measures within that set may be determined by situation-specific knowledge of the determinants of the team shared mental model, or the relative importance of team processes or outcomes. That is, it may be known that work teams in one organization may be characterized by a particularly strong culture or dominant leaders; thus, the choice of measures may need to be sensitive to those factors. Alternatively, if it is important to avoid breakdowns in team decision making, then measures that are the most likely to predict such processes may be preferred.

Clearly, the next step is to operationalize and test specific measures of shared mental model components. Given the complex nature of the construct, the development and testing of such measures would benefit by a construct-oriented measurement approach. For example, multiple measures of shared mental models may be collected before asking teams to perform complex tasks requiring multiple dimensions of team performance (e.g., communication, coordination, shared decision making). Alternatively, multiple measures may be collected prior to asking teams to perform distinct tasks each requiring a different dimension of team performance. In either scenario, predictions may be made about the relationship between components of a shared mental model and a specific dimension of team performance (e.g., teams high on a measure of shared expectations will perform better on tasks, or aspects of tasks, requiring coordination, but will not necessarily perform better on tasks requiring communication). By testing predictions such as these, we can learn not only about the convergent and discriminant validity of the measures but also about the relationships between shared mental model components and team performance.

REFERENCES

Altman, I. (1966) Aspects of the criterion problem in small group research: The analysis of group tasks (Vol. 2). *Acta Psychologica, 25,* 199–221.

Bettenhausen, K. L. (1991). Five years of group research: What have we learned and what needs to be addressed? *Journal of Management, 17,* 345–381.

Brehmer, B. (1972). Policy conflict as a function of policy similarity and policy complexity. *Scandinavian Journal of Psychology, 13,* 208–221.

Burgess, K. A., Salas, E., & Cannon-Bowers, J. A. (1993, May). *Training team leaders: "More than meets the eye."* Paper presented at the eighth annual conference of the Society for Industrial and Organizational Psychology, San Francisco, CA.

Cannon-Bowers, J. A., Oser, R., & Flanagan, D. L. (1992). Work teams in industry: A selected review and proposed framework. In R. W. Sweezey & E. Salas (Eds.), *Teams: Their training and performance.* Norwood, NJ: Ablex.

Cannon-Bowers, J. A., & Salas, E. (1990, April). *Cognitive psychology and team training: Shared mental models in complex systems.* Paper presented at the fifth annual Conference of the Society for Industrial Organizational Psychology, Miami, FL.

Cannon-Bowers, J. A., Salas, E., & Converse, S. A. (1993). Shared mental models in expert decision making teams. In N. J. Castellan, Jr. (Ed.), *Current issues in individual and group decision making* (pp. 221–246). Hillsdale, NJ: Lawrence Erlbaum Associates.

Cannon-Bowers, J. A., Tannenbaum, S. I., Salas, E., & Volpe, C. E. (1995). Defining team competencies: Implications for training requirements and strategies. In R. Guzzo & E. Salas (Eds.), *Team effectiveness and decision-making in organizations* (pp. 333–380). San Francisco: Jossey-Bass.

Cascio, W. (1989). *Managing human resources: Productivity, quality of work life, profits.* New York: McGraw-Hill.

Chidester, T. R., & Foushee, H. C. (1989). Leader personality and crew effectiveness: A full mission simulation to identify variables influencing crew effectiveness. In *Proceedings of the Fifth International Symposium on Aviation Psychology.* Columbus: Ohio State University.

Chidester, T. R., Kanki, B. G., & Foushee, H. C., Dickinson, C. L., & Bowles, S. V. (1990). *Personality factors in flight operations: Leader characteristics and crew performance in full-mission air transportation simulation* (NASA Technical Memorandum 102259). Moffett Field, CA: NASA-Ames Research Center.

Costa, P. T., & McCrea, R. R. (1992). *NEO PI-R professional manual*. Odessa, FL: Psychological Assessment Resources, Inc.

Cronbach, L. J., & Meehl, P. H. (1955). Construct validity in psychological tests. *Psychological Bulletin, 89,* 281-302.

Cropanzano, R., James, K., & Citera, M. (1992). A goal hierarchy model of personality, motivation, and leadership. In L. L. Cummings & B. W. Staw (Eds.), *Research in organizational behavior* (Vol. 15, pp. 267-322). Greenwich, CT: JAI Press.

Driskell, J. E., & Salas, E. (1992). Collective behavior and team performance. *Human Factors, 34,* 277-288.

Dyer, J. L. (1984). Team research and team training: A state of the art review. *Human Factors Review,* 285-323.

Fleishman, E. A., & Zaccaro, S. J. (1992). Toward a taxonomic classification of team performance functions: Initial considerations, subsequent evaluations and current formulations. In R. W. Sweezy & E. Salas (Eds.), *Teams: Their training and performance* (pp. 31-56). Norwood, NJ: Ablex.

Forward, J., & Zander, A. (1968). Choice of unattainable group goals and effects on performance. *Organizational Behavior and Human Performance, 6,* 184-189.

George, J. M . (1990). Personality, affect, and behavior in groups. *Journal of Applied Psychology, 75,* 107-116.

Goldsmith, T. E., & Johnson, P. J. (1990). A structural assessment of classroom learning. In R. W. Schvaneveldt (Ed.), *Pathfinder associative networks: Studies in knowledge organization* (pp. 241-254). Norwood, NJ: Ablex.

Goldsmith, T. E., Johnson, P. J., & Acton, W. H. (1991). Assessing structural knowledge. *Journal of Educational Psychology, 83,* 88-96.

Goldsmith, T. E., & Kraiger, K. (1997). Applications of structural knowledge assessment to training evaluation. In J. K. Ford (Ed.), *Improving training effectiveness in organizations* (pp. 73-96). Hillsdale, NJ: Lawrence Erlbaum Associates.

Gregorich, S. E., Helmreich, R. L., & Wilhelm, J. A. (1990). The structure of cockpit management attitudes. *Journal of Applied Psychology, 75,* 682-690.

Hackman, J. R. (1990). *Groups that work (and those that don't): creating conditions for effective teamwork*. San Francisco, CA: Jossey-Bass.

Hare, A. P. (1962). *Handbook of small group research*. New York: The Free Press.

Isen, A. M., Shalker, T. E., Clark, M., & Karp, L. (1978). Affect, accessibility of material in memory, and behavior: A cognitive loop? *Journal of Personality and Social Psychology, 36,* 1-12.

Jih, H. J., & Reeves, T. C. (1992). Mental models: A research focus on interactive learning systems. *Educational Technology, Research and Development, 40,* 39-54.

Jonassen, D. H., Beissner, K., & Yacci, M. (1993). *Structural knowledge: Techniques for representing, conveying, and acquiring structural knowledge*. Hillsdale, NJ: Lawrence Erlbaum Associates.

Kaplan, R. (1990). Collaboration from a cognitive perspective: Sharing models across expertise. *EDRA, 21,* 45-51.

Kleinman, D. L., & Serfaty, D. (1989). Team performance assessment in distributed decision-making. In R. Gilson, J. P. Kincaid, & B. Goldiez (Eds.), *Proceedings: Interactive Networked Simulation for Training Conference* (pp. 22-27). Orlando, FL: Naval Training Systems Center.

Klimoski, R., & Mohammed, S. (1994). Team mental model: Construct or metaphor? *Journal of Management, 20,* 403-437.

Kraiger, K. (1995). Integrating training research. *Training Research Journal, 1,* 5-17.

Kraiger, K., Ford, J. K., & Salas, E. (1993). Application of cognitive, skill-based, and affective theories of learning outcomes to new methods of training evaluation [Monograph]. *Journal of Applied Psychology, 78,* 311–328.

Kraiger, K., Salas, E., & Cannon-Bowers, J. A. (1995). Cognitively-based measures of learning during training. *Human Factors, 37,* 804–816.

Lawler, E. E., III. (1986). *High-involvement management.* San Francisco: Jossey-Bass.

Lawler, E. E., III. (1990). *Strategic pay: Aligning organizational strategies and pay systems.* San Francisco: Jossey-Bass.

Lesgold, A., Rubinson, H., Feltovich, P., Glaser, R., Klopfer, D., & Wang, Y. (1989). Expertise in a complex skill: Diagnosing X-ray pictures. In M. T. Chi, R. Glaser, & M. J. Farr (Eds.), *The nature of expertise* (pp. 311–342). Hillsdale, NJ: Lawrence Erlbaum Associates.

Margerison, C., & McCann, D. (1989). Managing high performance teams. *Training and Development Journal, 68*(11), 52–60.

McIntyre, R. M., Morgan, B. B., Jr., Salas, E., & Glickman, A. S. (1988). *Teamwork from team training: New evidence for the development of teamwork skills during operational training.* Paper presented at the 10th annual Interservice/ Industry Training Systems Conference, Orlando, FL.

McIntyre, R. M., & Salas, E. (1995). Team performance in complex environments: What we have learned so far. In R. Guzzo & E. Salas (Eds.), *Team effectiveness and decision making in organizations* (pp. 333–380). San Francisco: Jossey-Bass.

Means, B., & Gott, S. P. (1988). Cognitive task analysis as a basis for tutor development: Articulating abstract knowledge representations. In J. Psotka, L. D. Massey, & S. A. Mutter (Eds.), *Intelligent tutoring systems: Lessons learned* (pp. 35–57). Hillsdale, NJ: Lawrence Erlbaum Associates.

Minionis, D. P., Zaccaro, S. J., & Perez, R. (1995, May). *Shared mental models, team coordination, and team performance.* Paper presented at the 10th annual meeting of the Society for Industrial and Organizational Psychology, Orlando, FL.

Morgan, B. B., Glickman, A. S., Woodard, E. A., Blaiwes, A. S., & Salas, E. (1986). *Measurement of team behaviors in a Navy environment* (Tech. Rep. TR-86-014), Orlando, FL: Naval Training Systems Center.

Norman, D. A., Gentner, S., & Stevens, A. L. (1976). Comments on learning schemata and memory representation. In D. Klahr (Ed.), *Cognition and instruction* (pp. 177–196). Hillsdale, NJ: Lawrence Erlbaum Associates.

Orasanu, J. (1990). *Shared mental models and crew performance.* Paper presented at the 34th annual meeting of the Human Factors Society, Orlando, FL.

Orasanu, J., & Fisher, U. (1993, May). *Leadership in flight emergencies: Lessons from the flight deck.* Symposium paper presented at the eighth annual conference of the Society for Industrial and Organizational Psychology, San Francisco, CA.

Oser, R. L., McCallum, G. A., Salas, E., & Morgan, B. B. (1989). *Toward a definition of teamwork: An analysis of critical team behaviors* (Tech. Rep. No. 89-004). Orlando, FL: Naval Training Systems Center, Human Factors Division.

Ouchi, W. G. (1981). *Theory Z: How American business can meet the Japanese challenge.* Reading, MA: Addison-Wesley.

Peters, T. J., & Waterman, R. H. (1982). *In search of excellence: Lessons from America's best-run companies.* New York: Harper & Row.

Prince, C., Chidester, T. R., Cannon-Bowers, J. A., & Bowers, C. (1992). Aircrew coordination–achieving teamwork in the cockpit. In R. W. Sweezey & E. Salas (Eds.), *Teams: Their training and performance* (pp. 329–353). Norwood, NJ: Ablex.

Rentsch, J. R., Heffner, T. S., & Duffy, L. T. (1993). *Teamwork schema representations: The role of team experience.* Paper presented at the eighth annual conference of the Society for Industrial and Organizational Psychology, San Francisco, CA.

Rosen, N. (1989). *Teamwork and the bottomline.* Hillsdale, NJ: Lawrence Erlbaum Associates.

Rouse, W. B., Cannon-Bowers, J. A., & Salas, E. (1992). The role of mental models in team performance in complex systems. *IEEE Transactions on Systems, Man, and Cybernetics, 22,* 1296–1308.

Rouse, W. B., & Morris, N. M. (1986). On looking into the black box: Prospects and limits in the search for mental models. *Psychological Bulletin, 100,* 349–363.

Ruffel-Smith, H.P. (1979). *A simulator study of the interaction of pilot workload and errors* (Tech. Rep. No. TM-78482). Moffett Field, CA: NASA-Ames Research Center.

Rumelhart, D. E., & Ortony, A. (1977). The representation of knowledge in memory. In R. C. Anderson, R. J. Spiro, & W. E. Montague (Eds.), *Schooling and the acquisition of knowledge* (pp. 99–136). Hillsdale, NJ: Lawrence Erlbaum Associates.

Schein, E. H. (1990). Organization culture. *American Psychologist, 45,* 109–119.

Schvaneveldt, R. W., Durso, F. T., & Dearholt, D. W. (1989). Network structures in proximity data. In G. H. Bower (Ed.), *The psychology of learning and motivation* (Vol. 24, pp. 249–284). New York: Academic Press.

Shavelson, R. J. (1974). Methods for examining representations of subject-matter structure in a student's memory. *Journal of Research for Science Teaching, 11,* 231–249.

Shea, G. P., & Guzzzo, R. A. (1987). Group effectiveness: What really matters? *Sloan Management Review, 3,* 25–31.

Staw, B. M., & Ross, J. (1985). Stability in the midst of change: A dispositional approach to job attitudes. *Journal of Applied Psychology, 70,* 469–480.

Stogdill, R. M. (1972). Group productivity, drive, and cohesiveness. *Organizational Behavior and Human Performance, 8,* 26–43.

Suedfeld, P., & Coren, S. (1992). Cognitive correlates of conceptual complexity. *Personality and Individual Differences, 13,* 1193–1204.

Tannenbaum, S. L., Beard, R. L., & Salas, E. (1992). Team building and its influence on team effectiveness: An examination of conceptual and empirical developments. In K. Kelly (Ed.), *Issues, theory, and research in industrial/organizational psychology* (pp. 117–153). Amsterdam: Elsevier.

Travillian, K., Baker, C. V., & Cannon-Bowers, J. A. (1992, March). *Correlates of self and collective efficacy with team functioning.* Paper presented at the 38th annual meeting of the Southeastern Psychological Association, Knoxville, TN.

Triandis, H. (1972). *The analysis of subjective culture.* New York: Wiley.

Triandis, H. (1988). Collectivism vs. individualism: A reconceptualization of a basic concept in cross-cultural psychology. In C. Bagley & G. K. Verma (Eds.), *Personality, cognition, and values: Cross-cultural perspectives in childhood and adolescence* (pp. 60–95). London: Macmillan.

Triandis, H. (1989). The self and social behavior in differing cultural contexts. *Psychological Review, 96,* 506–520.

Vroom, V. H. (1964). *Work and motivation.* New York: Wiley.

Weiner, N. (1980). Determinants and behavioral consequences of pay satisfaction: A comparison of two models. *Personnel Psychology, 33,* 741–757.

Weiss, H. M., & Adler, S. (1984). Personality and organizational behavior. In B. M. Staw & L. Cummings (Eds.), *Research in organizational behavior* (Vol. 6, pp. 1–50). Greenwich, CT: JAI Press.

Wickens, C. D. (1984). *Engineering psychology and human performance.* Columbus, OH: Charles Merrill.

Willis, R. P., Hubert, T., Burgess, K. A., & Travillian, K. K. (1992). *Factors impacting distributed teamwork: Preliminary results.* Paper presented at the 100th annual meeting of the American Psychological Association, Washington, DC.

5 Team Workload: Its Meaning and Measurement

Clint A. Bowers
Curt C. Braun
Ben B. Morgan, Jr.
University of Central Florida

> Despite spectacular technological advances in controls, displays, and information handling, the effectiveness of military systems remains inextricably linked to the performance capabilities of human operators . . .
>
> —Boff (1990, p. 552)

One of the most widely studied areas of human capability has been concerned with the performance effects of operator workload. The significance of the effects of workload on performance is reflected in the fact that recent design standards require the evaluation and limitation of operator workload (U.S. Dept. of Army, 1987). Today, few systems are designed and produced without in-depth evaluations of operator workload. The critical importance of this factor has given rise to a vast literature related to the effects of workload on individuals. For example, it has been reported that more than 500 workload papers have been written since the early 1960s (Hancock, Mihaly, Rahimi, & Meshkati, 1988). The scope of this literature ranges from discussions of measurement techniques to workload modeling and computer simulation. A review of this literature indicates that workload assessment techniques have been applied to problem solving, flying, training, driving, and a host of other applied domains. However, although the importance of workload has been illustrated with respect to individuals, there has been virtually no research related to the effects of workload in teams.

As noted recently by others (e.g., Cannon-Bowers, Oser, & Flanagan,

1992), teams have become an increasingly important unit of performance in many military, industrial, medical, and public service environments. The increasing technological sophistication and complexity of operating systems, the reduced availability of highly skilled personnel, and the increasing importance of global competition in the international marketplace has led both military and civilian organizations to place greater reliance on the performance of teams. This increased utilization of teams in the workplace has resulted in a substantial body of research related to the factors that influence team performance and the ability of teams to coordinate effectively among team members. Indeed, one of the major thrusts of this research has focused on the relationship of coordination requirements and behaviors to team performance. Very early in the study of teams, coordination was identified as having a major impact on team performance. For example, Kidd (1961) highlighted the relationship between team coordination and performance when he observed that, "intrinsic to team performance is the requirement of coordination. This requirement is superimposed on the normal demands of the task itself and leads to a proportionate reduction of exclusively task-directed behavior" (p.199).

Thus, the effects of coordination requirements on team performance has been the focus of considerable research. For example, work conducted by Lauber (1979) and Ruffel-Smith (1979) revealed that airline pilots, although proficient in flying, experienced substantial difficulties with coordination. In an evaluation of the coordination demands associated with U.S. Navy helicopter crews, Bowers, Morgan, Salas, and Prince (1993) found that coordination demand and workload were highest in the nonroutine segments of flight. Outside the cockpit, Morgan, Glickman, Woodward, Blaiwes, and Salas (1986) studied the coordination of U.S. Navy gunnery teams (see also Glickman et al., 1987; McCallum, Oser, & Salas, 1989). These studies have typically reported that increased coordination demands produce increasing disruptions of team performance.

It appears that coordination in teams seems to produce effects that are similar to those produced by workload in individuals. In fact, it could be argued (as it is here) that coordination requirements impose a type of workload on teams. However, a review of the team literature, like that of the workload literature, reveals that since the 1950s, very few articles have discussed workload in teams (Bowers et al., 1993; Dyer, 1984; Morgan, Coates, Kirby, & Alluisi, 1984) and only a handful of studies have addressed this issue empirically (Beith, 1987; Thornton, Braun, Bowers, & Morgan, 1992; Urban, Bowers, Monday, & Morgan, 1995). Because of the increased use of teams in today's workplace and the pervasiveness of workload in these settings, and in view of the demonstrated deleterious effects of workload, it is important to explore the causes, components, and consequences of workload in teams. A number of questions need to be addressed in this regard. For example: How are teams impacted by workload? What are the critical elements of workload in teams? How does workload in teams differ from individual workload? And, how is workload measured in teams?

Thus, we explore issues related to the components and potential effects of workload in teams, hereafter referred to as *team workload*. Issues discussed include the basics of mental workload and task performance, the unique characteristics of and circumstances of teams, and the definition of team workload. The factors that influence team workload (e.g., coordination, communication, team experience, and team training) are also discussed. Finally, the assessment of team workload and its implications for task design and training are discussed.

Individual Workload and Task Performance

The conceptualization of team workload is developed from the application of individual workload concepts, principles, and relationships to the team environment. Therefore, it is important to examine briefly the major findings from prior studies of the performance effects of workload in individuals. A large body of literature has developed dealing with the relationship between task workload and individual performance (Navon & Gopher, 1979), and no attempt is made here to review all of this literature. Rather, this chapter focuses on a few of the major findings that seem to have the greatest relevance to teams.

It is widely accepted that the relationship between workload and individual performance is characterized by a curvilinear function where performance degrades at low and high levels of workload (Johannsen, 1979; O'Donnel & Eggemeier, 1986). The detrimental effects of high workload have been shown consistently in the workload literature. For example, Casali and Wierwille (1983) demonstrated that the frequency of pilot communication errors increased with increased workload. Wierwille, Rahimi, and Casali (1985) noted similar performance decrements when pilots operated in conditions of increased mediational load. As workload increased, subjects' performance on the mediational task degraded. Similarly, Vidulich and Wickens' (1984) assessment of workload dissociation revealed in compensatory tracking associated with increased workload. Performance decrements may also result when workload is below some lower threshold. In these conditions, the operator may become complacent or bored, and this can result in inattentiveness and reduced performance (Hart, 1986; Hart & Wickens, 1990; Kantowitz & Casper, 1988; Parasuraman, 1986).

Central to the concept of *workload* is the realization that task performance is a function of the cognitive resources dedicated to accomplishing a task. In fact, workload in individuals has been defined in terms of the relationship between the cognitive resources of the individual and the demands of the situation (Norman & Bobrow, 1975). The quantity of an individual's dedicated resources is a function of the individual's overall availability, the number of resources needed to attain a level of performance, and the efficiency with which the resources are administered (Navon & Gopher, 1979, 1980). Although there is some disagreement as to the attributes of cognitive resources (Navon & Gopher, 1979, 1980; Wickens, 1980, 1984), it is widely accepted that the quantity is limited. When total quantity and demand remain constant (Kerr, 1973), performance becomes a function of resource efficiency.

Navon and Gopher (1979, 1980) avoided an in-depth discussion of resource efficiency. However, available evidence clearly points to the fact that practice and training alter resource efficiency. William James (1890) first advanced the idea that practice alters the efficiency of cognitive resources. His "liberation of attention" implied that the quantity of cognitive resources required to perform a task diminished with practice. From James' days, this effect has been clearly demonstrated. Shiffrin and Schneider (1977), for example, tracked the performance of subjects on a visual search task. During initial trials, the task required the investment of considerable cognitive resources. Yet, with increased repetition, this investment decreased substantially. After 2,100 trials, the cognitive resources required to complete the task diminished from a resource-intensive controlled process to a reduced-resource automatic process. This transition from controlled to automatic processing has been demonstrated by many studies and is not limited to simple task performance (Boulter, 1977; Fisk & Schneider, 1983; Kramer, Wickens, & Donchin, 1983; MacLeod & Dunbar, 1988; Poltrock, Lansman, & Hunt, 1982; Schneider & Fisk, 1983, 1984).

Concomitant with the change in processing as a function of practice is a reduction in workload. Kramer, Wickens, and Donchin's (1983) study of complex perceptual-motor tasks revealed that workload, as measured by event-related brain potentials (ERP), diminished with extensive practice. This finding is consistent with previous studies by Poon, Thompson, Williams, and March (1974), and Rosler (1981), who also reported decreases in ERPs following practice. Finally, Gopher and Braune (1984), using a psychophysical assessment of workload, also reported a practice-workload interaction. They found that workload diminished with increased practice of seven different cognitive and psychomotor tasks.

Operational findings parallel those resulting from laboratory studies. Lindholm and Cheatham (1983) assessed the workload of student pilots being trained to execute carrier landings. Using physiological indices of workload, the authors found that workload diminished with increased practice and training. In a comparison of student and instructor pilots, Crosby and Parkinson (1979) found significant workload differences between the two groups. Using a secondary memory search task, the authors found that workload and training interacted such that student pilots, who had yet to complete training, evidenced significantly longer reaction times than their instructor counterparts. At the completion of training, however, these differences diminished substantially.

Although practice has been shown to increase resource efficiency, the stability of this state is tenuous. The processing gains achieved over time abate with the addition of other tasks. Duncan (1979) wrote, "performance decrements may often result from failure (or limits) of new or *emergent* processes whose existence depends on the particular set of tasks combined" (p. 216). The attributes of these emergent processes are the subject of much debate. Although the specific mechanisms are yet unknown, the effects are clear. For example, Bahrick and Shelly (1958) trained subjects on four visual discrimination tasks with an increasing degree of cue redundancy. Subjects practiced each task until their performance attained a level of automatic processing. The researchers then added an auditory task to the visual discrimination task. Subsequent performance of the visual task diminished as a function of the level of redundancy. Performance of 100% redundant visual tasks diminished less than 10%, but performance of tasks with no redundancy decreased almost 40%. In a similar fashion, Damos, Bittner, Kennedy, and Harbeson (1981) demonstrated a significant task performance decrement when a critical tracking task was combined with a compensatory tracking task. Prior to the merger, subjects performed both tasks independently until performance attained an asymptotic level (Damos, Kennedy, & Bittner, 1979). Yet, when combined, performance of both tasks decreased below the level of either performed independently. After 15 dual-task trials, performance only reached that attained after three single-task trials. Clearly, consideration must be given to the dual or multiple-task environment.

The influence of these emergent processes on the acquisition of complex skills has also been noted outside of the laboratory. Wightman and Lintern's (1985) review of training revealed that part-task training paradigms were inferior to their whole-task counterparts. In response to the poor transfer of training achieved via part-task training paradigms, Gopher, Weil, and Siegel (1989) suggest that such paradigms, although providing for individual task proficiency, fail to provide an opportunity to acquire skills necessary to perform multiple tasks simultaneously. Lintern and Wickens (1991) conclude that "Instruction with tasks in isolation (i.e., part training) could lead to poor dual-task performance because critical time sharing skills have not been practiced" (p.131).

In addition to the demands of the component tasks, the dual-task paradigm also imposes performance requirements associated with time sharing. Thus, it should be expected that the workload associated with multiple-task performance should be greater than that of the combined workload associated with the component tasks. Although this conclusion is generally reflected in the performance decrements exhibited, Gopher and Braune (1984) empirically evaluated the differences in single- and multiple-task workload. Subjects completed 14 single-task and 7 dual-task conditions. The dual-task conditions included tracking and either auditory or visual tasks. Using a psychophysical workload measurement technique, the authors noted that the dual-task conditions produced higher average workload than the combined workload for each individual task.

Team Workload

As an analogy to one of the major models of individual workload (cf. Norman & Bobrow, 1975), team workload can be characterized as the relationship between the finite performance capacities of a team and the demands placed on the team by its performance environment. According to this notion, when the team's resources are in reasonable balance with environmental demands, team performance will be optimized. However, when team tasks impose workload demands that exceed a team's ability to fulfill them, team coordination and performance may be diminished. The purpose of the current discussion is to focus on the workload demands associated with team performance environments. The capacity of teams to respond to those demands is not addressed here. Rather, a closer examination of the components of team workload will be given in order to provide further insight into the sources of workload associated with team performance requirements; further discussions of the nature of operational team performance situations are provided by Orasanu and Salas (1993).

In some respects, team performance environments can be viewed as being similar to that of a dual-task paradigm, wherein two tasks must be accomplished concurrently. That is, as suggested by the findings of Glickman et al. (1987; Morgan, Salas, & Glickman, 1994), team performance requires team members to engage concurrently in two broad categories of activities; namely, taskwork and teamwork activities. *Taskwork* refers to a team's interactions with tasks, tools, machines, and systems. It includes those efforts traditionally associated with individual task performance. However, in the team setting, it is assumed that team members must work together in order to perform the tasks that are assigned jointly to the team. *Teamwork* refers to the interpersonal interactions among individuals that are necessary for exchanging information, developing and maintaining communication patterns, coordinating actions, maintaining social order, and so on. In most team performance situations, team members must time-share the requirements for interaction and coordination (i.e., teamwork) with the demands imposed by performing their specifically assigned tasks (taskwork). Therefore, it is reasonable to conclude that team workload consists of workload demands associated with teamwork, taskwork, and the requirements to time-share task performance with team interactions. If the nature and effects of team workload are to be fully understood, it will be necessary to assess the relative workload associated with each of these three components of team performance. Furthermore, it is also reasonable to suggest that team workload differs from individual workload by virtue of the complex interactions among the requirements for taskwork and teamwork. That is, although each team member experiences some degree of individual workload, it is hypothesized that — because of the required time sharing of taskwork and teamwork processes — the team experiences overall demands that go beyond the sum of the workloads of individual team members. Clearly, this hypothesis and the relationship between individual and team workload needs to be studied further.

As indicated previously, prior research has focused on the workload associated with individual task performance. To the extent that this research generalizes to teams, it should apply primarily to the taskwork aspects of team workload. However, almost no effort has been made to understand how team workload relates to individual workload, or to measure the workload imposed by teamwork requirements and the requirement to time share taskwork and teamwork. Perhaps one reason for this lack of focus on the workload associated with teamwork is the relative difficulty of defining and evaluating teamwork workload as compared to the rather standard procedures for assessing taskwork workload. This difficulty results, in part, from an inability to define clearly the dimensions that constitute teamwork. Few efforts have been made to provide behavioral taxonomies of teamwork, and those that have been offered vary greatly in their specificity and depth.

For example, Hackman (1987; Hackman & Morris, 1975) outlined six general categories of teamwork behaviors that characterize effective teams. According to this schema, effective teams (a) minimize losses due to coordination and motivation, (b) create a sense of team spirit, (c) consider the competency of individual team members, (d) encourage individual members to learn from one another, (e) maximize the efficiency of performance strategies, and (f) foster creative planning. Although these behavioral categories are descriptive, they fail to provide detailed information concerning teamwork requirements.

Based on a review of flight crews, Franz and his colleagues (Franz, Prince, Cannon-Bowers, & Salas, 1990) outlined seven dimensions of teamwork behaviors. Specifically, teamwork behaviors were categorized as assertiveness, mission analysis, communication, decision making, adaptability, situational awareness, and leadership. In the communication dimension, for example, specific behaviors were identified as the use of standard terminology, concise and repeated transfer of information, communication of information required by other team members, and communication of information in the proper sequence. As reported by Franz et al. (1990), a complete listing of teamwork behaviors for flight crews is provided in Table 5.1.

It should be noted that the development of teamwork taxonomies is time consuming and may be nongeneralizable because teamwork behaviors vary with task demands. Hackman (1968), for example, concluded that 50% of the variance in team behaviors can be accounted for by task demands. This variability has also been noted by other authors who reported that task demands account for as much as 70% of teamwork behaviors (Hackman & Vidmar, 1970; Hare, 1962; Mann, 1961; Morris, 1966; Vidmar & Hackman, 1971). The paucity of teamwork behavioral taxonomies may reflect these findings. Nevertheless, the relative lack of understanding of the dimensions and effects of teamwork make it difficult to assess the workload associated with these behaviors. Clearly, additional research is needed to study both the effects of other sources of workload on teamwork behavior and the effects of teamwork requirements on overall team workload and performance.

TABLE 5.1
Specific Teamwork Behaviors for Flight Crews

Assertiveness	Decision-Making
Confront ambiguities and conflicts	Gather required information
Ask questions when uncertain	Identify alternatives and
Maintain position when challenged	contingencies
Make suggestions	Anticipate consequences of decisions
State opinion on	Cross-check information sources
decisions/procedures	Adaptability
Mission Analysis	Alter behavior to meet situational
Define tasks based on mission	demands
requirements	Step in and help others
Devise long- and short-term plans	Alter flight plans as required
Identify potential impact of	Situational Awareness
unplanned events on mission	Comment on deviations
Critique existing plans	Demonstrate an ongoing awareness
Communication	of mission status
Use standard terminology when	Identify problems
communicating information	Demonstrate awareness of task
Acknowledge communication by	performance of self/others
others	Leadership
Use nonverbal communication	Specify tasks to be assigned
appropriately	Ask for input, discuss problems
Provide information that is needed	Focus crew attention to a task
when asked for it	Provide feedback to other crew
Repeat vital information	members about performance

Although little is known about the potential effects of team workload, a number of hypotheses can be drawn from the brief review of individual workload just given. For example, it can be hypothesized that increases in demand associated with either taskwork or teamwork will result in increased workload and diminished performance. It should also be expected that the workload associated with these demands will decrease as a function of training, experience, and/or practice with the combined workload requirements. Furthermore, as suggested by the findings of Gopher and Braune (1984), the workload imposed by combinations of teamwork and taskwork requirements should also be expected to exceed the workload associated with teamwork or taskwork alone. In turn, this could lead to diminished performance in complex team performance situations, an expectation consistent with Steiner's (1966, 1972) concept of "process loss" and Navon and Gopher's (1979) notion of "concurrence cost." This latter point is particularly important because teams are almost always required to engage in teamwork and taskwork concurrently. Therefore, it seems particularly important to analyze, assess, and ameliorate the impact of team workload.

Beginning in the late 1950s, a number of studies directly compared the performance of teams to that of individuals. As a result of this research, some investigators concluded that teams have little advantage over individuals in complex systems where the requirements for teamwork is increased. Kidd (1961) evaluated the performance of individuals, dyads, and triads on a radar task. He reported that the performance of dyads and triads was inferior to that of individuals. Later, using a simulated target acquisition task, Naylor and Briggs (1965) also found individual performance to be superior to that of two-person teams.

The reduction in performance resulting from combined teamwork and taskwork is not limited to the laboratory. Examples of poor team performance in field operations are all too easy to find. As an example of the potential effect of teamwork on taskwork performance, Lauber (1979) recounted an airline accident where the crew became lethally preoccupied with an inoperative landing gear indicator. The crew became so engrossed in the pursuit of a solution to this situation, that they did not notice the aircraft's descent into the Florida Everglades. This disaster was not without warning. Review of the flight data recording revealed that the altitude alert sounded 1 min and 34 s before impact. The crew, then busily attempting to correct the landing gear problem, failed to react to the warning.

In order to identify the source of such errors, Lauber (1979) interviewed line pilots concerning specific problems that are commonly experienced in flight. Of those interviewed, many expressed concern over the lack of training, not in the technical aspects of the flight, but rather in the teamwork aspects of flight operations. One pilot wrote, "Pilots, particularly captains, ought to be given specific training in human behavior and human relationships . . . there is too much emphasis on the technical side of flying, and too little upon these 'softer' issues" (p. 3). It is apparent from these examples that the added task of teamwork can, and does, alter taskwork performance. Presumably, the time-sharing of teamwork and taskwork produces a combination of requirements that interact to determine the level of team workload experienced in a given situation.

Factors That Influence Team Workload

Several variables related to the team and the task it performs are likely to contribute to team workload. Some aspects of the task might serve to increase or decrease team workload. Similarly, variables related to team composition might serve to alter the workload of some teams. Although an exhaustive coverage of this topic cannot be attempted here, some of the important moderating elements of team workload are discussed here.

Coordination. As discussed earlier, the diversity of team tasks has inhibited exhaustive efforts to identify all possible team behaviors. In the absence of widely accepted team taxonomies, the literature has focused on two broad categories of team behaviors: coordination and communication. Intra-team interactions, termed *coordination*, is a major component of efficient, productive team operations. Coordination is the simultaneous and orderly action of several individuals in the performance of certain complex tasks (*Oxford English Dictionary,* 1989).

Following the framework just established, coordination behaviors can also be classified as either taskwork or teamwork coordination. Taskwork coordination represents the interactive behaviors that are elicited by the task. Task coordination is analogous to bottom up processes found in cognition in that bottom-up or data-driven processing is characterized by the requirements of the task. In this case, the stimulus serves to initiate and drive a particular process (Matlin, 1989). Team performance of the code lock solving task used in the Multiple Task Performance Battery provides an example of task-driven coordination (Morgan & Alluisi, 1972). The code lock solving task required five team members to determine the correct sequence for pressing five randomly ordered switches. With one switch per individual, the team coordinated its responses to systematically determine the correct order as quickly as possible. In this process, individual team members would call out their position to indicate that they had pressed their switch. A red or green light displayed to each team member would indicate a correct or incorrect sequence. Given an incorrect sequence, the team began the entire process again. In this situation, the requirements of the task dictated the majority of the coordinating behavior.

Navigation teams aboard large ships represent another example of task coordination. While navigating large naval ships in restricted waters, six different team members must interact. Bearing takers located on each side of the ship provide information concerning the ship's angular displacement from known landmarks. This position information is communicated to the bearing time recorder who logs the information. The plotter utilizes this information to plot the ship's current and projected position. The deck log keeper maintains a record of all the movements of the ship. Finally, the fathometer operator reads the depth of water under the ship and reports it to the bearing time recorder (Hutchins, 1990). Again, the majority of the coordinating behavior displayed by the navigation team is driven by an established system.

Teamwork coordination or top-down coordination consists of interactive behaviors that result from teamwork activities. This type of coordination stresses the initiative and flexibility of the individual in the process of teamwork (Matlin, 1989). In this case, teams use their special knowledge and distributed resources as a basis for initiating creative interactions that will help them cope with normal and non-normal task demands. An excellent example of this kind of top-down coordination can be seen in the recent emergency landing of a United Airlines Flight 232 in Sioux City, Iowa. Only 1 hr and 7 min into a flight from Denver, CO to Philadelphia, PA, the jet experienced a catastrophic engine disintegration that caused the loss of hydraulic fluid used to control the aircraft. Without control of the aircraft, the captain and first officer, aided by a check airman who had been riding in the passenger compartment, used asymmetrical thrust to control the aircraft's heading and altitude. During the course of events, the check airman got on his knees and moved the throttles as directed by the captain.

The obvious question is how do top-down and bottom-up coordination affect team workload? Furthermore, how does one assess the workload associated with two types of coordination requirement? Unfortunately, there are no data to provide answers to these questions. Beyond the obvious, however, it is essential to ascertain how the coordination demands of the team tasks can be manipulated in such a way as to minimize team workload.

Communication. Communications and team operations are inseparable. The very definition of teams dictates that individuals exchange information. Unfortunately, a series of early Ohio State studies painted a rather negative picture of the relationship between communication and performance. Following a survey of 12 years of research, Briggs and his colleagues (Johnston, 1966; Kidd, 1961; Lanzetta & Roby, 1956; Naylor & Briggs, 1965; Williges, Johnston, & Briggs, 1966), concluded that, "The available evidence favors the conclusion that team output is an inverse function of the extent to which teammates are required to coordinate, communicate, or otherwise interact with one another" (Johnston & Briggs, 1968, p. 89). Williges, Johnston, and Briggs (1966) went so far as to suggest that multiperson systems should be designed such that verbal communication is not required.

Very few studies have assessed the workload associated with communication. The available literature, however, suggests that communication does produce substantial task demands. For example, Casali and Wierwille's (1983) evaluation of workload assessment techniques used communication as a source of workload. Workload was manipulated by changing the frequency and combinations of aircraft call signs to which subjects responded. To increase workload, the presentation rate and the complexity of the call signs were increased. Complexity was gained by increasing the number of distractor call signs. For example, given a target call sign of "one-india-four-echo," a nontarget permutation [distractor] might be "india-one-four-echo" (p. 631). Of the 16 assessment techniques employed, 7 distinguished differences in communication workload.

Casali and Wierwille (1983) employed the tightest control of any of the communication and workload studies. All variables except the communications load remained constant. Yet, even in studies of less control, communications have been shown to alter workload. Hart, Hauser, and Lester (1984) assessed the relationship between a flight crew's communications and their concomitant workload. During flights of an airborne laboratory, an experimenter recorded all communications and assessed each crew member's overall workload, stress, mental effort, fatigue, time pressure, and performance for each of seven flight segments. To assess the relationship between communications and workload, the number of communications per minute was correlated with the workload data collected for each flight segment. Communications were found to correlate significantly with the flight crews' ratings of overall workload, stress, and effort.

Unfortunately, there are insufficient data to make more definitive statements concerning the relationship between communication and workload. This difficulty arises because communication and coordination have not been differentiated well in the literature. The communications assessed by Hart et al. (1984) represent a conglomerate of behaviors. Unfortunately, verbal communication is the primary medium through which these behaviors occur. A better approach to the issue of communication and workload would involve systematically evaluating specific communication behaviors, such as "acknowledge communication by others, provide information as required, etc." (identified by Franz et al., 1990), to determine their affect on workload.

Team Experience and Maturation.   The effect of experience on team workload remains to be investigated. In the absence of direct data, however, results from other areas can be generalized. Evident from previous discussions of practice, it has been shown that experience can alter an individual's form of processing from controlled to automatic. Although there is no direct evidence to suggest that this occurs in teams, experience has been shown to greatly influence team communication patterns. Communication within a team is greatly influenced by the extent of mutual knowledge developed and maintained within the team. Krauss and Fussell (1991) outlined three mechanisms of mutual knowledge.

First, direct knowledge depends on personal knowledge of an individual. The authors wrote, " . . . if you told a friend that you had seen the movie "Fatal Attraction" and were scared out of your wits by it, this information could be considered to be common ground between you and your friend" (p. 116). Direct knowledge can result from similar behaviors. Both you and your friend religiously read the sports page of the paper. The second mechanism of mutual knowledge can result from group membership. For example, one would expect that all pilots would know that flights in an easterly direction must be flown at odd altitudes and westerly ones at even altitudes. Finally, Clark and Marshall (1981) argued that any information given to two individuals at Time 1 will be mutual knowledge between the two at Time 1 + 1. Therefore, over the course of a conversation, units of shared information are transformed into mutual knowledge.

The most common means of evaluating these effects is via a referential communications task. This task requires an individual to communicate features of an object or problem to another teammate. The messages must provide sufficient information to allow the receiver to identify the object from a set of objects. Carroll (1985) used this methodology to assess the development of mutual knowledge. In this study, subjects repeatedly described the shape of a nonsense object to a fellow teammate. Once described, the teammate attempted to select the object from a set of objects. As proposed by Clark and Marshall (1981), each trial served to create a mutual knowledge concerning the nonsense object. The first trial required 10 words to describe the object, "looks like a martini glass with legs on each side." By the eighth trial, however, only one word, "martini," described the figure. Isaacs and Clark (1987) extended this methodology to include novices and experts in both homogeneous or heterogeneous teams. When presented with postcards of New York City, team members described a specific location on the postcard to the other teammate. As expected, homogenous teams of experts used the fewest number of words to describe the location, and homogeneous novices used the greatest number of words. Moreover, experts used the proper name of the location while novices used lengthy descriptions.

These systematic changes in mutual knowledge and communication behaviors reflect a team development process during which teams undergo a series of transformations that might influence their experience of workload. Morgan, Salas, and Glickman (1994; see also Morgan et al., 1986) characterize these transformations in their generalized model of *Team Evolution And Maturation* (TEAM). Based on work by several authors (Gersick, 1988; Tuckman, 1965; Tuckman & Jensen, 1977), the TEAM model depicts the evolution of teams in eight core phases. Over these phases, teams begin to form, explore the situation, develop norms, perform a task, evaluate their performance, reform their practices, continue performance of the task, and then complete the task. In addition to characterizing the phases of evolution, the TEAM model suggests the existence of taskwork and teamwork tracks of activity. According to the model, the taskwork and teamwork dichotomy diminishes with time. Related findings have been reported by other researchers. For example, Foushee and Manos (1981) found that airline flight crews displayed a refinement of cockpit communication only after 2 to 3 days of flight.

Morgan et al. (1994) studied teams at the U.S. Navy Gunfire School. During $4\frac{1}{2}$ days of training, teams were queried to assess the perceptions of individual and team ability, expertise, and motivation. Questions concerning individuals centered on knowledge of duties, motivation, role clarity, and experience and training. Questions dealing with team-level issues centered on communications, cooperation and coordination, experience and prior training, and power relationships. Each trainee completed the total questionnaire after each of four training phases. The data from each phase were then factor-analyzed to identify prominent sets of behaviors.

Analysis of data collected during the initial phase of training revealed three factors: taskwork, teamwork, and team/taskwork. The teamwork factor accounted for 22% of the variance and was typified by coordinating, cooperating, and communicating behaviors. The taskwork factor accounted for 5.5% of the variance and included items pertaining to team organization and performance. The final factor, team/taskwork accounted for 7.6% of the variance and consisted of items that characterized team forming behaviors. Similar task and teamwork factors were also noted in the second phase of training. During this second phase, however, a new factor developed. This factor included items that reflected an increase in the team's collaborative behavior. Instructors at the school construed this factor to be representative of the "jelling" experienced by teams. The third phase produced the same taskwork and teamwork factors, but the variance accounted for by the pair diminished to 8.8% and 6%, respectively. The team/taskwork factor reemerged to account for 26% of the variance. This factor included items that were included earlier in either team or taskwork factors, but which had merged into this more general factor as a result of training. Upon completion of training, the relationship between factors revealed in Phase 3 changed little. Thus, at the end of training, team/

taskwork accounted for 25.8% of the variance, yet teamwork and taskwork factors accounted for only 8.4% and 6.1%, respectively.

The research conducted by Foushee and Manos (1981) and Morgan et al. (1994) provide support for the TEAM model. As depicted by the model, team interactions mature over time. One might assume that these transformations might alter the level of workload experienced by the team. Unfortunately, no definitive answer can be given because workload has not been assessed under these circumstances. However, generalization from the literature on individual workload would predict a reduction in team workload as a function of the team's experience in working together.

Team Training.   Team training seems to represent a highly influential factor with regard to its potential impact on team workload. When task design remains constant, team training and experience can significantly influence team performance and workload. To reiterate a point made earlier, definitive research has not been conducted on the effect of training on team workload. There is, however, a large body of literature concerning team training and performance. It is reasonable to conclude that improved performance indicates a reduction in workload because increased performance suggests an increase in resource efficiency. Therefore, generalizations — albeit unproven — relating to workload can be drawn from the available literature.

The team training literature can be divided into two categories. In 1 group of studies, team training is carried out by allowing team members to practice together. The remaining group includes literature that specifically identifies teamwork tasks and provides training for those tasks (Meister, 1976). Applications of both types of training to laboratory and operational environments demonstrate mixed success.

In the laboratory, Naylor and Briggs (1965) compared the performance of two-member teams which received either individual or team training. Both groups of teams completed a simulated radar intercept task. During individual training, individuals worked independently and communicated to one another through a third supervisory team member. In the team training condition, individuals worked jointly and communicated directly. The performance of both types of teams revealed that individually trained teams performed better than teams trained as teams. Although Briggs and Naylor's findings were significant, the type of team training used represented more practice than training.

Consider 2 laboratory studies conducted by Hall and Williams (1970, 1971). They evaluated the effects of teamwork training on decision making. Using the 12 Angry Men group decision task and the NASA Moon Survival Problem, Hall and Williams found a distinct difference between teams trained in teamwork behaviors and their untrained controls. In both tasks, trained teams produced superior decisions when compared to their control counterparts. The authors reported that untrained teams demonstrated a variety of ineffective teamwork behaviors that reduced their performance. Team members "exhibited an apparently common need to coalesce rapidly so that they could reach a decision and discharge the responsibility with which they were charged" (p. 300). In pursuit of closure, team members actively pursued solutions and considered only a small portion of possible solutions. Furthermore, this apparent need to reach consensus created a perception of urgency not dictated by the problem. Finally, as the team approached consensus, its tolerance for differing opinions diminished and frustration increased.

Hall and Williams' team training centered around six simple guidelines: (a) avoid arguing; (b) avoid situations that can be characterized "win-lose;" (c) do not allow potential conflict to change your mind; (d) avoid the use of averaging, majority rules, and coin flipping as a means of reducing conflict; (e) accept differences of opinion as an advantage; and (f) question initial consensus. Following training in areas of teamwork, teams demonstrated a superior performance and avoided the detrimental behaviors displayed by their nontrained counterparts.

Sundstrom, De Meuse, and Futrell's (1990) review of team training effectiveness produced mixed results. Examination of 13 training interventions, conducted between 1980 and 1988, indicated that only 4 of the 9 reporting performance changes demonstrated increases in team performance. The successes include a training intervention conducted by Hughes, Rosenbach, and Clover (1983). Hughes et al. provided team training to 8 of 40 Air Force cadet squadrons. Prior to training, all of the squadrons were ranked according to their academic, military, and athletic performance. Eight teams were then selected from the middle of this distribution. Team training in the areas of feedback techniques, goal setting, stereotyping, and conflict resolution was provided over a period of 3 consecutive days. Six months after training, Hughes et al. compared the trained and untrained squadron. Upon reevaluation, the trained teams showed a significant increase in all three performance indices. Of the three areas, military and athletic performance displayed the largest improvements. Hughes et al. failed to provide an explanation or description of the measures, but they did report that their military and athletic indices were indicative of team performance.

Of the operational environments where team training has been applied, no one area has received as much attention as the airline industry. In an earlier review of such programs, White (1987) found that only 10% of the air carriers affiliated with the International Air Transport Association used coordination training. Although the training programs vary, the majority focus on issues germane to flight crews. This includes communication, situation awareness, mission analysis, decision making, team management, stress management, and interpersonal skills (Prince, Chidester, Cannon-Bowers, & Bowers, 1992). Although there is a large degree of variability among training programs, the overall response to this type of team training has been positive. A preliminary review of training effectiveness revealed that flight crew performance increased following training (Helmreich, Wilhelm, Gregorich, & Chidester, 1990).

In summary, the available literature suggests that the training of teamwork might reduce team workload. Without direct study, however, such a supposition is tenuous. Further research is needed to assess the extent to which team workload is ameliorated by team training.

The Assessment of Team Workload

In large part, team workload has been considered primarily as an independent variable. That is, the difficulty of the team task is typically manipulated in experiments, and resulting changes in performance are used as evidence of the validity of these manipulations. However, in order to fully understand the nature and role of team workload, it is important to develop measures of the construct that will allow researchers to quantify the resource demands placed on team members. By developing such a measure, it will be possible to avoid confounding team workload with other variables such as task difficulty, coordination requirements, and so forth. Toward that end, approaches to assessing team workload are presented here.

Although it may be possible to administer both subjective and objective techniques to assess team workload, characteristics of the team environment clearly favor some assessment techniques over others. Equipment intensive techniques such as EEG measures or other physiological indices would be impractical in most team settings. Use of subjective workload ratings like the NASA Task Load Index (TLX) or the Subjective Workload Assessment Technique (SWAT), by their nature, are more conducive to the team environment. Other assessment methodologies such as secondary or dual-task paradigms might also be easily administered to teams. Even though there remains a high degree of flexibility in the selection of an assessment technique, there are several additional issues that must be addressed.

For example, at what level of the team does one assess workload? How should the data from a team of individuals be combined and interpreted? Should team members be required to rate their subjective perception of overall team workload? Can team workload be defined as the total (or average) of the individual levels of workload experienced by team's members? What dimensions or components of team workload should be measured, and how should these measures be combined?

Unfortunately, the literature provides little guidance for answering these questions. Ongoing work by the current authors represents some of the first considerations of team workload. In order to address some of these questions, data from two previous studies have been analyzed to test preliminary assumptions regarding the measurement of team workload. One study (Thornton et al., 1992) investigated the workload of two-person teams performing a simulated flight task with varying levels of task demand. Workload was assessed using the NASA TLX, which was administered to team members individually. A modified version was also used to solicit member's perceptions of the overall team workload. The second study involved a Team Performance Assessment Battery (TPAB), which presented five team members with a simulated radar scope that displayed encroaching targets (Bowers, Urban, & Morgan, 1992; Urban et al., 1995). Successful performance required team members to work cooperatively in order to prosecute as many targets as possible. Over the course of the study, teams completed three, two-hour TPAB performance sessions. Performance was scored by cumulating the value of the targets that were successfully prosecuted by the team. Workload was assessed in terms of NASA TLX scores and performance on three secondary monitoring tasks.

In order to determine the best way to characterize overall team workload, performance was correlated with several representations of team workload: TLX score of the team member with the lowest performance score, TLX score of the member with the highest performance score, average TLX score, individual secondary task performance, and average secondary task performance. Results of the Thornton et al. (1992) study revealed no significant relationship between performance and any of the workload measures. In the TPAB study, the team's highest and lowest subjective workload score and the average of the team's workload were positively correlated with performance. When attenuated for the reliability of the measures used, the correlations revealed that the lowest workload score within the team accounted for 41% of variance in performance. The highest and the average scores accounted for 19% and 11%, respectively. Thus, the quality of team performance appears to be related to the quantity of available resources possessed by the team.

These studies included a manipulation of task difficulty. Consequently, another manner of determining the most advantageous method of assessing team workload might be to examine the sensitivity of each measure to this manipulation. The data reported by Thornton and her colleagues revealed no difference in TLX ratings as a function of task demand. The data from the Bowers et al. (1992) study also failed to yield a significant difference in TLX ratings of teams in the low and high task demand condition. Similar results are reported in the subsequent study by Urban et al. (1995), despite a deleterious effect of workload on task performance. Unfortunately, these findings provide no information concerning the relative sensitivity of the various team workload measures to manipulations of task difficulty. However, they do raise concerns about the overall utility and appropriateness of using modified TLX measures as indices of team workload. Although the TLX has been used successfully in studies of individual workload, the studies just mentioned suggest that other measures, or more sensitive modifications of the TLX, need to be developed to measure team workload.

Secondary task data from the decision-making studies also yielded equivocal results. In the Bowers et al. (1992) study, teams under high levels of task demand demonstrated higher latencies than those under low demand. However, this effect was observed for only one of three monitoring tasks, and no such difference was observed in the later Urban et al. (1995) study.

As noted earlier, the data from these studies demonstrate the apparent ineffectiveness of adapting existing measures of individual workload for use with teams. Certainly, one could question the effectiveness of the workload manipulation in each of these studies as a cause for the negative results. However, it is important to note that the workload manipulation was sufficient to produce performance changes in every case. That notwithstanding, there are data to indicate that the workload of teams performing problem-solving tasks is significantly lower than that of individuals performing the same task (Beith, 1987). It is possible that manipulations required to generate high levels of team workload have been consistently underestimated in the studies just reviewed. More likely, it is probably the case that any assessment that relies upon averaging individual workload sufficiently reduces the sample variance such that effects of task manipulations are masked. Consequently, there is a need to identify alternative measurement strategies. Measures such as using the lowest workload might hold some promise, as described previously. However, the research base regarding these types of measures is insufficient.

There is also a need for additional measures derived directly from models of team workload. It is possible, for example, that global measures of team workload are simply not sensitive to all of the demands imposed on teams. An alternative might be to specify the components of team workload and to combine these components into an aggregated team workload score. For example, Bowers and his colleagues have described a technique to assess the coordination demands of team tasks (Bowers et al., 1993). Data collected by these authors indicate that coordination demand is correlated with perceptions of team workload. Thus, it is possible that by using this instrument to assess coordination demand, another to assess task demands, and so forth, a useful composite index could be derived.

SUMMARY

Teams are becoming increasingly important in modern workplaces. Consequently, there has been a concurrent increase in research regarding factors that influence team performance. A variable that seems critical in this regard is team workload. However, this construct has received surprisingly little research interest. This chapter has attempted to improve the state-of-the-art by providing a conceptual description of team workload, the factors that may affect it, and possible directions in its measurement. As demonstrated by the results described here, current assessment techniques are simply inadequate to accelerate the understanding of the effects of the variable on team performance. Consequently, there is a clear and urgent need for additional research to develop more thorough, valid assessments of this construct and its component dimensions. Researchers should devote additional effort to specifying the components of team workload, developing sensitive measuring techniques based on these theories, and empirically establishing the construct validity of the resulting measures. It is hoped that this discussion will help to stimulate these much needed research efforts.

REFERENCES

Bahrick, H. P., & Shelly, C. (1958). Time sharing as an index of automatization. *Journal of Experimental Psychology, 56,* 288–293.

Beith, B. H. (1987). Subjective workload under individual and team performance conditions. *Proceedings of the Human Factors Society 31st Annual Meeting,* 67–71.

Boff, K. R. (1990). Meeting the challenge: Factors in the design and acquisition of human-engineered systems. In H. R. Booher (Ed.), *Manprint: An approach to systems integration.* New York: Van Nostrand Rheinhold.

Boulter, R. L. (1977). Attention and reaction times to signals of uncertain modality. *Journal of Experimental Psychology, 3,* 379–388.

Bowers, C. A., Morgan, B. B., Jr., Salas, E., & Prince, C. (1993). Assessment of coordination demand for aircrew coordination training. *Military Psychology, 5,* 95–112.

Bowers, C. A., Urban, J. M., & Morgan, B. B., Jr. (1992). *The study of crew coordination and performance in hierarchical team decision making* (Team Performance Laboratory Tech. Rep. No. 92-1). Orlando, FL: University of Central Florida.

Cannon-Bowers, J. A., Oser, R., & Flanagan, D. (1992). Work teams in industry: A selected review and proposed framework. In R. W. Swezy & E. Salas (Eds.), *Teams: Their training and performance* (pp. 355–377). Norwood, NJ: Ablex.

Carroll, J. M. (1985). *What's in a name?: An essay in the psychology of reference.* New York: Freeman.

Casali, J. G., & Wierwille, W. W. (1983). A comparison of rating scale, secondary-task, physiological, and primary-task workload estimation techniques in a simulated flight task emphasizing communications load. *Human Factors, 25,* 623–641.

Clark, H. H., & Marshall, C. E. (1981). Definite reference and mutual knowledge. In A. K. Joshi, I. Sag, & B. Webber (Eds.), *Elements of discourse understanding* (pp. 10–63). New

York: Cambridge University Press.

Crosby, J. J., & Parkinson, S. R. (1979). A dual task investigation of pilots' skill level. *Ergonomics, 22,* 1301-1313.

Damos, D. L., Kennedy, R. S., & Bittner, A. C. (1979). Development of a Performance Evaluation Test for Environmental Research (PETER): Critical tracking test. *Aerospace Medical Association,* 33-34.

Damos, D. L., Bittner, A. C., Kennedy, R. S., & Harbeson, M. M. (1981). Effects of extended practice on dual-task tracking performance. *Human Factors, 23,* 627-631.

Duncan, J. (1979). Divided attention: The whole is more than the sum of its parts. *Journal of Experimental Psychology Human Perception and Performance, 5,* 216-228.

Dyer, J. L. (1984). Team research and team training: A state-of-the-art review. *The Human Factors Review, 00,* 285-323.

Fisk, A. D., & Schneider, W. (1983). Category and word search: generalizing search principles to complex processing. *Journal of Experimental Psychology: Learning, Memory, and Cognition, 9,* 177-194.

Foushee, H. C., & Manos, K. L. (1981). Information transfer within the cockpit: Problems in intracockpit communications. In C. E. Billings & E. S. Cheaney (Eds.), *Information transfer problems in the aviation system* (NASA Tech. Rep. No. TP-1875). Moffett Field, CA: NASA-Ames Research Center.

Franz, T. M., Prince, C., Cannon-Bowers, J. A., & Salas, E. (1990). The identification of aircrew coordination skills. *Proceedings of the 12th annual Department of Defense Symposium,* Colorado Springs, CO (pp. 97-101).

Gersick, C. J. G. (1988). Time and transition in work teams: Toward a new model of group development. *Academy of Management Journal, 31,* 9-41.

Glickman, A. S., Zimmer, S., Montero, R. C., Guerette, P. J., Campbell, W. J., Morgan, B. B., & Salas, E. (1987). *The evolution of teamwork skills: An empirical assessment with implications for training* (NTSC Tech. Rep. No. TR-87-016). Orlando, FL: Naval Training Systems Center.

Gopher, D., & Braune, R. (1984). On the psychophysics of workload: Why bother with subjective measures? *Human Factors, 26,* 519-532.

Gopher, D., Weil, M., & Siegel, D. (1989). Practice under changing priorities: An approach to the training of complex skills. Special Issue. The learning strategies program: An examination of the strategies in skill acquisition. *Acta Psychologica, 71,* 147-177.

Hackman, J. R. (1968). Effects of task characteristics on group products. *Journal of Experimental Social Psychology, 4,* 162-187.

Hackman, J. R. (1987). The design of work teams. In J. W. Lorsch (Ed.). *Handbook of organizational behavior,* (pp. 315-357). Englewood Cliffs, NJ: Prentice-Hall.

Hackman, J. R., & Morris, C. G. (1975). Group tasks, group interaction process, and group performance effectiveness: A review and proposed integration. In L. Berkowitz (Ed.), *Advances in experimental social psychology* (Vol. 8, pp. 00). New York: Academic Press.

Hackman, J. R., & Vidmar, N. (1970). Effects of size and task type on group performance and member reactions. *Sociometry, 33,* 37-54.

Hall, J., & Williams, M. S. (1970). Group dynamics training and improved decision making. *The Journal of Applied Behavioral Science, 6,* 39-68.

Hall, J., & Williams, M. S. (1971). Personality and group encounter style: A multivariate analysis of traits and preferences. *Journal of Personality and Psychology, 18*(2), 163-172.

Hancock, P. A., Mihaly, T., Rahimi, M., & Meshkati, N. (1988). A bibliographic listing of mental workload research. In P. A. Hancock & N. Meshkati (Eds), *Human mental workload* (pp. 329-382). New York: North-Holland.

Hare, A. P. (1962). *Handbook of small group research.* New York: The Free Press of Glencoe.

Hart, S. G. (1986). Theory and measurement of human workload. In J. Zeidner (Ed). *Human productivity enhancement.* (Vol. 1, pp. 396-455). New York: Praeger.

Hart, S. G., Hauser, J. R., & Lester, P. T. (1984). Inflight evaluation of four measures of pilot workload. *Proceedings of the Human Factors Society 28th annual meeting* 945–949.

Hart, S. G., & Wickens, C. D. (1990). Workload assessment and prediction. In H. R. Booher (Ed.), *MANPRINT: An approach to systems integration*. New York: Van Nostrand Reinhold.

Helmreich, R. L., Wilhelm, J. A., Gregorich, B. A., & Chidester, T. R. (1990). Preliminary results from the evaluation of cockpit resource management training: Performance ratings of flightcrews. *Aviation, Space, and Environmental Medicine, 61,* 576–579.

Hughes, R. L., Rosenbach, W. E., & Clover, W. H. (1983). Team development in an intact, ongoing work group: A quasi-field experiment. *Group and Organization Studies, 8,* 161–186.

Hutchins, E. (1990). The technology of team navigation. In J. Galegher, R. E. Kraut, & C. Egido (Eds.), *Intellectual teamwork* (pp. 191–220). Hillsdale, NJ: Lawrence Erlbaum Associates.

Isaacs, E. A., & Clark, H. H. (1987). References in conversation between experts and novices. *Journal of Experimental Psychology: General, 116,* 26–37.

James, W. (1890). *Principles of Psychology* (Vol. 1). New York: Holt.

Johannsen, G. (1979). Workload and workload measurement. In N. Moray (Ed.), *Mental workload its theory and measurement* (pp. 3–12). New York: Plenum Press.

Johnston, W. A. (1966). Transfer of team skills as a function of type of training. *Journal of Applied Psychology, 50,* 102–108.

Kantowitz, B. H., & Casper, P. A. (1988). Human workload in aviation. In A. Weiner & D. C. Nagel (Eds.), *Human factors in aviation* (pp. 157–187). New York: Academic Press.

Kerr, B. (1973). Processing demands during mental operations. *Memory & Cognition, 1,* 401–412.

Kidd, J. S. (1961). A comparison of one-, two-, and three-man work units under various conditions of workload. *Journal of Applied Psychology, 45,* 195–200.

Kramer, A. F., Wickens, C. D., & Donchin, E. (1983). An analysis of the processing requirements of a complex perceptual-motor task. *Human Factors, 25,* 597–621.

Kraus, R. M., & Fussell, S. R. (1991). Constructing shared communication environments. In L. B. Resnick, J. M. Levine, & S. D. Teasley (Eds.), *Perspectives on socially shared cognition* (pp. 172–200). Washington, DC: American Psychological Association.

Lanzetta, J. T., & Roby, T. B. (1956). Effects of workgroup structure and certain task variables on group performance. *Journal of Abnormal Social Psychology, 53,* 307–314.

Lauber, J. K. (1979). Resource management on the flight deck: Background and statement of the problem. In G. E. Cooper, M. D. White, & J. K. Lauber (Eds.), *Resource management on the flight deck* (pp. 3–16). NASA Conference Publication 2120.

Lindholm, E., & Cheatham, C. M. (1983). Autonomic activity and workload during learning of a simulated aircraft carrier landing task. *Aviation, Space, and Environmental Medicine, 54,* 435–439.

Lintern, G., & Wickens, C. D. (1991). Issues for acquisition and transfer of timesharing and dual-task skills. In D. L. Damos (Ed.), *Multiple task performance* (pp. 123–138). London: Taylor & Francis.

MacLeod, C. M., & Dunbar, K. (1988). Training and stroop-like interference: Evidence for a continuum of automaticity. *Journal of Experimental Psychology: Learning, Memory, and Cognition, 14,* 126–135.

Mann, R. D. (1961). Dimensions of individual performance in small groups under task and social emotional conditions. *Journal of Abnormal Social Psychology, 62,* 674–682.

Matlin, M. W. (1989). *Cognition*. New York: Holt, Rinehart & Winston.

McCallum, G. A., Oser, R., & Salas, E. (1989). *Toward a definition of teamwork: Behavioral patterns of effective teams* (NTSC Tech. Rep. No. TR-89-018). Orlando, FL: Naval Training Systems Center.

Meister, D. (1976). *Behavioral foundations of system development.* New York: Wiley.

Morgan, B. B., Jr., & Alluisi, E. A. (1972). Synthetic work: Methodology for assessment of human performance. *Perceptual and Motor Skills, 35,* 835–845.

Morgan, B. B., Jr., Coates, G. D., Kirby, R. H., & Alluisi, E. A. (1984). Individual and group performances as functions of the team-training load. *Human Factors, 26,* 127–142.

Morgan, B. B., Jr., Glickman, A. S., Woodard, E. A., Blaiwes, A. S., & Salas, E. (1986). *Measurement of team behaviors in a Navy environment* (NTSC Tech. Rep. No. TR-86-014). Orlando, FL: Naval Training Systems Center.

Morgan, B. B., Jr., Salas, E., & Glickman, A. S. (1994). An analysis of team evolution and maturation. *Journal of General Psychology, 120,* 277–291.

Morris, C. G. (1966). Task effects on group interaction. *Journal of Personality and Social Psychology, 4,* 545–554.

Navon, D., & Gopher, D. (1980). Task difficulty resources and dual-task performance. In R. S. Nickerson (Ed.) *Attention and performance VIII.* Hillsdale, N.J.: Lawrence Erlbaum Associates.

Navon, D., & Gopher, D. (1979). On the economy of the human processing system. *Psychological Review, 91,* 216–234.

Naylor, J. C., & Briggs, G. E. (1965). Team training effectiveness under various conditions. *Journal of Applied Psychology, 49,* 223–229.

Norman, D. A., & Bobrow, D. G. (1975). On data-limited and resource-limited processes. *Cognitive Psychology, 7,* 44–64.

O'Donnell, R. D., & Eggemeier, F. T. (1986). Workload assessment methodology. In K. R. Boff, L. Kauffman, & J. P. Thomas (Eds.), *Handbook of perception and human performance* Vol. 2. pp. 42:1–42:49). New York: Wiley.

Orasanu, J., & Salas, E. (1993). Team decision making in complex environments. In G. A. Klein, J. Orasanu, R. Calderwood, & C. E. Zsambok (Eds.), *Decision making in action: Models and methods* (pp. 327–345). Norwood, NJ: Ablex.

Parasuraman, R. (1986). Vigilance, monitoring and search. In K. R. Boff, L. Kauffman, & J. P. Thomas (Eds.), *Handbook of perception and human performance.* (Vol. 2, pp. 00). New York: Wiley.

Poltrock, S. E., Lansman, M., & Hunt, E. (1982). Automatic and controlled attention processes in auditory target detection. *Journal of Experimental Psychology: Human Perception and Performance, 8,* 37–45.

Poon, L. W., Thompson, L. W., Williams, R. B., & March, G. R. (1974). Changes of anterior-posterior distribution of CNV and late positive component as a function of information processing demands. *Psychophysiology, 11,* 660–673.

Prince, C., Chidester, T. R., Cannon-Bowers, J., & Bowers, C. (1992). Aircrew coordination-achieving teamwork in the cockpit. In R. Swezey & E. Salas (Eds.), *Teams: Their training and performance.* Norwood, NJ: Ablex.

Rosler, F. (1981). Event-related brain potentials in a stimulus-discrimination learning paradigm. *Psychophysiology, 18,* 447–455.

Ruffell-Smith, H.P. (1979). *A simulator study of the interaction of pilot workload with errors, vigilance, and decisions* (NASA TM-78482). Moffet Field, CA: NASA-Ames Research Center.

Shiffrin, R. M., & Schneider, W. (1977). Controlled and automatic human information processing: II. Perceptual learning, automatic attending, and a general theory. *Psychological Review, 84,* 127–190.

Schneider, W., & Fisk, A. D. (1984). Automatic category search and its transfer. *Journal of Experimental Psychology: Learning, Memory, and Cognition, 10,* 1–15.

Schneider, W., & Fisk, A. D. (1982). Concurrent automatic and controlled visual search: Can processing occur without resource cost? *Journal of Experimental Psychology: Learning, Memory, and Cognition, 8,* 261–278.

Steiner, I. D. (1966). Models for inferring relationships between group size and potential group productivity. *Behavioral Science, 11,* 273–283.

Steiner, I. D. (1972). *Group process and productivity.* New York: Academic Press.

Sundstrom, E., De Meuse, K. P., & Futrell, D. (1990). Work teams application and effectiveness. *American Psychologist, 45,* 120–133.

Thornton, C., Braun, C., Bowers, C., & Morgan, B. (1992). Automation effects in the cockpit: A low-fidelity investigation. *Proceedings of the Human Factors Society, 36th Annual Meeting, 1,* 30–34, Atlanta, GA: Human Factors Society.

Tuckman, B. W. (1965). Developmental sequences in small groups. *Psychological Bulletin, 63,* 384–399.

Tuckman, B. W., & Jensen, M. (1977). Stages of small group development revisited. *Group and Organizational Studies, 2,* 419–427.

Urban, J. M., Bowers, C. A., Monday, S. D., & Morgan, B. B., Jr. (1995). Communication for effective team performance. *Military Psychology, 7,* 123–139.

U. S. Dept. of Army. (1987). Manpower and personnel integration. (MANPRINT) in material acquisition process (Tech. Rep. No. 602-2). Washington, DC: Author.

Vidmar, N., & Hackman, J. R. (1971). Interlaboratory generalizability of small group research: An experimental study. *The Journal of Social Psychology, 83,* 129–139.

Vidulich, M. A., & Wickens, C. D. (1984). Subjective workload assessment and voluntary control of effort in a tracking task. *Proceedings, 20th Annual Conference on Manual Control and Mental Workload, 2,* 57–72. Moffett Field, CA: NASA Ames Research Center.

White, L. (1987). Cockpit resource management training (an international survey). In H. W. Orlady & H. C. Fourshee (Eds.), *Cockpit resource management training* (Tech. Rep. No. NASA CP-2455). Moffett Field, CA: NASA Ames Research Center.

Wickens, C. D. (1980). The structure of attentional resources. In R. S. Nickerson (Ed.), *Attention and performance VIII* (pp. 239–257). Hillsdale, N.J.: Lawrence Erlbaum Associates.

Wickens, C. D. (1984). Processing resources in attention. In R. Parasuraman & D. R. Davies (Eds.), *Varieties of attention* (pp. 63–102). New York: Academic Press.

Wierwille, W. W., Rahimi, M., & Casali, J. G. (1985). Evaluation of 16 measures of mental workload using a simulated flight task emphasizing mediational activity. *Human Factors, 27,* 489–502.

Wightman, D. C., & Lintern, G. (1985). Part-task training for tracking and manual control. Special Issue: Training. *Human-Factors, 27,* 267–283.

Williges, R. C., Johnston, W. A., & Briggs, G. E. (1966). Role of verbal communication in teamwork. *Journal of Applied Psychology, 50,* 473–478.

III METHODOLOGICAL DEVELOPMENTS AND ISSUES

6

Team Decision-Making Accuracy Under Difficult Conditions: Construct Validation of Potential Manipulations Using the TIDE² Simulation

John R. Hollenbeck
Douglas J. Sego
Daniel R. Ilgen
Michigan State University

Debra A. Major
Jennifer Hedlund
Jean Phillips

Although there has been a long standing interest in group dynamics, recent trends in business, medical, aerospace, and military contexts have pushed group-oriented issues to the forefront of the social science research agenda. In particular, the emergence of work teams that bring together people of different backgrounds or different areas of expertise, who must often make decisions under stressful conditions, is of increasing interest for those managing many kinds of social organizations.

In business, the popular press is replete with articles on the increased use of team-based structuring in both manufacturing and service industries (e.g., cover stories in *Time* and *Fortune* magazines in 1990). For example, manufacturers traditionally differentiated groups by functions, such as market research, product design, production, and sales, and these groups performed their tasks sequentially. In order to enhance competitiveness and improve efficiency, many manufacturers now bring experts from these four divergent functional areas together and have them work as re-engineered teams.

In the aerospace industry, the functioning of aircrew teams under conditions of stress has also emerged as a critical problem. In several cases, large-scale tragedies like the Tenefire accident (where two jumbo jets collided on the ground in the Canary Islands) have been traced to communication breakdowns among pilots, co-pilots, navigators, air controllers, and ground controllers (Foushee, 1984).

Finally, in the military context, events like those of the U.S.S. Stark and

U.S.S. Vincennes have highlighted the importance of team dynamics. In the U.S.S. Stark incident, an air patrol team that included the U.S.S. Stark, an AWACS reconnaissance plane, an Aegis Cruiser, and a land-based radar unit allowed an Iraqi jet to position itself and then launch an attack that led to the death of 37 U.S. servicemen. The immediate reaction to this incident was simply to "loosen the rules of engagement" for ships operating in the gulf. These measures backfired 13 months later when the Aegis Cruiser U.S.S. Vincennes mistakenly shot down an Iranian airbus killing over 150 civilians. The salience of teamwork and coordination was reinforced by the military's experience in the war with Iraq, where over half of the coalition forces casualties were attributable to "friendly fire." Indeed, these problems persist even in post-war Iraq, as evidenced by the recent incident involving U.S. F-15 jets shooting down two U.S. helicopter patrols over the "no fly zone."

Thus, whether one is concerned with performance in business, medicine, or the military, the need for rigorous research addressing issues associated with teams of experts making decisions under stressful conditions has never been greater. The purpose of this discussion is to help stimulate research on this topic by describing a newly developed computer simulation task that was designed to assist empirical inquiry in this area. First, we describe a new computer simulation task and show how it can be used to study many variables that might be of interest to team researchers. Second, we present empirical data from two studies that test the degree to which certain experimental manipulations can invoke conditions that have deleterious effects on team decision-making accuracy. Specifically, we wish to simulate the psychological conditions confronting teams that are working in environments that can be characterized as stressful and uncertain. If we can generate reliable manipulations that create uncertain and stressful conditions that lead to decrements in decision-making accuracy, future research can then incorporate these manipulations into studies that examine programs (e.g., training, selection, job/team structure, or leader-based interventions) designed to ameliorate these problems.

By separating construct validation from substantive research, one can examine the effects of various manipulations with a precision and fidelity that cannot be achieved in studies whose primary purpose is ameliorative. In particular, a narrowed focus allows us to examine the *multilevel* (physiological-, individual-, and team-level) effects of various manipulations in a *longitudinal context* where there is *random assignment* of subjects to conditions, and *objective indicators* of arousal, performance, and team processes. This research is in line with calls by many methodologists for holding off substantive research until rigorous empirical construct validation efforts are complete (Cook & Campbell, 1979; Cronbach & Meehl, 1995; Schwab, 1980).

TIDE²: A PROGRAM AND PARADIGM FOR TEAM-BASED RESEARCH

Groups have been defined as configurations of more than two interdependent individuals who interact over time. Teams are special cases of groups. Teams meet all the defining characteristics of groups, but in addition, teams incorporate skill differentiation in a context where there is a common fate (i.e., success or failure at the team level has consequences for all team members).

Ilgen, Major, Hollenbeck, and Sego (1995) have argued that the existing group literature is limited in its ability to answer questions about the kinds of teams just described for several reasons. First, most current research focuses on the ability of the group to reach consensus regarding a decision, and often does not focus on the accuracy of the decision rendered by the team. Second, many real-world work teams are comprised of members with heterogeneous skills and differentiated expertise. Exisiting group research that focuses on individuals with homogeneous skills and expertise cannot deal with the source from which many of the problems confronting current work teams emerge. Finally, one last feature of current work teams that is not well addressed by the current groups' literature is the geographically dispersed nature of team members. Most group research deals with face-to-face interactions. Members of many current work teams, however, are often physically separated and communicate through technologically mediated methods (fax, electronic mail, conference calls, etc.), which greatly complicates and changes the nature of team processes. The degree to which research on face-to-face interactions–that are rich in information redundancy, plus verbal and nonverbal feedback–will generalize to more confined technological media is an open question (Hedlund, Ilgen, & Hollenbeck, 1994).

Overview of TIDE²

TIDE² is a series of computer programs that constitute a vehicle for conducting team research. TIDE² stands for Team Interactive Decision Exercise for Teams Incorporating Distributed Expertise. It was developed to provide a paradigm for studying team decision making in the kinds of contexts that confront many work teams. These contexts can be characterized as complex, uncertain, and fast-paced. In addition, confronting problems in these contexts requires differentiated expertise embodied in persons who are often geographically dispersed and working under tight time constraints where decision quality is important.

Team members communicate through the network, and the program records virtually every keystroke, message, and decision made by every member. The program also compares team decisions to "true scores" and provides both team and individual level feedback. Sessions typically include multiple trials, and hence the package is conducive to longitudinal research and repeated measures designs (Hollenbeck, Ilgen, & Sego, 1994).

The program allows for wide flexibility in terms of specifying the content area in which the paradigm will be invoked. Thus, teams can be working on almost any type of decision-making task, such as a personnel selection decision where multiple job applicants are assessed on multiple dimensions, or an investment banking scenario where the team makes investment decisions, or a medical scenario where a team of medical specialists make decisions regarding patient treatment.

As a set, the programs (a) provide a standardized decision-making stimulus for people who communicate with each other over dedicated lines; (b) support programs for manipulating cues associated with decision alternatives; (c) support programs for radically changing the decision-making context confronting participants; (d) support programs for sorting, summarizing, and analyzing quantitative data generated by teams working on the task; and (e) support programs for aiding the content analysis of qualitative data generated by teams working on the task.

The purpose of the first part of this chapter is to familiarize the reader with TIDE^2. It contains five subsections that describe (a) the initial TIDE^2 scenario, (b) how to use the "cue-changing" capacities of TIDE^2 to establish different types of context effects, (c) how to use the "task-changing" capacities of TIDE^2 to establish other types of context effects, (d) how to change the initial scenario from naval command and control to some other applied problem, and (e) the types of output and analyses that can be readily obtained with TIDE^2. The interested reader can find documentation for the software in Hollenbeck, Sego, Ilgen, and Major (1991), and the program itself is freely available from the authors for research purposes.

Initial Scenario, Task, and Targets

The initial scenario associated with TIDE^2 is that of a four-person naval command and control team assigned the task of monitoring the airspace in the vicinity of an aircraft carrier battle group. Table 6.1 shows an overview description of the roles assigned to the four players as well as the types of judgments they need to make.

The team can measure each incoming aircraft on nine attributes. The names and descriptions of all the attributes are shown in Table 6.2. This table also shows the scale associated with each characteristic as well as its possible range. The degree of threat represented by the target can be ascertained by knowing (a) the target's standing on these nine attributes and (b) the five rules that describe how target characteristics combine to

TABLE 6.1
Description of Roles and Decision Alternative in the
Initial TIDE² Configuration

There are four roles in this simulation, one for each member of a 4-person team. The leader is the commanding officer (CO) of the aircraft carrier. The other team members include the CO of an AWACS air reconnaissance plane; the CO of an Aegis Cruiser, and the CO of a Coastal Air Defense (CAD) unit located on the mainland. The team's task is to decide what response the carrier group should make toward incoming air targets. Teams base their decisions on data they collect by measuring characteristics of aircraft that enter the group's airspace. These measures are obtained from sophisticated radar equipment. Aircraft that are being tracked on radar are called *targets*. There are 7 possible choices to make for each incoming target. These responses are graded in terms of their aggressivenes. Each of these is described here, moving from least to most aggressive:

(1) **IGNORE:** This means that the carrier group should devote no further attention to the target, but instead should focus on other possible targets in the area. The group should never ignore a target that might possibly attack, for obvious reasons. (0–2)

(2) **REVIEW:** This means to leave this target momentarily, so that the team can monitor other targets, but to return to this target after a short period of time to update its status. A carrier group can review a number of targets, but not an infinite number of targets. (3–5)

(3) **MONITOR:** Here the carrier group should continuously track the target on radar. A carrier group can monitor fewer targets than it can review, and thus monitoring diminishes the groups' overall patrol capacity. (6–8)

(4) **WARN:** In this case the carrier group sends a message to the target identifying the group and alerting the target to steer clear. Warning targets that should be ignored detracts from the salience of legitimate warnings. Warning targets that intend to attack is also bad, since the warning makes it easier for the attacker to locate the ship. (9–11)

(5) **READY:** This means to steer the ship into a defensive posture and to set defensive weapons on automatic. A ship in a readied position is rarely vulnerable to attack. This stance should not be taken to non-threatening targets as weapons set to "automatic" can fire mistakenly at innocent targets that fly to close to the carrier group. A ship in this position cannot readily use offensive weapons on the target. (12–14)

(6) **LOCK-ON:** This synchronizes the ship's radar and attack weapons so that the weapons fix themselves on the target. A ship at Lock-On position can use offensive weapons at a moment's notice. A ship's capacity to track other targets is severely constrained once it has Locked-On a single target, however. Thus, this should be reserved for targets that are almost certain to be threatening. (15–17)

(7) **DEFEND:** Defend is "weapons away." A defend decision cannot be aborted once initiated and thus must only be used when the group feels attack is imminent. (18–20)

TABLE 6.2
The Dimensions, Scale Values, and Ranges Associated With Incoming
Aircraft, and the Areas of Expertise for Each Staff Member

Dimensions	Scale and Range
(1) Speed	150 to 800 mph
(2) Altitude	5,000 to 35,000 ft
(3) Size	15 to 50 m
(4) Angle	minus 15 deg to plus 15 deg
(5) IFF	.2 Mhz to 1.6 Mhz
(6) Direction	plus 40 deg to 00 deg
(7) Corridor Status	1 mile to 50 miles
(8) Radar Type	Class 1 to Class 9
(9) Range	20 miles to 200 miles

Carrier:
>   Altitude; IFF; Radar Type;
>   Other Staff Members' Expertise
>   Angle–Range Combination Rule

AWACS:
>   Speed; Altitude; Size; Angle; IFF
>   Speed–Direction Combination Rule

Cruiser:
>   Angle; IFF; Direction; Corridor Status; Radar Type
>   Altitude–Corridor Status Combination Rule

Coastal Air Defense:
>   Corridor Status; Radar Type; Range; Speed; Altitude
>   Size–Radar Type Combination Rule

determine the level of threat. The five rules associated with the initial scenario are shown in Table 6.3. The last four rules are called "combination rules" because the degree of threat associated with knowledge of one attribute can only truly be ascertained if one also has knowledge of the attribute with which it combines.

Mathematical Structure of the Decision Task. At the core of this simulation is a mathematic linear combination of the form shown below in Equation 1, where W is a cue weight and B is a cue value:

$$\text{True Score} = W_1 B_1 + W_2 B_2 + W_3 B_3 + W_4 B_4 + W_5 B_5 \qquad (1)$$

The resulting value attained by assigning weights and inserting cue values into this linear combination determines the "true score" for each aircraft. Each "rule" that was described to participants in the instructions coincides with one term in the equation that gives the true score for each aircraft.

The linear combination associated with the initial version of TIDE[2] therefore has five components, four of which are combinations of multiple cues that create the four combination rules. The exact linear combination

TABLE 6.3
Determining Levels of Threat and Forming Judgments

In general, the degree to which an incoming target is threatening depends on its standing on the 9 attributes. There are five simple rules to remember in determining the danger associated with any target:

(a) all else equal, in terms of IFF, *military targets* are more threatening than civilian targets (see attribute #5 in Table 6.2)
(b) SPEED and DIRECTION go together, so that *fast targets coming straight in* are most threatening (see #1 and #6 in Table 6.2). Speed alone and direction alone mean nothing. There is nothing to fear if fast targets are not headed toward the group. There is nothing to fear from slow objects headed directly for the group.
(c) ANGLE and RANGE go together, so that *descending targets that are close* are especially threatening (see #4 and #9 in Table 6.2). Angle alone and range alone mean nothing. Descending targets that are far away, or close targets that are on the way up are not threatening.
(d) ALTITUDE and CORRIDOR STATUS go together, so that *low flying targets that are way outside the corridor* are especially threatening (see #2 and #7 in Table 6.2). Altitude alone and corridor status alone mean nothing. There is nothing to fear from high flying targets well outside the corridor or low-flying targets in the middle of the corridor.
(e) SIZE and RADAR go together, so that *small objects with weapons radar* are especially threatening (see #3 and #8 in Table 6.2). There is nothing to fear from small targets with weather radar only or from large targets with weapons radar.

The five rules combine to determine the overall threat represented by the target. So for example, if the team detected a (a) military aircraft that is (b) flying in straight and fast, (c) was close and descending, (d) was flying low and way outside the corridor, and (e) was small and had weapons radar; the ship is being attacked and should DEFEND.

If the team detected(a) a civilian aircraft, that is (b) passing slow at an angle, (c) was far away and ascending, (d) was flying high and in the middle of the corridor and (e) was large and had weather radar; this is a passenger plane that should be IGNORED.

Intermediate responses like MONITOR, WARN, or READY are to be used when the target is threatening according to some of the rules but not all. For example, a military aircraft that is close and descending (see Rule c), small and with weapons radar (see Rule e), but is traveling slowly at an angle to the group (see Rule b), and is high and in the middle of the corridor (see Rule d) might need to be WARNED. It should not be IGNORED, but neither should it be shot down.

used in the initial version of TIDE[2] is shown in Equation 2, where the parenthetic value is the cue weight, and the # indicates the number of the attribute described previously (i.e., #1 is speed, #2 is altitude, #9 is range, etc.):

$$\text{True Score} = (2)(\#5) + (1)(\#1)(\#6) + (1)(\#2)(\#7) + \\ (1)(\#3)(\#8) + (1)(\#4)(\#9) \tag{2}$$

The cues can take on values of 0 (i.e., nonthreatening), 1 (i.e., somewhat threatening), or 2 (i.e., very threatening). So, for example, the first rule deals with the attribute IFF (Identification Friend or Foe; i.e., #5). This attribute, from Equation 2, has a weight of 2. Thus, if the cue value takes on a value of 0, this component of the overall linear combination becomes 0. If the cue takes on a value of 1, this component of the linear combination takes on a value of 2. If this cue takes on a value of 2, this component of the linear combination takes on a value of 4.

Thus, in the initial version of TIDE^2, the true score for each aircraft ranges from 0 (i.e., a completely nonthreatening aircraft where all cue values equal 0) to 20 (i.e., a very threatening aircraft where all cue values equal 2). Verbally, a very threatening aircraft would appear similar to the aircraft described in the first paragraph in the section "How Rules Combine . . ." in Table 6.3. Verbally, a completely nonthreatening aircraft would appear similar to the aircraft described in the second paragraph of that section.

Intermediate values between 0 and 20 call for decisions that are more aggressive than IGNORE and less aggressive than DEFEND. The parenthetic values presented at the end of the description of each decision alternative in Table 6.1 shows how true scores on aircraft are translated into the "Correct Decisions" that serve as the criteria against which team decisions are evaluated. The aircraft described in the third paragraph of the bottom section of Table 6.3 has a true score of 10. This score comes about as shown in Equation 3:

$$\text{True Score} = (2)(2) + (1)(0)(0) + (1)(2)(2) + (1)(0)(0) + (1)(1)(2) \\ 10 = 4 + 0 + 4 + 0 + 2 \tag{3}$$

For researchers familiar with Multiple Cue Probability Learning (MCPL) tasks, the core of this simulation can be construed as an MCPL task with feedforward instructions. Feedforward simply refers to the fact that participants perform the task after being instructed in the weights assigned to cues.

Distributed Nature of Team Members. One feature of TIDE^2 that makes it unique relative to other MCPL tasks is that the task is performed in a team context where individual members have different areas of expertise. In the naval command and control scenario, the participant playing the role of the commanding officer (CO) of the carrier is the team leader and the person who ultimately decides what action should be taken toward each aircraft. Each of the other team members makes recommendations to the leader.

Each team member has expertise that is unique to his or her role. That expertise comes in two forms, (a) the ability to measure and translate raw attributes of the aircraft into opinions regarding how threatening the aircraft is on that attribute (see Table 6.2) and (b) the knowledge of rules (see Table 6.3). For example, although all team members know that aircraft within close range are generally more threatening than those far away, only one person in the team can actually measure range (i.e., Attribute #9). Also, this person is the only one trained in how to translate raw data on range (i.e., 20–200 miles) into precise judgments about threat (i.e., nonthreatening, somewhat threatening or very threatening). Also, each team member has to *memorize* one of the four combination rules (e.g., one member must memorize how speed and direction go together). Thus, at least one member of every team (including the carrier) will be an expert on one of the combination rules. The carrier can only measure a small number of aircraft attributes. The distinctive competency of the carrier is that this person knows the expertise of all the other team members.

A Typical TIDE² Trial.   To gain a better appreciation of this task, it is worthwhile to examine what a "typical trial" might look like for a "typical team." We cannot emphasize enough, however, the freedom team members have to structure their own activities and how variable their approaches tend to be. Team members can communicate whatever they want to whomever they want whenever they want via the computer network (we typically restrict face-to-face communication in order to ensure that all message traffic is captured electronically). Thus, depicting a "typical trial" as we do later, provides an overly simplistic representation of the variability in behavior across and even within teams.

For instance, the first thing some teams do is find out precisely who can measure what and permanently enter the answer into a computer log for future reference. Members of other teams may find out precisely who has the piece of information that they themselves need, and then, via trial and error, develop a ritual for moving needed information around. Other teams go for long periods of time asking and re-asking each other "can you measure this or that" and never seem to standardize their procedures. Thus, with the caveat established that variance is the norm, we provide one "typical scenario" here.

Typically, at the start of each trial, each team member measures everything that can be measured from his or her position. This is followed by transferring raw data around to people who need it (e.g., the cruiser might need data on speed from the AWACS every time). Once everyone has all the information they need, the staff members consider their recommendation, often discussing it with other staff members or the leader. They might also try to expand their areas of expertise by learning how to interpret raw data that was not originally part of their expertise (or expand the expertise of others by teaching them how to interpret raw data that was not part of their original area of expertise). When there is about 30 seconds left in the trial, a warning indicator starts to "beep." At this point, staff members send their judgments to the leader, who studies the recommendations as they come up on his or her screen. The leader considers these judgments along with whatever raw data or impressions he or she has about the aircraft, and then enters the team's decision, usually right before the countdown clock reaches 0.

Establishing Context Effects by Changing Aircraft Characteristics

By manipulating a set of aircraft characteristics, an experimenter can create several contextual effects that are often relevant to researchers in the area of team decision making. We examine several of these later.

Manipulating Stress Through Time Pressure. Stress is typically perceived as a negative emotional reaction and physiological change that occurs when someone is confronted with a challenge or problem. Stress is particularly acute under conditions where there is uncertainty regarding one's capacity to alleviate or meet the demand imposed by the threatening stimulus (McGrath, 1976). In this simulation, stress is manipulated by varying the amount of time pressure associated with specific aircraft. Thus, by decreasing the amount of time associated with a given trial, stress levels for participants should be higher. Later, the results of an empirical study aimed at establishing the construct validity of this type of manipulation are presented.

Creating Uncertainty. Often experimenters are interested in decisions where information is ambiguous on one or more dimensions. In the initial version of this simulation, the participants' training on cues leaves a range of values that are somewhat indeterminate as to their degree of threat. In other words, there are "grey zones" associated with all cues. For example, a speed of 500 mph falls in a grey zone between "somewhat threatening" and "very threatening." Similarly, 25,000 ft. falls somewhere between "nonthreatening" and "somewhat threatening" on altitude. Thus, the exact level of threat associated with the object on that cue is not always clear to the participants. Thus, by specifying the exact raw value for each cue, and placing this in a grey zone, the experimenter can create a relatively ambiguous aircraft. The results of a construct validitation study related to this manipulation is also described later.

Creating Vigilance Contexts.   One important component of performance that is embodied in many current jobs deals with vigilance. Vigilance has been defined as a requirement that observers maintain their focus of attention and remain alert to stimuli over prolonged periods of time while engaged in monotonous monitoring (Davies & Parasuraman, 1982). This particular aspect of human performance has always been present in many types of jobs, however, increased levels of automation have made this a particularly salient issue in modern work organizations.

This condition can be simulated with TIDE^2 by generating a set of aircraft that is dominated by almost all "threatening" or all "nonthreatening" aircraft. In this overall set, one can then introduce an "ambiguous" aircraft and see how participants' reactions are affected by the overall context that precedes the "critical aircraft." The damaging effect of this type of context on decision-making accuracy was shown by Hollenbeck, Ilgen, Tuttle, and Sego (1995). This study showed that teams encountering a critical aircraft in a vigilant context were 5 to 10 times more likely to make a serious error (resulting in a disaster) compared to teams reacting to an identical aircraft in a nonvigilant contexts (where there was a varied distribution of aircraft).

Creating Group Conflict.   Group conflict is a condition where there are multiple instances of different team members coming to different opinions. Experimenters can generate "conflict-generating" aircraft that look one way to one team member, but look entirely different to another team member. For example, the distributed nature of expertise among team members creates a situation where an aircraft could appear threatening on all the dimensions assessed by one team member, but non-threatening on all the dimensions assessed by a different team member. By generating aircraft this way, it is possible to generate a context where two team members almost always disagree. Researchers can then examine what effect this has on team processes and outcomes.

Manipulating Tempo.   There are two kinds of pressure created by time in this simulation. One deals with the time available to respond to aircraft, and the other deals with tempo, that is, the time between aircraft (i.e., the time a feedback screen is displayed). In fast tempo environments, one aircraft follows another in quick succession. There is little time to rest or reflect between trials. Tempo can be manipulated in this simulation by varying the time available to examine feedback. Short duration (e.g., 5 seconds) feedback screens create a fast tempo, whereas long duration (e.g., 60 seconds) feedback screens create a slow tempo.

Establishing Prototypes.   In cognitive psychology, a "prototype" is a simplistic frame used to interpret and make sense of more complex information (Lord, 1985). So for example, if someone suggests that another person is a "yuppie," this conjures up an image in the listener's mind about what the person will probably be like on a number of dimensions such as profession, political attitudes, dress and demeanor, or purchasing preferences. In the TIDE^2 simulation, one can create prototypes by generating aircraft that are categorical and configural (i.e., a limited number of ways in which the nine separate cues can come together).

For example, the environment that a participant encounters may be consist of only four kinds of aircraft (fighters, bombers, airliners and private airplanes) each of which can assume only two states (e.g., an attacking fighter vs. an innocent fighter flyover or a lost private airplane vs. a terrorist attack from a private airplane). In this kind of context, the participant's task is to sort aircraft into categories depending on their critical attributes. Some of the attributes may overlap across categories. For example, an innocent fighter flyover and a private plane on a terrorist mission may be similar on some dimensions (such as size and speed), but differ on others (e.g., radar and IFF). The development and use of these kinds of prototypes often separates experts from novices and may be of interest to researchers in team decision making.

Creating Trends, Cycles, and Seasonality.   *Trends* refer to relationships between adjacent aircraft within experimental sessions. Trends can be established by creating aircraft that steadily increase or decrease in terms of their threat level during the experiment. *Cycles* can be established by creating, and then changing, the direction of trends systematically. Thus, aircraft can increase in their level of threat up to some point, then begin to decrease up to some point and then start increasing again. *Seasonality* can also be established by having the degree of threat covary with some unit of time. For example, trials can be described as seasons, in that the first 10 are summer, the next 10 are fall. Scenarios can be written to suggest that hostility levels are always low in winter.

In summary, this section has described and shown a number of ways to use the initial version of TIDE^2 for various kinds of team research, where the task and scenario are as just described. That is, the context is a naval command and control context where there are nine specific cues that combine in five specific ways to generate one of these seven criterion decisions. In all cases, four players measure the specific cues, and communicate in specific fashions to reach one of seven possible decisions.

TIDE^2 is a much more flexible program than has been implied so far. We focus on its flexibility in the next section. First, we show how to change the nature of the task, yet maintain the naval command and control scenario. Then, we show how to change the nature of the scenario so that it has nothing to do with naval command and control.

Establishing Context Effects by Changing the Task

Up until this point, we have been only dealing with the option for creating and changing aircraft. One can also change many features of the basic underlying nature of the simulation, and some of the options available are described here relative to certain aspects of decision contexts that one might wish to manipulate.

Task Complexity. Wood (1986) noted that there are three primary dimensions of task complexity: component complexity, coordinative complexity, and dynamic complexity. Component complexity refers to the number of pieces of information that have to be processed to perform the task. This is readily manipulated in TIDE^2 by simply altering the number of attributes that can be measured. The coordinative aspect of task complexity deals with the degree to which information on one dimension changes the implications of information on another dimension. Weighting the interactions between dimensions more than the main effects, will increase coordinative complexity because no one piece of infomation can be interpreted without the corresponding piece of information with which it interacts. Finally, dynamic complexity can be manipulated by inferring that multiple trials actually correspond to subsequent time units associated with monitoring a single aircraft over time. For example, Trial 1 could describe the aircraft at the first time interval, and Trial 2 could be used to describe the same aircraft one minute later. Certain characteristics, such as speed, direction, altitude, corridor status, range, and/or angle could then be manipulated to create an aircraft that can change course while being monitored.

Required Interdependence. The initial version of TIDE^2 uses combination rules, and then nests information within roles such that no one role can get all the information on any combination rule. This creates interdependence among players. Interdependence can also be manipulated by adjusting who can measure various aircraft characteritics. High redundancy, where many roles can measure all the same attributes, leads to low interdependence. Taken to an extreme, this could mean that all players can measure all attributes by themselves. Low redundancy, on the other hand, means everyone measures unique attributes, and this creates high interdependence. Taken to an extreme, one could employ an eight attribute system where each of four roles can measure two unique attributes.

Required Precision.   The initial version of TIDE^2 uses seven judgment categories and allows for the possibility of five different outcomes; a hit (exactly correct), a near miss (the team's decision was off by 1 point relative to the true score), a miss (2 points off), an incident (3 points off) and a disaster (4 or more points off). This could be considered a precise decision making context. One could replace this with a system that requires much less precision. For example, a situation could be constructed so that there are only two types of judgments (standby and fire), and two types of outcomes (hit or miss). One may wish to require less precise decisions in highly speeded contexts, where there might be five or six decisions made a minute. In this context, the number of trials for a team within a specified time period could be increased relative to the number that might be possible for teams making more finely graded judgments.

Group Size.   The initial version of TIDE^2 uses four players, but this number can be reduced to triads and dyads. It can even be run as a single subject simulation.

Communication Networks.   Many of the conventional communication networks studied in the groups literature, such as "wheels," "lines," "circles," and "comcons" can be invoked in TIDE2. *These can be created by manipulating the options on who can send messages to whom.*

Speed of Communications.   Communications in the initial version of TIDE^2 move relatively quickly and efficiently between players, with a maximum transmission time of 3 seconds. Communications can be made much slower, and therefore become more costly and less helpful to players by manipulations of the "message wait time."

Feedback Variations.   In the initial version of TIDE^2 the team receives feedback on their performance after each trial. Also, the performance history for the team is displayed at that time. Individual members get to see each others' decisions for the previous trial, but are not given specific feedback on their performance, nor are their personal performance histories presented with the feedback screen. These can be made available to participants by manipulating task parameters.

In addition, the initial version of TIDE^2 gives feedback immediately with respect to the aircraft that the players just encountered. Feedback can be delivered in two other ways, however. First, one can obtain trial-delayed feedback, where the feedback coming up on the screen actually refers to an aircraft experienced a specified number of trials prior to the aircraft just encountered. In other words, participants act on an aircraft at Time 1, but do not receive feedback on this aircraft until Time 4, after acting on three other aircraft in the meantime.

Second, feedback can also be summative over many trials rather than provided after every single trial. That is, participants could act on five aircraft in a row before receiving any feedback. Then, the feedback they do receive would just be for the five aircraft as a whole (e.g., three hits, a near miss, and a miss), with no way of tying specific decisions to specific outcomes.

Finally, the feedback screen can be turned off altogether. There are two ways of doing this. First, one can set the feedback time to 0. If one does this, then aircraft appear one after another with no break in between them. If one wished to eliminate feedback, but not increase tempo, then a second means of eliminating feedback should be used. Specifically, one could delay feedback over x trials where x equals the total number of trials that make up the session. This method allows one to create rest periods (where players get a blank screen) where feedback screens used to appear.

Goal and Projection Variations.   The initial version of TIDE[2] has a team goal option, which includes a projection that tells participants what their performance will be at the end of the trial if they continue to perform at the same level experienced to that point. The team goal is also displayed along with the feedback allowing one to constantly monitor progress toward the goal. One can also create individual goals and projections for team members.

Changing the Scenario

Up to this point we have been changing the various aspects of the task, but we have retained the scenario of naval command and control. The TIDE[2] program allows much more radical changes in the context so that one can even create different scenarios. For example, by changing cue names, cue values, ranges, player names, judgments and outcomes, entirely different scenarios can be developed. For example, TIDE[2] could be turned into a personnel selection task where there are four team members: an interviewer, a testing specialist, a recruiter, and a plant manager (the leader). The applicant becomes the object of decision making (rather than an aircraft) and he or she might be assessed on eight dimensions; interpersonal skills and experience (measured by the interviewer); verbal and quantitative ability (measured by the testing specialist); strength of academic program and GPA (measured by the recruiter); fit with current employees and fit with future organizational strategy (measured by the plant manager). These four team members could then pool their judgments and come up with a team decision either graded (the desirability of hiring the individual) or dichotomous (hire or not hire), which then can be evaluated against some criterion developed for the scenario.

$TIDE^2$ could also be turned into an investment banking scenario where the four players might be a CEO (the leader), a production specialist, a financial specialist, and a marketing specialist that have to come together to make recommendations about investment opportunities (e.g., whether to purchase another company). Potential takeover targets then become the object of decision making and decisions can be based on measures of: interest rate projections, capital availability projections, company ledgers, company performance history, company technology, industry analysis, or analysis of competitors within the industry.

$TIDE^2$ could in the same manner be turned into a medical scenario where medical specialists such as a cardiologist, an anesthetist, an admitting emergency physician, and a nurse make decisions regarding the treatment of a patient based on information dealing with initial onset of symptoms, test results, and behavioral monitoring.

Scenarios described so far have typically involved simulations where the criterion was determined by the experimenter, but studies in ecological prediction could also be conducted with $TIDE^2$. For example, teams of participants could be given "live" information taken from actual investment sources via TIDE2 and asked to make purchasing decisions regarding different types of corporate stock at Time 1. Members could exchange information and then make predictions about which stocks would do best over the course of some time period (e.g., 6 months). These decisions could then be compared with the real stock price at Time 2. Thus, users of $TIDE^2$ are not limited to hypothetical decision contexts and researchers can take advantage of the many archival sources available to come up with real and interesting contexts where teams might come together to make decisions.

Output and Analyses from $TIDE^2$

One of the advantages of using $TIDE^2$ in research is that large amounts of information are automatically collected during the simulation sessions. This simplifies the transition in going from data collection to data analysis.

As an overview, $TIDE^2$ can be used to produce three types of output files at the end of every session. The first file provides an easy to read "box score" summary of several important objective measures of group outcomes and processes that occured during the experimental session (e.g., the team's decision, the recommendation of each staff member, who talked to whom with what frequency, etc). The second file provides a written record of every typewritten text message sent during the session. This includes the trial number, the source, the destination and time of every message. The third file converts virtually every keystroke made during the sessions into a quantitative file in SPSS format. Many conventional analyses in the groups and decision-making literatures can be run using the TIDE^2 files, some of which are described here.

Judgment Accuracy.   One of the critical dependent variables in either individual decision making or team decision making is the accuracy of judgments. Accuracy is typically operationalized as the absolute difference between the team/individual decision and the true score. Accuracy is also sometimes operationalized by the correlation over multiple trials between the decision and the true score. Other variables can then be related to accuracy to test theories about the effects of various kinds of independent variables or process variables on decision-making accuracy.

Policy Capturing.   One common practice in the decision-making literature is to conduct policy-capturing research. In policy-capturing studies, actual decisions are regressed on various aspects of the decision object (e.g., aircraft in the command and control scenario) to determine empirically what information is driving decisions. This can be accomplished in a variety of ways.

First, one can policy-capture the decisions of team members by regressing their judgments on raw attribute information. Therefore, one would regress the decisions on the attribute information or the known characteristics of the decision object. Second, one could policy-capture the decision of the leader in terms of the summary recommendations of the other players. Here, one regresses the leader's decision on the recommendations of other team members.

Process Tracing.   Another common analysis in the decision-making literature deals with process tracing. In process tracing, the experimenter attempts to capture the information seeking processes of participants in terms of what information was sought, from whom, and at what time (e.g., Ford, Schmitt, Schechtman, Hults, & Doherty, 1989). This can be accomplished by examining the timing of various information requests and transmissions.

Process tracing and policy capturing come together in studies that examine primacy and recency effects. That is, studies examining primacy and recency effects look at the differential impact of various pieces of information on decisions, as affected by the order or timing of information acquisition. Primacy studies focus on the effects of early information, and recency studies focus on the effects of information that comes in late.

Sociograms of Communication Flows.   In groups' literature, sociograms are used to provide a picture of the communication channels that develop in groups. That is, they attempt to generate quantitative indices of who talks to whom with what frequency. These can also be generated from the TIDE^2 program.

CONSTRUCT VALIDATION OF TIDE^2 MANIPULATIONS OF STRESS AND UNCERTAINTY

Clearly, we have implied that there are a large number of contextual factors relevant to team decision making that can be manipulated through TIDE^2. Although we could obviously not document the construct validity of each of these suggestions within one chapter, there are two constructs critical to this area of research that we do wish to validate. These two constructs are related to various aspects of the environment that are typically perceived as being detrimental to effective team functioning—stress and uncertainty.

These variables are important because research is often interested in discovering factors that lead to effective team decision making, despite unfavorable conditions. As a first step, the research reported here attempts to show that the TIDE^2 simulation can effectively create these debilitating conditions. With this established, subsequent research will focus on factors that are believed to ameliorate the detrimental effects of these conditions.

The efficiency gained by separating construct validation research and substantive research comes from the ability to use the former to infer about conditions created in the latter, without establishing these directly. In other words, if we can show here that certain manipulations (e.g., decreasing response times) have predictable effects on physiological responses (e.g., higher heart rate, blood pressure), subjective perceptions (e.g., higher perceived stress), and performance (e.g., lower decision accuracy), then these reactions may be inferred in future studies that utilize the same manipulations in substantive studies.

By freeing these substantive studies from establishing construct validity, research resources can be used more efficiently. For example, if a reliable manipulation of stress is established in construct validation studies, subsequent studies can focus their limited measurement resources on substantive variables (e.g., team cohesiveness, leader experience, team member cognitive ability) rather than obtaining multiple measurements of stress (e.g., pulse rate, blood pressure, and subjective stress experiences).

STUDY 1: STRESS

We attempted to evaluate the potential of several manipulations of the environment to create stress for teams. Based on findings in the stress literature (McGrath, 1976), we evaluated two manipulations: time pressure and instability in time allotments. The goal of this study was to determine which manipulation or combination of manipulations was most effective in creating a stressful context that inhibits accurate decision making. The a priori belief that guided this research was that stress would be high and decision accuracy would be low in situations characterized by high time pressure and high instability. In addition, the effects of each manipulation were studied over time to see how each interacted with task experience. An ideal manipulation would be one whose detrimental effects persisted despite increases in task experience on the part of the subject.

Method

Participants.   One hundred and sixty undergraduate students at a large midwestern university participated in this research. Each was randomly assigned to one of 40 four-member teams. Research participants received extra course credit in return for their involvement. In addition, to enhance motivation and stress-generating potential, the top 3 performing teams in each condition (out of 10) received a monetary bonus of $40 to $100 per team. Thus, poor performane during the trials had economic consequences.

Research participants were trained on the task in the typical manner employed with TIDE^2 (see Hollenbeck et al., 1991, for more details). This training included a reading component, a video component, and a "hands-on" interactive training tutorial component. Due to the complexity of the task, training required approximately 90 minutes. Participants were trained to mastery level in terms of the mechanics of using the simulator for measuring attributes and communicating with other team members. Participants were also allowed sufficient time to learn their area of expertise, which included how to interpret cues, and the rules by which cues combined to determine threat levels associated with various aircraft.

Design.   The 40 teams were divided into four sets of 10 teams and each set was assigned to a different condition. The four conditions were used to create a 2 × 2 design where initial time pressure (high vs. low) and instability in time pressure (constant vs. changing) were varied.

Time pressure was manipulated by giving one set of teams 5 minutes per target, whereas the other set of teams were given only 2.5 minutes per aircraft. These values were based on pilot work that suggested that 5 minutes was more than enough time to evaluate each aircraft, whereas 2.5 minutes required people to work at extreme speeds to effectively share information and arrive at decisions.

Although time pressure itself could be stressful and detrimental to decision-making accuracy, we also wished to explore the effect of *changes in time pressure*. To do this, we included two more conditions. One set of teams initially worked under high time pressure and then shifted to low time pressure. Another set of teams experienced just the opposite, that is, they initially worked under low time pressure and then shifted to high time pressure. Although not manipulated, we also explored how each manipulation interacted with the team's level of experience. For obvious reasons, experience is likely to have strong effects on stress and decision-making accuracy. The degree to which the effects of these manipulations persisted despite increased level of experience was also a consideration. Experience was added as a third, within persons variable, resulting in two 2 (high vs. low initial time pressure) × 2 (constant vs. changing time pressure) × 3 (low, moderate, and high experience) design.

An additional benefit of the within-persons facet of the design is that it enhances statistical power in a situation where there are only 10 groups per cell in the between persons design. Power is enhanced because we can (a) isolate systematic variance attributable to individual differences and (b) increase the number of observations (and hence degrees of freedom) per group or team member.

Dependent Variables.   Because the situation we wished to create in the simulation was one of high stress and low decision accuracy, we looked at multiple measures of each of these two outcomes. Perceived levels of subjective stress were measured with a seven-item questionnaire administered at three times (early, middle, and late) during the experimental session. Factor analyses of these items confirmed their unidimensionality. Coefficient alpha for the subjective stress measure ranged from .84 to .86 across the three time periods. This dependent variable (DV) was measured at the individual level at three time periods and thus created 480 (40 * 4 * 3) observations (prior to missing data) for each analysis.

Since enhanced physiological reactions are also considered to be indicative of stress, yet less reactive than self-report perceptual measures, we also assessed subjects' heart rate and blood pressure once prior to the experiment and three times during the experimental sessions. These measurements were taken through Dinamap Robotic Monitors that automatically record heart rate, systolic and diastolic pressure at predefined time intervals. We used the conventional formula for translating systolic and diastolic readings into a single measure of blood pressure.

We had only two such monitors, and because teams were run two at a time, only one subject per group was assessed in this way. These DVs were at the individual level, taken at four periods and this created 160 observations (40 * 1 * 4) prior to missing data. For these two DVs the design actually becomes a 2 × 2 × 4 design.

Performance at the individual level was obtained by creating a deviation score for each person by subtracting the person's judgment from the correct decision. Performance was measured at three time periods, thus creating 480 observations for analyses at the individual level. The team's decision, registered by the carrier, was also compared to the "true score" to get a measure of team decision accuracy. Because this is at the team level, and is measured at three time periods, there were 120 observations available for analyses. All bonus money awards were contingent on team decision-making accuracy.

Results

Analyses.   Five separate repeated measures ANOVAs were conducted for each DV (subjective stress, heart rate, blood pressure, individual accuracy, team accuracy) for each of the two separate 2 × 2 × 3 designs (2 × 2 × 4 for heart rate and blood pressure). These analyses provided the statistical significance and effect sizes for three sources of between-subject variance (each manipulation and their interaction) and four sources of within-subject variance (experience and its interaction with the three sources of between-groups variation). Because all hypotheses were directional, one-tailed tests of significance were employed. Cohen (1977) recommended the use of partial eta^2 as the effect size estimate in this type of design.

Effects of Initial Time Pressure and Instability.   Table 6.4 presents the results where the between-group factors were initial time pressure and instability. Entries in this table reflect partial eta^2 values for each effect.

As a whole, the manipulations and experience had statistically significant effects on all outcomes, explaining 40%, 49%, 28%, 19%, and 37% of the variance, respectively, in subjective stress, heart rate, blood pressure, individual and team performance. Although there were a few scattered main effects and two-way interactive effects, the most important finding in this table is the three-way interaction that was significant for four out of five outcomes.

Plots of these cell means clearly indicated that the effects were associated with the condition where teams started off under low time pressure and then shifted to high pressure during the course of the session. Whereas the general pattern was one of decreasing stress and increasing accuracy as people gained experience, the opposite was the case in the condition where time pressure started off low and then changed to high. Shifting from a low to high time pressure environment led to higher stress and lower accuracy, despite the fact that subjects were gaining experience.

TABLE 6.4
The Effects of Initial Time Pressure, Instability and Experience on Stress,
Physiological Arousal, and Decision Accuracy

	Stress and Physiological Arousal			Decision Accuracy	
	Subjective Stress	Heart Rate	Blood Pressure	Individual Performance	Team Performance
Between Subjects					
(1) Initial time pressure (IT)	.01	.00	.05	.01	.00
(2) Instability	.01	.26*	.02	.00	.00
(3) IT * IN	.00	.03	.00	.01	.05
Within Subjects					
(4) Experience (E)	.16*	.13*	.07*	.15*	.22*
(5) IT * E	.10*	.02	.04	.01	.00
(6) IN * E	.01	.00	.01	.00	.02
(7) IT * N * E	.10*	.05*	.09*	.01	.08*
Total Eta^2	.40*	.49*	.28*	.19*	.37*
	$N=150$	$N=31$	$N=30$	$N=152$	$N=38$

Note. Table entries reflect partial eta^2.
*$p \leq .10$. **$p \leq .05$.

STUDY 2: UNCERTAINTY

Many of the interesting questions that deal with team decision making involve performance under conditions of informational uncertainty. Because this was an issue that we wished to explore in our research, we attempted to validate a manipulation of uncertainty.

In TIDE^2, uncertainty can be manipulated via cue values and instructions. Specifically, each aircraft can be assessed on nine dimensions, and these assessments are reported in "raw values" (e.g., mph for speed, feet for altitude, mi for range, etc.). As part of their training, subjects were instructed how to translate raw values on any attribute like "speed" into judgments regarding the degree of threat associated with that attribute. For example, team members who had expertise on assessing "speed" learned that targets flying "100 to 275 mph" were "nonthreatening." They also learned that aircraft traveling "325 to 500 mph" were "somewhat threatening" and the targets in the "600 to 800 mph" range were "very threatening."

When a manipulation of uncertainty is desired, this training leaves specific "areas of doubt" or "grey zones" where team members cannot make definite assessments. In this study, for example, a speed of 299 or 312 fell in such a "grey zone" between "nonthreatening" and "somewhat threatening." A speed of 595 or 611 fell in the grey zone between "somewhat threatening" and "very threatening." If a majority of the aircraft's attribute values fell in such grey zones, it was difficult—even for the experts—to translate raw values into threat judgments with much certainty.

To test whether such a manipulation actually leads to uncertainty on the part of subjects, we ran two studies, one of which used a between-subjects design, and the other conducted with a within-subjects design. Our overall belief was that a manipulation of uncertainty should (a) create perceptions of ambiguity in the minds of team members, and (b) take the team members (especially the staff) a longer time to evaluate. In addition, these effects would result in (c) more instances where the team failed to register a decision in the time allotted, and (d) lower decision accuracy.

Method

Participants.   Study 2a employed 160 undergraduate students at a large midwestern university. Study 2b employed 416 undergraduate students. In both studies, the same rewards were offered as in Study 1 for their participation. That is, we offered course credit that was not contingent on team performance, and a pay bonus that was contingent on team performance. Research participants were trained on the task in the typical manner employed with TIDE[2].

Design.   Study 2a manipulated uncertainty between subjects, along with time stress as part of a 2×2 design. We also controlled for experience within subjects (high vs. low) to create an overall $2 \times 2 \times (2)$ design.

Uncertainty was manipulated by assigning one set of 20 teams to an "ambiguous condition" where all nine raw values for attributes fell in "grey zones." The other 20 teams were assigned to a "certain condition," where all nine attributes fell in clearly defined ranges. Stress and experience were operationalized as in Study 1.

Study 2b manipulated uncertainty within-subjects, so that half of the aircraft seen by each team member had all their cue values falling in grey zones, whereas the other half of the aircraft they experienced were unambiguous on all nine dimensions.

Dependent Variables.   Study 2a employed four dependent variables. Two of these could be considered process variables that should be affected by uncertainty. The first was perceptions of uncertainty on the part of subjects. Second was the amount of time it took staff members to render and forward their recommendations to the leader. The manipulation should create perceptions of uncertainty on the part of subjects and should force them to consider the aircraft longer.

Two of the dependent variables could be considered outcome variables. The first was overall team decision-making accuracy and the second was the frequency of "no call" responses, that is, incidents where the team failed to respond to the aircraft in the allotted time. Overall decision accuracy should be lower, and specific incidents of performance failures (no calls) should be higher, with uncertain targets.

Study 2b, the within-subjects replication of Study 2a, employed only two dependent variables, time required of the staff to render judgments, and overall team decision accuracy.

Results.   As shown in Table 6.5, for perceptions of uncertainty there was a simple main effect for the manipulation, indicating that subjects perceived more uncertainty in arriving at judgments when in the ambiguous relative to unambiguous condition. Although there was no main effect of uncertainty on "no call" incidents, there was a strong uncertainty by time interaction. The nature of this interaction was such that there were significantly more failures to register a decision (i.e., no calls) under high uncertainty—high time pressure conditions (mean of 10.11) relative to the other three conditions (5.38).

Turning to the remaining dependent variables, the uncertainty manipulation had a strong effect on the time it took staff members to make their judgments (eta of .44), as well as the team's overall performance (eta of .36). In both cases, the manipulation also interacted with experience (eta of .07 and .17 for timing and performance respectively). The nature of this

TABLE 6.5
The Effects of Ambiguity, Time Pressure, and Experience on
Perceptions of Uncertainty, Decision Processing Times, "No Call" Cases, and
Team Decision Accuracy

	Consequences of Uncertainty			
	Perceptions of Uncertainty	Decision Processing Time	"No Call" Cases	Team Decision Accuracy
Between Subjects				
(1) Ambiguity	.53*	.44*	.01	.36*
(2) Time Pressure	.00	.19*	.00	.02
(3) A * TP	.00	.01	.16*	.02
Within Subjects				
(4) Experience	.00	.00	.01	.00
(5) A * E	.01	.07*	.01	.17*
(6) TP * E	.00	.00	.00	.01
(7) A * TP * E	.00	.00	.00	.00
Total Eta^2	.54*	.73*	.19*	.58*
	N=155	N=155	N=39	N=39

Note. Table entries reflect partial eta^2.
*$p < .05$.

interaction suggested that the manipulation, while detrimental to the performance of all teams, was especially harmful to teams at relatively low levels of experience.

Turning to Study 2b, the effects found when manipulating uncertainty between-subjects generalize to within-subject manipulations. Teams evaluating uncertain aircraft took longer to process the aircraft and performed worse on those targets relative to their performance with unambiguous aircraft. As was the case previously, uncertainty interacted with experience when overall team performance was the dependent variable. The nature of this interaction was identical to that found with between-subject manipulations; that is, uncertainty had particularly detrimental effects on inexperienced teams.

SUMMARY

The purpose of this discussion was to set the stage for future research on team decision making by describing a research task that can be used to create conditions that are detrimental to decision accuracy. We also described several manipulations of the TIDE^2 simulation that could create contexts that may be of interest to researchers in this area. As a first step, the empirical studies reported attempted to validate situational manipulations that might reliably create stress and uncertainty within-teams. The analyses of these studies indicated that these manipulations did have most of the intended effects. The manipulation of stress led to both perceptual and physiological reactions that are consistent with a stress response and decreased team decision-making accuracy. The manipulation of uncertainty led to perceptions of uncertainty, longer processing times, more instances where no decision could be arrived at in the allotted time, and decreased team decision-making effectiveness. Future research using this task and paradigm may be able to document the construct validity of other manipulations of this simulation, as well as elucidate more substantive findings associated with enhancing the decision-making effectiveness of teams and team members.

ACKNOWLEDGMENTS

This research was supported, in part, by Grant No.N00014-90-J-1788 from the Office of Naval Research as part of the technical base research for the Cognitive and Neural Sciences Division. Although support for this research is gratefully acknowledged, the ideas expressed within are those of the authors and not necessarily the funding agency.

REFERENCES

Cohen, J. (1977). *Statistical power analysis for the behavioral sciences*. New York: Academic Press.

Cook, T. D., & Campbell, D. T. (1979). *Quasi-experimentation: Design and analysis issues for field settings*. Chicago: Rand McNally.

Cronbach, L. J., & Meehl, P. E. (1955). Construct validity in psychological tests. *Psychological Bulletin, 52,* 281–302.

Davies, D. R., & Parasuramen, R. (1982). *The psychology of vigilance*. London: Academic Press.

Ford, J. K., Schmitt, N., Schechtman, S. L., Hults, B. M., & Doherty, M. L. (1989). Process tracing methods: Contributions, problems and neglected research questions. *Organizational Behavior and Human Decision Processes, 43,* 58–74.

Foushee, H. C. (1984). Dyads and triads at 35,000 feet. *American Psychologist, 39,* 885–893.

Hedlund, J., Ilgen, D. R., & Hollenbeck, J. R. (1994). *Computer-mediated versus face-to-face communication in hierarchical team decision making*. Unpublished manuscript, Michigan State University, East Lansing.

Hollenbeck, J. R., Ilgen, D. R., & Sego, D. J. (1994). Repeated measures regression: Enhancing the power of leadership research. *Leadership Quarterly, 5,* 3–23.

Hollenbeck, J. R., Ilgen, D. R., Tuttle, D., & Sego, D. J. (1995). Team performance on monitoring tasks: An examination of decision errors in contexts requiring sustained attention. *Journal of Applied Psychology, 80,* 685–696.

Hollenbeck, J. R., Sego, D. J., Ilgen, D.R., & Major, D. A. (1991). *Team interactive decision exercise of teams incorporating distributed expertise (TIDE²): A program and paradigm for team research* (Office of Naval Research Tech. Rep. No. RA 014-91-1).

Ilgen, D. R., Major, D. A., Hollenbeck, J. R., and Sego, D. J. (1995). Decision-making in teams: A levels perspective on an individual difference analog. In R. Guzzo & E. Salas (Eds.), *Team decisions in organizations* (pp. 113–148). San Francisco: Jossey-Bass.

Lord, R. G. (1985). An information processing approach to social perceptions, leadership, and behavioral measurement in organizations. In B. M. Staw & L. L. Cummings (Eds.), *Research in organizational behavior* (pp. 87–128). Greenwich, CT: JAI Press.

McGrath, J. E. (1976). Stress and behavior in organizations. In M. D. Dunnette (Ed.), *Handbook of industrial/organizational psychology* (pp. 1320–1365). Chicago: Rand McNally.

Schwab, D. P. (1980). Construct validity in organizational behavior research. In B. M. Staw & L. L. Cummings (Eds.), *Research in organizational behavior: An annual series of analytical essays and critical reviews* (pp. 51–80). Greenwich, CT: JAI Press.

Wood, R. (1986). Task complexity. Definition of a construct. *Organizational Behavior and Human Decision Processes, 37,* 60–82.

7

Team Performance Measurement in Distributed Environments: The TARGETs Methodology

Daniel J. Dwyer
Naval Air Warfare Center

Jennifer E. Fowlkes
Summit Technologies, Inc.

Randall L. Oser
Eduardo Salas
Naval Air Warfare Center

Norman E. Lane
Summit Technologies, Inc.

In today's workforce, many teams – particularly military teams – are distributed (i.e., separated by space). These teams are often large in size and composed of members with different backgrounds and areas of expertise. Teaching team members to maximize coordination and synchronization skills necessary to function successfully in distributed environments poses a tremendous modern day training challenge. Fortunately, technologies for distributed training are emerging. Advances in hardware, software, and network development will eventually make distributed training more commonplace. However, along with these advancements, one of the most critical training components that must also be developed for effective distributed training is team performance measurement. This chapter describes an extension of a measurement technique from conventional team training settings to a distributed training environment and discusses the lessons learned resulting from this application.

Distributed training refers to training that is generally managed from a central control site and that is provided to individuals or teams who are located at one or more remote sites. In recent years, the U.S. military has been active in the design and development of technologies that support distributed training. These include simulator networking (SIMNET) and Distributed Interactive Simulation (DIS), both of which allow the interaction of trainees who are operating simulation devices at geographically dispersed locations. In addition, technologies now exist that link live forces on instrumented ranges with constructive (e.g., war gaming) and virtual (e.g., conventional) simulation.

The development of technologies that support distributed training offers several benefits. The economic benefits of providing training to participants at their home facilities—rather then requiring them to travel to a central site—are obvious. In addition to the cost benefits afforded by distributed training, there is the ability of this type of training to create environments similar to the real world, where team members must face the constraints imposed by physical separation. Bringing participants together at a central site may create artificial situations that would not be encountered in operational settings. For example, walking across a room to resolve an interteam communication problem may not be the same as resolving that problem when the team members are miles apart. Thus, the ability to mimic reality through a distributed training environment can maximize the opportunity for transfer to real world operations.

Additionally, distributed teams are often characterized by differences other than geography. In industry, distributed team members will likely represent different areas of expertise. Similarly, in the military, differences between team members may exist with regard to their service, doctrine, tactics, techniques, procedures, communication patterns, and expertise. Distributed training can provide an opportunity to assess the implications of these differences, and to resolve them if necessary, prior to encountering them in an operational setting. Thus, distributed training technologies have the potential to economically create synthetic environments that replicate real-world constraints imposed by separation. Furthermore, these technologies allow teams to identify disparities, determine performance strategies, and apply the strategies in a safe, but highly realistic setting.

DIS is an emerging technology that enables distributed training. The development of DIS is a result of a joint government–industry–academia venture to develop the techniques, protocols, and general infrastructure that will allow multiple simulators and simulations of various types to be networked. The intent is to "bring together systems [simulations] built for separate purposes, technologies from different eras, products from various vendors, and platforms from various services" in a manner that allows them to interoperate (IEEE, 1994, p. 2). In its military applications, DIS-based training allows geographically dispersed participants to "congregate" in a simulated "combat arena."

The potential training value of DIS is tremendous, yet the technology must continue to mature before its benefits can be realized fully. Similarly, the "training system" that must ultimately be superimposed onto this technology must also continue to evolve if DIS is to be used effectively and efficiently. Indeed, given the cost and level of effort devoted to this technology development, the assessment of training effectiveness will be demanded. One area that must be enhanced within this realm is team performance measurement.

To determine effectiveness and to pinpoint performance strengths and weaknesses in any team training environment, training should be assessed from a number of perspectives. These perspectives include reactions to training, attitudes toward teamwork, knowledge of key teamwork concepts, and actual team performance (Cannon-Bowers et al., 1989; Cannon-Bowers & Salas, chapter 3, this volume). Typically however, when team training is assessed, only the first three of these dimensions are examined. What is as important, more difficult to accomplish, and less frequently assessed, is the fourth dimension: actual team performance — that is, the extent to which team behaviors are successfully exhibited during a training evolution. Despite the importance of assessment, virtually every major review of the team training and performance literature has identified the lack of team performance measures as a hindrance to the development of effective team training systems (Baker & Salas, 1992; Dyer, 1984; Modrick, 1986; O'Neil, Baker, & Kaslauskas, 1992).

Most typically, when team performance is assessed, the evaluation method relies on instructors or other subject matter experts (SMEs) to provide numerical ratings of performance (Modrick, 1986). Even when rating scales are carefully constructed (e.g., behaviorally anchored), they have several deficiencies that limit them as evaluation tools. First, because ratings tend to be global, they lack diagnostic specificity (i.e., they do not point out specific performance deficiencies). For example, outstanding performance on a given dimension during one point in training may be tempered by poor performance on that dimension at other points in training. A single rating cannot accurately capture both "good" and "poor" performance. Second, rating techniques typically require several highly trained SMEs to achieve adequate measurement properties. Baker and Salas' (1992) review of team performance measurement suggested that although moderate levels of interrater reliability can be obtained, they are generally unacceptably low. Finally, unless there is considerable opportunity for preselecting the measurement system, the content of the rating constructs and their relevance are essentially unknown.

Because of these deficiencies, a number of researchers have begun advocating the use of event-based measurement techniques that assess team processes more objectively, provide diagnostic capabilities for identifying specific problem areas, and provide psychometrically sound metrics for tracking training progression (Cannon-Bowers & Salas, chapter 3, this volume; Dwyer, Oser, & Fowlkes, 1995; Fowlkes, Lane, Salas, Franz, & Oser, 1994; Hall, Dwyer, Cannon-Bowers, Salas, & Volpe, 1993; Johnston, Smith-Jentsch, & Cannon-Bowers, chapter 14, this volume; Oser, Dwyer, & Fowlkes, 1995). One technique that accommodates these components is the Targeted Acceptable Responses to Generated Events or Tasks (TARGETs) methodology (Fowlkes et al., 1994).

TARGETs and other event-based measurement techniques create measurement opportunities by systematically identifying and embedding events within training exercises that provide known opportunities to observe behaviors of interest (Dwyer et al., 1995; Hall et al., 1993; Wigdor & Green, 1991). Having a number of such opportunities present within an exercise provides a sound observation base, controls the nature of the observations, and reduces the judgment and biases typically associated with rating techniques. Event-based approaches have been associated with excellent reliability and sensitivity (Fowlkes et al., 1994; Wigdor & Green, 1991).

The TARGETs methodology has been successfully applied to small team training settings in which teams were composed of members who were physically located with one another (Fowlkes et al., 1994). However, the extent of this methodology's applicability to distributed training environments, in which training participants are geographically dispersed, is uncertain.

In distributed training environments, measurement challenges are likely to be exacerbated over those encountered in conventional training environments (Fowlkes, Lane, Dwyer, Willis, & Oser, 1995). For example, Fowlkes et al. (1995) suggested that (a) the fact that real-world tasks are often replicated means that the task content will be less certain and therefore harder to measure; (b) because of the greater number of participants, and their possible interactions, control of the training exercise will be harder to achieve; (c) the potential impact of training equipment failures may be greater because there are more potential sources; and (d) the differences between training devices in the extent to which they replicate reality will create unlevel playing fields, giving some team members artificial advantages. The use of TARGETs and other event-based approaches in distributed training environments is problematic because of the much greater difficulty in controlling the training exercise to ensure that intended events are presented. Yet, this may be exactly the type of strategy needed to ensure training value in distributed environments.

This chapter describes the lessons learned resulting from an application of an event-based measurement approach—the TARGETs methodology— within the context of a distributed training environment. Prior to describing the application and lessons learned, the TARGETs methodology is described in detail.

THE TARGETs METHODOLOGY

Requirements

The original impetus for TARGETs development was a need to evaluate team performance in complex and dynamic environments, specifically aircrew coordination training (Fowlkes et al., 1994). The methodology had to be responsive to several requirements for assessing team performance in these types of settings. The TARGETs methodology had to produce a measurement tool that (a) was able to capture team processes and identify performance deficiencies, (b) could produce a psychometrically sound metric for monitoring training progression, (c) was sensitive to training constructs of interest, (d) had to be responsive to the practicalities of measurement in applied team training contexts, and (e) minimized rater bias and error. Although TARGETs was developed for military applications, these requirements apply equally well to most situations in which team performance must be assessed. These requirements are discussed here.

Capture Team Processes.   The focus of the TARGETs method was on capturing team processes to provide greater diagnostic capability than can be provided by outcome measures. Outcome measures reveal very little concerning "why" something happened; process measures, however, provide the level of granularity necessary for determining why something happened. A focus on team performance processes was the first requirement for the TARGETs methodology.

Provide Satisfactory Metric Properties.   The evaluation of training interventions with *experienced* teams is complicated by the tendency for the intervention effects to be quite small. Therefore, unusually sensitive measurement is necessary, demanding both high measurement reliability and measurement relevance (i.e., what is measured must be modifiable by the intervention). Consequently, the TARGETs methodology had to produce a metric that was sensitive enough to detect even slight variations between performance levels.

Sensitive to Relevant Constructs.   To achieve sensitivity to the training constructs of interest, it is important to link performance measures to training objectives. One way to do this is to systematically design events into scenarios to provide opportunities for teams to demonstrate specific team behaviors related to the training objectives. These events create situations that act as cues for the team to take some action. The actions they take as a result of an event provide an opportunity for evaluators to observe critical behaviors and to assess how well they perform relative to the training objectives. The goal for TARGETs was to create links among scenario events, team behaviors, and training objectives.

Responsive to Practical Constraints.   The TARGETs method had to be usable in applied training situations. This implied that (a) performance had to be scorable off-line by non-SME evaluators when SMEs were not available, (b) measures had to have diagnostic and debriefing value (the ability to point out specific performance deficiencies), and (c) the methodology had to be generalizable across multiple domains.

Control Rater Bias and Error.   The TARGETs methodology required observers to determine the presence or absence of predetermined, acceptable behaviors. This feature, perhaps more than any other, separates TARGETs from rating techniques. The TARGETs method required that numerical judgments associated with rating scales be replaced with dichotomous judgments. This requirement was intended to remove much of the subjectivity associated with rating scales.

Development

The TARGETs methodology produces assessment tools that are developed with the requirements just cited at the forefront. The methodology results in a measurement instrument organized as an event-based, behaviorally focused checklist. This format allows observers to collect structured observations of team behaviors in a manner that flows in parallel with the exercise (Fowlkes et al., 1994). The methodology calls for the checklist to be organized by scenario events (i.e., the prompts that create opportunities for performance of a set of behaviors related to the training objectives) in the approximate sequence in which the events will appear in the associated exercise. Thus, each TARGETs checklist is exercise-specific.

Once the events and the training objectives they represent are identified, a set of team-related behaviors for each event is identified and positioned in the checklist in the appropriate section for that event. Thus, Event A may be associated with six behaviors, Event B with five related behaviors, and so on. Each of the behaviors associated with a given event are placed together in the section of the checklist devoted to that event.

The identification of acceptable team behaviors is conducted a priori, according to doctrine, task analyses, standard operating procedures, SME input, and other documented tactics, techniques, and procedures. Thus, the responses are the job-specific manifestations of critical team behaviors. Consequently, the method provides a means for maintaining an explicit link among the training objectives, exercise events, and the critical team behaviors.

Many of the events that typically would be included in an exercise would be routine, for example passing through standard mission phases, each of which requires a number of actions to be performed. However, additional events should also be introduced to serve as cues for nonroutine tasks such as those that require (a) behaviors with a low frequencies of occurrence, or (b) behaviors that are not ordinarily observable. The effective use of this methodology is directly tied to the control of exercises (i.e., through the event-based exercise structure) to ensure that the intended events are presented.

As an exercise unfolds, assessors score each of the checklist items as either acceptable or unacceptable. The technique of dichotomous assessment significantly reduces the level of subjectivity often associated with performance assessments that rely on observations.

Due to the nature of the TARGETs checklist, team performance can be analyzed in a number of ways. One method involves calculating the proportion of acceptable behaviors relative to the total set of behaviors that should have been performed. This metric provides a general indication of how well the team processes were performed. A second, supplemental method involves dividing groups of behaviors into functionally related clusters, for example those linked to a specific training objective or those for a particular event. These clusters can then be examined separately in order to provide an indication of how teams performed within certain functional areas, provided that each is based on a sufficient number of observations. Assessment of performance for these clusters can then serve as a source of feedback and can be used for monitoring training progress over a series of training exercises.

The event-based emphasis of the TARGETs methodology is a deliberate attempt to acquire performance scores with sound psychometric properties. Control over the number of events enhances reliability by controlling the number of observations obtained. The advantage of this approach is that during an exercise, a large number of cued events can be presented to a team, providing a stable base for observation. Control over the nature of events enhances the relevance of the resulting observations to team theory or training objectives. That is, this approach fuses measurement with those specific team behaviors intended to be modified by the training.

Benefits

As discussed previously, the requirements imposed on the TARGETs methodology and the actual development approach result in advantages over traditional rating scales as measurement tools. Next, we briefly expand on these benefits. Table 7.1 compares the TARGETs methodology to traditional rating approaches on several factors. These comparison factors are describe here.

Observation Procedure. The observation task is simpler with TARGETs compared to that generally required with rating techniques. With TARGETs, each "entry" requires the observer to determine the presence or absence of a specific, observable behavior, thus minimizing judgment. In

TABLE 7.1
Comparison of the TARGETs Methodology to
Traditional Rating Methodologies

Factors	TARGETs	Ratings
Observation Procedure	Present-absent scoring of observable behaviors or actions	Generally, unobservable constructs are rated based on "behavioral markers"
	A priori knowledge of task events and observation requirements	Generally, task events and observation requirements are not as rigorously specified
	Judgment entails determining the acceptability of specific behaviors	Generally, judgments are based on a large number of observations made over some period of time; generally, rater must judge performance as it relates to more than one construct
Observer Training	Training of observers is required, subject matter experts are not always required for scoring	Extensive training required; subject matter experts are critical for ratings
Observation Forms	Specific to exercise or scenario	Most often are generic
Scores	Each score is based on a large number of predetermined observations	Each score is based on an indeterminate number of observations that may not even occur
	Scores have inherent meaning given SME input in identifying behaviors. Higher scores indicate that a greater number of behaviors have been correctly performed	Meaningfulness of scores directly related to validity of underlying constructs

addition, because of the event-based approach, the observer has knowledge of what events will occur, when they will occur, and a list of team behaviors to anticipate for each event. In contrast, with rating approaches, observations are generally less well-defined. If the exercise is not controlled, the rater must try to observe behaviors that might only occur infrequently, and the sampling base is left to chance. Moreover, the rater must generally consider, simultaneously, different aspects of performance related to the constructs to be evaluated (e.g., adaptability, communication, and situation awareness).

Observer Training.   On TARGETs checklist forms, events and behaviors to be observed are presented in the approximate order in which they will occur in the exercise. This, coupled with the dichotomous nature of the judgments required, means that less observer training is required with the TARGETs methodology. In addition, in some applications, individuals who are not SMEs can be employed, easing the burden of identifying SMEs for the time-consuming task of scoring performance. With traditional rating approaches, extensive rater training is generally required to provide ratings that are free of bias. One would be hesitant to employ individuals who are not SMEs for the rating task, especially for complex jobs.

Observation Forms.   A generic rating form may apply to a variety of situations, exercises, or scenarios in which rating scales are used. The opposite is true with TARGETs for which scenario-specific, tailored forms are developed. Although the up-front work is greater, the scenario-specific nature of TARGETs checklists increases the specificity of observations and enhances their diagnosticity.

Scores.   Higher scores from TARGETs indicate that more behaviors have been correctly performed. Thus, TARGETs scores have inherent meaning apart from the theory or guidance used to generate the scenario events. In contrast, the meaningfulness of scores obtained with rating techniques is directly dependent on the validity of the underlying theory.

APPLICATIONS OF THE TARGETs METHODOLOGY

Aviation Team Training

Fowlkes et al. (1994) demonstrated the utility of the TARGETs methodology in a military cargo helicopter community. It was shown that the insertion of events into scenarios, the specification of acceptable behavioral responses for each event, and the organization of the TARGETs checklist in a manner parallel to scenario flow, permitted the capturing of team processes for a training evolution. The ability to quantify performance, based on the proportion of acceptable responses performed, allowed the creation of a metric for training performance assessment.

The methodology was sensitive to the practicalities in applied training settings as evidenced by the ability of non-SMEs to score performance. Also, the event-based approach allowed a traceable link among the training objectives, scenario events, performance measures, and feedback components. And finally, the evidence of sound psychometric properties (interobserver reliability = .94, internal consistency = .97, and sensitivity in the ability to detect performance differences between trained and untrained groups; $p < .05$) demonstrated that the TARGETs methodology could control rater bias and minimize error. Satisfactory reliability and sensitivity have also been obtained across three additional military aviation communities, although these findings are unpublished.

Distributed Training

The successful TARGETs applications were obtained in situations composed of small teams in which 2 to 3 team members were co-located. The small team size made exercise control feasible, and it was relatively easy to monitor the interactions among the participants. Also, because team members were co-located, it was easy for assessors to observe behaviors among team members during scenario execution. Furthermore, in most cases, audiovisual recordings were made and assessments were conducted post hoc, where performance could be systematically and repeatedly reviewed.

Several issues surfaced when the TARGETs methodology was adapted to a distributed training environment. How well the methodology could be extended to training domains composed of larger numbers of participants was unknown. Also unclear was the extent to which the method would lend itself to training environments where team members were physically separated from one another, and where assessors were dependent on only those communications that they could monitor and on observations of those participants at the site where the assessors were located. The need to support rapid, postexercise feedback posed additional challenges. It is toward this type of training setting that we examined extending the TARGETs methodology.

Testbed.   The initial extension of the TARGETs methodology into the realm of distributed training environments involved the military mission known as Close Air Support (CAS). CAS is a complex mission that requires coordination among several teams from different military services. In general, the objective of CAS is to conduct air strikes against hostile targets that are located in close proximity to friendly forces. A research testbed, known as the Multi-service Distributed Training Testbed (MDT2), provided the distributed training vehicle for the effort (Bell, 1995; Moses, 1995). The testbed linked several teams and their respective simulators at different sites via a longhaul electronic network. The network allowed training to occur real-time between distant sites and across different military services for teams using simulators located at the various sites.

The testbed provided an opportunity to implement TARGETs and assess team performance in a distributed setting. Several subteams were aggregated into a larger collective whose overall mission was to conduct CAS as one component of a larger ground battle. The training was performed over 5 days and focused on behaviors performed by 19 key participants who were responsible for the interteam interactions necessary to successfully plan and execute CAS. The general flow of a training day consisted of a pre-exercise briefing, conduct of the exercise, and a feedback session that focused on the behaviors contained in the TARGETs checklist.

TARGETs Development. Twenty-five training objectives, and the associated tasks that defined the interservice interactions necessary to successfully conduct CAS missions, were identified during front-end analyses. The key personnel involved in executing those tasks were also identified. Scenario flow was examined and an assessment was made of where routine multiservice tasks were expected to be performed (e.g., enemy tanks encountered). For the tasks that were less likely to be performed, specific events (e.g., losing a critical communication link, encountering heavy enemy artillery) were identified and embedded at certain points in the scenario. The appropriate behaviors for routine and nonroutine events were then delineated. Finally, a checklist was created that paralleled the scenario flow. This procedure was followed for each of the scenarios used in training. Figure 7.1 provides a sample section from one of the TARGETs checklists.

Although the TARGETs checklist contained separate multipage sections — each section devoted to a specific phase of the CAS mission — the example in Fig. 7.1 depicts only a small sample from one mission phase. This sample however, is representative of the organization and format used throughout all phases.

As can be seen in Fig. 7.1, the mission phase (pre-attack in the sample) is provided at the top of the checklist. The body of the TARGETs checklist is arranged in a manner such that the left side of the form reflects behaviors associated with routine events, whereas the right side of the form focuses on behaviors linked to nonroutine events.

On the left side of the checklist, the main column lists the behaviors that were expected to be routinely performed during that mission phase. The second, smaller column, provided an area for the assessors to record their observations (i.e., the presence or absence of the behaviors) related to the routine events. The right side of the form was constructed similarly, except that the focus was on the behaviors that were expected to be performed in response to nonroutine events introduced during the scenario.

Assessors used the coding scheme listed at the bottom of the checklist to record their observations in the appropriate columns. Each section of the TARGETs checklist also contained an area for note-taking and comments by the assessor.

Event A: Heavy Enemy Artillery

Fighter authenticates		Fighters informed of situation	
Fighter provides brief to FAC		Fighters told to orbit at safe distance	
- Mission number		Fighter plan time considered	
- Number/type of aircraft		Informal ACA established/re-established	
- Ordnance		Alternate ACA considered	
- Time on Station		ACA	
- Abort code		- Protects fighters	
		- Allows fighter maneuverability	
9-line provided to fighters		- FSO ensures indirect fires conform to ACA	
- IP		- Clearly defined (e.g., suitable landmarks identified)	
- Heading (IP to target)		TOT revised	
- Distance (IP to target)		Availability of SEAD established	
- Target description		FSO established that SEAD can comply with TOT	
- Type mark, laser code, target line		Fighters briefed	
- Friendly location		- ACA clearly communicated	
- Egress directions		- TOT communicated	
- Remarks: SEAD, ACA clearly described, etc.			
- TOT/TTT			
TTT/TOT retransmitted by fighter to acknowledge			
Fighter brief passed to MULE team			
TOT passed to FSO			

Comments:_____
_____
_____
_____
_____

1 = Observed/Performed Satisfactorily
0 = Omitted/Failed to Perform Satisfactorily
X = No Opportunity to Perform/Not Required

FIG. 7.1.   Sample from the TARGETs checklist for the CAS pre-attack phase.

Procedure.   Two scenarios, one offensive and one defensive in nature, were run alternately on 5 consecutive days. Each scenario lasted approximately 2 to 3 hours, and generally prompted four to six CAS missions. Although there were numerous military personnel involved in the training exercise, 19 key participants who were responsible for planning and executing CAS were the focus of the case study. Assessors (SMEs) were located at each of the training sites involved in the distributed training exercise. The assessors' job involved monitoring the participants' communications over radio nets during the exercise, observing the behaviors, and completing the TARGETs checklist as the exercise was conducted. The TARGETs data would then be used to support postexercise feedback to the participants and to generate metrics for examining performance trends across 5 days of training.

Findings.   Figure 7.2 presents a plot of the TARGETs data from the planning phase of the CAS missions. (Plots from two other phases — pre-attack and attack — are not presented, although similar patterns emerged. Those plots can be found in Oser et al., 1995.) The plot in Fig. 7.2 represents the averaged TARGETs scores from all assessors for all CAS missions conducted on a given day. As can be seen in Fig. 7.2, overall performance generally improved across the 5 days. This trend indicates that task performance improved as a function of MDT2 practice.

In an attempt to further examine specific clusters of behaviors, the TARGETs data were broken out into the functional areas of Target Selection, Airspace Coordination Areas (ACA), Control of Aircraft, and Synchronization. All components except Control of Aircraft appeared to asymptote at high performance levels by Day 3; performance related to the Control of Aircraft peaked on Day 4 before declining slightly on Day 5. These patterns in the data served as valuable discussion topics during the feedback sessions. For example, "Target Selection" received very little attention during the feedback session early in the week because of the relatively high performance in that area. "Airspace Coordination Areas" however, received considerable attention early in the week because of the relatively poor performance in that area.

Comments from assessors concerning the use and utility of the checklist were highly favorable, suggesting the format was practical for use in applied settings. Finally, interrater reliability estimates ranged from the middle .50s for the dynamic, fast-paced attack phase to the high .90s for scores based

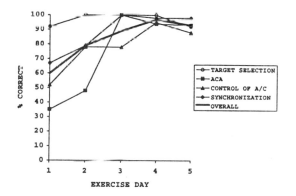

FIG. 7.2.   Overall TARGETs scores and subscores for each exercise day (planning phase).

on observations made during the slower paced, more deliberate actions of the planning phase. This suggested that while adequate control of rater bias and error can be achieved, improvement is needed in some areas.

LESSONS LEARNED

The initial extension of the TARGETs methodology to the distributed training environment was successful. The checklist flow allowed assessors to monitor and capture team processes during the exercises. Conversion of the data into metrics allowed assessors to track progress over several exercise days. The steady increase in performance across days of training — that one would expect — was detected by the TARGETs checklist. However, many lessons learned were obtained that not only pointed to strengths of the method, but also to areas in which the method needed to be improved. Several of these lessons are discussed here.

First, the scenarios successfully prompted the employment of CAS, allowing several repetitions of the behaviors associated with CAS to be observed during each exercise day. However, exercise control leading to the introduction of events prompting nonroutine behaviors was difficult to achieve. Thus, assessment was limited chiefly to observation of routine behaviors.

Despite the limitations with respect to scenario control, the TARGETs checklists were sufficiently sensitive to detect improvements in performance. Just as important, they were robust with respect to data loss. Because DIS is an emerging technology, system reliability often caused one or more training sites to "fall off the network." Consequently, training for those participants came to a temporary stop. Additionally, assessors were often called away from their job as assessors to perform unplanned duties.

In these cases, portions of the exercise went unobserved and consequently, sections of the TARGETs checklists were uncompleted. Computing the metrics for assessing performance could have unfairly penalized participants because checklist items that were left blank may have suggested a failure of the team to perform those behaviors. However, by noting and subsequently omitting those items from the computation, the performance metrics reflected only those checklist items that were "fair game" during the exercise. The final metric was still based on a percent correct "score," however it reflected only those segments of the exercise that the assessors could reasonably observe. This permitted fair comparisons of performance scores across exercise days.

Related to the issue of unplanned duties for the assessors was the fact that several assessors were also assigned collateral duties (e.g., role-playing higher echelon positions, or coaching individuals within one of the subteams). Competition for assessors' attention and their resulting focus on several facets of the exercise clearly interfered with their assessment and feedback duties. Future applications of distributed training should use a dedicated cadre of skilled assessors whose only job is to assess performance and participate in the feedback sessions.

One lesson learned that probably could have been avoided concerned assessor access to the trainees' communication nets. Because multiple teams and team members were widely dispersed, radio communications were frequently the only method of interaction. Consequently, assessors must have access to those communication channels in order to assess the interactions. In this application however, the assessors had insufficient access to these communications. To get around this problem, different assessors were assigned to focus on certain phases or segments of the CAS missions and shared access to monitoring equipment as necessary. Nonetheless, this was a cumbersome work-around procedure that limited thoroughness. Ensuring that sufficient hardware and space are available for this function is critical for future applications.

Another lesson learned from the case study extension of the TARGETs methodology focused on the different vantage points available to assessors at the different training sites. Whereas an assessor at one site might not have observed a behavior or series of behaviors, an assessor at another site might have witnessed the performance of the behaviors because of a viewing advantage due to the perspective at a particular site. Although this could have been problematic, the assessors discussed their differing observations during the preparation period for the feedback session, reached a consensus, and decided how it would be discussed during the feedback. In many ways, this multiple perspective worked as a backup system for the assessors.

A valuable lesson learned concerned the amount of time needed to convert input from multiple TARGETs forms and from multiple assessors into a format for feedback. This proved to be a time-consuming process that seriously challenged the ability to provide timely feedback to training participants. Techniques for speeding up this process are needed.

Another lesson learned concerned the inability of the TARGETs checklist to take into account and assess behaviors associated with spontaneous events; that is, those unplanned events that teams often unintentionally introduce into an exercise. Because the TARGETs methodology relies on prespecified events and the associated behavioral responses—and the checklist is laid out to follow that flow—unanticipated, and possibly very creative behaviors may go unassessed. Furthermore, depending on when these unplanned events occur, they may interfere with preplanned events, thereby obscuring or preventing opportunities to assess behaviors associated with the intended events.

Although the performance measurement tools resulting from the TAR-

GETs methodology appeared to be manageable by observers, as distributed systems increase in size, the methodology may require modification so that assessors are not overwhelmed by the number of items on the tools. The selection of specific behaviors to be included on a TARGETs measurement tool may need to be limited to those that are most likely to discriminate between more and less effective teams.

A final lesson learned concerned the observation that the primary strength of the TARGETs checklist — dichotomous scoring — is in some way also a limitation. Although the binary assessment indicates the presence or absence of an acceptable behavior, it is possible that the behavior could have been performed to varying degrees of thoroughness, efficiency, accuracy, and so forth. A dichotomous score does not reflect the degree of success. One possible solution for this dilemma is to supplement TARGETs-based assessments with additional measurement tools (e.g., the Teamwork Observation Measure; Dwyer et al., 1995) that incorporate qualitative assessments. A second potential solution, already incorporated, is to provide commentary on the TARGETs checklist for specific behaviors that were performed, but still had room for improvement. The commentary can then be used to provide feedback that is more focused on the degree of successful performance.

CONCLUDING REMARKS

The extension of the TARGETs methodology from small team training applications with co-located team members to distributed training environments with team members dispersed throughout the country, was largely a successful one. Although the performance data reported for this application are based on a case study, they are the first of their kind. During this trial application, both researchers and practitioners were content with the methodology. However, this extension is only the first step. The lessons learned must be addressed and strategies for resolving the associated problems must be developed and incorporated in order to further enhance the utility of the methodology. No doubt, distributed training will continue to expand in the future. Assessment of performance in this type of training environment will similarly expand. The TARGETs methodology offers tremendous potential to support this expansion.

REFERENCES

Baker, D. P., & Salas, E. (1992). Principles for measuring teamwork skills. *Human Factors, 34,* 469–475.

Bell, H. H. (1995). The engineering of a training network. *Proceedings of the Human Factors and Ergonomics Society 39th Annual Meeting* (pp. 1311–1315). Santa Monica, CA: Human Factors and Ergonomics Society.

Cannon-Bowers, J. A., Prince, C., Salas, E., Owens, J. M., Morgan, B. B. Jr., & Gonos, G. H. (1989). Determining aircrew coordination training effectiveness. *Proceedings of the 11th Interservice/Industry Training Systems Conference* (pp. 128–136). Arlington, VA: American Defense Preparedness Association.

Dwyer, D. J., Oser, R. L., & Fowlkes, J. E. (1995). A case study of distributed training and training performance. *Proceedings of the Human Factors and Ergonomics Society 39th Annual Meeting* (pp. 1316–1320). Santa Monica, CA: Human Factors and Ergonomics Society.

Dyer, J. L. (1984). Team research and training: A state-of-the-art review. In F. A. Muckler (Ed.), *Human factors review: 1984*. Santa Monica, CA: Human Factors Society.

Fowlkes, J. E., Lane, N. E., Dwyer, D. J., Willis, R. P., & Oser, R. (1995). Team performance measurement issues in DIS-based training environments. *Proceedings of the 17th Interservice/Industry Training Systems and Education Conference* (pp. 272–280). Arlington, VA: American Defense Preparedness Association.

Fowlkes, J. E., Lane, N. E., Salas, E., Franz, T., & Oser, R. (1994). Improving the measurement of team performance: The TARGETs methodology. *Military Psychology, 6*, 47–61.

Hall, J. K., Dwyer, D. J., Cannon-Bowers, J. A., Salas, E., & Volpe, C. E. (1993). Toward assessing team tactical decision making under stress: The development of a methodology for structuring team training scenarios. *Proceedings of the 15th Interservice/Industry Training Systems and Education Conference* (pp. 87–98). Arlington, VA: American Defense Preparedness Association.

IEEE. (1994). *Recommended practice for distributed interactive simulation: Exercise management and feedback* (Draft IEEE Standard). Orlando, FL: Simulation, Training, and Instrumentation Command.

Modrick, J. A. (1986). Team performance and training. In J. Zeidner (Ed.), *Human productivity enhancement: Training and human factors in systems design* (Vol. I). New York: Praeger.

Moses, F. L. (1995). The challenge of distributed training. *Proceedings of the Human Factors and Ergonomics Society 39th Annual Meeting* (pp. 1306–1310). Santa Monica, CA: Human Factors and Ergonomics Society.

O'Neil, H. F., Baker, E. L., & Kaslauskas, E. J. (1992). Assessment of team performance. In R. W. Swezey & E. Salas (Eds.), *Teams: Their training and performance*. Norwood, NJ: Ablex.

Oser, R. L., Dwyer, D. J., & Fowlkes, J. E. (1995). Team performance in multi-service distributed interactive simulation exercises: Initial results. *Proceedings of the 17th Interservice/Industry Training Systems and Education Conference* (pp. 163–171). Arlington, VA: American Defense Preparedness Association.

Wigdor, A. K., & Green, B. F., Jr. (1991). *Performance assessment for the workplace*. Washington, DC: National Academy Press.

8 The Measurement of Team Performance With a Standardized Survey

Glenn Hallam
David Campbell
Center for Creative Leadership
Colorado Springs, CO

"How are we doing?" This is a natural and seemingly simple question for members of a team to ask. Answering it, however, is not so simple. If members of a team want to know how well they performed in the last 30 minutes while working on a particular problem, that might well be quantifiable, but most team members usually want a more complicated answer. For example, they want to know how they performed over the last 6 months while tackling a number of different projects, sometimes simultaneously. They want to know how well they performed while doing actual work under typical day-to-day conditions, not while performing simulated tasks under controlled conditions. If encouraged to clarify their question, members of a team will often say they want to know how they are doing in a wide range of areas, from team coordination and conflict resolution to customer satisfaction and productivity.

Furthermore, most team members believe that the evaluation of their performance should be adjusted for a unique set of forces that may help or hinder them, factors that are out of their control, such as the actions of their competitors, changes in the market, or new demands from the organization. They are essentially asking, "Given the circumstances, how are we doing?" They want an answer to this question even though they may not have produced any tangible results nor are there any hard data (financial or otherwise) to reflect their performance. They often want to know how they compare to other teams, even though "other teams" is usually ill-defined and may be embedded in different organizational contexts with different tasks, customers, and ways of measuring their performance.

155

In spite of their demand for this information, few teams are interested in elaborate methods for tracking their performance. They do not want researchers following them around with clipboards nor video cameras peering down on them; they are too busy to constantly record their observations or complete rating forms; and they rarely, if ever, have the money to fund a study of their performance. Still, they want to know, "How are we doing?"

There are at least three ways to respond to this question: (a) "I don't know," (b) "Fund a study and I might be able to tell you," and (c) "Let's take a survey and find out." For most teams, the method of choice is the psychological survey. Surveys are inexpensive, measure a wide range of topics, focus on how the team has functioned over relatively long time periods, and are useful for a wide variety of teams doing different kinds of work in highly diverse settings.

In this chapter, a commercially available survey called the Campbell–Hallam Team Development Survey™ (TDS™) is described, and results from 194 teams are presented. Applications for this measurement device are discussed. It is argued that administering a well-designed team survey is the best way to answer the deceptively simple question, "How are we doing?"

PURPOSE OF THE TDS

The TDS™ differs from other performance measurement methods in many ways, the most important one being its purpose. The purpose of the TDS™ is to measure the perceptions of team members and return this information back to the members in a form they can use for identifying strengths to celebrate and problems to address. The survey is designed to give a comprehensive answer to the question, "How is the team doing . . . according to the members of the team and their observers?" Ultimately, the purpose of the survey is to stimulate and guide the team in the process of finding ways to improve.

SURVEY CONTENT AND SCORING

The TDS assesses the perceptions of the team members by presenting 72 specific statements about the team. Each team member responds to the statements using a six-point scale ranging from *strongly agree* to *strongly disagree*. Each survey item is a statement about the team or its members such as "Team members offer help when I need it." Example items appear

TABLE 8.1
Example TDS Member Items

Our work is high quality.
When we disagree, we usually work out our differences in an honest, healthy way.
This team often laughs together.
Our team meetings are well organized.
Our team members are skilled and competent.
We have a reputation for being innovative.
We are overwhelmed with things to do. *
Team members compete with each other rather than cooperate.

*Items in italics are negatively weighted.

in Table 8.1. The items are organized into 18 short scales, measuring a wide array of areas related to the team's needs and effectiveness:

Time and Staffing
Information
Material Resources
Organizational Support
Skills
Commitment
Mission Clarity
Team Coordination
Team Unity
Individual Goals
Empowerment
Team Assessment
Innovation
Feedback
Rewards
Leadership
Satisfaction
Performance

Each scale contains three to six items, with most of the scales having four or five items. Scale scores are computed by mathematically combining the responses to the items on each scale. Items that reflect a negative opinion about the team (e.g., *"Team members compete with each other rather than cooperate."*) are weighted negatively in this process. An Overall Scale Score is also reported, based on a sum of all the items (again, negatively worded items are weighted negatively).

Scores are reported as *T* scores, that is, standard scores, with a mean of 50 and a standard deviation of 10. A score of 50 represents the typical or average team that has completed the survey (the norming sample is described here). Each scale produces an approximately bell-shaped curve, with about two thirds of team members falling between scores of 40 and 60 on each scale. Thus, scores above 60 can be considered "high," and scores below 40 can be considered "low."

DEVELOPMENT OF THE TDS

The selection of topics for measurement was based on both theoretical and practical considerations. For example, the Mission Clarity scale was derived from early work by Zander (1968) showing that groups' goals can affect group behavior just as individuals' goals affect individual behavior. Similarly, the Individual Goals scale was suggested by the literature documenting the positive effects of goals on individual performance (Locke, Shaw, Saari, & Latham, 1981). Also, the Team Unity scale was suggested in part by the extensive research on group cohesiveness (e.g., Brawley, Carron, & Widmeyer, 1988; Evans & Dion, 1991) showing that cohesive groups are easier to maintain and often perform better than groups that are not cohesive.

Other scales were developed based on well-established principles in psychology. For example, the Feedback scale was created because of the well-known effect that feedback can have on performance and the Rewards scale stems from the axiom that people tend to do that for which they are rewarded. Similarly, the Skills scale was developed because of the obvious effect that training, experience, and general competence can have on performance.

The TDS scales were initially developed conceptually, then refined empirically through an iterative process of collecting data and modifying the survey. In initial tryouts, response data were collected on several early versions of the survey booklet from a wide range of teams. These data were used to make improvements in the item statements themselves and in the measured constructs. Items were dropped, new ones were added, scales were combined or dropped, items were moved from one scale to another — all of this guided by the collected data.

Observer Survey.   Because teams often benefit from the perspective of people outside the team, a shorter (22-item) parallel observer survey was developed, designed to be completed by at least three knowledgeable observers from outside of the team. These observers, who are normally selected by the survey administrator with help from the team, are often managers supervising the team, customers or clients served by the team, or other colleagues working in the same organization as the team. Example questions from the Observer Booklet appear in Table 8.2.

The Survey Report. The survey is computer scored and each member of the team receives a 10-page report of both the team and their individual results. This report includes the standard T scores for each of the 18 scales as well as item-level summaries for the 72 items presented to the members and the 22 items presented to the team's observers.

The Norming Sample. A standard score of 50 represents the typical team that has completed the survey. All of the teams in the norming sample purchased the TDS™, and were processed and scored through the normal sales channel of National Computer Systems, the publisher. Persons were screened from the database if they reported that they were neither a team member nor a team leader. This final norming sample included 1,881 people on 194 teams. Following are examples of the teams in this sample:

Administrative teams
Career development teams
Customer service teams
Engineering teams
Human resource teams
Inventory control teams
Manufacturing and assembly teams
Marketing teams
Medical teams
Middle-management teams
Product development teams
Public utility teams
Purchasing teams
Research and development teams
Sales teams
School administrators
Security teams

TABLE 8.2
Example TDS Observer Items

I am happy with the team's results.
The team is organized and plans well.
They work together in harmony.
They receive accurate and timely feedback about how they are doing.
Their organization supports the team and its mission.

Senior management teams
Social service teams
Study groups
Teams of accountants
Teams of lawyers
Teams of psychological counselors
Teams of trainers
Teams from university settings
Technical support teams

All of the teams in the norming sample had at least 3 members; on average there were about 10 members per team. Of the sample, 90% were White, 3% African American, 2% Asian Americans, 3% Hispanic, and 2% Native American. The gender split was fairly even, with 54% male, 46% female.

Of the respondents, 83% said they worked with at least some of their team members daily, 15% said weekly, and 2% said monthly. The ratio of team leaders to team members was about 7 to 1, with 12% of the respondents indicating that they were team leaders and 88% indicating that they were team members, not leaders. The occasional outsider who completed the survey, usually a consultant working with the team, was screened from the normative sample.

In this sample, 69% of the leaders were male and 31% female. The average age of the team leader was 43 and the average age of the other team members was 39.

SURVEY APPLICATIONS

In the most typical application of the TDS™, an outside group facilitator is often asked to handle the entire process of administration, scoring, feedback, action planning, and follow-up. The facilitator will usually meet first with the team leader to discuss the purpose of the survey and the action planning sequence, and then to go over the logistics of data collection and processing. When the results are ready, the facilitator again meets with the team leader to discuss the results and to prepare for the team feedback session.

The whole team then meets to discuss the results with the help of the facilitator. In this meeting the team discusses the results and works to develop an action plan for team improvement. The team also takes certain actions, such as circulating their team action plan, to ensure that the team follows up with the plans it has developed for team improvement.

The survey has many features to facilitate team communication and action planning: confidentiality, broad coverage, individual–group comparisons, outside observers, ideas for improvements, and a recommended process for using the survey with teams.

Confidentiality.   The individual results are handled confidentially so that each team member will feel free to express his or her opinions without fear of reprisal from other team members. Yet each person has the opportunity to have his or her opinions addressed in the team discussion because each individual's scores are included in the group mean scores, and his or her responses are included in the response counts that appear on the report for each item of the survey. Thus, opinions become public though confidentiality is maintained.

Broad Coverage.   The survey measures a broad array of specific topics. Scales that might have been combined because of their relatively high intercorrelation (e.g., *Feedback* and *Rewards*) have been kept separate to facilitate focused discussions about each topic. By measuring a broad array of topics, the survey gives the team a wide range of topics to think and talk about. At least some of these topics are relevant to each team and how it can improve.

Individual–Group Comparisons.   Each team member gets to see how his or her scores compare to the average scores for the team. This can be particularly powerful for the team leader, who may learn for the first time how the others view the team and what their unique needs may be. Also, team members naturally want to explore why their individual scores are different from the scores of the rest of the team, so they are usually eager to talk about the results. Similarly, by showing the spread of scores on each scale, the results can help motivate team members to focus on different viewpoints so that they can understand and perhaps reconcile differences among the members of the team.

Outside Observers.   The results include those from observers outside of the team. Team members will learn how they are perceived by key outsiders, such as customers or the managers they report to within the organization. Learning about these perspectives usually generates interesting and constructive discussion within the team about possible improvements, both in actually changing their performance, and in managing the perceptions of others.

Ideas for Improvements.   The survey report includes specific, practical ideas for improvements in each of the areas measured by the survey. For example, in the area of Team Coordination, team members are advised to meet briefly each Monday to discuss the week ahead, choose a time and place to do team long-range planning, write a clear definition of their jobs and share the definitions with each other. These suggestions are intended to stimulate each team member to generate other ideas for helping the team to improve, especially ideas that are particularly appropriate for this specific team. If at least one team member mentions one of the suggestions in the team discussion, this can help the team to begin solving problems rather than just talking about them.

Recommended Process.   Without following a prescribed process in studying and discussing the survey results, some teams will simply study the data, conclude that they are disappointing, even depressing, and never get to the stage where they generate ways to improve the team. Therefore, a facilitator's guide has been developed that outlines a recommended process for discussing the results. This process is the result of several years of experimentation with survey feedback methods.

PSYCHOMETRIC CHARACTERISTICS AND OTHER RESEARCH RESULTS

There are several ways to evaluate the value of a survey instrument such as the TDS™. The most typical method is to examine its psychometric characteristics. Because team members are quickly frustrated by long surveys yet also want a wide variety of information, the scales on the TDS™ cover a wide range of topics, but each scale is quite short. Reassuringly, the scale scores have moderate to high reliability (median alpha = .69 and median test–retest reliability = .80). Scores on the survey, reflecting the perceptions of the team members, have also been shown to correlate highly with the perceptions of the team's observers. Among the items on the Observer Survey, the following items most directly relate to the performance of the team:

1. The team's work is high quality.
7. They are meeting their team objectives.
15. I am happy with the team's results.
19. Reports on their performance are favorable.
22. So far, the team has been a great success.

Responses to these items have been averaged to form an Observer Performance Scale Score. Another measure of the team's overall performance is their average score on the team member Performance Scale, which contains the following set of items parallel to the Observer Performance Scale:

40. Our work is high quality.
17. We are meeting our team objectives.
60. The people who evaluate our team performance are happy with our results.
 2. Reports on our performance are favorable.
72. So far, our team has been a great success.

This team score can be separated into two more specific scores: the average score for the *team leader(s)* on the Performance scale, reflecting the perceptions of the team leaders, and the average score of the other *team members*, reflecting the perceptions of the team members, excluding the leader.

To what extent are scores on the other TDS™ scales related to how well the team is performing, as assessed by the team's observers, by the team's leader(s), and by the team members, excluding the leader? This is the question addressed by Table 8.3, which shows the correlations between the average team member's TDS™ scores and three indications of the team's performance: the Observer Average Performance score, the Team Leader Average Performance score, and the Team Member Average Performance score.

The overall correlations between the Team Member Performance score, the Team Leader Performance score and the Observer Performance score were reassuringly high, both .70. Among the specific scales, the highest correlations between the three measures of performance and the other TDS scores were with the Skills scale (.66, .50, and .66), Commitment scale (.58, .43, and .66), Innovation scale (.56, .41, and .61), and the Leadership scale (.58, .36, and .60). The lowest correlations were dramatically lower: Material Resources (.12, .19, and .16) and Time and Staffing (.18, .29, and .39). This pattern suggests that a team's "soft," or more psychologically based, resources are more related to perceived performance than are its "hard" resources, that is, those more economically based. Furthermore, these dramatic differences in correlations cannot be accounted for by differences in the reliabilities of the scales. For example the internal consistency and test–retest reliabilities for the Commitment scale (.66 and .78) are not appreciably higher than the corresponding reliabilities for the Material Resources (.61 and .78) and Time and Staffing scales (.68 and .76).

The reader may notice a consistent trend in these correlations. Correlations with the team average scores tend to be highest, followed by correlations with the average observer scores, and correlations with the average team leader scores. The reason for this may be that the team

TABLE 8.3

Correlations Between Average Team Scale Scores and Performance as Assessed by the Observers, the Team Leader, and the Members

	Average Observer Performance Score	Average Leader Performance Score	Average Member (Excluding the Leader) Performance Score
	(N = 107)	(N = 162)	(N = 194)
Time and staffing	.18	.29	.39
Information	.47	.40	.57
Material resources	.12	.19	.16
Organizational support	.31	.33	.52
Skills	.66	.50	.66
Commitment	.58	.43	.66
Mission clarity	.52	.35	.63
Team coordination	.49	.45	.62
Team unity	.52	.39	.55
Individual goals	.33	.22	.46
Empowerment	.42	.29	.49
Team assessment	.36	.32	.50
Innovation	.56	.41	.61
Feedback	.44	.30	.60
Rewards	.51	.37	.57
Leadership	.58	.36	.60
Satisfaction	.50	.38	.64
Performance	.70	.70	.98
Overall index	.63	.53	.79
Median correlation	.50	.37	.60

performance scores are based on more people (an average of about nine people) and the leader's performance scores are based on the fewest people (teams with leaders usually have only one leader). A measure that is based on responses from several people tends to be more reliable and thus more highly related to other measures than is a measure based on responses from a single individual.

Leader–Member Differences

Do all members of a team share the same perception of their team? Clearly, the answer is no. A wide range of scores is common within any team, as each team member has unique experiences and expectations. Perhaps understandably, leaders tend to evaluate their teams more favorably than do the other members of their teams. Overall, leaders score about one-half standard deviation (5 points) higher than members, indicating that, on average, leaders have a more positive view of their team than do their team members. This means that during the team feedback session, team leaders will often be in the situation of learning why their team members have a more negative view of the team than they do.

Interestingly, some of the largest discrepancies between leaders and members are on the scales of Leadership and Empowerment. On average, leaders have a more favorable view of themselves in these areas than do their followers. A similar finding, called the "Hierarchy Effect," has been obtained with other surveys, such as the Campbell Organizational Survey (Campbell & Hyne, 1994). Managers who are higher in the hierarchy of the organization tend to have more favorable impressions of the organizational climate than do their subordinates. Whether this is because being higher in an organization, or in charge of a team, makes one more satisfied with the organization or team, or because people who are satisfied with the organization or team are more likely to be promoted, is not clear. Probably both factors are operating in most settings. Whatever the explanation, the consistency of this effect over different work settings is remarkable.

A different way to view the relationship between the scores of the leaders and those of the other members is to examine how their scores correlate. For each team, an average leader score was computed (in teams with only one leader these averages are the same as the leader's scores). An average team member score was also computed, so that the average member score could be correlated with the average leader scores, where the unit of analysis is the team. Table 8.4 reports these correlations. The numbers in the diagonal are the correlations between the leader and the team members for each scale. Essentially, they reflect the relationship between how the leader sees the team and how the members see the team.

Although most of these correlations were high, there were several notable exceptions. In particular, the leader and member scores correlated only .10 on the Leadership scale, and only .12 on the Empowerment scale. Thus, there was typically little agreement between members and leaders in their perception of Leadership and Empowerment. On the other hand, there was much more congruence between members and leaders in their assessment of Team Coordination (.54), Performance (.58), and Team Unity (.64). Curiously, the differences between leader and member perceptions were greatest in those areas concerned solely with leader behavior—Leadership and Empowerment—whereas in those areas concerning team member behavior, perceptions were more congruent. Again, these data suggest that the survey will tend to reveal important discrepancies in the perceptions of leaders and members.

Scale Scores by Team Composition

How do scores on the survey relate to various team characteristics, such as how large the team is, or whether the team is led by a man or woman, or

TABLE 8.4
Correlations Between Team Member and Team Leader Scores (N = 160 Teams)

	Average Member Scores (Excluding Leader)																		
Average Leader Scores	Time and Staffing	Information	Material Resources	Organizational Support	Skills	Commitment	Mission Clarity	Team Coordination	Team Unity	Individual Goals	Empowerment	Team Assessment	Innovation	Feedback	Rewards	Leadership	Satisfaction	Performance	Overall Index
Time and staffing	**.34**	.12	.13	.27	.25	.13	.12	.18	.16	.05	.05	.16	.17	.06	.16	.10	.10	.30	.23
Information	.25	.24	.08	.24	.18	.08	.09	.18	.07	.06	.07	.16	.14	.11	.12	.08	.05	.26	.19
Material resources	.20	.12	**.37**	.30	.08	-.11	-.07	-.02	-.08	-.06	.04	-.09	-.02	-.01	.10	.05	-.06	.00	.05
Organizational support	.36	.27	.25	**.50**	.21	.08	.14	.22	.09	.06	.14	.11	.20	.15	.20	.15	.13	.36	.28
Skills	.22	.26	.08	.23	**.42**	.34	.18	.31	.36	.13	.13	.26	.25	.20	.28	.19	.18	.48	.37
Commitment	.08	.39	.09	.17	.47	**.55**	.38	.49	.58	.25	.36	.36	.37	.33	.46	.43	.42	.42	.53
Mission clarity	.08	.29	.16	.20	.24	.26	**.42**	.29	.29	.16	.16	.21	.22	.27	.29	.24	.23	.39	.36
Team coordination	.12	.42	.11	.15	.33	.30	.34	**.54**	.39	.13	.28	.34	.19	.32	.35	.37	.23	.42	.43
Team unity	.13	.33	.06	.20	.44	.54	.39	.49	**.64**	.22	.43	.34	.36	.31	.48	.47	.46	.39	.53
Individual goals	.06	.15	.12	.08	.17	.17	.23	.25	.19	**.11**	.10	.18	.12	.10	.19	.17	.13	.32	.23
Empowerment	.09	.19	.13	.14	.13	.16	.15	.21	.19	.05	**.12**	.24	.14	.09	.17	.10	.11	.22	.22
Team assessment	.04	.23	.06	.09	.28	.31	.28	.28	.34	.18	.21	**.44**	.20	.26	.25	.27	.20	.31	.34
Innovation	.07	.22	.10	.07	.21	.22	.12	.15	.23	.04	.17	.19	**.29**	.17	.26	.21	.11	.25	.25
Feedback	.04	.27	.14	.17	.19	.19	.24	.26	.18	.18	.13	.14	.10	**.38**	.30	.25	.13	.38	.29
Rewards	.14	.24	.19	.24	.31	.20	.19	.25	.24	.11	.17	.16	.09	.19	**.41**	.27	.09	.27	.30
Leadership	.15	.22	.10	.17	.23	.16	.14	.26	.18	.05	.03	.16	.17	.09	.19	**.10**	.03	.36	.23
Satisfaction	.15	.37	.18	.26	.26	.35	.35	.43	.41	.28	.35	.28	.26	.38	.42	.42	**.28**	.42	.45
Performance	.24	.34	.18	.28	.39	.35	.27	.38	.36	.15	.24	.26	.31	.24	.33	.30	.31	**.58**	.44
Overall index	.24	.41	.22	.32	.43	.39	.35	.45	.44	.19	.29	.35	.31	.32	.44	.38	.29	.53	**.50**

whether the team members are old or young? Such questions can be addressed by using the background information gathered from each survey respondent, such as sex, age, and role on the team, along with the three Performance Scores (Team Member, Team Leader, and Observer). Table 8.5 reports the three average *Team Performance* scores for various types of teams: teams that are all men, teams that are all women, small teams, large teams, teams whose members are relatively young, and so forth. Three distinct perspectives on the team's performance are reported: the perspectives of members, leaders, and observers. The sample sizes (N) reported in this table are the numbers of teams falling into each category.

The overall impression gained from studying this table is that team member and team leader demographic characteristics, such as age and gender, generally make little difference in how teams score. As expected, the Leader Performance scores were higher than the Observer or Member Performance scores, almost without exception, but the other demographic variables seemed to have little relation to the performance of the team. For example, looking down the far-right column, which contains the mean Observer Performance scores, one will note that most team means fell within the range of 48 to 52, which is quite typical.

The importance of demographic characteristics can also be examined by correlating these characteristics with scores on the other TDS™ scales. Table 8.6 reports such correlations. These correlations are essentially another way to express the relationships that have already been expressed in Table 8.5. As can be seen, none of these characteristics were related to the TDS scales. All of the correlations clustered around 0, with the highest being .28.

Overall, this table of correlations and the previous table of means both indicate that factors such as whether the team has a leader or not, or whether the leader is a man or woman or whether the team is young or old, have little impact on the TDS™ scores. In this sense, the TDS™ scores are not biased by extraneous demographic factors or other team characteristics (Hallam & Campbell, 1994a).

VALUE IN HELPING TEAMS IMPROVE

Given that the purpose of the instrument is to help teams find ways to improve, another important measure of the value of the survey is whether it does, in fact, achieve this end. Does the survey generate a lively and productive discussion of the team's strengths, weaknesses, and ways to improve? To answer this, we can only speak from our experience in working with teams and talking to people who have used the survey. The survey can be extremely effective in generating a discussion and helping teams find ways to improve. The team facilitator, however, must know how to create

TABLE 8.5
Mean Team Performance Scores for Selected Subgroups

	Team Members (Excluding Leader)			Leaders			Observers		
	N	Mean	SD	N	Mean	SD	N	Mean	SD
Teams without leaders	32	49	8	–	–	–	14	52	7
Teams with one leader	124	50	7	124	54	9	74	49	8
Teams with multiple leaders	38	51	6	38	53	7	19	54	6
Teams that are all men	26	48	9	20	52	9	14	49	11
Teams that are all women	9	50	4	8	51	8	6	46	10
Teams that are an even mix of men and women	70	50	7	57	55	9	40	51	6
Teams with male leaders	109	50	7	109	53	9	61	50	8
Teams with female leaders	37	50	6	37	55	7	24	51	7
All female teams with female leaders	7	49	4	7	50	8	6	46	10
All male teams with male leaders	19	50	7	19	53	8	11	50	10
Mixed-sex teams with female leaders	11	51	5	11	54	9	7	52	5
Mixed-sex teams with male leaders	38	49	7	38	54	10	25	50	7
All white teams	103	51	7	89	55	7	59	51	7
Teams with racial mix	12	50	6	9	58	6	7	51	9
Teams whose leader is under 42 years old	74	49	7	74	53	9	45	48	8
Teams whose leader is over 42 years old	75	51	6	75	55	8	43	52	6
Teams whose average age is under 40	92	50	7	73	53	8	52	51	7
Teams whose average age is over 40	96	50	7	86	54	9	54	50	8
Young team members led by young leaders	53	49	6	53	53	9	33	49	8
Older team members led by older leaders	60	51	6	60	55	8	34	52	7
Young team members led by older leaders	15	53	5	15	55	8	9	55	4
Older team members led by younger leaders	21	48	7	21	54	10	12	47	8
Teams whose leader is newer than the average non-leader	70	49	7	70	53	8	38	50	7

(Continued)

TABLE 8.5 (Continued)

	Team Members (Excluding Leader)			Leaders			Observers		
	N	Mean	SD	N	Mean	SD	N	Mean	SD
Young teams (average member has been on team less than 2.8 years)	96	48	7	77	53	9	46	49	8
Older teams (average member has been on team more than 2.8 years)	97	51	6	85	55	8	60	51	7
Teams whose members all meet or work at least once a day	79	50	7	65	54	8	50	51	7
Teams that meet or work together less often	112	50	7	97	54	9	56	50	8
Small teams (8 or fewer members)	97	50	7	78	54	8	49	50	8
Large teams (9 or more members)	97	50	6	84	54	9	58	51	7

Scores on the Performance Scale (3 Perspectives)

N = number of teams.

an environment in which team members feel comfortable discussing the results and offering ideas for team improvement. This is why there is a recommended process for the facilitator to follow in preparing for and conducting the feedback session with the team (Hallam & Campbell, 1994b).

CONCLUSIONS

The TDS is a useful tool primarily because it provides a response to the difficult question, "How are we doing?" In spite of the complexities of quantifying the effectiveness of the team, most team members find the survey items easy to respond to, and most members find the feedback accurate, relevant, and helpful.

Such useful measurement is made possible by focusing on the perceptions of the team members and their observers. Although perceptions are not always reality, the perceptions of the team and their observers can have real consequences for the team. For example, if one team member is unhappy about the progress that the team has been making on a particular project, this dissatisfaction can be both a cause for frustration and burnout, and a potential catalyst for team improvement—the team member may share valuable ideas about how to speed up the project. Perceptions can affect the

TABLE 8.6
Correlations Between Average Scale Scores and Team Characteristics

Team Means	Average Member Age (N = 188)*	Average Leader Age (N = 149)*	Proportion Female (N = 192)*	Proportion Leader Female (N = 160)*	Number Leaders (N = 194)*	Number Members (N = 194)*	Proportion Non-White (N = 192)*	Times Meeting Weekly (N = 191)*	Average Years on Team (N = 193)*
Time and staffing	-.04	.08	.11	-.06	.03	.03	.07	.05	.09
Information	.13	.07	-.03	-.09	.07	-.11	.02	**-.16**	-.01
Material resources	**.23**	**.20**	-.06	**-.15**	.02	**-.14**	.04	-.12	-.01
Competence	**.14**	**.16**	.09	.03	.06	-.03	-.03	**-.14**	.12
Organizational support	.13	.12	-.09	**-.19**	.12	-.08	.06	-.04	.10
Mission clarity	.03	.00	-.11	-.04	.07	-.09	.00	-.10	-.07
Coordination	-.05	-.11	.03	.01	.08	-.08	.01	**-.22**	-.08
Commitment	-.01	.07	.03	.02	.07	-.09	-.10	-.01	-.04
Unity	-.01	-.01	-.10	-.05	.05	-.13	.02	**-.15**	**-.14**
Goal setting	.13	.10	-.10	-.05	**.15**	-.07	.03	.04	**.16**
Team assessment	-.02	-.03	-.01	-.01	.11	.01	.01	-.06	-.13
Innovation	.08	.10	-.03	-.04	**.18**	-.09	-.09	**-.14**	-.07
Feedback	**.16**	.07	-.12	-.09	**.15**	-.04	-.04	-.12	.05
Empowerment	**.16**	.02	-.13	**-.15**	.11	-.05	-.05	**-.16**	-.08
Leader	**.17**	.06	-.07	-.08	.13	-.05	-.05	**-.17**	-.03
Rewards	**.28**	.18	-.13	-.13	**.15**	**-.14**	-.08	-.09	.02
Satisfaction	.04	-.02	-.08	-.09	.06	-.02	-.12	-.10	.03
Overall index	.11	.09	-.04	-.07	.12	-.10	-.03	**-.14**	.00
Performance	.07	**.14**	.07	.02	.12	-.05	-.06	-.08	**.18**
Performance (nonleaders)	.06	.12	.06	.00	.10	-.03	-.05	-.06	**.19**
Performance (leaders)	.08	.12	.09	.07	-.02	-.03	.00	-.05	.11
	(N = 159)	(N = 149)	(N = 162)	(N = 160)	(N = 162)	(N = 162)	(N = 162)	(N = 162)	(N = 162)
Performance (observers)	-.05	**.21**	.10	.09	.10	-.05	-.06	**-.16**	.05
	(N = 106)	(N = 088)	(N = 107)	(N = 092)	(N = 107)	(N = 107)	(N = 106)	(N = 106)	(N = 106)

*Except as noted; correlations significant at $p = .05$ (two-tailed) are in **bold**.

mood and level of motivation of the team members. In other words, when the team members ask "How are we doing?" it is appropriate and useful to respond with standardized information about how the team thinks it is doing.

REFERENCES

Brawley, L. R., Carron, A. V., & Widmeyer, W. N. (1988). Exploring the relationship between cohesion and group resistance to disruption. *Journal of Sport Exercise Psychology, 10,* 199–213.

Campbell, D. P., & Hyne, S. A. (1994). *Manual for the Campbell Organizational Survey* (2nd ed.). Minneapolis: National Computer Systems.

Evans, C. R., & Dion, K. L. (1991). Group cohesion and performance: A meta-analysis. *Small Group Research, 22,* 175–186.

Hallam, G. L., & Campbell, D. P. (1994a). *Manual for the Campbell-Hallam Team Development Survey.* Minneapolis: National Computer Systems.

Hallam, G. L., & Campbell, D. P. (1994b). *Facilitator's guide for the Campbell-Hallam Team Development Survey.* Minneapolis: National Computer Systems.

Locke, E. A., Shaw, K. N., Saari, L. M., & Latham, G. P. (1981). Goal setting and task performance: 1969-1980. *Psychological Bulletin, 90,* 125–152.

Zander, A. (1968). Group aspirations. In D. Cartwright & A. Zander (Eds.), *Group dynamics: research and theory* (3rd ed.). (pp. 418–421). New York: Harper & Row.

9

Assessing Processes Within and Between Organizational Teams: A Nuclear Power Plant Example

John E. Mathieu
David V. Day
Penn State University

As we turn the corner in the 1990s and head toward the 21st century, it is clear that organizations of the future will be more technologically sophisticated and team-based. Gone are the behemoths operating in stable environments—today's organizations tend to be high-tech fluid entities interacting with dynamic environments. This changing nature of the world of work presents many challenges to human resource professionals, not the least of which is the necessity to develop assessment strategies for diagnosing and developing team-based organizations (Cohen, 1993). The purpose of this chapter is to illustrate a methodology for assessing processes within and between organizational teams operating in nuclear power plants (NPPs). We begin by sculpting a brief theoretical overview of team processes in the context of sociotechnical systems theory. Next, we outline a method for gathering and analyzing team process assessment data using a small demonstration sample. Finally, we discuss the application of our approach to other high-tech dynamic settings.

Despite the technological wizardry of the weapon systems exhibited worldwide on nightly news shows, the key reason for success of the Coalition Forces in the 1991 Gulf War was teamwork. General Horner (USAF) stated after the war that "We had an unusually strong team, and trust was a key factor. Land, sea, air, and space were all subelements of the overall campaign; there was no room for prima donnas. You need people schooled and trained in their own type of warfare, and then you need trust in each other." Similarly, events that have occurred in the nuclear industry within the past 2 decades have highlighted the fact that the coordination of work behaviors, both within and between plant departments, are related to the safe operation of NPPs. Problems relating to the behavior of humans in the nuclear environment have been found to influence the likelihood that a NPP will be involved in an incident, as well as how well the organization can deal with an incident once it has begun (cf. Frye, 1988; Sokolowski, 1985). Frye (1988) noted that greater than 50% of the nuclear power industry's significant events have been attributable to human error and that a large portion of such errors were due to some sort of breakdown in the coordination of control room teams. He likened the operation of nuclear control room teams to those of airline cockpit crews and critical military task teams such as flight crews, tank crews, and combat squads or platoons. Frye (1988) suggested that accidents and performance deficiencies often occur not because the team members were incapable of performing appropriate action, but because they failed to coordinate their efforts effectively. Clearly, gaining a better assessment and understanding of team processes will provide valuable insights regarding influences on team performance.

Assessing team-based processes in technologically intensive organizations such as aircraft carriers, transit facilities, many flexible manufacturing plants, and NPPs presents some unique challenges for human resource (HR) professionals. These organizations operate around the clock and strive to minimize outside intrusions. The workloads and information processing demands of these environments are daunting, thereby necessitating complex coordinating of activities both within and across teams (Roberts & Gargano, 1990; Roberts, LaPorte, & Rochlin, 1987). In addition, many of these settings have particularly intensive work periods where the consequences of organizational breakdowns could be catastrophic. Such instances would include rush periods for transit operators, combat situations for aircraft carriers, and refueling or unplanned shutdowns for NPPs. At issue is the fact that although effective HR practices are critical for the safe and effective operation of these organizations, the opportunities to conduct thorough assessments of team processes are extremely limited. Accordingly, it is important to develop assessment strategies and tools that are simultaneously sensitive to subtle HR needs, yet minimize data collection demands and system intrusion.

Theoretical Overview

One cannot conduct an organizational assessment in the absence of some theoretical framework (Hausser, 1980). We adopted an integrated systems model that focused both upon the characteristics of the entire plant as well as the processes that develop within and between different departments or subunits (Van de Ven & Ferry, 1980). Our approach is also rooted in sociotechnical systems theory and research. The basic idea behind sociotechnical theory is that one must arrange a *joint optimization* of the interacting technical and social systems in the organization (Miles, 1980). Three concerns most clearly distinguish this approach: (a) an open systems perspective that views organizations and environments as constantly changing; (b) considerations of the interface between physical and technological systems and the organizational social systems; and (c) explicit plans for implementing changes to enhance such interfaces (Robinson, 1982).

Sociotechnical studies have, as their units of analysis, organizational systems and subsystems. It is important to note that any assessment effort must specify the level(s) of analysis of interest, whether they be specific functional teams, organizational subunits, organizations, or even organization populations. Although clearly important, we do not devote attention to the organizational or more macrolevels of analysis in this chapter. Rather, we concentrate our attention on strategies for identifying critical NPP departments, their internal team processes, and their interfaces with other NPP departments. This operationalization is somewhat coarser than most "team studies" that concentrate on task or work teams. Our team focus is broader and on larger interdependent collectives of employees, but follows from recent efforts to create team-based organizations. Indeed, Cohen (1993) argued that the dominant form of future organizations is likely to be networked teams. We recognize that varying numbers and types of teams operate in different NPP departments with varying ties to other departments. Nevertheless, for consistency and ease of presentation we treat departments as though they are unique operational teams.

Functional Analysis

Functional analysis is simply an umbrella term for a set of fairly qualitative activities that occur at the beginning of an organization assessment/ development effort. Table 9.1 contains a synopsis of the key features of a functional analysis. The goals of a functional analysis are to identify critical organizational activities, positions, roles, and individuals, and basically to learn about the operations of the organization (see Jacobs et al., 1992). We reviewed previous research conducted in nuclear and other organizational settings, Nuclear Regulatory Commission (NRC) Technical Reports, Nuclear Industry License Event Reports (LERS), summaries of nuclear Human Performance Evaluation System reports (HPES), and a variety of other written information sources. In addition, we discussed the influence of team processes on NPP safety with professors of nuclear engineering, consultants to the nuclear power industry, and NPP employees and management.

We next conducted a preliminary assessment of our demonstration plant in order to derive three types of information. This activity was performed

TABLE 9.1
Key Features of a Team-Based Functional Analysis

Goals
To identify:
- processes that exist within and between teams,
- task or environmental influences on team performance,
- critical team-to-team interfaces,
- important positions, roles, and individuals,
- organizationally specific language and terminology, and
- sources of assessment data.

Approach
Fairly qualitative relying primarily on:
- semi-structured interviews,
- review of documents (e.g., organizational charts),
- observations,
- archival data, and
- consultation with subject matter experts.

---

primarily through a company HR liaison assigned to our project. Our liaison knew both the functional characteristics of our pilot plant as well as personnel who occupied critical positions throughout the organization. The functional analysis proceeded as an interactive discussion between the research team and the liaison, in conjunction with input from other NPP personnel and organizational documents (e.g., organizational charts and, when available, job descriptions), with the following goals. First, the functional analysis was designed to reveal the critical areas or departments in the organization as well as which departments worked closely with which other departments. Identifying the critical areas in each department then guided the determination of which individuals were best suited to provide assessments of different types (Seidler, 1974). Second, identifying which departments worked with one another guided the interdepartmental process assessment effort. Figure 9.1 presents a hypothetical illustration of the type of relationship network that will emerge from this effort. For example, Department A can be seen to be very central or interdependent with numerous other departments, yet Departments D and E are rather isolated. Thus, all else being equal in terms of the criticality of linkages, the team processes related to Department A have a larger impact on the performance of the entire NPP system than do others.

The third purpose for conducting the functional analysis was to capture the specific terminology, job titles, and so on, that were used at the plant in order to customize the assessment instruments (Alderfer & Brown, 1972). Following the functional analysis we sought to assess the quality of team processes that operate *within* various NPP departments, as well as the quality of processes that characterized how well different departments dealt with each other. These two focuses are detailed here.

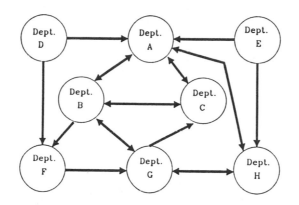

FIG. 9.1. Hypothetical linkages between NPP departments.

Department-Level Processes

Department-level processes deal with the ways in which individuals and subgroups' efforts are organized and coordinated within each department. Reviews in the organizational psychology and sociology literature have repeatedly underscored the importance of the structuring of departmental work activities (Berger & Cummings, 1979; Hall, 1991; James & Jones, 1976; Payne & Pugh, 1976). The logic underlying these writings is that once the organization grows beyond a certain size a diversity of subunit structures is likely to emerge. For example, the structuring of outpatient services, admissions, surgery, rehabilitation, administration, support services, and the pharmacy within a hospital vary markedly. Within NPPs, operations, maintenance, radiological control, engineering, and training departments are also likely to have differing structures and work processes. Accordingly, it is important to understand what structures are most appropriate for the various departments, taking into consideration their characteristics and various missions.

There has been a resurgence of interest in team processes lately and in particular how they relate to effectiveness in high-tech organizations operating in dynamic environments (Swezey & Salas, 1992). Several generic taxonomies of team functioning have been advanced (e.g., Fleishman & Zaccaro, 1992; Shiflett, Eisner, Price, & Schemmer, 1982) and the importance of team processes for team effectiveness have been illustrated repeatedly (see Swezey & Salas, 1992). The influence of team skills on performance in NPPs has also received attention recently. Frye (1988) and Davis, Gaddy, Turney, and Koontz (1986) recommended that control room crews receive training not only on technical matters, but also on team processes. Frye (1986), Davis et al. (1989), Gaddy and Koontz (1987), and

Gaddy and Wachtel (1992) also underscored the importance of team processes for the safe and effective operation of NPPs.

Although a detailed review of the nature of theses processes is beyond the scope of this chapter (see Gaddy & Wachtel, 1992), what is clear is that the safe operation of NPPs relies heavily on effective coordination of multiple teams. The complexity of work and the consequences of errors make it imperative that teams function effectively. The quantity and quality of communication, the coordination of activities, the problem-solving and decision-making strategies employed, as well as the degree of team spirit are all signs of the extent to which teams are functioning effectively. These team skills are important aspects of safe and efficient power generation during normal plant operations, more important during anticipated intensive activities such as planned shutdowns and refuelings, and are most critical for effective responses to crisis situations (Jacobs et al., 1992).

Based on our review of the literature and the functional analysis, we decided to assess eight attributes of departmental team processes. From the more macro organizational perspective, (cf. Berger & Cummings, 1979; Hall, 1991; James & Jones, 1976) we chose four variables: (a) *centralization*—the extent to which decision making and power are localized in one area, typically in the hands of the department head; (b) *formalization*—the extent to which there are formalized rules and procedures governing departmental activities; (c) *coordination*—the extent to which the efforts of different individuals or subgroups are integrated and coordinated; and (d) *goal priority*—the extent to which members set departmental goals, and agree about the relative priority of goals.

From the team-based literature (e.g., Gaddy & Koontz, 1987; Gaddy & Wachtel, 1992), we selected four additional measures: (a) *information exchange and evaluation*—the extent to which departmental members share information and provide useful feedback; (b) *task coverage*—the extent to which members are cross-trained and cover for one another; (c) *performance direction*—the extent to which there are standards and norms governing departmental behavior; and (d) *decision making*—the extent to which members remain flexible and adapt their working styles to changing circumstances. Our assumption was that, in general, to the extent that departments exhibited higher levels of these variables they would be better able to function effectively and to deal with work challenges.

Interdepartmental Processes

The coordination of work between different departments has been recognized as an important component of the effectiveness of organizations (cf. Hall, 1991), but has not been studied extensively. Our reviews of HPES reviews, LERs, and other post-hoc accounts of NPP mishaps or near misses revealed that many problems occurred when work needed to be coordinated across departments. Scant research attention has been devoted to how such processes operate in NPPs. Our assumption is that when employees from different departments who have inconsistent interpersonal styles or formality of work structures must coordinate their efforts, it is not clear how joint work will actually be performed. This may easily lead to breakdowns in communication as employees from one department may, for example, perceive others as "rude and stiff" as the second set may consider the first to be "lazy and unprofessional." These differing perceptions will detract from the quality of joint work the two groups of employees must perform.

The nuclear industry is not alone in its lack of attention devoted to interdepartmental processes. Van de Ven and Ferry (1980) noted that *intra*organizational interdependencies are highly neglected topics in organizational research. They drew parallels between organizational–environment relations and intraorganizational departmental relations. The basic idea from this literature is that to the extent that internal organizational processes are not consistent with the demands of the environments, they will be less effective. Extended to interdepartmental relations, we submit that the extent to which the relationships between different NPP departments are strained and/or inconsistent, their joint functioning will be compromised.

Based on our functional analysis and organizational–environment relations focused writings (e.g., Aldrich, 1979; Hall, 1991) we decided to assess five between-departmental dimensions, several of which parallel the within-department processes previously described: (a) *formalization*—the extent to which there are rules, procedures, and standard methods for coordinating activities; (b) *coordination*—which refers to the sequencing of activities between departments to accomplish a common goal; (c) *cooperation*—the extent to which employees from different departments interpersonally get along with one another; (d) *goal priority*—the extent to which employees from different departments agree about the priority of organizational goals; and (e) *interdependence*—the extent to which the actions of one department affect the operations of the other department. We contend that to the extent that interdepartmental relations break down along these lines, employees will become frustrated and work processes will be ineffective. These breakdowns, then, can create a less safe work environment.

Generalizability Analysis Framework

Echoing back to our earlier comments, the primary challenges for HR specialists working with teams in high-tech and dynamic environments are to (a) gather high-fidelity information for diagnosing within- and between-team processes; and (b) minimize the time and intrusiveness of assessment activities. The functional analysis described here can be linked with powerful data analyses techniques to offer an insightful means of meeting these challenges. One such analytic technique is Generalizability (G) theory. Although originally proposed as a tool for analyzing the dependability (i.e., reliability) of behavioral measurements (Cronbach, Gleser, Nanda, & Rajaratnam, 1972), G theory can be adopted to provide valuable information regarding ratings of team processes within and between departments. In particular, G-theory analysis (typically called a G study) allows for the estimation of the amount of systematic variance associated with an effect. In the case of our application, the larger the estimated variance component, the greater the disagreement across people, departments, or another effect of interest. Large variance components reduce the degree with which one can generalize from the sampled cases to others. In the present application, a large variance component associated with the Department variable, for example, would reduce the confidence we would place in generalizing results to other NPP departments in this organization. As such, there is an inherent link between generalizability and reliability.

Whereas G theory can be viewed as a specific application of the general linear model (DeShon, 1995), it has become associated with its own particular terminology. We attempt to minimize the use of confusing jargon that is typical of many G-theory presentations; nevertheless, a few key terms must be defined. Every source of potential systematic variance is termed a *facet*. For example, the different departments will comprise one facet in our design. The various process scales on which departments are rated will comprise another facet. The amount of variance associated with each facet is estimated by means of analysis of variance. Thus, a distinct advantage of G theory is that it partitions variance into multiple dimensions associated with the sampled facets; classical reliability analysis, on the other hand, attributes systematic variance to only one source and assumes the remaining unexplained variance is random error. G theory recognizes that multiple sources of measurement error can operate simultaneously (Cronbach et al., 1972).

Another key term is *condition*, which refers to the number of specific observations for a given facet. One way to reduce a variance component is to increase the number of conditions. As long as there is a positive covariance among facet conditions, increasing the number of conditions will decrease error variance and heighten the dependability of measurement. Therefore, a typical means of reducing measurement error and increasing generalizability is to increase the number of conditions for a particular facet. The manner in which overall generalizability is estimated is by means of a generalizability coefficient. The G coefficient represents the proportion of observed score variance that is true score variance; it is conceptually the same as an intraclass correlation coefficient (Shrout & Fleiss, 1979).

It is also important to recognize that there are conceptually different types of facets. Most G-theory applications assume facets to be random. That is, conditions were selected arbitrarily from a larger possible set. For example, the eight within-team processes examined here can be thought of as a sample from the infinite universe of the ways that team processes could be described. However, it is also possible to consider a facet to be fixed. Treating a facet as fixed assumes that all relevant conditions were selected and that we do not care to generalize beyond this given set of conditions. In initially estimating variance components, it is typically recommended that all facets be treated as random (Shavelson & Webb, 1991) because there is no variance associated with a fixed facet. Researchers and practitioners are also rarely concerned with just the observations they have on hand. If desired, however, a facet can be considered fixed in subsequent analyses to determine the resulting effect on generalizability.

G theory is also sufficiently flexible to handle complicated designs. For example, our application is formally a nested design because only team members provide assessments of their team processes. In other words, different people rate the different teams. Compare this with a crossed facet where, for example, a single group of outside consultants observes the operations of all teams and provides ratings for each one. Unfortunately, the variance associated with respondents cannot be separated from the variance associated with departments in nested designs such as ours. Whether this shortcoming outweighs the time, effort, and expense that would be required to employ a cadre of consultants is an important question organizations must consider when determining their strategic human resource needs. Because the current application was a demonstration project, the resources necessary to establish a fully crossed design were not deemed warranted.

More detailed discussions of generalizability theory and analysis can be found in Brennan (1983), Cronbach et al. (1972), and Shavelson and Webb (1991). For now, we turn our attention to providing a small demonstration of how this approach was used to assess the team processes that exist within and between-departmental teams in a NPP. Our expectations going into this project were that some teams would be functioning better than others, and that some interteam relations would be better than others. Thus, we were expecting to find some significant differences in team processes across teams, as well as differences in terms of how well teams interfaced with others.

SAMPLE ILLUSTRATION

Site Identification

To illustrate our assessment methodology we use data that were collected as part of a larger project concerned with the assessment of organizational factors related to NPP safety (see Jacobs et al., 1992, for details). The particular plant selected for study had an excellent operating record and was viewed as well organized by the researchers as well as by NRC personnel. Survey instruments were developed and administered during one-on-one interviews with plant personnel.

Respondents[1]

For illustration purposes, we present data from 16 employees, 2 each from 8 departments, who responded to the within-department measures. Departments included in the analyses were: Maintenance, Operations, Radiological Control, Plant Engineering, Training, Technical Functions, Nuclear Safety, and Quality Assurance. However, because of confidentially concerns, we randomly ordered departments and will simply refer to them as A through F. A list of the number of items, reliability, and definitions for each of the eight within-department scales appears in Table 9.2. All items were responded to using 6-point Likert-type scales ranging from 1 (*not at all*) to 6 (*a very great extent*). Scale scores were calculated by averaging the items responded to by each person.

For the between-department illustration we used data from 12 individuals representing six departments. In this case, each participant rated how he or she viewed the working relationship between his or her department and five other departments using five scales. A list of the number of items, reliability, and definitions for each of these scales appears in Table 9.3. The 6-point extent scale was also used for these ratings. The five "target departments" that appeared on each between survey were identical for respondents sampled from the same department, but differed for respondents from other departments. In actuality, these forms were constructed in a balanced fashion to yield reciprocal ratings. In other words, Department

---

[1]Given the nature of the assessment data to be collected, there is some question as to who should be interviewed. A second issue concerns which NPP departments should receive high levels of attention as related to other chosen departments. In terms of sampling, a guiding philosophy we subscribed to was the concept of "key respondents" as vital for the accurate assessment of organizational processes. Key respondents are defined as those individuals who have access to relevant information for making specific evaluations (Seidler, 1974). For example, lower level employees are not well positioned for judging how the plant manager and departmental managers coordinate their efforts and make decisions. Alternatively, upper level managers are not well positioned for providing insight as to how daily departmental activities are performed. Thus, we believe that the critical first step of an accurate assessment of team processes is the identification of individuals who are best suited for making judgments of different types. A corollary of this approach, then, is that no one individual (or set of individuals) is (are) best positioned for making all judgments, and that the most accurate picture of team processes will emerge by collecting a variety of perceptions from people who are best suited for making such judgments.

TABLE 9.2
Within-Department Scale Labels, Definitions, Reliabilities, and Sample Items

Centralization: The extent to which decision making and power are localized in one area, typically in the hands of the department head. (7 Items, $\alpha = .80$)
"To what extent are employees in your department encouraged to make their own decisions concerning work related matters?"

Formalization: The extent to which there are formalized rules and procedures governing departmental activities. (6 Items, $\alpha = .65$)
"To what extent are there written rules for coordinating the activities of the employees in your department"

Coordination: The extent to which the efforts of different individuals or subgroups are integrated and coordinated. (9 Items, $\alpha = .76$)
"How well do employees in your department plan and coordinate their activities?"

Goal priority: The extent to which members set departmental goals, and agree about the relative priority of goals. (3 Items, $\alpha = .66$)
"To what extent do employees in your department agree on the [priority of departmental goals?"

Information Exchange & Evaluation: The extent to which departmental member share information and provide useful feedback. (13 Items, $\alpha = .88$)
"Do employees in your department provide information to others when or before it is needed?"

Task coverage: The extent to which members are cross-trained and cover for one another. (4 Items, $\alpha = .75$)
"Do employees in your department fill in for one another when someone is tied up with a task?"

Performance direction: The extent to which there are standards and norms governing departmental behavior. (3 Items, $\alpha = .73$)
"To what extent do employees in your department teach one another their uniquely held knowledges, skills, and experiences?"

Decision making: The extent to which members remain flexible and adapt their working styles to changing circumstances. (5 Items, $\alpha = .62$)
"Once a performance problem is recognized, to what extent do departmental members develop an accurate solution quickly?"

TABLE 9.3
Between-Department Scale Labels, Definitions, Reliabilities, and Sample Items

Formalization: The extent to which there are rules, procedures, and standard methods for coordinating activities. (6 Items, $\alpha = .72$)
"How well established are the routines when your department works with . . ."

Coordination: Which refers to the sequencing of activities between departments to accomplish a common goal. (7 Items, $\alpha = .71$)
"To what extent are the activities between your department and the following departments coordinated?"

Cooperation: The extent to which employees from different departments interpersonally get along with one another. (6 Items, $\alpha = .72$)
"Do employees in your department resolve personal conflicts with employees in the following departments that could interfere with work?"

Goal priority: The extent to which employees from different departments agree about the priority of organizational goals. (3 Items, $\alpha = .62$)
"To what extent do employees from your department and each of the following departments agree on the priority of plant goals?"

Interdependence: The extent to which the actions of one department effect the operations of the other department. (6 Items, $\alpha = .78$)
"To what extent will the operations of each of the following departments be affected if work in your department is not done well?"

A respondents rated how they worked with Departments B, C, D, and E; Department B respondents rated how they dealt with departments A, C, D, and E, and so forth such that each department rated, and was rated by, all others in the set.

Analyses

The G and D study analyses were performed using GENOVA (Crick & Brennan, 1983), which is a Fortran-type program developed especially for G-theory applications. GENOVA stands for "*GEN*eralized analysis *Of VA*riance system," and as the acronym suggests, it is a general purpose ANOVA program for complete and balanced designs. GENOVA is designed especially to handle large data sets with numerous factors (i.e., facets); it is a very efficient program, as well as user friendly. The primary output of GENOVA is an ANOVA source table, along with estimated variance components for all main effects and interactions. In the present study, the sources of variance — called G-study variance components (Brennan, 1983) — for the *within-department* analyses are associated with the main effects for Departments (D), Persons Within Departments (P:D), and Scales (S); and a two-way interaction between Departments and Scales (DS). The Persons × Departments × Scales facet constitutes the error term for these analyses.

The *between-department analyses* has a more complicated design, that is depicted in Fig. 9.2. It includes main effects for Departments (D), Persons within Departments (P:D), Targets (T; i.e., target departments), and Dimensional Scales (S); two-way interactions for Departments × Targets (DT), Departments × Scales (DS), Targets × Scales (TS), Persons Within Departments × Targets (P:DT) and Persons Within Departments × Scales (P:DS); and the three-way interaction for Departments × Targets × Scales (DTS), and Persons Within Departments × Targets by Scales (P:DTS), which is also confounded by error.[2]

---

[2]Notably, the between department assessment data were collected in a reciprocal manner such that respondents from six departments all rated how they interacted with the five other departments in the set. Collectively, this yields a 6 × 6 balanced design *except* for the fact that the diagonal cells (i.e., 1 × 1, 2 × 2, etc.) are empty since departments did not rate themselves. Therefore, we initially used a missing values algorithm to estimate variance components (cf. DeShon, 1995) which were then input to GENOVA for the generalizability analyses.

GENOVA provides an overall generalizability coefficient based on one randomly sampled condition for each facet of generalization (e.g., one random rater and performance dimension), as well as *F* statistics and quasi *F* ratios (Winer, 1971). Researchers are advised to also construct confidence intervals around the estimated variance components, using methods proposed by Satterthwaite (1946). Brennan (1983, pp. 137–140) presents an understandable overview of this procedure and provides corresponding tables to facilitate their computation. An estimated confidence interval that includes zero indicates that the variance associated with

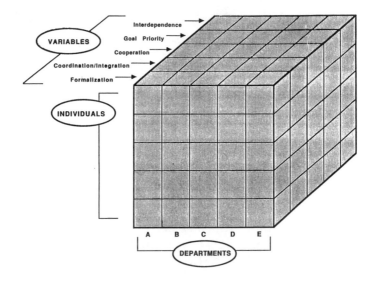

FIG. 9.2.   Interdepartmental data.

A secondary output of GENOVA are D-study results, which estimate generalizability coefficients under various user-specified facet conditions (i.e., number and type of conditions). This allows the researcher, for example, to estimate the number of facet conditions necessary to generalize at a certain level. Since G coefficients are analogous to classical reliability estimates, convention would suggest that values greater than or equal to .70, or better still greater than or equal to .80, should be considered reasonable (Kraiger & Teachout, 1990; Nunnally, 1982).

---

that facet may be entirely due to sampling error. Estimates of practical effect sizes compare the percent of variance explained by each variance component relative to total variance.

As noted by Shavelson and Webb (1991), this provides "a heuristic in interpreting the relative magnitudes of estimated variance components" (p. 30). By comparing these estimates in a relative manner, the researcher can determine which facets account for sizeable (and conversely, trivial) amounts of variance. It is also true that researchers can conduct more focused follow-up tests to identify the source of significant overall effects. For example, a significant department × scale interaction in the within-department analyses would prompt follow up tests, such as one-way ANOVAs or paired T tests, to identify which departments are high and low on which dimensions. For the between-department analyses, a department by target department interaction indicates that the relationships across departments are not uniform. A series of more focused analyses, taking pairs of departments at a time, would reveal where the discrepancies lie and where additional assessment or development efforts are probably most warranted.

WITHIN-DEPARTMENTS FINDINGS AND DISCUSSION

G Study

The ANOVA source table, along with the estimated variance components and 90% confidence intervals (i.e., precision indices) for each facet of the within-department analyses are presented in Table 9.4. Results show that the *persons* (i.e., respondents) facet had the largest estimated variance component ($\hat{\sigma}^2_P = .13$; 29% of total variance), indicating that process ratings varied considerably as a function of the person providing the ratings. In addition, the relatively large variance component for *scales* ($\hat{\sigma}^2_S = .09$; 20% of total) indicated that departments were not perceived as uniform across the different scales. This finding means that respondents did not simply rate their department as high or low across the different measures. Importantly, there was also a substantial *Department* × *Scales* interaction component ($\hat{\sigma}^2_{D:S} = .05$; 11% of total variance), which means that departments were not seen as uniformly high or low. In other words, the rank order of departmental quality would differ depending on which process measure was considered. Indeed, the overall variance for *departments*, which does not take into consideration the different scales, was actually *negative* ($\hat{\sigma}^2_D = -.03$), which should be interpreted as accounting for zero total variance.

Follow-Up Analyses

We next conducted follow-up mean comparisons to decipher the nature of the department × scales interaction. We found, for example, that Department A was rated the highest on centralization, yet the lowest on formalization. Elsewhere, we found that Department B was among the lowest rated on task assignment and formalization, yet among the highest on strategy development. This level of detailed analysis would enable HR

TABLE 9.4
Within-Department Generalizability Results

Source	df	MS	$\hat{\sigma}^2$	SE ($\hat{\sigma}^2$)	90% Confidence Interval
Departments (D)	7	.93	−.03	.04	$-.11 < \hat{\sigma}^2 < .06$
Persons in Departments (P:D)	8	1.24	.13	.07	$-.01 < \hat{\sigma}^2 < .27$
Scales (S)	7	1.70	.09	.05	$-.01 < \hat{\sigma}^2 < .19$
DS	49	.28	.05	.03	$-.01 < \hat{\sigma}^2 < .12$
PS:D (error)	56	.18	.18	.03	$.11 < \hat{\sigma}^2 < .25$

$\hat{\sigma}^2$ = estimated variance component; $SE (\hat{\sigma}^2)$ = standard error.
$N = 16$, 2 respondents per 8 Departments.

specialists to identify areas of strengths and weaknesses throughout the plant, and to target better development efforts.

D Study

Whereas the primary purpose of a G study is to estimate variance components, D studies apply G-study results in tailoring a measurement procedure for future decision making (Shavelson, Webb, & Rowley, 1989). Specifically, D studies allow for the estimation of generalizability under various facet conditions (numbers) and types (i.e., random vs. fixed). At issue here is the determination of whether we have collected sufficient information to draw dependable inferences from the above comparisons. In other words, how reliable are the above results and can we be confident that we have not missed important departmental differences?

The size and organizational structure of the plant is going to dictate the number of departments that exist, and the functional analysis will determine, in large part, the number of measures that are included in the assessment effort. The primary facet of concern here is how many respondents per department do we need to sample in order to get reliable assessments? Using the variance components derived in the G study, we varied the number of respondents per department from one to eight. The resulting generalizability coefficients were .75 for one respondent, .83 for two respondents, and surpassed .90 with seven respondents. Based on these results, we are confident that our findings based on two respondents were fairly reliable. In instances where the reliability of measurements is deemed critical, however, based on these findings, we would recommend collecting data from at least eight respondents per department.

BETWEEN-DEPARTMENTS FINDINGS AND DISCUSSION

G Study

The estimated variance components, standard error estimates, and approximate Wald Z-statistics for each facet and their interactions for the between department analyses are presented in Table 9.5. The strongest effects with significant Z-statistics were evident for the interactions involving the P:D facet ($\sigma^2_{P:DxT} = .17$; $\sigma^2_{P:DxS} = .13$; and $\sigma^2_{P:DxTxS} = .23$). The only other variance component estimate that was found to have a confidence interval excluding zero was the Target × Scale interaction ($\sigma^2_{TxS} = .10$). Taken together, these G-study results indicate that there are differences among persons within departments on the ratings of targets (i.e., other departments), and to a lesser degree, disagreement on the different dimension

TABLE 9.5
Between-Department Generalizability Results

Source	δ^2	SE (δ^2)	Z
Departments (D)	.032	.087	0.37
Persons within Departments (P:D)	.123	.071	1.71
Targets (T)	.088	.094	0.95
Scales (S)	.046	.051	0.91
D × T	.114	.064	1.77
D × S	.000	.000	0.00
P:D × T	.170	.039	4.34**
P:D × S	.131	.028	4.67**
T × S	.099	.037	2.72**
D × T × S	.015	.013	1.16
P:D × T × S (residual)	.231	.020	11.40**

Note. δ^2 = estimated variance component; SE (δ^2) = standard error; Z approximate Wald Z-statistics, which are compared to the standard normal distribution.
**$p < .01$.

scale ratings, collapsing across target departments. The latter result is indicative of rating biases that are systematically affecting results. The relatively large Target × Scale interaction is interesting in that it suggests that the rated target departments varied by dimension scale, collapsing across persons within departments. That is, there is systematic variance associated with reported target department functioning on the different dimensions, as rated by other department members.

Follow-Up Analyses

Because of the noted systematic interaction effects for the Target facet, it was decided to run 15 separate G studies analyzing each possible combination of departments (e.g., Departments A and B rating each other; A and C rating each other; etc.). In essence, these follow-up analyses will allow us to better understand which particular departments most *disagree* on their ratings of functioning. These results are summarized in Table 9.6. For the most part there were no systematic effects associated with the Department facet. There were two specific comparisons, however, in which the proportion of total variance associated with the Department effect exceeded .10 (viz., B × E and C × E). This result indicates a systematic difference in the way the two focal departments view each other's functioning, collapsing across Persons and Scales.

Overall, the most consistent systematic influences across analyses were found for the Persons Within Department facet, which explained an average of approximately 14% of total variance for each comparison. This

TABLE 9.6
Generalizability Analysis Variance Components for 15 Departmental Pairings

Department Pairings	Facets				
	D	P:D	S	D × S	P:D × S
1. A × B	.00 (00)	**.14** (17)	.04 (05)	.00 (00).	**13** (16)
2. A × C	.00 (00)	**.09** (11)	.07 (09)	.00 (00)	.07 (09)
3. A × D	.00 (00)	**.17** (22)	.04 (05)	.00 (00)	.00 (00)
4. A × E	.10 (07)	**.41** (29)	.05 (03)	.00 (00)	.00 (00)
5. A × F	.00 (00)	**.15** (19)	**.09** (11)	.00 (00)	.03 (04)
6. B × C	.01 (01)	.04 (05)	.06 (08)	.00 (00)	.07 (09)
7. B × D	.06 (07)	**.12** (13)	.04 (04)	.00 (00)	.02 (02)
8. B × E	**.45** (27)	**.21** (12)	.02 (01)	.02 (01)	.00 (00)
9. B × F	.02 (02)	**.09** (10)	.03 (04)	.05 (05)	.05 (05)
10. C × D	.00 (00)	.08 (09)	.06 (07)	.00 (00)	.07 (08)
11. C × E	**.24** (16)	**.18** (12)	.06 (04)	.00 (00)	.06 (04)
12. C × F	.00 (00)	.03 (03)	**.12** (13)	.00 (00)	**.10** (11)
13. D × E	.08 (06)	**.26** (20)	.04 (03)	.00 (00)	.00 (00)
14. D × F	.00 (00)	**.11** (13)	.07 (07)	.00 (00)	.04 (05)
15. E × F	.08 (05)	**.32** (21)	.10 (06)	.00 (00)	.00 (00)
Average %	4.7%	14.4%	6.0%	0.0%	4.9%

Values in parentheses are approximate percentages of total variance for each component. All components ≥ 10% of total variance are bolded.

effect can be interpreted as meaning that differences exist in dimensional ratings collapsing across Departments and Persons Within Departments. As such, those effects do not provide very much diagnostic information. The only other result of interest is the lack of any systematic Department × Scale variance across the comparisons. These trivial interactions tell us that the focal departments do not differ on their dimensional ratings, collapsing across raters within departments. That is, representatives of the departments in question view each other's functioning as uniformly good, bad, or whatever across the various scale dimensions.

CONCLUSIONS

Our goal for this chapter was to illustrate the application of functional and generalizability analyses to the diagnosis of within- and between-team processes. We hope the message is clear that such efforts are not simply statistical exercises. In particular, the role of the functional analysis is critical. It helps to determine which organizational subunits or teams and which cross-team linkages should be assessed. It also helps to ground the effort in the organizational milieu and to identify critical challenges that teams face. In our application, the functional analysis turned out to be one of the more challenging aspects of this effort. Initially, we and corporate HR personnel believed that the identification of interrelated NPP teams would be an easy exercise. In practice, we encountered a web of ties and had to distill a wide assortment of information before we could begin to locate the critical links. Even so, because of the critical role that some departments occupied (e.g., Operations, Radiological Control), we ended up creating multiple linkage assessments (only one of which was presented here) and needed to draw multiple samples from some departments. This effort, however, in and of itself signaled to the organization the undeniable fact that the functioning of some teams, and their linkages with others, were far more critical than were others. Accordingly, when resources such as time and money are scarce, the functional analysis makes it clear where HR professionals should direct their efforts.

Once preliminary data were collected, generalizability analyses helped to determine where significant differences existed throughout the organization. Through use of the Decision (D) studies, generalizability analyses also permitted HR specialists to conduct preliminary analyses sampling relatively few respondents and to determine empirically whether additional data collection effort is warranted. In our case, it was clear that sampling only a few people was sufficient for some purposes but substantially larger samples would have been necessary to confidently draw other conclusions. This does not mean that a full scale organizational assessment must commence. It simply suggested that the time and effort required to gather additional data would be well spent.

Finally, supplemented with more traditional analyses such as ANOVA and mean comparisons, this approach facilitates the identification of where significant differences exist. Such follow-ups are important because there is little justification for "developing" teams that are already doing well when there are others that are doing poorly. The contrast analyses, in conjunction with the functional analysis, should guide HR professionals to the critical levers in the organization most in need of attention. This is not to say that even good teams cannot be improved, or that organizations should not strive for overall enhancement. It simply acknowledges that in environments such as NPPs, attention should first be directed at potentially dangerous weaknesses and then toward continuous improvement. It is also worth noting, however, that these contrast analyses can highlight exceptionally well-functioning teams or particularly smooth team interfaces. Once identified, such circumstances can be studied further, insights gained, and lessons learned for use with other teams.

Several important caveats or limits to this approach must be kept in mind. First, because generalizability analysis is an ANOVA-based model, the approach is limited to organizations with fairly distinct team boundaries. It would be much harder to employ these techniques in more fluid organizations with permeable boundaries (such as matrix-designed organizations), because respondents must be unequivocally assigned to only one team. Further, the boundaries of "teams" needs to be explicit in any application. We fixed such boundaries in terms of departmental membership for our application, but clearly more micro (e.g., workgroups, shifts) and/or macro (e.g., production vs. office, different plants at multiplant sites) frames may be suitable as the situation warrants. Whatever frame(s) that is(are) adopted, however, should guide the wording of measures and of the "target other" ratings.

A second caveat concerns the necessary sample sizes for generalizable results. Based on our within-department analyses, it would be tempting to conclude that reliable team assessments can be conducted using only two or three respondents. On the other hand, the between-department analyses indicated samples of 25 or more per department would be necessary to yield reliable conclusions. We therefore caution against overgeneralizing these interpretations because our findings are likely to be idiosyncratic due to the nature of our sample. We included only management employees who tend to have significantly different perceptions of organizational practices than do bargaining-unit employees (Tesluk, Vance, & Mathieu, 1994).

Furthermore, we sampled only *key respondents* who, by definition, are assumed to be well-positioned to provide ratings. A more random sample of employees would likely introduce greater variance in the ratings and, we believe, yield more stable estimates of relationships. We also believe that the *nature of the respondents' positions* could be introduced as a facet of inquiry for these types of analyses. In other words, if assessment data are collected from, say bargaining-unit employees, lower and upper level management, and position was used as a facet, generalizability analyses would reveal: (a) if perceptions of within-team relationships are uniform across the vertical hierarchy; and (b) if the inter-team relationships vary as a function of the level(s) at which they come in contact and are rated. Although necessitating larger samples that could prove difficult in these types of organizations, we believe that the diagnostic information yielded would be quite valuable. In any event, a few respondents per position could be drawn initially, and D-study results would suggest how many more respondents are necessary to draw reliable conclusions.

An alternative strategy might be to first sample a limited number of respondents per department and to follow-up disagreements by having individuals (whether they be from within the same team regarding the "within" ratings, or from different teams regarding the "between" ratings) meet to derive a consensus rating (see Kumar, Stern & Anderson, 1994, for an example along these lines). This latter strategy, though offering a promising alternative, might be perceived as too intrusive for delicate situations. In any case, the preliminary small sample G study will provide a solid foundation for such targeted follow-up efforts.

Finally, the reader may have noticed that we have been silent as to the substantive meaning of significant effects—do they always suggest a problem? At issue here is whether: (a) all teams should have high scores on all scales; (b) the relationships between some teams are more critical than those among others; and (c) teams should maintain one profile of processes across time. The framework and analytic techniques we described simply signal whether statistically significant differences exist. Such differences must be interpreted in light of presumed appropriate profiles of scores. For example, we suspect that the ideal set of within-departmental processes for operations differs from that for human resources. We further believe that the relationships among some departments (e.g., Maintenance and Operations) are far more critical to plant operations and safety than are other linkages (e.g., Maintenance and Security). In other words, the nature of the team task may significantly moderate the effectiveness of different process profiles.

We also agree with Perrow (1984), who suggested that high reliability organizations such as NPPs must often adopt different work processes in response to changing circumstances (e.g., operate fairly bureaucratically during normal operations, yet operate quite fluidly during intensive activities such as refuelings). In short, the numbers from a team-based assessment, and whether they differ significantly in various comparisons, cannot be interpreted in a vacuum. Whether they depict a suitable profile or not is a question for organizational design and strategy decision makers and subject to outside forces (e.g., NRC regulations). Our purpose was simply to illustrate how to sculpt such profiles and to compare them.

ACKNOWLEDGEMENTS

The authors contributed equally to the preparation of this work. We thank Mike Brannick and Ed Salas for their many helpful comments on an earlier version of this chapter. We are also indebted to Rick DeShon for his help with many of the generalizability analysis issues.

REFERENCES

Alderfer, C. P., & Brown, L. D. (1972). Questionnaire design in organizational research. *Journal of Applied Psychology, 56,* 456–460.
Aldrich, H. E. (1979). *Organizations and environments.* Englewood Cliffs, NJ: Prentice-Hall.

Berger, C. J., & Cummings, L. L. (1979). Organizational structure, attitudes, and behaviors. *Research in Organizational Behavior, 1,* 169–208.

Brennan, R. L. (1983). *Elements of generalizability theory.* Iowa City, IA: American College Testing Program.

Cohen, S. G. (1993). New approaches to teams and teamwork. In J. Galbraith & E. Lawler & Associates (Eds.), *Organizing for the future: The new logic for managing complex organizations.* San Francisco: Jossey-Bass.

Crick, J. E., & Brennan, R. L. (1983). *Manual for GENOVA: A generalized analysis of variance system.* Iowa City: American College Testing Program.

Cronbach, L. J., Gleser, G. C., Nanda, H., & Rajaratnam, N. (1972). *The dependability of behavioral measurements.* New York: Wiley.

Davis, L. T., Gaddy, C. D., Turney, J. R., & Koontz, J. L. (1986). Team skills training. *Performance & Instruction, 25,* 12–17.

DeShon, R. P. (1995). *Restricted maximum likelihood estimation of variance components in generalizability theory: Overcoming balanced data requirements.* Paper presented at the 10th annual conference of the Society of Industrial and Organizational Psychology, Orlando, FL.

Fleishman, E. A., & Zaccaro, S. J. (1992). Toward a taxonomy of team performance functions. In R. W. Swezey & E. Salas (Eds.), *Teams: Their training and performance* (pp. 31–56). Norwood, NJ: Ablex.

Frye, S. R. (1988). An approach to enhanced control room crew performance. *IEEE 4th Conference on Human Factors and Power Plants.* Monterey, CA: IEEE.

Gaddy, C. D., & Koontz, J. L. (1987). Evaluation of team skills for control room crews. *Proceedings of the 7th Symposium on Training of Nuclear Facility Personnel* (CONF-870406). Springfield, VA: National Technical Information Services.

Gaddy, C. D., & Wachtel, J. A. (1992). Team skills training in nuclear power plant operations. In R. W. Swezey & E. Salas (Eds.), *Teams: Their training and performance* (pp. 379–396). Norwood, NJ: Ablex.

Hall, R. H. (1991). *Organizations: Structures, processes, & outcomes* (5th ed.). Englewood Cliffs, NJ: Prentice-Hall.

Hausser, D. L. (1980). Comparison of different models for organizational analysis. In E. E. Lawler, D. A. Nadler, & C. Cammann (Eds.), *Organizational assessment: Perspectives on the measurement of organizational behavior and the quality of work life* (pp. 132–161). New York: Wiley.

Jacobs, R. R., Mathieu, J. E., Landy, F. L., Barratta, A., Robinson, G., Hofmann, D. A., & Ringenbach, K. (1992). *Draft NUREG-5750: Organizational processes and nuclear power plant safety—A structured interview approach.*

James, L. R., & Jones, A. P. (1976). Organizational structure: A review of structural dimensions and their conceptual relationships with individual attitudes and behavior. *Organizational Behavior and Human Performance, 16,* 74–113.

Kraiger, K., & Teachout, M. S. (1990). Generalizability theory as construct-related evidence of the validity of job performance ratings. *Human Performance, 3,* 19–35.

Kumar, N., Stern, L. W., & Anderson, J. C. (1994). Conducting inter-organizational research using key informants. *Academy of Management Journal, 36,* 1633–1651.

Miles, R. H.(1980). *Macro-organizational behavior.* Santa Monica, CA: Goodyear.

Nunnally, J. (1982). *Psychometric theory* (2nd ed.). New York: McGraw-Hill.

Payne, R., & Pugh, D. S. (1976). Organizational structure and climate. In M. D. Dunnette (Ed.), *Handbook of industrial and organizational psychology* (pp. 1125–1176). Chicago: Rand McNally.

Perrow, C. (1984). *Normal Accidents.* New York: Basic Books.

Roberts, K. H., & Gargano, B. S. (1990). Managing a high-reliability organization: A case for interdependence. In M. A. Glinow & S. A. Mohrman (Eds.), *Managing complexity in high technology organizations* (pp. 146-159). New York: Oxford University Press.

Roberts, K. H., LaPorte, T. R., & Rochlin, G. I. (1987). The self-designing high-reliability organization: Aircraft carrier flight operations at sea. *Naval War College Review, 40,* 76-91.

Robinson, G. H. (1982). Accidents and socio-technical systems: Principles for design. *Accident Analysis and Prevention, 14,* 121-130.

Satterthwaite, F. E. (1946). An approximate distribution of estimates of variance components. *Biometrics Bulletin, 2,* 110-114.

Seidler, J. (1974). On using informants: A technique for collecting quantitative data and controlling for measurement error in organizational analysis. *American Sociological Review, 39,* 816-831.

Shavelson, R. J., & Webb, N. M. (1991). *Generalizability theory: A primer.* Newbury Park, CA: Sage.

Shavelson, R. J., Webb, N. M., & Rowley, G. L. (1989). Generalizability theory. *American Psychologist, 44,* 922-932.

Shiflett, S. C., Eisner, E. J., Price, S. J., & Schemmer, F. M. (1982). *The definition and measurement of team functions.* Bethesda, MD: ARRO.

Shrout, P. E., & Fleiss, J. L. (1979). Intraclass correlations: Uses in assessing rater reliability. *Psychological Bulletin, 86,* 420-428.

Sokolowski, E. (1985). Human error as a source of disturbance in Swedish nuclear power plants. *IEEE 3rd Conference on Human Factors and Power Plants,* Monterey, CA: IEEE.

Swezey, R. W., & Salas, E. (1992). *Teams: Their training and performance.* Norwood, NJ: Ablex.

Tesluk, P., Vance, B., & Mathieu, J. (1994, August). Examining employee involvement in the context of participative work environments: A multi-level approach. In R. Vance (Chair), *Organizational, group, and individual determinants of employee involvement program success.* A symposium presented at the annual meeting of the Academy of Management, Dallas, TX.

Van de Ven, A. H., & Ferry, D. L. (1980). *Measuring and assessing organizations.* New York: Wiley-Interscience.

Winer, B. J. (1971). *Statistical principles in experimental design* (2nd ed.). New York: McGraw-Hill.

10

Task and Aggregation Issues in the Analysis and Assessment of Team Performance

Paul Tesluk
Tulane University

John E. Mathieu
The Pennsylvania State University

Stephen J. Zaccaro
Michelle Marks
George Mason University

This chapter is concerned with some factors that need to be considered by researchers and practitioners when assessing performance in organizational teams. By way of illustration, we describe the nature and activities of teams in hospital environments. Hospitals provide fascinating portrayals of individuals, placed into different kinds of work arrangements, who integrate their activities in various ways to produce effective collective and organized responses. Often, these actions occur through split-second coordination where the results have literal life and death implications. Hospitals are likely to be divided into groupings that represent different functional activities. Each of these groups may be subdivided into smaller groups also differentiated by function, albeit more specialized than the larger groupings. Also, some teams (e.g., surgical teams) are ad hoc ones that come together for a limited period of time and for a specific purpose and then disband. Still others, such as nursing teams, are loose configurations where each member has a specialized function and their organization into a team is designed to facilitate the rotation of personnel to different performance settings (Denison & Sutton, 1990). Finally, the hospital as a whole may be directed by a top management team (Cohen, 1990).

Such complex arrangements are typical of most organizations. Accordingly, what are some critical considerations that should be attended to when assessing work performance in such settings? The basis for addressing this question resides in the fundamental nature of organizations. The essence of organizational action is the coordination, synchronization, and integration of the contributions of all organizational members into a series of collective responses (Katz & Kahn, 1978; Weick, 1979). Typically, these members are

197

organized into various organizational subsystems (called departments or divisions) that may be divided further into a number of teams and groups. These teams may be structured in a variety of different ways according to their functional requirements within the organization. For example, members of one team may work relatively independently, yet members of another team may interact in a manner that makes the decomposition of their collective response into smaller units impossible. The performance of the organization as a whole requires the effective integration of these different teams with their varying structure. Furthermore, sustained organizational effectiveness requires that managers assess and facilitate the performance of these organizational units and simultaneously attend to the alternate work arrangements and structures of the different teams.

The assessment of team performance within organizations requires, as well, a consideration of individual versus collective contributions. If managers simply evaluate the product of a team as a whole, they are assuming that each member contributed equally to the collective product. Yet, as we indicate later in this chapter, this assumption is valid only for some collective work arrangements. In other arrangements, individuals contribute independently and sometimes disproportionately to the collective effort. Limiting one's evaluation to the team product as a whole obscures these individual contributions. Likewise, interventions directed at improving team performance that target the team as a whole (e.g., process consultant, team building) may be misplaced because the critical determinants of collective performance may reside at the individual level and therefore require different kinds of interventions.

We hasten to add that merely focusing on individual contributions versus the collective product as a whole is simplistic. Although some team outcomes reflect the mere compilation of individual efforts, such work arrangements do not preclude group level effects. For example, how each team member completes his or her work within the team may still be affected by the speed and motivation of other team members. Thus, although the team product is easily decomposed into individual contributions, there still exists a group level effect that should be considered in assessments of performance in this setting.

This chapter focuses on the nature of work team arrangements and levels of analysis as necessary considerations in the assessment of team-based performance. In the next section we describe four basic work arrangements that typically characterize collective action. We use different types of hospital teams as illustrations of these arrangements. We then examine implications of these work arrangements and their critical "team levers" for the measurement and diagnosis of team performance. For those work arrangements that yield identifiable individual products, measurement and analysis need to occur at multiple levels. Indeed, researchers and practitioners need to understand the nature of "group-level" effects in such arrangements. Accordingly, we also discuss levels of analysis issues in team performance assessment. We conclude with some prescriptions for interventions designed to improve team performance appropriate for different team work arrangements. We begin with a description of different team tasks and their corresponding work arrangements.

TEAM PERFORMANCE TASKS AND MEMBER WORK ARRANGEMENTS

Four Patterns of Teamwork

The nature of the work activities performed by the team, or its task characteristics, serves to specify the requisite actions, behaviors, and processes that lead to effective team performance (Cannon-Bowers, Tannenbaum, Salas, & Volpe, 1995; Fleishman & Zaccaro, 1992; Goodman, 1986; Shaw, 1976; Steiner, 1972). Therefore, interventions aimed at improving team performance are likely to be more successful when they take into account the team's specific task functions and requirements. For instance, Goodman and his associates (Goodman, Devedas, & Hughson, 1988; Goodman, Ravlin, & Argote, 1986) argued that self-managing work team interventions could be more effective if greater attention was given to understanding the teams' critical behaviors and functions. They define such teams as "groups of individuals who can self-regulate work on their interdependent tasks" (Goodman et al., 1988, p. 296).

Although self-managing work teams are based on the principle of sociotechnical theory, that work effectiveness is enhanced when the technical and social systems are jointly optimized (Pasmore, Francis, Haldeman, & Shani, 1982), most self-managing team interventions focus on changes in the social system and do not adequately address the technical nature of the team's task (Goodman et al., 1988; Kelly, 1978). The result is that although changes in the social system that provide more responsibility, variety, and autonomy may have motivational benefits, they only have limited impact on actual team performance. This is because the instrumental team behaviors that link the effort and knowledge of team members to performance criteria are not identified and enhanced.

Given the importance of team task characteristics, the diagnosis, design, and implementation of interventions to improve team performance should be guided by an understanding of the team's task requirements. This allows a more clear identification of the critical levers that influence team performance. By critical levers we mean the most important factors or work processes that underlie a particular team's performance. In certain types of work-flow arrangements, particular individual and synchronized activities are more critical for effective performance than they are in other task situations. In other arrangements, more integrated and full interdependent activities form the basis for effective team performance. Figure 10.1 presents and describes four basic work flow arrangements (Thompson, 1967; Van de Ven & Ferry, 1980) that are used to characterize the work of different types of team interdependencies. This approach to analyzing the nature of the task has been applied to the team context (Kozlowski & Salas, in press). Examples of teams in a typical hospital setting are used to illustrate the point that for different team work flow arrangements, different levers are especially critical for effective team performance.

Pooled Interdependence. When team performance is an additive function of individual performance, or in other words, a simple aggregation of individual performance, the team task is pooled or additive in nature (Steiner, 1972). In pooled tasks, each individual contributes incrementally to overall task completion, and hence, team performance. Minimal coordination and communication are required of team members in order to accomplish the task. This is not to say that team members are not interdependent. For example, if one employee's work begins to drag behind that of others, other employees will have to increase their efforts to compensate for the loss. But, essentially each individual's performance is a function of his or her efforts and does not depend directly on the performance of others.

In a hospital setting, the work performed by janitorial, laboratory, pharmacy, and data processing teams and work groups are examples of pooled performance task arrangements. For instance, with custodial crews, the entire crew is responsible for cleaning restrooms, removing trash, mopping floors, and so on on a particular wing of the hospital. For the most part, each member of the custodial crew works independently on a number of different tasks in a particular area of the hospital wing. It is the sum of their individual work efforts that determines custodial crew performance. Work in the hospital laboratory also is structured in a pooled/additive manner. Typically, laboratory technicians work independently in performing requested laboratory tests. Similarly, in the hospital pharmacy, pharmacists and their assistants work independently to fill prescription orders. The ability of the pharmacy unit to purchase and distribute medicine in a timely manner depends to a large extent on the summed contributions of these individuals. A final example in a hospital setting involves data processing teams, where data are divided and parcelled out to data entry staff, who then independently type in the data.

Sequential Interdependence. Whereas in pooled work flow arrangements team performance is based on individual team member contribu-

Work Flow Description

Pooled/Additive: Work and activities are performed separately by all team members and work does not flow between members of the team

Sequential: Work and activities flow from one member to another in the team, but mostly in one direction

Reciprocal: Work and activities flow between team members in a back-and-forth manner over a period of time

Intensive: Work and activities come into the team and members must diagnose, problem solve, and/or collaborate as a team in order to accomplish the team's task.

Diagram

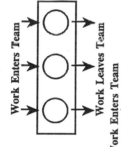

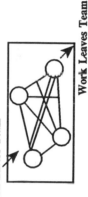

Work Enters Team — Work Leaves Team

Work Enters Team — Work Leaves Team

Work Enters Team — Work Leaves Team

Work Enters Team — Work Leaves Team

Examples From a Hospital Setting

- Housekeeping Services
- Pharmacy
- Laboratory
- Data Processing

- Accounting
- Radiology
- Admissions Registration
- Purchasing
- Medical Records

- Respiratory Care
- Social Services
- Psychiatry
- Human Resources
- Fiscal Services

- Physical Therapy
- Operating Room
- Emergency Room
- Intensive Care Unit
- Public Relations

FIG. 10.1. Taxonomy of team work processes.

tions, in other settings team performance is more dependent on systematic unidirectional interfaces between team members. In a hospital environment, this type of work flow arrangement typically exists in purchasing, food services, medical records, accounting, admissions registration, and radiology. Contrast, for example, the nature of the tasks facing custodial crews or data processing teams to that of a hospital's purchasing department. In purchasing, each member of the unit makes a contribution to the unit's total performance (i.e., pooled interdependence). However, in addition to the importance of individual contributions, synchronization between unit members is required for effective management of needed materials and supplies. Performance resembles that of an assembly line; orders for new materials and supplies are completed, then incoming shipments are handled in shipping and receiving, stored and tracked by warehousing, and finally, distributed to various units in the hospital. Work flows in a consistent unidirectional pattern through each of these stages. In teams of this type, the linkage between individual and team performance is not simply additive. If one member of the purchasing unit fails to complete his or her task adequately, then the work of those further along in the process will be stymied. In essence, then, in sequential interdependent teams there are premiums placed not only on the performance of individuals, but also in the interfaces or "hand-offs" as work moves from one member to another.

In using the more traditional technologies in radiology departments (e.g., x-rays, fluoroscopies), physicians, radiologists, and technologists form a similar sequential group task. The process starts with the physician making a referral for a patient that is sent to the radiology department. A technologist in the radiology department performs the procedure (e.g., chest x-ray) and the results are then provided to the radiologist. The radiologist then provides an interpretation of the results to the referring physician. In radiology, as in purchasing and other hospital units such as admissions, accounting, and medical records, work flows in a coordinated but unidirectional fashion between team members. For instance, in radiology, once the technician completes an x-ray, he or she provides the film to the radiologist. The radiologist then interprets the films for the referring physician. The sequential order and direction of the work flow is relatively stable. For example, the radiologist would rarely talk directly with the technician unless there was an undetected problem with the film and a technician would very rarely interact directly with a referring physician over an x-ray procedure.

Reciprocal Interdependence. When team members' roles become less distinguishable and highly interdependent, team performance is a function of more complex forms of coordination. These types of tasks build on the unidirectional flow of departments just described but also introduce a feedback or bidirectional feature. In other words, in reciprocal interdependent team settings, interactions are more dynamic in nature and work flows back and forth between team members. A number of hospital departments have team processes that are reciprocal in nature. These include respiratory care, social services, human resources, and fiscal services. In many of these cases, the bidirectional interfaces between team members can largely be anticipated.

Consider, for example, mental health treatment teams. Located in the hospital's psychiatric unit, a mental health treatment team typically consists of a psychiatrist, a psychologist, a social worker, a nurse, and one or more psychiatric nursing assistants (Shaw, 1990). Collectively, these individuals are responsible for developing and putting into place a therapeutic program for the unit's patients. Although the team members represent different functions that place alternative emphases on the treatment of mental disorders, they are interdependent with one another in assessment, treatment planning, patient education, coordination of care, and medication management (Yank, Barber, & Spradlin, 1994).

For instance, a psychiatrist depends on other team members to provide information about a patient's mental functioning and behavior to make the most appropriate decisions regarding the type of psychotropic medication to prescribe. In a similar manner, other team members conducting rehabilitative activities (e.g., psychologist, social worker) depend on the psychiatrist's prescription practices when they are engaged in counseling activities. Most of these back-and-forth type interactions that occur during treatment team meetings can be anticipated. If during a team meeting the psychiatrist suggests altering a patient's medication, certainly the psychologist and nurses need to know how this may impact the patient's behavior and if they, in turn, need to adjust their treatment strategies. Hence, anticipated coordination and reciprocal interdependencies between mental health care team members are critical points for effective team performance defined in terms of improvement of the patient's condition.

Intensive.   In intensive work arrangements, team members work together closely to diagnose and solve problems in performing the task. Interfaces between team members require well-orchestrated teamwork, but often it is impossible to fully anticipate when and where these interfaces will occur because the nature of the task is so dynamic and complex. Many of the prototypical team arrangements that come to mind when we think of hospitals, such as operating room (OR) and emergency room (ER) teams, demonstrate intensive work flow patterns. Others include intensive care units (ICUs), physical therapy units, and hospice facilities.

Operating room surgery teams, typically consisting of surgeons, anesthesiologists, and operating room nurses, provide an excellent example of an intensive task. Because of the often highly stressful, quick-paced, real-time nature of the task and the serious consequences that may result from poor performance, members of OR teams share a high level of interdependence that requires a high level of synchronization, communication, and coordination between team members. For these reasons, compared to individual factors (e.g., differences in aptitude or skill), or environmental conditions (e.g., differences in operating room design, equipment), group process factors play a considerable role in predicting differences in the performance of OR teams (Helmreich & Schaefer, 1994).

The types of group processes that differentiate OR teams in their level of performance, however, go beyond simple coordination. They include factors such as mutual situational awareness, where team members are able to predict, adapt, and coordinate with one another successfully, even under stressful or novel conditions. This requires training that can enhance the development of shared mental models or the formation of expectations and explanations that reflect an accurate understanding of the entire team's task requirements (Cannon-Bowers, Salas, & Converse, 1993). Training strategies that require team members to verbalize expectations and explanations for the team's functioning are one possible means to develop shared mental models. An alternative and possibly complementary method is through the use of cross-training, where team members learn the tasks involved in each other's role (Rouse, Cannon-Bowers, & Salas, 1992).

Patterns of Team Work and Team Problem Diagnosis

Identification of Critical Team Levers.   Understanding the nature of the task performed by the team is critical for proper diagnosis of problems in team performance. If the critical levers for team performance are not identified, measurement efforts may be targeted at the wrong level of analysis and may miss important individual and team activities and processes. For instance, at first glance we may consider the members of a mental health treatment team as working relatively independently of each other. In such teams, members represent distinct and separate disciplines that are primarily concerned with particular tasks involving the patient's treatment. For instance, the psychiatrist is primarily concerned with developing a treatment plan and prescribing appropriate medication; nurses are involved in the patient's routine care and in administering medication; yet, a social worker is primarily involved in patient and family education and coordination of care across facilities.

We may therefore decide to assess the treatment team's performance by measuring the performance of each individual on their tasks and summing across individuals. The problem with this method of measurement lies in a misperception or poor understanding of the nature of the treatment team's task. As we noted earlier, work in a mental health treatment team typically occurs in a reciprocal interdependent fashion. Thus, beyond the performance of various individuals, the ultimate effectiveness of the team depends on well-coordinated "hand-offs" or transitions between members. Accordingly, for teams operating in these types of environments, the measurement of those key reciprocal interactions are the critical levers where there should be emphasis.

Linking Critical Team Levers to Measurement Strategies. Once the critical levers of team performance have been identified (providing an answer to the question of what to measure), we can then determine the particular method of measurement that is most appropriate for assessing team performance (providing an answer to the question of how to measure it). There are a variety of strategies available for measuring team performance and process. The choice between them involves selecting among potential: (a) sources of information, and (b) methods of measurement. Table 10.1 contains examples of studies that have measured team or group process and/or performance for each of these possible source by method combinations. Some of the possible combinations have been used very rarely by previous researchers. For those instances, however, we have provided an example of how such combinations could be used to assess hospital teams.

Sources of information refer to who provides the information on a team's processes or level of performance. Sources may be either incumbents (i.e., team members) or observers of some sort. The most common source for assessing team process and performance has been team members themselves, in part because they often are best positioned to provide certain kinds of information such as member's affective reactions and feelings about one another (e.g., esprit de corps). However, members have a stake in the team's outcomes and might provide biased assessments for other variables such as team processes or performance. This is likely to be particularly true when the information is evaluative in nature. Various types of observers who differ according to their functional relationship to the team can also serve as sources of information on team process and performance. Such people would include subordinates, peers, supervisors, or managers, or external experts (e.g., team instructors, researchers).

Because different sources of information are more qualified to provide assessments on particular aspects of behavior and performance (Borman, 1974), several sources may be used in combination to provide a more holistic view of team functioning and effectiveness (Brannick, Roach, & Salas, 1993). Each source of information (e.g., team members, peers in other teams, supervisors, team trainers) provides relevant and meaningful

TABLE 10.1
Examples of Alternative Ways to Assess Team Process and Performance

Sources of Information	Methods of Measurement			
	Surveys	*Observations*	*Interviews*	*Archival*
Incumbents	*Cohen & Ledford (1994)* Autonomous workgroup members rated group performance on quality, productivity, QWL, costs, & safety *Gladstein (1984)* Marketing workgroup members rated group on maintenance and task behaviors and group performance *Kane, Marks, Zaccaro, & Blair (in press)* Wrestling team members rated team on collective efficacy, task and social cohesion	*Mirvis (1980)* Minor league baseball players used diary to record team conditions and performance	*Eisenhardt & Bourgeois (1988)* Interviews with top management team members on member interactions and decision making	*Andrews, Wang, & Bell (1992)* Display and debriefing of squadron performance (maneuvering, weapon employment effectiveness in kills, misses, etc.) recorded on audio, video, and electronic means *Gladstein (1984)* Sales revenue of marketing workgroups as measure of performance

206

		Example	
Subordinates	*Deluga (1991)* Subordinates of health care managers rated work unit effectiveness *Tesluk, Vance, & Mathieu (1994)* Subordinates rated interactions within work unit (e.g., cooperation, decision making, interpersonal relations)	*Example* Hospital middle-level managers assess top management team performance-based on observations of changes in available resources, etc. *Example* Interviews with hospital employees on their perception of the hospital's functioning and performance	*Watson, Michaelsen, & Sharp (1991)* Results from standard objective true-false, multiple-choice tests competed by group consensus
Peers	*Mathieu & Day (in press)* Key informants rated all other departments on department processes (e.g., decision making) in a nuclear power plant	*Example* Members of other area hospital management teams based on observation of team's handling of recent events (e.g., doctor's strike) *Example* Interviews with top-level managers in all area hospitals on what are the most effective hospitals and top management teams	*Pritchard, Jones, Roth, Steubing, & Ekberg (1988)* Unit productivity assessed based on objective performance information

(Continued)

TABLE 10.1 (Continued)

	Methods of Measurement			
Sources of Information	Surveys	Observations	Interviews	Archival
Supervisors or Managers	*Breuer, Wilson, & Beck (1994)* Police sergeants' supervisors rated sergeants' teams on 12 performance dimensions *Cohen & Ledford (1994)* Autonomous workgroup supervisors rated group performance on quality, productivity, QWL, costs, & safety *Mathieu, Hofmann, & Farr (1993)* Supervisor ratings on department characteristics (e.g., standardization) *Tziner & Eden (1985)* Unit commander ratings of tank crew performance	*Andrews, Wang, & Bell (1992)* Senior commanders view battalion performance (in terms of individual and vehicle location and status) in battlefield simulation exercises via computer consoles *Zaccaro, Zazanis, Diana & Greathouse (1994)* Team supervisors rates Army soldier teams on performance demerits and time spent on task	*Inkson, Pugh, & Hickson (1970)* Interviews with CEOs on organizational formalization	*Cohen & Ledford (1994)* Managers used performance records to rank order autonomous workgroups on quality, efficiency, and overall performance

External Experts	Dailey (1989) Directors of R&D labs' ratings of R&D team coordination and performance	Andrews, Wang, & Bell (1992) Instructors view team real-time air combat performance through Air Combat Maneuvering Instrumentation Display Units McIntire & Salas (1995) Team instructors observing Navy teams in training used a behavioral checklist to record effective and ineffective team behaviors Morgan, Salas, & Glickman (1993) Mission performance in simulator exercises of Navy command Information Center teams observed and then assessed by instructors	McIntire & Salas (1995) Open-ended interviews with Navy team instructors as to what constitutes effective teamwork and performance Murningham & Conlon (1991) Interviews with teachers of string quartets on what constitutes effective group processes and performance	Murningham & Conlon (1991) String quartet performance rated by: (a) newspaper and magazine review rated by independent expert evaluators, (b) concert fees, albums, quartet stability

yet different information. Thus, team members may be used to collect information on team processes (e.g., team cohesion) and outcomes (e.g., member satisfaction, team viability; Sundstrom, De Meuse, & Futrell, 1990) that are not obvious to outside observers. Other aspects of team process and performance that either may be less evident to team members or where assessments may be influenced by the emotional stake members have in their team can be measured by team instructors, supervisors, or other types of observers. This perspective is very similar to the 360° feedback approach for individual performance assessment, where differences in ratings from multiple sources (e.g., self, supervisor, peers, subordinates) are treated as a rich and complex source of information for individual development, instead of treated as error variance that needs to be reduced (Tornow, 1993).

Although most of the examples provided in Table 10.1 are of studies that have utilized only one source of information for assessing team process or performance, a few have included multiple sources. For example, Glickman and his associates (1987) collected team processes and performance information on three types of Naval teams from two different sources. Overall teamwork processes (e.g., communication, cooperation, and coordination) were collected from team members' ratings. More specific aspects of team process and performance, which team members may have been less immediately aware themselves, were gathered from team instructors who observed and rated critical team behaviors and performance during team training.

The method of measurement specifies how data on team process and performance are collected. In other words, team measurement strategies refer to the vehicle or instruments used to scale various team attributes and include surveys or questionnaires, observations, interviews, or archival data. An important factor in team performance assessment is that the nature of the team's task and the particular processes or aspects of performance that are being measured should play an important role in determining which particular method of measurement to use. For example, the work of OR teams is highly intensive (i.e., highly integrated and interdependent) and team coordination requirements are fairly subtle. Therefore, these aspects of team process may not be readily obvious to team members themselves. Accordingly, measures of such processes may be gathered best through observations of OR teams in intensive "after-action" interviews of OR team members.

Alternatively, similar measurement strategies can be employed using different sources. For instance, interviews to measure the performance of a top management team of a private hospital may be conducted with team incumbents (e.g., CEOs, senior vice presidents), subordinates (e.g., middle-level managers), peers (e.g., members of top management teams in other area hospitals), superiors (e.g., influential members of the hospital's board of directors), or external experts (e.g., experts in hospital administration). Each of these different sources is likely to offer a unique vantage point on how the top management team operates and performs. We should note, however, that archival methods of measurement may be by-products of other data collection activities, or may not be tied to a source at all. For example, many of the high-tech and low-fidelity computer team simulations incorporate features that monitor team processes and performance. In this sense, the source of the information is more inherent to the task than stemming from any external source.

Just as most studies of team process or performance have utilized single sources of information, most have also generally employed a single method of data collection. Again, however, there are exceptions where studies have collected information on team process and/or performance using multiple methods. For example, Zaccaro, Zazanis, Diana, and Greathouse (1994) had soldiers complete surveys to assess team climate variables (e.g., collective efficacy, group cohesion). They also retrieved assessments of members' skills and attributes from archival records and recorded multiple objective indices of team performance. Gladstein (1984) surveyed sales team members about team processes (e.g., communication supportiveness, boundary management) and aspects of group effectiveness, including group members' satisfaction with their team and perceptions of team performance. She also used more objective measures of group performance from archival data on team's sales revenue. A similar approach was taken by Cohen and Ledford (1994) in their study of the effectiveness of autonomous work groups by using group members' ratings of different dimensions of team performance (i.e., quality, productivity, quality-of- work life [QWL], costs, and safety) as well as manager's rank-ordered ratings of groups on performance. In an attempt to ground manager ratings in actual performance data, managers used archival data on group performance (e.g., reports on quality of service) in ranking groups on performance.

Studies that combine the use of multiple methods with multiple sources of measurement (i.e., multitrait–multimethod approaches) can provide valuable information for selecting the most appropriate team performance assessment strategy. If measures of team process and performance assessed by different methods and sources of measurement demonstrate convergent and discriminant validity, then there is evidence that the measures are valid (Campbell & Fiske, 1959). Using both multiple sources of information and multiple methods of measurement is important for accurate assessment of team performance because if sources or methods do not agree, then the most appropriate measure can be selected from those that are available.

One study that highlights this point particularly well was conducted by Brannick et al. (1993) and focused on the team process and performance of two-person teams performing a low-fidelity fighter simulation exercise.

They measured team processes using questionnaire ratings from team incumbents and behavioral checklists of critical team behaviors completed by on-site observers during observations of team performances and off-site observers who listened to audiotapes of the team's interactions. Team performance was also collected from each of these three sources (team members, on-site, and off-site observers) with the use of ratings of overall team performance as well as with objective measures of the time taken to shoot down enemy planes and the number of radar locks on enemy targets. By comparing multiple measures of team processes across combinations of sources and methods of measurement and relating these measures to team performance, Brannick et al. (1993) were able to identify which aspects of team behavior and process were best measured by a particular source by method combination.

TEAM PERFORMANCE ASSESSMENT AND ISSUES OF AGGREGATION-LEVEL INFLUENCES

When researchers and practitioners assess team activities, behaviors, processes, or dimensions of performance, they typically use such measures to make inferences about team attributes. That is, they attempt to describe team performance, team cohesion, or other qualities of the team as a whole. However, to make such inferences, researchers and practitioners need to consider the issue of data aggregation and the appropriate level of analysis. Data on team cohesion, communication, and coordination, for example, are often collected through members' ratings. These scores supplied by individuals are typically then aggregated (e.g., averaged) to form a single score that describes the team's level of cohesion, communication, coordination, or whatever other team-level variable is of interest to the team assessor.

In order to aggregate individual level data to the team level, however, certain theoretical and empirical guidelines need to be observed (George & James, 1993; Kenny & La Voie, 1985; Roberts, Hulin, & Rousseau, 1978; Rousseau, 1985). First, it is important that an appropriate theoretical rationale exists for considering the variable a team-level construct. Second, in designing measures of team-level constructs that are to be assessed at a lower level, it is critical that lower level data be matched to teams and that the measures specifically refer to team properties (e.g., by using team item referents in surveys, such as, "My team is a cohesive one"; Rousseau, 1985). Third, shifting levels of analysis may change the psychometric characteristics of the variables (Hulin & Rousseau, 1980); thus it is important to address the measurement properties and validity of team-level variables at their proper level of analysis (see Mathieu, 1991; Sirotnik, 1980).

Finally, in order to justify that individual-level scores indeed reflect team-level attributes, team assessors need to empirically demonstrate adequate within-group agreement. The premise of such agreement is that individuals who work together on a team over a period of time become more homogeneous with respect to one another on perceptions of team attributes. When a certain attribute characterizes a team as a whole (e.g., cohesiveness), then members should rate their team on this characteristic in similar ways. Thus, to infer a team-level process or attribute, statistical criteria need to be applied to the aggregation of individual-level data. Such criteria have been described by James, Demaree, and Wolf (1984; 1993) who provided an index of interrater agreement, r_{wg}, that can be used to assess the homogeneity of members' perceptions when they are considered to be random (i.e., not occupying specific roles).

Other options, such as multitrait-multisource analyses (cf. Thomas, Shankster & Mathieu, 1994), are available for instances where members' roles are consistent and comparable across teams. Also, Kenny and La Voie (1985) described the use of the intraclass correlations (ICC), where within-team variance is compared to between-team variance, to infer the presence of aggregate level effects. In instances where members or observers fail to demonstrate adequate agreement initially, Kumar, Stern, and Anderson (1993) suggested that they be brought together to reach some form of consensus about the appropriate levels of team attributes.

We should add a note of caution here. The demonstration of high within-team homogeneity in member perceptions of team attributes may not always mean the presence of a team attribute. Kenny and La Voie (1985) stated that the use of the ICC to infer group-level effects necessitates the assumption that team members were initially randomly assigned to teams. In such cases, the variance within teams is equal to the variance between teams—that is, team-level characteristics have not yet emerged. When team members interact, and teams acquire unique qualities and attributes, members' perceptions of these attributes become more similar to one another and less similar to those of members of different teams.

James et al. (1984) argued that using within-team versus between-team comparisons to infer team attributes can be problematic when teams are selected from a common organizational climate. For example, members of different military teams may have common perceptions of their team's attributes, not because of team level influences, but instead because all of the teams share a common environment. James et al. (1984) recommended using interrater agreement indices to avoid this problem. However, if team membership is not formed randomly (as is the case in most naturally occurring teams), then selection biases can create artificial within-team homogeneity (or heterogeneity). For example, in a hospital environment an ad hoc team may be created to assess emergency room procedures and policies. Members may be selected for this team because they (a) work well together, (b) have similar functional perspectives, and/or (c) have similar attitudes about what are appropriate emergency room procedures. This a priori similarity is likely to produce homogeneity in perceptions of team properties that does not result from a history of member interactions, and therefore should not signify a unique property of this team. Thus, the inference of a team attribute follows not only from high within-team homogeneity, but also from some evidence that this homogeneity results from a history of shared team experiences (see, e.g., Zaccaro et al. 1994).

Team performance assessment typically involves the formation of inferences about a team as a whole, its dominant processes, and the quality of its performance. Although data are often collected from each individual team member, conclusions from the data are generalized to the team as a whole. Unfortunately, many team researchers and practitioners will make such generalizations without attending to the empirical criteria necessary to derive aggregate level attributes. Thus, team performance assessment requires consideration not only of the pattern of work arrangements within the team, but also of the patterns of team interactions that signal the existence of meaningful team properties.

THE OPERATION OF MULTIPLE AND SIMULTANEOUS LEVERS IN TEAM ACTION

Because more interdependent forms of team task arrangements are built on less dynamic and interactive work patterns (Cannon-Bowers et al., 1995; Penner & Craiger, 1992), there are often several critical levers that operate to influence team performance. For instance, in order for members of an OR team to be able to fully anticipate the requirements for a complex surgical procedure and to be able to quickly and accurately anticipate each others' actions and needs during the different stages of the operation, all individuals must have the necessary knowledge, skills, and abilities required for their position in the OR team.

These individual-level capabilities are a necessary, but not sufficient, condition for effective team functioning. In other words, in general, the more complex task designs subsume the requirements of the simpler ones, yet introduce further demands. This generalization, however, does not hold completely. For example, the effectiveness of teams operating in sequential or reciprocal task designs can be undermined by the failure of a single individual (i.e., a "weak-link" phenomenon). However, in the demanding and complex intensive settings, there are often opportunities for load shifting or compensatory behaviors such that other teammates might cover or compensate for a given individual's weakness. Nevertheless, the main point here is that the more complex the task demands are on the team, the more likely that any remedial or developmental activity will need to and be multifaceted consider multiple levels of critical levers.

IMPLICATIONS FOR TEAM PERFORMANCE ENHANCEMENT

What implications do our points in this chapter have for improving poorly performing teams? As just described, the team task analysis guides researchers and practitioners to the critical levers that exist for any given type of team. That, in combination with the use of one or more of the assessment strategies discussed, permits the diagnosis of the roots of any performance problem. In all probability, poorly performing teams will be suffering from several decrements, whereas high performing teams will be doing many things well and few things poorly. Thus, there will not likely be a single cure-all or simple response to the question "What do we do?"—the answer will depend on the particular shortcomings of the types of teams in the kinds of situations that one is reviewing.

Some trends, however, are likely to emerge. As illustrated in Table 10.2, teams operating under different task conditions should be more amenable to certain types of human resource programs and performance interventions. For example, pooled/additive team designs place a premium on maximizing aggregate individual performance. Indeed, there is very little "teamness" about this situation. Consequently, programs focused on enhancing individual task-related knowledge, skills, abilities, and other factors (KSAOs), such as selection, training, and task design efforts, will be most suitable here. Motivational programs and leadership behaviors should be designed to facilitate and reward the contributions of individuals. For example, piece-rate compensation or competitive bonus systems tend to maximize individual contributions. Indeed, in these situations organizations are free to adopt policies and practices that maximize aggregate individual contributions even if they lead to a large variance across individuals. Such discrepancies would generally cause coordination problems in more complex task settings.

Teams operating in sequential task settings still ought to have a primary emphasis placed on individual task-related KSAO development. However, some attention should also be focused on facilitating the sequential coordination activities required by this work arrangement. Because the exchanges can be anticipated and are unidirectional, enhancing them is not likely to be a daunting task. It is true, however, that selection, placement, training, and other personnel programs should be designed to minimize "false positives." In other words, teams operating in sequential (as well as

TABLE 10.2
Targeted Human Resource Problems Based on Team Tasks

			Team Tasks		
Human Resource Programs	Pooled/Additive	Sequential	Reciprocal	Intensive	
Selection	Focus on task-related KSAOs Maximize average individual performance	Focus on task-related KSAOs and some coordination skills Maximize false positives Consider placement implications	Focus on task- and team-related KSAOs Consider team composition issues Consider placement implications and maximize "hub" performers	Focus on task- and team-related KSAOs Consider team composition issues Emphasize team competencies Select requisite competencies for the team	
Training	Focus on task-related KSAOs	Focus on task-related KSAOs and some coordination skills Train dyads on their particular exchanges	Focus on task- and team-related KSAOs Train dyads on their particular exchanges Introduce whole-team or part-team training on scripted sequences Consider within-team training	Focus on task- and team-related KSAOs Introduce whole-team training Develop shared mental models of task- and team-work Consider within-team cross-training Foster a team learning environment	

Work Design	Time-in-motion studies Clarify job/role requirements	Minimize bottleneck Work-flow analyses and load balancing JIT approaches	Work-flow analyses and load balancing Sociotechnical approaches Incorporate member monitoring/feedback mechanisms	Sociotechnical approaches Incorporate member monitoring/feedback mechanisms
Motivation	Individual-based incentives (e.g., piece rate) Individual competitions Individualized feedback	Individual-based incentives (e.g., piece rate)	Team-based incentives and feedback Team-building interventions Introduce employee involvement programs	
Leadership		Dyadic approach	Average leadership style	

reciprocal) task settings may be stymied by "weak-link" contributors (Steiner, 1972). It is far better to have several average team members than some "stars" and some "laggards" in these situations. Similarly, work redesign efforts should be targeted at bottlenecks, perhaps by adopting programs such as just-in-time delivery systems and considering redistribution of tasks along the sequence.

Motivation and leadership programs should still emphasize individuals' contributions but also focus on the exchange sequences between members. For example, piece-rate compensation systems may still be applicable, but a portion of the rate should probably be tied to team performance rates. Providing a vehicle for employee input into the sequencing of activities is valuable for these settings. Also, leaders should establish common understandings, or shared mental models, about expected interactional sequences in collective action within teams (Cannon-Bowers et al., 1993). Such shared understandings facilitate team coordination activities, making them more predictable (Minionis, Zaccaro, & Perez, 1995). Further, when directing team actions, leaders need to monitor not only the level of contributions by each individual team member (as would be the case in pooled/additive arrangements) but also how successfully these contributions are "handed-off" across the team.

Reciprocal team tasks place a premium not only on individual task-related KSAOs, but also on team-related KSAOs. Thus, selection systems should assess and weight more heavily those factors that facilitate teamwork and social coordination, some of which have traditionally been labeled *Other* characteristics (e.g., *social intelligence, social values,* and *commitment to others;* Mumford, Zaccaro, Harding, Fleishman, & Reiter-Palmon, 1993; Zaccaro, Gilbert, Thor, & Mumford, 1991) Training interventions should also emphasize the development of both task- and team-related behaviors. Cross-training in other team members' roles may be a particularly beneficial way to build appreciation of the importance of coordinating behaviors. Given the nature of the work flow between members in these settings, as compared to the simpler ones, attention should focus on the exchanges between them. Not only do the exchanges occur more frequently, but now they must be coordinated in multiple directions.

Motivational and leadership efforts should be directed to the team as a whole in these settings. Reward and feedback programs should be based more on team processes and performance, and less on individual outputs. Teams should be empowered and have a much greater degree of control over how their work gets accomplished. Recently, leadership theories have emphasized the critical role of organizational and team leaders in creating such empowerment and galvanizing individuals toward collective and integrated action (Bass, 1985; Tichy & Devanna, 1986). Although this role is applicable to all of the work arrangements outlined in Fig. 10.1, it becomes doubly important as greater integration of member effort is necessary for effective collective performance. In these instances, individual effort and costs may be perceived as higher, personal benefits lower and less tangible. Thus, team leaders need to tie collective goal attainment clearly to team members' personal well-being in order to generate their willingness to contribute the sometimes extraordinary effort needed of integrated action.

Teams operating in intensive designs place a premium on whole team-focused programs. Naturally, the individual members must still possess the requisite task-related KSAOs for the position they occupy, but a greater emphasis is now placed on team-related KSAOs and team synergy. Selection systems should expand to incorporate and weight more highly these team-related skills. Further, the unit of analysis should shift off the traditional individual level to the team level for these settings. For example, it may be important for someone in the team to possess a certain KSAO in order for a team to be successful (e.g., knowledge of a certain procedure or source of information), but that particular KSAO may not be required to successfully perform each of the team roles. In other words, selection systems need to ensure that someone in the team has that KSAO, even though it would be inappropriate to insist that everyone in the team (or any given person) possess it.

Training programs should also shift their focus to the team level of analysis and place greater emphasis on team-related KSAOs. In addition, efforts to establish shared mental models and greater understanding of other teammates' jobs (perhaps through cross-training) should enhance the implicit synergy of the team. Work design efforts should ensure that the team has a clear agenda, time frame, and well-articulated span of influence to better facilitate its effectiveness. These efforts are particularly important in instances where the team operates in a fluid or confusing environment (cf. Hackman, 1990).

Motivational programs should clearly focus on team level processes and outcomes by providing team-level feedback and incentives. Self-directed or autonomous work group designs are most appropriate for teams operating in these settings. Likewise, leadership-based interventions should focus more clearly on enabling self-management functions within-team (Manz & Sims, 1989). Intensive team task arrangements often mean greater diffusion of responsibility for team leadership functions. Such tasks require that members share in problem diagnosis, solution generation, and planning of solution implementation — activities that are often the responsibility of single individuals who occupy team leadership roles in other teamwork arrangements. Thus, performance enhancement for teams working under intensive work arrangements may require training interventions that foster team-centered approaches to leadership (Bradford, 1976; Goodman et al., 1988).

CONCLUSIONS

This chapter emphasizes two factors, teamwork arrangements and levels of analysis, that researchers and practitioners should consider when assessing the performance and processes of teams. Too many researchers erroneously generalize principles and models of individual performance to collective performance, without justifying such a leap. Although issues related to individual performance assessment (e.g., rater biases, criterion properties) are certainly applicable to team performance assessment as well, the latter also requires attention to unique properties and concerns that emerge as one moves from an individual to a team or higher level of aggregation. Team performance assessment requires an analysis, not only of individual attributes and contributions, but also how well the team as a whole combines these contributions.

As shown in this chapter, this analysis begins with an understanding of the structure of work flow within the team that is demanded by team task requirements. Further, different work flow arrangements have separate implications for the influence of individual- versus team-level effects. A fully inclusive approach to team assessment should proceed from the goal of identifying influences and components of collective performance (i.e., the critical levers) that may be operating simultaneously at multiple levels of aggregation. Such an effort would result in more accurate assessment of team performance as well as a more comprehensive approach to team performance enhancement.

REFERENCES

Andrews, D. H., Wang, W. L., & Bell, H. H. (1992). Training technologies applied to team training: Military examples. In R. W. Swezey & E. Salas (Eds.), *Teams: Their training and performance* (pp. 283–328). Norwood, NJ: Ablex.

Bass, B. M. (1985). *Leadership and performance beyond expectations.* New York: Free Press.

Borman, W. C. (1974). The rating of individuals in organizations: An alternative approach. *Organizational Behavior and Human Performance, 12,* 105–124.

Bradford, L. P. (1976). *Making meetings work.* San Diego, CA: University Associates.

Brannick, M. T., Roach, R. M., & Salas, E. (1993). Understanding team performance: A multimethod study. *Human Performance, 6,* 287–308.

Brewer, N., Wilson, C., & Beck, K. (1994). Supervisory behavior and team performance amongst police patrol sergeants. *Journal of Occupational Psychology, 67,* 69–78.

Campbell, D. T., & Fiske, D. W. (1959). Convergent and discriminant validation by the multitrait-multimethod matrix. *Psychological Bulletin, 56,* 81–105.

Cannon-Bowers, J. A., Salas, E., & Converse, S. A. (1993). Shared mental models in expert team decision making. In N. J. Castellan, Jr. (Ed.), *Current issues in individual and group decision making* (pp. 221–246). Hillsdale, NJ: Lawrence Erlbaum Associates.

Cannon-Bowers, J. A., Tannenbaum, S. I., Salas, E., & Volpe, C. E. (1995). Defining competencies and establishing team training requirements. In R. A. Guzzo, E. Salas, & Associates (Eds.), *Team effectiveness and decision making* (pp. 333–380). San Francisco: Jossey-Bass.

Cohen, S. G. (1990). Hilltop hospital top management group. In R. Hackman (Ed.), *Groups that work (and those that don't): creating conditions for effective teamwork* (pp. 36–55). San Francisco: Jossey-Bass.

Cohen, S. G., & Ledford, G. E., Jr. (1994). The effectiveness of self-managing teams: A quasi-experiment. *Human Relations, 47,* 13–43.

Dailey, R. C. (1980). A path analysis of R&D team coordination and performance. *Decision Sciences, 11,* 357–369.

Deluga, R. J. (1991). The relationship of subordinate upward-influencing behavior, health care manager interpersonal stress, and performance. *Journal of Applied Social Psychology, 21,* 78–88.

Denison, D. R., & Sutton, R. I. (1990). Operating room nurses. In R. Hackman (Ed.), *Groups that work (and those that don't) creating conditions for effective teamwork* (pp. 293–308). San Francisco: Jossey-Bass.

Eisenhardt, K. M., & Bourgeois, L. J. III. (1988). Politics of strategic decision making in high-velocity environments: Toward a midrange theory. *Academy of Management Journal, 31,* 737–770.

Fleishman, E. A., & Zaccaro, S. J. (1992). Toward a taxonomy of team performance functions. In R.W. Swezey & E. Salas (Eds.), *Teams: Their training and performance* (pp. 31–56). Norwood, NJ: Ablex.

George, J. M., & James, L. R. (1993). Personality, affect, and behavior groups revisited: Comment on aggregation, levels of analysis, and a recent application of within and between analysis. *Journal of Applied Psychology, 78,* 798–804.

Gladstein, D. L. (1984). Groups in context: A model of task group effectiveness. *Administrative Science Quarterly, 29,* 499–517.

Glickman, A. S., Zimmer, S., Montero, R. C., Guerette, P. J., Campbell, W. J., Morgan, B. B., Jr., & Salas, E. (1987). *The evolution of teamwork skills: An empirical assessment with implications for training* (Tech. Rep. No. 87-016). Orlando, FL: Naval Training Systems Center.

Goodman, P. S. (1986). The impact of task and technology in group performance. In P. S. Goodman (Ed.), *Designing effective work groups* (pp. 120–167). San Francisco: Jossey-Bass.

Goodman, P. S., Devedas, R., & Hughson, T. L. C. (1988). Groups and productivity: Analyzing the effectiveness of self-managing teams. In J. P. Campbell & R. J. Campbell (Eds.), *Productivity in organizations* (pp. 295–327). San Francisco: Jossey-Bass.

Goodman, P. S., Ravlin, E., & Argote, L. (1986). Current thinking about groups: Setting the stage. In P. S. Goodman (Ed.), *Designing effective work groups* (pp. 1–33). San Francisco: Jossey-Bass.

Hackmann, J. R. (1990). *Groups that work (and those that don't): creating conditions for effective teamwork.* San Francisco: Jossey-Bass.

Helmreich, R. L., & Schaefer, H. G. (1994). Team performance in the operating room. In M.

S. Bogner (Ed.), *Human error in medicine*. Hillsdale, NJ: Lawrence Erlbaum Associates.

Hulin, C. L. & Rousseau, D. M. (1980). Analyzing infrequent events: Once you find them your troubles begin. In R. H. Roberts & L. Burnstein (Eds.), *Issues in aggregation: New directions for methodology of social and behavioral science* (Vol. 6). San Francisco: Jossey-Bass.

Inkson, J. H. K., Pugh, D. S., & Hickson, D. J. (1970). Organizational structure and context: An abbreviated replication. *Administrative Science Quarterly, 15*, 318–329.

James, L. R., Demaree, R. G., & Wolf, G. (1984). Estimating within-group interrater agreement. *Journal of Applied Psychology, 69*, 85–98.

James, L. R., Demaree, R. G., & Wolf, G. (1993). r_{wg}: An assessment of within-group interrater agreement. *Journal of Applied Psychology, 78*, 306–310.

Kane, T. D., Marks, M. A., Zaccaro, S. J., & Blair, V. (in press). Applying goal theory to examine athletes' self-regulation and performance. *Journal of Sports and Exercise Psychology*.

Katz, D., & Kahn, R. L. (1978). *The social psychology of organizations* 2nd ed.). New York: Wiley.

Kelly, J. E. (1978). A reappraisal of socio-technical systems theory. *Human Relations, 31*, 1069–1099.

Kenny, D. A., & La Voie, L., (1985). Separating individual and group effects. *Journal of Personality and Social Psychology, 47*, 339–348.

Kozlowski, S. W. J., & Salas, E. (in press). A multilevel organizational systems approach for implementation and transfer of training. In J. K. Ford (Eds.), *Improving training effectiveness in work organizations*. Mahwah, NJ: Lawrence Erlbaum Associates.

Kumar, N., Stern, L. W., & Anderson, J. C. (1993). Conducting interorganizational research using key informants. *Academy of Management Journal, 36*, 1633–1651.

Manz, C., & Sims, H. P. (1989). *Superleadership: Leading others to lead themselves*. Englewood Cliffs, NJ: Prentice-Hall.

Mathieu, J. E. (1991). A cross-level nonrecursive model of the antecedents of organizational commitment and satisfaction. *Journal of Applied Psychology, 76*, 607–618.

Mathieu, J. E., & Day, D. V. (in press). Assessing processes within and between organizational teams: A nuclear power plant example. In M. T. Brannick, E. Salas, & C. Prince (Eds.), *Assessment and measurement of team performance: Theory, methods, and applications*.

Mathieu, J. E., Hofmann, D. A., & Farr, J. L. (1993). Job perception–job satisfaction relations: An empirical comparison of three competing theories. *Organizational Behavior and Human Decision Processes, 56*, 370–387.

McIntyre, R. M., & Salas, E. (1995). Measuring and managing for team performance: Lessons from complex organizations. In R. A. Guzzo, E. Salas, & Associates (Eds.), *Team effectiveness and decision making* (pp. 9–45). San Francisco: Jossey- Bass.

Minionis, D. P., Zaccaro, S. J., & Perez, R. (1995). *Shared mental models, team coordination, and team performance*. Paper presented at the 10th annual meeting of the Society for Industrial and Organizational Psychology, Orlando, FL.

Mirvis, P. H. (1980). Assessing physical evidence, documents, and records in organizations. In E. E. Lawler, II, D. A. Nadler, & C. Cammann (Eds.), *Organizational assessment*. New York: Wiley.

Morgan, B. B., Jr., Salas, E., & Glickman, A. S. (1993). An analysis of team evolution and maturation. *The Journal of General Psychology, 120*, 277–291.

Mumford, M. D., Zaccaro, S. J., Harding, F. D., Fleishman, E. A., & Reiter-Palmon, R. (1993). *Cognitive and temperament predictors of executive ability: Principles for developing leadership capacity*. Alexandria, VA: U.S. Army Research Institute for Behavioral and Social Sciences.

Murninghan, J. K., & Conlon, D. E. (1991). The dynamics of intense work groups: A study of British string quartets. *Administrative Science Quarterly, 36,* 165–186.

Pasmore, W., Francis, C., Haldeman, J., & Shani, A. (1982). Sociotechnical systems: A North American reflection on empirical studies of the seventies. *Human Relations, 35,* 1179–1204.

Penner, L. A., & Craiger, J. P. (1992). The weakest link: The performance of individual team members. In R. W. Swezey & E. Salas (Eds.), *Teams: Their training and performance* (pp. 130–141). Norwood, NJ: Ablex.

Pritchard, R. D., Jones, S. D., Roth, P. L., Steubing, K. L., & Ekberg, S. E. (1988). Effects of group feedback, goal setting, and incentives on organizational productivity. *Journal of Applied Psychology, 73,* 337–358.

Roberts, K. H., Hulin, C. L., & Rousseau, D. M. (1978). *Developing an interdisciplinary science of organizations.* San Francisco: Jossey-Bass.

Rouse, W. B., Cannon-Bowers, J. A., & Salas, E. (1992). The role of mental models in team performance in complex systems. *IEEE Transactions on Systems, Man, and Cybernetics, 22,* 1296–1308.

Rousseau, D. M. (1985). Issues of level in organizational research: Multi-level and cross-level perspectives. In L. L. Cummings & B. Staw (Eds.), *Research in organizational behavior.* (Vol. 7, pp. 1–38). Greenwich, CT: JAI Press.

Shaw, R. B. (1976). *Group dynamics: the psychology of small group behavior.* (2nd ed.). New York: McGraw-Hill.

Shaw, R. B. (1990). Mental health treatment teams In J. R. Hackman (Ed.), *Groups that work (and those that don't): creating conditions for effective teamwork* (pp. 330–348). San Francisco: Jossey-Bass.

Sirotnik, K. A. (1980). Psychometric implications of the unit of analysis problem (with examples from the measurement of organizational climate). *Journal of Educational Measurement, 17,* 245–282.

Steiner, I. (1972). *Group process and productivity.* New York: Academic Press.

Sundstrom, E., De Meuse, K. P, & Futrell, D. (1990). Work teams: Applications and effectiveness. *American Psychologist, 45,* 120–133.

Tesluk, P. E., Vance, R. J., & Mathieu, J. E. (1994). Examining employee involvement practices in the context of a participative work environment: A multi-level approach. In R. J. Vance (Chair), *Organizational, group, and individual determinants of employee involvement program success.* Symposium conducted at the annual meeting of the Academy of Management, Dallas, TX.

Thomas, J. B., Shankster, L. J., & Mathieu, J. F. (1994). Antecedents to organizational issue interpretation: The roles of single-level, cross-level, and content cues. *Academy of Management Journal, 37,* 1252–1284.

Thompson, J. D. (1967). *Organizations in action.* New York: McGraw-Hill.

Tichy, N., & DeVanna, M. A. (1986). *Transformational leadership.* New York: Wiley.

Tornow, W. W. (1993). Perceptions or reality: Is multi-perspective measurement a means or an end? *Human Resource Management, 32,* 221–229.

Tziner, A., & Eden, D. (1985). Effects of crew composition on crew performance: Does the whole equal the sum of the parts? *Journal of Applied Psychology, 70,* 85–93.

Van de Ven, A. H., & Ferry, D. L. (1980). *Measuring and assessing organizations.* New York: Wiley-Interscience.

Watson, W., Michaelsen, L. K., & Sharp, W. (1991). Member competence, group interaction, and group decision making: A longitudinal study. *Journal of Applied Psychology, 76,* 803–809.

Weick, K. E. (1979). *The social psychology of organizing.* New York: Random House.

Yank, G. R., Barber, J. W., & Spradlin, W. W. (1994). Mental health treatment teams and leadership: A systems model. *Behavioral Science, 39,* 293–310.

Zaccaro, S. J., Gilbert, J. A., Thor, K. K., & Mumford, M. D. (1991). Leadership and social intelligence: Linking social perceptiveness to behavioral flexibility. *Leadership Quarterly, 2,* 317–347.

Zaccaro, S. J., Zazanis, M., Diana, M., & Greathouse, C. (1994, April). *The antecedents of collective efficacy over a team's lifespan.* Paper presented at the 9th annual meeting of the Society for Industrial and Organizational Psychology, Nashville, TN.

IV APPLICATIONS

11

Behind the Scenes: Fieldtesting a Measure of Effectiveness for Theater Teams

Judith L. Komaki
Baruch College
City University of New York

> It's very hard for us . . . to come to terms with the fact that our most public feedback may literally have little or nothing to do with our own efforts
>
> — Arvin Brown, former Artistic Director, Long Wharf Theatre, New Haven

Arvin Brown vents his frustration at the way in which he and other theater professionals are typically evaluated. He said:

> I mean, if it were a matter of being damned for what you can't do well and being praised for doing what you do well, as much as anyone hates to be criticized, one could live with it far more easily. . . . Very often you're overpraised (by critics) for things that you know damned well don't represent you or the other artists at their best, and you can be cruelly taken to task for things that are simply not true. (Bartow, 1988, p. 34)

Teams putting on theater productions, launching satellites, or doing open-heart surgery are sights to behold. Yet, our knowledge of how to enhance and measure these efforts borders on the archaic. In the past two decades, reviewers of the group literature have concluded that "although literally thousands of studies of group performance have been conducted, . . . we still know very little about why some groups are more effective than others. We know even less about what to do to improve the performance of a given group working on a specific task" (Hackman & Morris, 1975, p. 2).

227

In a subsequent review, Hackman and Morris (1978) bemoaned that "there has hardly been a pouring forth of conceptual and empirical attacks on the group effectiveness problem" (p. 58). Six years later, Dyer (1984) concluded that "despite all of the small-group research that has been conducted, one sometimes feels that, in fact, this is all we know: It's just teamwork" (p. 294). In 1986, Goodman and his colleagues expressed chagrin about the "dearth of information about permanent groups in organizations," estimating the number of research studies to be "limited to an average of about 12 studies per year" (p. 22). Bettenhausen (1991) admitted that "managers are often exasperated by what they see as the irrelevant outcomes of scholarly research," but his prospects are limited to promises of what new scholars *may* do. In the present volume, the chapters by Brannick and Prince and Salas and Baker reveal similar sentiments.

LACKING SUITABLE MEASURES OF GROUP EFFECTIVENESS

Among the reasons for the disappointing lack of progress is the failure to develop suitable measures of effectiveness. Despite the fact that practitioners and academics alike agree about the importance of well-functioning teams (Blake, Mouton, & Allen, 1987; Levine & Moreland, 1990; McGrath, 1984; Mitchell, 1982), relatively little attention has been paid to what can be done to develop better criterion measures of effectiveness about "permanent groups in organizations" (Goodman et al., 1986, p. 2).

The bulk of the writing about the criterion problem is nonempirical. News of findings are scarce in comparison with words of advice. Furthermore, many of the recommendations are vague. Binning and Barrett (1989), after an extensive review, concluded that "perhaps the greatest advancement for the science of personnel psychology will come only when the values driving organizational administrators' decisions about behavioral science research are changed" (p. 490). Exactly what these changes should be and how they will affect what we do, however, they do not identify. Other authors recommended guidelines (e.g., Baker & Salas, 1992; Blum & Naylor, 1968; Campbell, Dunnette, Lawler, & Weick, 1970) or standards (Hackman, 1987), but with the exception of behaviorally based checklists, examples in which the recommendations are implemented are rare.

Unfortunately, Georgopoulos and Mann's (1962) contention that mere "lip service" has been paid to "coordination as an organizational problem" (p. 597) is still, unfortunately, true today. Although Hackman and Morris (1978) pointed out that "group members are particularly likely to be working interdependently on complex tasks — especially when (as is usually the case) the group is located in an organizational milieu" (p. 61), the bulk of the research in work settings has *not* dealt with these interdependent tasks (McGrath, 1986).

Moreover, the typical study of teams in ongoing organizations includes only predictor variables about the team's inputs—for instance, group norms, team composition. Researchers sometimes look at the group's process—such as the interactions of group members. But what is generally missing is the criterion variable or outcome of the team. Rarely is it reported in studies of team-building (cited in Bettenhausen, 1991) how the teams fared against one another. When outcomes of group effectiveness do exist, they are traditionally limited to nonrealistic contexts with "ad hoc groups which are convened for such a short time that the group does not have a chance to develop its own history or its own unique normative structure" (Hackman & Morris, 1975, p. 59). Even when positive results are found, questions are raised about the external validity of their findings (Guzzo & Shea, 1992).

Outcomes of group effectiveness in work settings (as enumerated in Schmitt and Klimoski's detailed chapter about the effectiveness of groups [1991]), are categorized as (a) objective indices—for instance, Komaki, Desselles, and Bowman's (1989) win-loss records of racing crews; (b) subjective ratings such as Tziner and Eden's (1985) ranking of tank crews by their commanding officers; and (c) assessments of emotional tone—for example, Campion, Medsker, and Higgs' (1993) measure of employee satisfaction. Although these criteria have been used to reflect the outcomes of teams, many complaints have been lodged. McGrath (1986) ended his chapter on groups at work by lamenting that "we have a powerful array of sophisticated tools for data processing and analysis. They are, if anything, too strong for the data we usually feed them. We need better data to put into them" (p. 365). Three specific problems exist.

The first criticism, highlighted by the Artistic Director, Arvin Brown, concerns the *unresponsiveness* of many of the indices to the efforts of the entire team. The second problem involves the *incompleteness* of many of the measures in reflecting the intricacies of the process and the outcome of teams working on interdependent tasks (as noted by Schmitt & Klimoski [1991]). The third objection deals with the perennial *unreliability* of raters with different perceptions and expectations (as identified by Dyer [1984] in her review of 20 years of group studies).

MEASUREMENT CHALLENGES IN THE NONPROFIT SECTOR

These criterion problems are painfully evident in the nonprofit sector (Alexander, 1980; Anthony, Deardon, & Bedford, 1989; Gies, Ott, &

Shafritz, 1990; Powell, 1987). In nonprofit organizations such as symphony orchestras, universities, and most non-Broadway theater companies, the absence of the profit motive complicates the assessment process. The principal goal of many nonprofit organizations is the rendering of service; an elusive and difficult-to-quantify aim to measure. In contrast, in the for-profit sector, the "bottom line" provides a metric by which to judge how well the team is doing. Moreover, the fact that professionals tend to predominate in nonprofit organizations complicates matters further. Professionals, by the nature of their tasks, do not lend themselves to being assessed using typical outcome measures. Hence, the fact that so few models exist for assessing teams in the nonprofit sector is not surprising.

All of these problems are particularly true in the theater community. An acceptable measure of effectiveness is not only problematic, but skeptics question whether effectiveness can even be quantified (Langley, 1990). "Theatre is notoriously collaborative," Jones (1986, p. 6), a director, contends. "Weeks, months, and sometimes years elapse between the initial doodling or dreaming and the final technical rehearsals with their split-second electronic calibrations" (p. 6). With circumstances constantly changing and deadlines looming, he contends that "the director's world is . . . resistant to coherent intellectual or critical treatment" (p. 6). Furthermore, theater productions themselves are elusive. Before 8 p.m., they never existed and after midnight, as one director describes, they turn "into vapor" (Jones, 1986, p. 10). Hence, a formidable challenge is to capture the quality of the "product" being delivered.

Another daunting challenge to the measurement process is the fact that putting on a production involves a variety of highly skilled professionals. The director interprets the play and works with cast members to bring his or her interpretation to fruition. The director also works with designers who have their own visions. A director, David Belasco (1963), described how he works, beginning with the scenic designer, and how the scenic designer takes the empty stage and makes sketches of the scenes. Once the scenes are set, then comes the lighting of the scenes and the "evolving [of] our colors by transmitting white light through gelatin or silk of various hues. Night after night we [Belasco and the lighting designer] experiment together" (p. 127). One lighting designer, Allen Lee Hughes, described how he lit *Fantasio* like a fairy tale: "We have attempted here to heighten the presentational effect by layering the lighting, with wash for color and highlights on the soldiers and the ballerina . . ." (Pearce, 1993, p. 26).

Moreover, producing a play provides an excellent example of a team doing an interdependent task (Clurman, 1972). Interdependence, in this case, means that crew members must coordinate together in order to accomplish the task. Thompson (1967) referred to these tasks as serially or reciprocally interdependent rather than pooled in which team members make independent contributions to the whole. David Ives (1995), a playwright, described the process:

> Over weeks of planning, weeks of rehearsal and weeks of performance, all the people in that group have to agree. This doesn't mean. . . . they don't have political and philosophical or racial and religious differences. It doesn't mean there isn't a hierarchy of power. . . . It doesn't mean everyone is equal in talent. It means that all those people have to work together and negotiate decisions and delegate authority together, whether they like one another or not, in the interest of some agreed-upon greater good. (p. H 13)

Because of the interdependence involved in putting on a production, theater teams were sought out as subjects of a study conducted under the auspices of the Army Research Institute. The purpose of the research was to identify how leaders such as directors promoted tasks requiring coordination among group members. One requirement of being in the study was that the group had to be composed of two or more people who are "mutually aware of one another and are potentially in interaction with one another" (McGrath, 1984). The group must also have some continuity over time so that the "relationships have, or quickly acquire, some history and some anticipated future" (McGrath, 1984). Another requirement was that the group be hierarchically based in which one member was identified, from the onset of the task, as the leader; in this case, it was the director in charge of the production. The last condition was that the group must be performance-based and doing what Hackman and Walton (1986) referred to as "real work" (ranging from conducting a mission to actually producing things) in a purposive social system (p. 73).

REACTIONS BY THE THEATER COMMUNITY TO THE TRADITIONAL MEASURES OF EFFECTIVENESS

To study theater teams, it was necessary to identify a suitable index of effectiveness. Not surprisingly, however, none of the current indices of effectiveness generates much enthusiasm in the theater community: (a) critics' reviews of the production; (b) ticket sales; (c) awards such as Tonys and Obies given for direction, acting, and technical aspects such as costumes, set design, lighting, and sound effects, and, lastly, within the theater community itself; (d) peer; (e) cast; (f) crew; and (g) designer evaluations. Ball (1984), when he directs, likes "to project for the actors some standard by which we all, the ensemble, may consider ourselves successful at the outcome" (p. 103). Among those he recommends are "a good time working together" or exploring "Chekhov's technique of indirect action to the fullest" (p. 103). Particularly pertinent to our discussion here is what he does not recommend: the measure of success will *not* be "rave critical notices, nor box-office success. Nor will the measure of success be a production that runs for three years and has five touring companies" (p. 103). The same three problems—the lack of responsiveness, the incompleteness, and the unreliability of raters—surfaced again and again when examining these traditional measures of effectiveness.

Lack of Responsiveness

> *. . . a crap shoot.*
> —Arvin Brown, Artistic Director

The major complaint with indices such as critics' reviews and ticket sales is that they are "excessive . . .beyond what the manager can do himself to affect outcome" (Campbell et al., 1970, p. 107). The artistic director, Arvin Brown, readily admits he doesn't like being evaluated. At the same time, he doesn't feel he's been unduly battered by critics. But he has strong reservations when the indices are *not under the control* of the team. Likening the evaluation process to a "crap shoot," Brown bemoaned that ". . . our most public feedback may literally have little or nothing to do with our own efforts" (Bartow, 1988, p. 34). Other directors point to the same lack of responsiveness in the way in which they are evaluated. Andrei Serban claimed that if he were to do a traditional piece in a nontraditional way, "critics would tear me to pieces" (Bartow, 1988, p. 294). Peter Sellers contended challenges to the audience are "not allowed in new plays by reviewers. There is this odd notion that everything in the theater should be . . . smoothly digestible, . . . like a McDonald's milk shake that will not melt in the sun" (Bartow, 1988, p. 277).

Even indices like Tony or Obie awards are affected by extraneous factors such as whether the shows are open or closed. One disgruntled nominator for the Tony awards complained about some of his fellow nominators who were reluctant to nominate shows that had closed: "Are there people working on Broadway who are so obsessed with profits that they are not only willing but eager to ignore artistic merit unless it also means big bucks?" (Witchel, 1992, p. C2). As the artistic director of the Lincoln Center Theater, Andre Bishop has had plays close for contractual reasons just as nominations are being made on major awards. He charged: "Artistic excellence and economic well-being do not always go hand in hand. It doesn't seem fair that a play's excellence be based on whether it is still open or has closed" (Witchel, 1992, p. C2). Shows close for many reasons such as the schedule of the theater and the actors, the advertising, the choice of the play, and the economy, precious few of which are related to the efforts of the entire team. To better reflect the team's efforts, the focus should be on a measure that includes aspects that the team can more readily control.

Problems Reflecting Complexity

> . . .*a sculpture in motion.*
> —Marshall W. Mason, Director

The second reservation about the measures of effectiveness in theater concerns the extent to which the group as a whole is reflected, what Campbell et al. (1970) referred to as the "sampling of the job behavior domain" (p. 111). The adequacy of the sampling of the group is particularly germane with theater teams because of the *intricacies* of putting up a show. The former artistic director of Arena Stage in Washington, DC, Zelda Fichandler, talks about how she "leads the other contributing artists— designers, composers, actors—to find their keys [to the play], harmonious with her own." She discusses how they "make it specific in terms of their own special domains: light, sound, environment, behavior" (Bartow, 1988, p. 114). Another director, Marshall Mason, referred to "the concept of directing as a sculpture in motion" (Bartow, 1988, p. 198). Along the same lines, Lloyd Richards, renown for his direction of August Wilson's plays, goes so far as to liken the act of directing to "Picasso's painting, Guernica. The many components of that genius reflected themselves in just where each little or big element existed in that picture—what shapes they began to take, where they appeared before they were finally in the right place, in the right color . . ." (Bartow, 1988, p. 259).

Criticisms have been lodged against seemingly straightforward but sterile measures. Hackman (1987) holds that "most organizational tasks do not have clear right-or-wrong answers, for example, nor do they lend themselves to quantitative measures that validly indicate how well a group has done its work. Moreover, one needs to be concerned about more than raw productivity or decision quality" (p. 323). In fact, he recommends using a three-part evaluation system, composed of system-defined rather than researcher-defined assessments of a group's output, as well as social and personal criteria. Highlighting the importance of the group and their working conducively together, he argues for including the team members and their process of interactions as vital components in the evaluation process. Schmitt and Klimoski (1991) agreed on the significance of including more than one viewpoint when evaluating teams. In fact, to more sensitively reflect the entire team's efforts, they recommend that the evaluation should be made by multiple interested constituencies.

Disagreements Among Raters

> . . .*his own ax to grind, his own vendettas and resentments.*
> — Rocco Landesman, President of Jujamcyn Theaters

A final misgiving about the traditional indices of effectiveness concerns the lack of agreement among the raters. Rocco Landesman describes theater professionals as a diverse group, each with "his own ax to grind, his own vendettas and resentments" (Witchel, 1992, p. C2). It would not be surprising to see that casts, technical crews, designers, and directors might have different expectations. Lighting designers would probably have a different perspective about a production than the cast. Even within groups, disagreements are common. In compiling interviews with professional directors in the U.S., Arthur Bartow (1988) ruefully noted:

> even among those directors whose belief systems are similar, the work of each has its distinctness. Together, they serve to prove that there is no "correct" method of directing. As soon as one points to a director whose technique results in success, one can then look to another director whose method contradicts the first and whose work is also recognized as significant. (p. xii)

To ensure that the evaluation not be subject to "response sets, chance response tendencies, and differing expectations of observers" (Campbell et al., 1970), it would be important to return to the traditional psychometric concern for interrater reliability.

In short, as we have seen, teamwork is readily acknowledged as being a key factor in the success of any group effort. Unfortunately, few indices exist identifying the effectiveness of teams particularly those doing interdependent tasks. When evaluating theater teams, three complaints predominate. The first involves the method — in this case, the interrater reliability — of the evaluations. The other two problems concern the content of the index — how well what is measured reflects the complexity of putting on a clean, tight show and how much the index is under the control of the team itself.

What Is Needed: Criteria for Criteria

In response to the problems of method and content in the traditional measures of team effectiveness, we propose 3 criteria. Just as we can have criteria for selecting restaurants (e.g., a rating above 20 for food quality in Zagat's *Restaurant Survey*) or for identifying estimators in classical statistical theory (e.g., lack of bias, small variance, linearity), so we can have principles for criterion variables, what Weitz (1961) refers to as *criteria for criteria*. The advantage of these criteria for criteria is that they can be used to constructively judge existing criterion variables and improve future ones.

Tailored to Assessments of Team Effectiveness

Not just any criteria will do, however. The criteria must be tailored to the particular population, in this case teams, and the particular task, in this case, interdependent ones. If one were limiting the measurement to independent tasks, then it might not be necessary to include criteria that addressed this aspect of the task. At the same time, if one were primarily interested in a descriptive study of the team, it might be sufficient to have criteria such as mutual exclusivity (i.e., ensuring the categories are non-overlapping) and exhaustiveness (i.e., identifying each and every behavior the crew does; Fleishman & Quaintance, 1984). However, when one wants to measure the performance-based nature of the work the team is doing together, then the criteria must be tailored to reflect this aim.

About What Is Measured

The criteria should shed light on what should be measured. As discussed earlier, questions about *what* to address have been raised: Is it adequate to reflect the complexities of the group relying on a single perspective such as that of the critic? Should the team be appraised on more than a single aspect? If so, what different aspects should be included? Does it matter that ticket sales are largely out of the hands of the team?

About How Effectiveness Is Measured

The criteria should also reflect *how* the data are obtained. As we have seen, even within the same constituency, in this case directors, disagreements occur in assessing a given team. A major issue is what can be done to shore up the interrater reliability among raters so that an evaluation is not subject to the idiosyncratic perceptions and response sets of a particular coder.

A NEW SET OF CRITERIA FOR CRITERIA: CRU

We propose 3 criteria for criterion variables. Like a good white wine, the criteria can be referred to by the mnemonic CRU:

C: Reflects the *complexity* of the team's effort. The intricacy can be expressed in a variety of ways — by including both the product and the process of the team (Hackman, 1987), multiple constituencies (Schmitt & Klimoski, 1991), and/or the part(s) of the task requiring coordination among team members for successful completion (Komaki et al., 1989).

R: Indicates that independent raters consistently agree on their recordings and obtain interrater *reliability* scores of 90% or better during the formal data collection period.

U: Is primarily *under* the control of the team, responsive to their efforts, and minimally affected by extraneous factors.

Two standards (C, U) deal with substance, and one (R) with the method used in assessing effectiveness. Two criteria (R, U) can be seen in the author's earlier work (Komaki, Collins, & Temlock, 1987); one (C) is discussed here for the first time.

To illustrate how and why to use the CRU criteria, an example follows. Although the illustration takes place in a particular setting, the CRU criteria can be applied to a variety of teams doing a variety of interdependent tasks.

DEVELOPING A CRITERION USING THE CRU CRITERIA: THE THEATER TEAMWORK EFFECTIVENESS MEASURE

The Theater Teamwork Effectiveness Measure (TTEM) is an index of the success of a team in putting up a theater production.

TTEM Aspects

The TTEM includes three aspects: (a) excellence in execution, (b) fulfillment of the staff's vision, and (c) factors affecting the morale of the group. The three aspects of execution, vision, and morale are calculated and aggregated for a TTEM score, as shown in Table 11.1.

Excellence in execution refers to the percentage of production elements deemed to be in line with the standard operating procedures (SOP) of any theater production. The SOP are the production elements audience members expect to be in place when viewing a play. Audiences assume, for example, that the lights and sound will be in synchrony with the action of the play. Other elements include the set, costumes, props, and the curtain/bows at the end. For example, the lighting was judged unsatisfactory when the lights came on too late after an actor flipped a light switch or when the blackout lights at the beginning of the play were on for longer for 5 seconds.

TABLE 11.1
Calculation and Aggregation of Theater Teamwork
Effectiveness Measure (TTEM)

Excellence in Execution (E%)

$E\% = \frac{E1}{E2} \times 100$

where:

E1 = # of production elements (e.g., lights, sound,
      costumes) judged satisfactory (+)

   = # +

E2 = sum of # of elements judged satisfactory (+) and # of
      unsatisfactory (−)

   = (# +) + (# −)

Fulfillment of the Staff's Vision (V%)

$V\% = \frac{V1}{V2} \times 100$

where:

V1 = # of visions implemented

V2 = # of visions expressed

Factors Affecting Group Morale (M%)

M% = (p% + g%) − (o%)

where:

$p\% = \frac{p1}{p2} \times 100$

   p1 = # of mins. productively (p) spent during rehearsal

      = total # of mins. of rehearsal (p2) minus # of mins.
        in which the rehearsal is delayed from the
        scheduled beginning time (dt) or from breaks (db)
        or from outbursts (dd)

      = p2 − (#dt + #db + #dd)

   p2 = total # of mins. of rehearsal (from scheduled
        beginning to actual end)

o% = # of outbursts (o) times 10%

   = #o × 10%

g% = # of gracious remarks (g) times 5%

   = #g × 5%

Theater Teamwork Effectiveness Measure (TTEM)

TTEM = E% × V% × M%

A portion of the execution data sheet is shown in Table 11.2; each element
is judged satisfactory (+), unsatisfactory (−), or not applicable (NA)
during each 15 minutes of the production. For the many ways the elements
were judged unsatisfactory, refer to Table 11.3. The execution score is
calculated as the number of production elements judged satisfactory/the
total number of production elements judged or the number of elements
deemed satisfactory or unsatisfactory.

The *fulfillment of the staff's vision* is defined as the percentage of staff's
visions that are implemented. There may be many ways to furnish a room

TABLE 11.2
TTEM Data Sheet for Excellence in Execution

Date __/__/__ Production _____ Primary coder _____ Rel _____

Circle + for satisfactory, − for unsatisfactory[1] or NA (not applicable).[2] Score during each 15-min. period. Describe if unsatisfactory.

1–15 minutes
+ −NA Lights _____
+ −NA Sound _____
+ −NA Set _____
+ −NA Costumes _____
+ −NA Props _____
+ −NA Curtain/bow/other _____

15–29 minutes
+ −NA Lights _____
+ −NA Sound _____
+ −NA Set _____
+ −NA Costumes _____
+ −NA Props _____
+ −NA Curtain/bow/other _____

Excellence in Execution score (E%) = # of production elements (e.g., lights, sound) judged satisfactory (+)/# satisfactory (+) # unsatisfactory (−) × 100.

[1]Refer to Table 11.3 for definitions and elements.

[2]Some elements such as the curtain or bows were limited to specific times during the production; at other times they were checked as not applicable.

or clothe a character, but only a few that express the way the staff wants the show to look and feel. The staff's visions refer to these discretionary wishes about the desired look, sound, and "feel" of the production. The staff could include the director, the lighting, sound, set, and costume designers, as well as the cast and technical crew.

A vision was counted when it was expressed and agreed on during the technical or tech rehearsal. A vision that was implemented was accomplished, typically the next night, during the dress rehearsal. For example, at the tech rehearsal, the director might suggest a layer of wet ocher mud on the bottom one eighth of an actor's dress. When the coder saw this suggestion had been realized at the dress rehearsal, it was coded as a vision that had been implemented. A portion of the vision data sheet is shown in Table 11.4; on the sheet, the coder first lists expressed visions, and then identifies whether or not it was implemented. The vision score is calculated as the number of successfully implemented visions/the number of expressed visions.

Group morale consists of three subaspects identified by members of the theater community as affecting the morale of the group: (a) the time productively spent, (b) outbursts, and (c) gracious acts. Higher morale was

TABLE 11.3
TTEM Definitions and Examples of Unsatisfactory Execution of Production Elements

Lights

House
1. Timing: Blackout for longer than 5 seconds.
2. Inappropriate: Ghosting (lights not turned down all the way).

Stage
   a. *Specials out of sync with action:* For instance, actor flips a light switch and the light is delayed *or* comes on before the switch is touched.
   b. *Not following action:* Lights come up on the actor/location after the focus of attention has switched to another spot.
   c. *Late cue:* Lights abruptly moved to actor after she has begun speaking.
2. Inappropriate:
   a. *Worklights visible:* Worklights seen backstage, in wings, or off-stage.
   b. *Abrupt up-and-down:* Lights come up and suddenly go down especially on part of stage where no action is taking place.
   c. *Sudden change:* Level abruptly changes (up or down) without clear indication from the action of its appropriateness.

Equipment
1. Inappropriate:
   a. *Messy:* Stray, low hanging cable, for example, that looks like it might fall.
   b. *Obstructive:* An impediment such as a cable in front of another instrument's light beam.
   c. *Misfocused:* For example, a stage light shining in the audience's eyes or lighting a wall of the seating area.

Sound

1. Missing or incomplete:
   a. *Absent reference:* Sound referred to in the text is not made (e.g., not a single hoot before the line "Even the owls are restless tonight").
   b. *Sound-making props don't sound:* For instance, the phone doesn't ring or the doorbell doesn't buzz.
2. Timing
   a. *Too soon:* Sound cue that inappropriately covers dialogue.
   b. *Too late:* Pause between reference and the start or stop of the sound.
   c. *Misplaced:* Illogical sound from props (e.g., actress talking on the phone and phone rings).
   d. *Start/stop/restart:* Abrupt stopping and restarting of same sound or music without transition such as actors staring to speak or house lights coming on.
3. Inappropriate:
   a. *Too loud:* Level covers dialogue or causes pain to listeners.
   b. *Too soft:* Sound only faintly heard when should be more audible.
   c. *Equipment noise:* Feedback, audible tape hiss, or props occur when sound starts or stops.
   d. *Wrong Sound:* Referenced sound is not the one heard (e.g., "Even the owls are restless tonight" and frogs croak).

(Continued)

TABLE 11.3 (*Continued*)

Set

1. Missing or incomplete:
   a. *Masking missing:* Backstage or wings inappropriately visible.
   b. *Set element missing:* Actors mime door opening instead of having actual door to use.
   c. *Wet paint:* Actors skirting some portion of set because the paint is not dry.
2. Inappropriate:
   a. *Prevents action from taking place as directed:* For example, door does not open or does not stay shut.
   b. *Breaks during use:* Banister falls off wall when actor grabs it for normal support, for instance.
   c. *Causes injury to people or things:* For example, actor scrapes arm or costume catches on protruding screw head.

Costumes

1. Missing or incomplete:
   a. *Absent reference:* Piece referred to is not present (e.g., reference to beard on clean-shaven actor; reference to hair on bald actor).
   b. *Obvious substitution:* Out-of-period piece of clothing substituted for correct one.
   c. *Unfinished:* For example, sleeve starts unraveling: unhemmed edges of skirt or coat visible but not appropriate for character.
   d. *Insufficiently constructed:* Tears apart at seams in normal use.
2. Timing
   a. *Costume change takes too long:* Actor appears on stage incompletely costumed or finishes fastening costume piece; actor makes late entrance in new costume when others are already in place.
3. Inappropriate:
   a. *Prevents action from taking place as directed:* Restricts movement otherwise expected, including exists.

Props

1. Missing or incomplete.
   a. *Absent:* Actors miming use of item referred to in dialogue or otherwise indicated.
   b. *Insufficiently constructed:* Falls apart in normal use.
2. Inappropriate:
   a. *Obvious substitution:* Prop in use does not match references made in dialogue (e.g., a different size or color).
   b. *Prevents action from taking place as directed:* For instance, book does not open for actor to look in; bottle is empty when actor needs to pour.

Scene Changes

1. Timing:
   a. *Too soon:* For example, the change begins while actors are still speaking; before lights change to worklights or blackout; or before the curtain is completely down (feet visible).
   b. *Too long:* Covering music or sound runs out before change is completed (e.g., the change is completed in silence of 15 seconds); actors are on stage and beginning next scene before change is completed; curtain rises with technicians still on stage.
   c. *Too late:* 15 seconds or more with worklights on empty stage before change starts.

(*Continued*)

TABLE 11.3 (*Continued*)

2. Inappropriate:
   a. *Too loud:* Sounds indicating bumping, dropping, breaking, talking, or walking are heard.
   b. *When visible, not fluid:* Movement is not continuous throughout.
   c. *When visible, confused:* For example, technicians shift pieces more than twice after placing them or run into one another.

Curtain call / final bow

1. Timing
   a. *Too late:* For instance, an empty stage in which the curtain call lights and sound are up, but no actors are on the stage.
   b. *Too soon:* Light change to curtain call and curtain call sound starts before the actions ends.
2. Inappropriate:
   a. *Confused:* For example, actors are running or bumping into each other on entrances and/or exists.
   b. *Not coordinated with front-of-house:* House lights are up full before stage lights are down and actors have cleared the stage.

thought to occur when a relatively small percentage of the rehearsal time was spent in a nonproductive way, when outbursts were nonexistent or kept to a minimum, and when an occasional gracious act occurred.

The first subaspect of group morale, the percentage of time productively spent, was calculated as the number of minutes productively spent/number of minutes of rehearsal. Productive was defined as the number of minutes of rehearsal minus the number of minutes of delays following the scheduled start time and scheduled break ending(s), as well as time spent in outbursts.

The second subaspect was the number of "outbursts." Outbursts occurred when a team member, usually in a supervisory role, expressed displeasure. Only expressions that resulted in a stopping of the work flow of persons by persons not directly involved in the vicinity were counted. Outbursts could involve yelling, walking out, or gesturing. They could also be calm and lower in tone such as the director pausing and asking calmly for waiting actors and actresses to be quiet so the stage manager can hear the cues. The important thing is that persons other than the actors and the director stopped their work. If the crew working on the lights paused, this constituted an outburst.

The third subaspect was the number of "gracious acts." Graciousness occurred when any team member was recognized for facilitating the efforts of the team. To count, the gracious act had to be delivered directly rather than indirectly, it had to occur publicly rather than privately, and it had to be clearly positive as judged by the nature of the act or by context. Some examples would be a lighting designer expressing appreciation after an actress had repeated a tough scene four times or the production manager

TABLE 11.4
TTEM Data Sheet for Visions Fulfilled

Date __/__/__ Production _____ Primary coder _____ Rel _____
Write verbatim statements[1] about technical problems/issues/concerns/discrepancies
  expressed in which the staff agrees it can be done by dress rehearsal.[2]

Time Expressed vision about li/sp/se/pr/co/c/cc[3]
__ : __ _____
_____
_____
_____

Only relative ("louder") _____ Who identified?[4]: D TF SM LD SD CD Act
Implemented: +?-?[5] _____
_____
_____

Vision score (V%) = # visions implemented / # visions expressed.

[1]More specific, the better: time (ghosting at *top,* light switch *throughout*), cue (missing when *criminals apporoaching*), location/scene (chandelier missing in *living room*), role (sweater too baggy on *female lead*).

[2]Whether the vision is doable is often implied. Assume this is the case in the absence of any discussion to the contrary.

[3]Production elements: li = lighting, so = sound, co = costumes, se = set, pr = props, c = curtain, cc = curtain call.

[4]Staff: D = director, TD = technical director, SM = stage manager, LD = lighting, SD = sound, CD = costume designer, Act = actor.

[5]Implemented: + = yes (1), ? = yes but (.5), − = no (0).

thanking actresses specifically for their patience in repeating their entrance at the start of the show. Perfunctory "thank you's" did not count.

In computing the morale score, outbursts were weighted at −10% apiece and were subtracted, whereas gracious acts were valued at +5% and were added . The total morale score, not to exceed 100%, was the sum of the Productive Time % and the Gracious Act %, minus the Outburst %, as shown in Tables 11.1 and 11.5.

TTEM Score

To calculate the TTEM score, we multiplied the execution, vision, and morale scores, as shown in Table 11.5. Let's say, for example, that director Joanne Akalaitis' team received a 90% for its execution, 90% for the implementation of its vision, but only 60% for group morale, for a product of 486,000. Director Lloyd Richards' team, on the other hand, received scores of 80%, 80%, and 80%, for a product of 512,000.

Multiplying the scores reflects our belief in what is termed a *noncompen-*

TABLE 11.5
Aggregation of TTEM for Two Teams

	Teams	
TTEM Aspects	Richards'	Akalaitis'
E%: Excellence in execution	80	90
V%: Fulfillment of vision	80	90
M%: Attention to group morale[a]	80	60
p%: Productive time	80	80
o*: Lack of "outbursts"	(0)	− .30
g%: Gracious acts	(0)	+ 10
TTEM[b]	512,000	486,000

[a]$M\% = p\% + o\% + g\%$
[b]$TTEM = E\% \times V\% \times M\%$

satory model. That is, we assume that each aspect is critical and that one score should not compensate for another. By multiplying the scores, a score of 60% for group morale, for example, could not be compensated for by a high score of 90% in execution and 90% in vision.

Another way of aggregating the scores would have been to sum them. Summing the scores, however, implies a compensatory or additive model, a commonly used technique and assumption (Brannick & Brannick, 1989). To illustrate, when Akalaitis' and Richards' scores are added, they both get the same score of 240: execution 90% + vision 90% + morale 60% = 240 for Akalaitis, and execution 80% + vision 80% + morale 80% = 240 for Richards. What this means is that when Akalaitis' team does well in execution and vision, but poorly in morale, then the high execution and vision scores make up or "compensate" for the low morale score. Because we assumed a noncompensatory model, we decided to multiply the scores together.

Although we recommend the method of combining the aspects and subaspects into an overall TTEM score, Brannick (personal communication, August 3, 1995) admits being "uncomfortable adding some pieces and multiplying others." He offers several salient suggestions. One is to create a profile instead, reporting individual aspect scores (e.g., excellence in execution, factors affecting group morale) and subaspect scores (e.g., the percentage of time productively spent, and the number of outbursts and gracious remarks). Another possibility, which we also recommend, is to explore using different aggregation methods until one agrees with your subjective assessment of the relative ordering of the teams. His last noteworthy but difficult-to-implement (because of the lack of an appropriate criterion) suggestion is to empirically validate the scale.

Observational Procedures

Subjects and Settings.   Thus far, we have fieldtested the TTEM in six productions. One was a college production, the other five were Off-Off Broadway. All the plays were realistic or naturalistic rather than surrealistic or musical. The intricacy of each play's technical requirements was moderate. On a 7-point scale (where 1 is for a monologue with no more than one lighting or sound changes during each scene and 7 represents 2 or more components such as an orchestra or dancers as well as actors), each of the productions was rated either a 3 or 4.

The supervisory personnel in each production included a director in charge of the entire production; a stage manager; and lighting, costume, and sound designers. The other personnel consisted of the designer's technical crews, production crew members who built the sets and ran operations like the ticket office, and running crews behind the stage.

Raters.   Six raters collected data. With the exception of the author, five were theater majors in college with backstage experience as either production or stage managers or technical crew such as sound board operator.

Data Collection.   The coders obtained data during tech and dress rehearsals. During the tech rehearsal, elements of the show such as the lights and sound are practiced and finalized. During dress rehearsal, the entire production is run straight through from the beginning to the end. For a description of the aspects coded and the times during which data were collected, refer to Table 11.6.

TABLE 11.6
Observational Procedures of TTEM

Technical rehearsal
  Observe from scheduled start to actual end of rehearsal.
  Assess:
    Visions expressed (V1) in Vision score
    Productive time (p1) in Morale score
    Outbursts in Morale score
    Gracious acts in Morale score

Dress rehearsal
  Observe from beginning to end of production.
  Assess:
    E1 and E2 in Execution score
    Visions implemented (V2) in Vision score

Limitations. Because cast rehearsals were off limits to the raters, the interactions with the cast could not be included. Hence, the TTEM emphasizes the technical aspects of putting on a clean, tight show rather than its artistic merit.

APPLYING CRU CRITERIA

Reflecting Complexity (C)

The TTEM reflected the intricacies of putting on a production by including the three aspects of execution, vision, and morale. Both product and process were represented. The product was reflected in the execution score; with a high execution score, the audience got to see the fruits of the crew's labor, that is, the lights and sound operating as planned. The process can be seen in the morale score, which indicates the behind-the-scenes actions of the team during rehearsal. Both the product and process were reflected in the vision score. Information was obtained about the process or expression of the visions; the implementation of the vision resulted in a visible product (e.g., the change in costume) that could be seen in the production.

Another way in which the TTEM reflected the complexity of the team effort was its inclusion of multiple constituencies. The director was coded, as well as the designers and their crews, and the production crew.

The reciprocal interdependence of the team was most directly reflected in the vision score. For a vision to be considered implemented, the vision had to be expressed by one member of the team, typically the director or one of the designers, and agreed to by at least one other team member, often the technical crew such as the costumer's assistant, and lastly, it had to be implemented by one or more members of the crew.

Ensuring the TTEM Was Under the Control (U) of the Team

Care was taken to ensure that the TTEM was minimally affected by extraneous factors. In operationalizing execution, for instance, a team could be operating on a shoestring budget of $15 (this happens!) for the entire production, but they could still obtain a score of 100% for execution if all the elements were in place.

Similarly, in defining vision, the vision could be expressed by the director or one of the designers or even one of the cast or crew; the primary stipulation was that a decision had to be made to do it and it had to be possible to do by dress rehearsal. If objections were made by any member of the team, it was not counted as a vision.

In the same way, the operationalization of morale did not depend on the length of the rehearsals but rather on whether the time, however long, was spent productively. Along the same lines, an outburst in and of itself did not doom the team to a miserably low morale score. Joanne Akalaitis, who prides herself on treating actors decently, admitted that she has yelled and once thrown "a pumpkin muffin at an actor" (Bartow, 1988, p. 8). This outburst on her part could be made up or compensated for by her acting graciously. In short, the emphasis of the TTEM is to ensure that all aspects of the TTEM were within the grasp of the team and not subject to extraneous influences over which they bore little control.

Another extraneous factor that was eliminated was the choice of the play itself, the interpretation by the director, and the acting on the part of the cast. These aspects, falling under the rubric of artistic merit, reflected a single person's vision rather than the team as a whole. That is, critics could castigate a show for the choice of the play or the interpretation of the director and individual cast members, even though the team met the technical requirements of the production. Hence, the Excellence score was defined to reflect whether the show, whatever its plot or period, was well-executed.

Enhancing Interrater Reliability (R)

To ensure that the TTEM met the criterion of being reliable, tests of interrater reliability were assessed. To do this, two raters independently go to the setting using the same coding system and simultaneously watch what was happening. Afterward, they check for agreements and disagreements. An agreement occurs when the two raters agree, for example, on the number of visions that were expressed. Interrater reliability is calculated as a percentage figure: [# of agreements/(# of agreements + # of disagreements) × 100]. When reliability scores of at least 90% for an established measure and at least 80% for a new measure (Miller, 1997) are obtained during the formal data collection on approximately 10% of the observations, then the target behavior is considered to be reliably defined. (Note: These reliability scores will vary depending on the way in which it is calculated. For further discussion of this consequential topic, refer to Sulzer-Azaroff and Mayer, 1991, and Volume 10 of the *Journal of Applied Behavior Analysis*, 1977).

Two steps are used to enhance reliability. The first step occurs during the *developmental stage* when defining terms. The aim is to define terms "unambiguously" until reliability scores of ideally 90% to 100% are obtained three times in a row on representative occasions. It does not matter how objective the terms or procedures appear. The proof is in the agreement between the observers. The second step takes place during the *training stage*. For example, each rater has to obtain three consecutive, representative reliability scores of at least 90% or better before she or he is considered trained and ready to formally collect data. During the formal data collection, reliability checks are then conducted at least 10% of the time.

To date, satisfactory reliability scores have yet to be reached during the developmental stage, and revisions of the TTEM continue. Disagreements continued to occur over whether or not a particular vision had been implemented. Some lighting and sound changes were notoriously difficult for the rater to discern. A director might say: "Let's brighten up the corner a bit." The lighting designer could precisely increase the number of lumens. But even the most experienced rater could not readily discern if the change had been made the next night. These differences occurred despite the fact that the raters were technically proficient. To resolve the disagreements, a general rule was instituted: Visions had to be discrete ("Let's light the corner") rather than relative and in terms of degrees ("Let's brighten up the corner a bit"). Using the new rule, reliability checks were again conducted. Although the scores increased, it was not a sufficient and sustained increase. Only when reliability scores of 90% or better are obtained on three consecutive, representative occasions for all of the elements of light, sound, and so forth will this developmental stage be considered complete.

This discussion of the ongoing fieldtesting of the TTEM we hope, will illustrate how, and more important why, the CRU criteria are integral to the development of criterion variables.

USING CRU CRITERIA TO ANALYZE OPTIONS

The CRU criteria can also be used to judge potential candidates for criterion variables. Few of the traditional theater measures met the CRU criteria, as shown in Table 11.7. Critics' reviews are judged incomplete and unresponsive, with some questions as to their reliability. Ticket sales are thought to be reliable for the most part. (Note: Some stars such as Glenn Close in "Sunset Boulevard" have questioned how accurately producers reported the ticket sales. When she took a vacation, the sales purportedly declined, but the producers maintained that the sales held steady.) But ticket sales are deficient in reflecting the complexity of the team effort and excessive in including extraneous factors. Awards given for particular aspects of the show such as costumes are by their nature incomplete, although they would probably receive high marks for reliability. Evaluations by peers, cast, crew, and designers are problematic in that they represent only one constituency, their reliability is questionable, and they may or may not be subject to factors out of the team's control.

TABLE 11.7
Use of Criteria in Evaluating Measures of Effectiveness

Criteria			
C *Complexity*	R *Reliability*	U *Under Control*	*Measures of Effectiveness*
–	?	–	Critics' reviews
–	+	–	Ticket sales
–	+	?	Awards (Tonys, Obies)
–	?	?	Peer evaluations
?	?	?	Cast evaluations
?	?	?	Crew evaluations
?	?	?	Designer evaluations

DISCUSSION

The present chapter responds to Weitz' (1961) call for criteria for criteria over three decades ago. First, it recommends three criteria, referred to by the mnemonic CRU (like a fine white wine). Meeting the *complexity* (C) criteria means that the intricacies involved in conducting an interdependent task will be reflected. The fact that the measure is responsive to the team's effort means that it will be *under* (U) their control. The fact that the measure is *reliable* (R) means that the data will be more likely to reflect the actions of the team rather than dependent on the idiosyncrasies of a particular rater. The advantage of these higher order principles is that they provide guidelines to judge and use in determining effectiveness. With criteria, the discussion is more likely to be constructive for both practitioners and researchers. Formulating the problem in terms of failing to meet the criterion of complexity is more likely to result in indices meeting this criterion.

Second, the chapter addresses "industrial psychology's major bugaboo since its inception . . . quantifying job effectiveness" (Campbell et al., 1970, p. 101). The TTEM illustrates how one can quantify the effectiveness of teams putting on theater productions. Jones (1986) makes a similar recommendation in his discussion of stage directing. "What," he asks, "do we know of an art without a body of great, authoritative instances? What does 'sublime' mean in visual art without Michelangelo, in music without Beethoven, in drama without Sophocles?" (p. 7). As an example, the TTEM presented here demonstrates that it is possible to reflect the quality of the teamwork that goes on behind the scenes during a theater production.

Finally, by applying these criteria for criteria with theater teams, one can begin to blend theory and research as recommended by McGrath (1984). By applying standards such as the complexity criteria, one can actually see how to translate principles into action. This attempt to forge a combination of criteria for criteria and data on an index of effectiveness will hopefully point the way to further development as we continue to be fascinated with enhancing and measuring teams in action.

ACKNOWLEDGMENTS

This resarch was supported by the U.S. Army Research Institute contract MDA903-91-K-0136. The views, opinions, and findings contained in this article are those of the authors and should not be construed as the official position of the U.S. Army Research Institute or as an official Department of the Army position, policy, or decision.

A special thanks to Suzanne Fass, Scottie Harwood, Patricia Wilson, Chris Murphy, and Laura Romanowski for their technical expertise and to Asli Gevgilili, Michelle Reynard, Luis Colon, Tom Redding, and Talia Heimovich for their teamsmanship.

REFERENCES

Alexander, J.O. (1980). The nonprofit organization handbook. In T. D.Connors (Ed.), *Planning and management in nonprofit organizations* (pp. 155–161). New York: McGraw-Hill.

Anthony R. N., Deardon J., & Bedford N. M. (1989). Nonprofit organizations. In *Management control systems* (6th ed.) (pp. 804–858). Homewood, IL: Richard D. Irwin.

Baker, D. P., & Salas, E. (1992). Principles for measuring teamwork skills. *Human Factors, 34*(4), 469–475.

Ball, W. (1984). *A sense of direction: Some observations on the art of directing*. New York: Drama Book.

Bartow, A. (1988). *The director's voice* [Interviews with A. Brown, pp. 20–35, Z. Fichhandler, pp. 105–127, J. Akalaitis, pp. 1–19, M. W. Mason, pp. 194–211, L. Richards, pp. 255–268, P. Sellers, pp. 269–285, & A. Serban, pp. 286–299]. New York: Theatre Communications Group.

Belasco, D. (1963). Creating atmosphere. In T. Cole & H. K. Chinoy (Eds.), *Directors on directing: A source book of the modern theater* (pp. 125–137). New York: Macmillan.

Bettenhausen, K. L. (1991). Five years of groups research: What we have learned and what needs to be addressed. *Journal of Management, 17*(2), 345–381.

Binning, J. F., & Barrett, G. V. (1989). Validity of personnel decisions: A conceptual analysis of the inferential and evidential bases. *Journal of Applied Psychology, 74*, 478–494.

Blake, R. R., Mouton, J. S., & Allen, R. L. (1987). *Spectacular teamwork: How to develop the leadership skills for team success.* New York: Wiley.

Blum, M. L., & Naylor, J. C. (1968). *Industrial psychology* (Rev. ed.). New York: Harper & Row.

Brannick, M. T., & Brannick J. P. (1989). Nonlinear and noncompensatory processes in performance evaluation. *Organizational Behavior and Human Decision Processes, 44*, 97–122.

Campbell, J. P., Dunnette, D. M., Lawler, E. E., III, & Weick, K. E., Jr. (1970). *Managerial behavior, performance, and effectiveness.* New York: McGraw-Hill.

Campion, M. A., Medsker, G. J., & Higgs, A. C. (1993). Relations between work group characteristics and effectiveness: Implications for designing effective work groups. *Personnel Psychology, 46,* 823–850.

Clurman, H. (1972). *On directing.* New York: Collier Books.

Dyer, J. L. (1984). Team research and team training: A state-of-the-art review. In F. A. Muckler (Ed.), *Human factors review: 1984* (pp. 285–323). Santa Monica, CA: Human Factors Society.

Fleishman, E. A., & Quaintance, M. K. (1984). *Taxonomies of human performance.* Orlando: Academic Press.

Georgopoulous, B. S., & Mann, F. C. (1962). *The community general hospital.* New York: Macmillan.

Gies, D. L., Ott, J. S., & Shafritz, J. M. (Eds.) (1990). *The nonprofit organization: Essential readings.* Pacific Grove, CA: Brooks/Cole.

Goodman, P. S., Ravlin, E. C., & Argote, L. (1986). Current thinking about groups: Setting the stage for new ideas. In P. S. Goodman & Associates (Eds.), *Designing effective work groups* (pp. 1–33). San Francisco: Jossey-Bass.

Guzzo, R. A., & Shea G. P. (1992). Group performance and intergroup relations in organizations. In M. D. Dunnette & L. M. Hough (Eds.), *Handbook of industrial and organizational psychology:* (Vol. 3, 2nd ed., pp. 269–313). Palo Alto, CA: Consulting Psychologists.

Hackman, J. R. (1987). The design of work teams. In J. W. Lorsch (Ed.), *Handbook of organizational behavior* (pp. 315–342). Englewood Cliffs, NJ: Prentice-Hall.

Hackman, J. R., & Morris, C. G. (1975). Group tasks, group interaction process, and group performance effectiveness: A review and proposed integration. *Advances in Experimental Social Psychology, 8,* 45–99.

Hackman, J. R., & Morris, C. G. (1978). Group process and group effectiveness: A reappraisal. In L. Berkowitz (Ed.), *Group processes* (pp. 57–66). New York: Academic Press.

Hackman, J. R., & Walton, R. E. (1986). Leading groups in organizations. In P. S. Goodman & Associates (Eds.), *Designing effective work groups* (pp. 72–119). San Francisco: Jossey-Bass.

Ives, D. (1995, February 26). The ancient Greeks did it; Why can't we? *The New York Times,* p. H13.

Jones, D. J. (1986). *Great directors at work: Stanislavsky, Brecht, Kazan, Brook.* Berkeley, CA: University of California Press.

Komaki, J. L. (in press). *Leadership from an operant perspective.* London: Routledge.

Komaki, J. L., Collins, R. L., & Temlock, S. (1987). An alternative performance measurement approach: Applied operant measurement in the service sector. *International Review of Applied Psychology, 36*(1), 71–89.

Komaki, J. L., Desselles, M. L., & Bowman, E. D. (1989). Definitely not a breeze: Extending an operant model of effective supervision to teams. *Journal of Applied Psychology, 74,* 522–529.

Langley, S. (1990). *Theatre management and production in America.* New York: Drama Book.

Levine, J. M., & Moreland, R. L. (1990). Progress in small group research. *Annual Review of Psychology, 41,* 585–634.

McGrath, J. E. (1984). *Groups: Interactions and performance.* Englewood Cliffs, NJ: Prentice-Hall.

McGrath, J. E. (1986). Studying groups at work: Ten critical needs for theory and practice. In P. S. Goodman & Associates (Eds.), *Designing effective work groups* (pp. 362–391). San Francisco: Jossey-Bass.

Miller, K. (1997). *Principles of everyday behavior* (3rd ed.). Pacific Grove: Brooks/Cole.

Mitchell, T. R. (1982). Motivation: New directions for theory, research, and practice. *Academy of Management Review, 7,* 80–88.

Pearce, M. (1993, October). Behind the design: A portfolio. *American Theatre,* 24–32.

Powell, W. W. (Ed.) (1987). *The nonprofit sector.* New Haven, CT: Yale University.

Schmitt, N. W., & Klimoski, R. J. (1991). *Research methods in human resources management.* Cincinnati, OH: South-Western.

Sulzer-Azaroff, B., & Mayer, G. R. (1991). *Behavioral analysis for lasting change.* Fort Worth: Holt Rinehart & Winston.

Thompson, J. D. (1967). *Organizations in action.* New York: McGraw-Hill.

Tziner, A., & Eden, D. (1985). Effects of crew composition on crew performer: Does the whole equal the sum of its parts? *Journal of Applied Psychology, 70,* 85–93.

Weitz, J. (1961). Criteria for criteria. *American Psychologist, 16,* 228–232.

Witchel, A. (1992, June 2). On stage, and off. *The New York Times,* pp. C2.

Zagat New York City restaurant survey: 1996. (1995). New York: Zagat Survey.

12 Assessment of Nuclear Power Plant Crew Performance Variability

Jody L. Toquam
Jennifer L. Macaulay
Curtis D. Westra
Battelle Seattle Research Center

Yushi Fujita
Technova, Inc.

Susan E. Murphy
Claremont McKenna College

Effective nuclear power plant operation is a complex process that requires reactor operators to work together as a crew and follow prescribed procedures to ensure continuous, safe operations. These operations crews undergo extensive training to ensure consistent peak performance. Unfortunately, even highly trained crews who perform, on average, very effectively, may vary in their performance. Although performance inconsistencies may be inconsequential for some work groups, inconsistency can produce serious consequences in nuclear plant operations. What factors influence crew performance variability, and how can these factors be influenced by organizational actions so as to reduce such variability?

This study explores the measurement of one important factor of crew performance: performance variability. The type of performance variability of interest in this study is within-crew performance variability. That is, variability in crew performance effectiveness over time and across situations. The study further examines the factors that may influence within-crew performance variability in nuclear power plant operations using an adaptation of the Nieva, Fleishman, and Reick (1978) model of team performance as presented in Fig. 12.1. External demands, such as organizational policies, practices, and organizational culture, certainly influence task characteristics, as well as the way in which individuals utilize abilities, skills, and other characteristics in performing a task, and may influence the processes teams use to perform a task. Here, *task characteristics* are those elements of the task that determine process and performance requirements. *Team member characteristics* are the knowledge and those skills, abilities, and experiences that members bring to the team. Team characteristics and

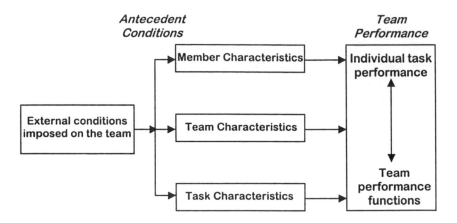

FIG. 12.1.   Conceptual model of team performance (adapted from Nieva, Fleishman, & Reick, 1978).

processes are those that apply to the team as a whole rather than the individuals that make up the team. These include group cohesion, size, and communication patterns.

In accordance with the model, three major factors are considered in this chapter as sources of within-crew performance variability, including: (a) task characteristics, (b) team member characteristics, and (c) team characteristics and processes. The fourth major factor, external conditions imposed on the team, is not examined as these external conditions were basically constant in the study reported here. Scores on measures of the three factors were examined to determine their relationship with crew performance and within-crew performance variability.[1]

Models such as the one presented in Fig. 12.1 are based on an extensive body of literature that has examined factors that influence individual or crew performance effectiveness. Fewer studies, however, have been designed to examine within-individual or within-group performance variability. Researchers have developed methods and approaches for assessing within-individual performance variability (Ghiselli, 1956; Glass, Willson, & Gottman, 1975; Hanges, Schneider, & Niles, 1990; Kane, 1986; Komaki, Collins, & Penn, 1982; McCain & McCleary, 1979). Borman (1991), for example, argued that performance measures that only take into account average individual performance are missing vital information dealing with performance variability. Despite his arguments, however, very little research has shown attempts to examine factors that influence performance

---

[1]Crew performance was included in this analysis to provide a benchmark of the factors that correlate with overall mean performance assessed at the crew level.

variability. One exception is a study by Hanges, Schneider, and Niles (1990) that attempted to determine if performance variability could be explained by person or situation variables. These authors found surprising stability of performance across the person variables, suggesting that performance variability is most likely caused by situational factors.

This chapter serves as a preliminary investigation to identify factors that influence within-crew performance variability and crew effectiveness. Because the bulk of the literature focuses on performance effectiveness, rather than performance variability, we examined the performance effectiveness literature and used this to generate hypotheses about within-crew performance variability. The literature concerning performance effectiveness is examined here.

LITERATURE REVIEW

Major factors that have potential for influencing within-crew performance variability are identified by the Nieva, Fleishman, and Reick (1978) model adapted in Fig. 12.1. In the following section, we examine the literature on task characteristics, team member characteristics, and team characteristics and processes and summarize how each of these three factors has been shown to influence performance effectiveness for teams or groups. Following this review, we generate hypotheses about how these factors may influence within-crew performance variability.

Task Characteristics

Although characteristics of the task are expected to contribute to differences in performance, there is little agreement among researchers about the critical features of tasks. Because no well-accepted comprehensive taxonomy of critical features exists, no research has examined how these features impact performance.

Nevertheless, several researchers have proposed non-comprehensive taxonomies to classify tasks along some dimensions. Galbraith (1977) classified tasks using an information-processing approach along three dimensions: task complexity, task interdependence, and environmental uncertainty. To be effective, groups must posses information-processing capabilities that match task demands along each of the three dimensions. Wood (1986) further developed and defined the concept of *task complexity* by hypothesizing a curvilinear relationship between task complexity and performance. As complexity increases, performance first increases as interest and motivation increase, then decreases as capacity is exceeded. Dickinson (1969) defined *task structure* as involving task complexity, task interdependencies, and work coordination. He hypothesized that effective communication patterns depend on the three elements of task structure. When the task structure is characterized by high complexity, high interdependencies, and a decentralized work structure, communication networks must be well developed.

In addition to these models, researchers have gathered supporting empirical evidence that suggests that features of tasks influence group processes, which in turn influence group performance outcomes. For example, research using Dickinson's model has shown that communication and coordination training increase the performance of groups involved in complex, interdependent, and decentralized tasks more than in less complex, less interdependent, and hierarchical tasks (Bass & Barrett, 1981). Furthermore, in support of Wood's model, task difficulty was shown to moderate the communication processes of groups. Research has also shown that groups perform best in tasks with uncertain environments when their communication is decentralized (Tushman, 1979) and internal coordination is flexible (Argote, 1982). Morris (1966) showed that both task type and task difficulty influenced group interaction and communication. Further, Hanges, Schneider, and Niles (1990) found that situational variables accounted for substantially more variance for instructors than did person variables.

The current literature suggests that task characteristics are likely to influence group performance outcomes. Moreover, the relationship is made more complex by suggesting that task characteristics influence group processes, which in turn influence group performance. The current literature, however, does not provide an agreed upon taxonomy of task features that influence group performance.

Team Member Characteristics

Several researchers have theorized that the attributes and characteristics of individual members determine the performance of the group or aggregate (Bass, 1980; Schnieder, 1987). This hypothesis has been supported by results from several research programs (Hill, 1982; Terborg, Castore, & DeNinno, 1976; Tziner & Eden, 1985; Wright, McMahan, Smart, & McCormick, 1995). Because it is expected that individual characteristics play a role in group performance outcomes, we attempted to identify those characteristics that have been shown to influence individual performance in power plant operations or similar occupations. For example, Dunnette et al. (1982) identified a number of individual characteristics that contributed to individual performance in nuclear power plant operations. These included general intelligence, specific cognitive abilities (e.g., spatial ability, numerical ability, mechanical comprehension), personality characteristics (e.g., potency, adjustment, dependability), experienced stress (e.g. recent life changes), and background factors (e.g., tenure on the job and tenure in the industry). Itoh, Yoshimura, Ohtsuka, and Matsuda (1990) also reported that cognitive abilities, such as perceptual speed and memory, predict performance in power plant operators. Schmidt, Hunter, and Caplan (1981) reported that for operators in the petroleum industry, measures of general intelligence and arithmetic reasoning were valid predictors of performance.

Dunnette, Bownas, and Bosshardt (1981) and Gertman, Haney, Jenkins, and Blackman (1985) demonstrated that emotional stability as measured by several personality scales predicts performance for power plant operators. Other personality variables found to correlate with individual job performance in operations occupations include impulsivity, work motivation, emotional stability, and conscientiousness (Barrick & Mount, 1991; Helmreich, Sawin, & Carsud, 1986; Picano, 1991; Rouse & Rouse, 1982).

Team Characteristics and Processes

The dynamics of groups as they perform can influence group performance. Research involving three team characteristics and process variables—group member homogeneity, group cohesion, and group communications—is summarized here.

Group Homogeneity. Group homogeneity or heterogeneity indicates the degree of similarity or dissimilarity among group members. Although the characteristics on which group members could be compared is endless, only a few characteristics have been found to influence group dynamics. Characteristics of interest for this study—personality, cognitive abilities, and previous job experience—were identified from studies focusing on individual operator performance.

Research findings indicate that groups composed of individuals all scoring high on certain personality characteristics (homogeneous groups), perform more effectively than groups heterogeneous on these same variables. For example, groups composed of members high in task orientation and need for achievement perform more effectively than groups average or low in these characteristics (Cooper & Payne, 1972; Klein & Christiansen, 1969; Martens, 1970).

Heterogeneity of attitudes and personality traits has been found to positively affect group performance under some conditions (Kanas, 1985). For example, in tasks requiring creativity or novel solutions to problems, groups composed of individuals with dissimilar personality profiles have been found to perform better than groups composed of individuals with similar personality profiles (Stein, 1982). Further, heterogeneous groups have been reported to outperform homogeneous groups when members have experience with the task at hand (Triandis, Hall, & Ewen, 1965).

Homogeneity and heterogeneity of group members on cognitive abilities have been shown to influence group outcomes. Hill (1982), Tziner and Eden (1985), and Fernandez (1992) reported that groups composed of all high-ability members outperformed groups of all low-ability members and of mixed high- and low-ability members. Interestingly, Tziner and Eden reported a cumulative effect such that all high-ability member groups performed much better than expected, while all low-ability member groups performed much worse than expected.

Homogeneity of group members can also influence group dynamics, which in turn, affect performance. For example, Pfeffer (1983) suggested that group homogeneity on characteristics, such as job tenure, may produce conflict within work groups, which in turn interferes with performance. Other researchers have provided supporting evidence to suggest that group members more similar in age and length of job experience are more effective groups and communicate with one another more frequently (O'Reilly, Caldwell, & Barnett, 1989; Wagner, Pfeffer, & O'Reilly, 1984; Wiersema & Bird, 1993; Zenger & Lawrence, 1989).

Group Cohesion.   Cohesion is frequently defined as group spirit, group morale, or group commitment. Results from studies investigating this construct indicate that cohesive groups demonstrate more effective performance than less cohesive groups (Keller, 1986; Miesing & Preble, 1985; Sherif, 1966; Tziner & Vardi, 1983). In a meta-analysis of more than 372 groups, Evans and Dion (1991) reported that group cohesion leads to increased performance. This effect, however, is fairly small and appears to depend on other factors (moderators).

Communication.   Studies of group communication processes have frequently revealed that certain types of communication between group members influence the overall performance of the group. Frequency of communication has been found to affect group performance. Those groups who perform effectively spend more time on communication than do those groups who perform more poorly (Foushee, Lauber, Baetge, & Acomb, 1986; McBride, 1988). Although this appears true in studies using a fairly unstructured task, the reverse is true if the task is highly structured (Steiner & Dodge, 1956). For example, in studies using vigilance-monitoring tasks, the relationship between frequency of communication and performance is negative (Johnston, 1966; Naylor & Briggs, 1965).

Patterns of communication have also been found to be related to group performance (Foushee, Lauber, Baetge, & Acomb, 1986; Foushee & Manos, 1981; Kanki, Lozito, & Foushee, 1989; Ruffell-Smith, 1979). For example, Foushee and his colleagues (1986) found that airplane cockpit crews performed best when there were more commands, more suggestions, more acknowledgements, and more statements of intent. Similar findings are reported in Foushee and Manos (1981). These same researchers also reported that crews that performed poorly engaged in more tension release and more nontask-relevant communications. Helmreich, Wilhelm, Gregorich, and Chidester (1990) reported that the best performing cockpit crews more frequently engaged in communications involving inquiry, advocacy, decision making, and concern for group.

Kanki (1989) and Kanki, Lozito, and Foushee (1989) explored variation in communication and crew performance. Results from these studies indicated that, for airplane cockpit crews, the best performing crews had similar and consistent communication patterns. These crews seemed to follow closely a procedure-based pattern of communication. The poorest performing crews did not demonstrate a consistent pattern of communication. Similarly, Tushman (1977) found that flexible communication patterns were associated with high performing groups only when the task was uncertain.

Implications for the Present Study

Based on the research summarized here, it is clear that task characteristics, team member characteristics, and team characteristics and processes can influence group performance effectiveness. For the present study, it is possible to examine the effects of these three broad classes of variables on group performance and within-crew performance variability. The general hypothesis related to each class of variables is discussed in turn.

Task Characteristics. It has been theorized that features of the task will influence group performance, but the actual linkage between task features and group performance may be less direct (e.g., influence group processes and, in turn, influence group performance). Although several models or task feature taxonomies have been proposed, there is no agreed upon method for characterizing task features that ultimately influences group performance, and the models suggest that the relationship between task demands and group performance is complex rather than a simple linear equation. In the present study, we attempt to demonstrate the presence of within-crew performance variability and then to examine the source of this variability. The first analyses conducted are designed to demonstrate that the source of this variability is not simply a function of task difficulty. Nonsignificant results from this first analysis are used to support conducting more in-depth analyses to determine other potential sources of within-crew performance variability.

Team Member Characteristics.   Research has shown that individual team member's abilities, personality characteristics, and background experiences can influence group performance effectiveness. Results from this body of literature have been extended to within-crew performance variability outcomes in the hypotheses appearing here.

H1: Groups scoring high on cognitive ability and background experience factors will perform more consistently than groups scoring low on these factors.

Team Characteristics and Processes.   Research has shown that group composition (homogeneity and heterogeneity) on individual characteristics can influence group performance outcomes. For example, group composition (homogeneity) on cognitive abilities and background experience may result in higher performance, whereas group heterogeneity in personality characteristics is likely to contribute to increased performance. Research has also shown that cohesive groups, in general, are more effective than less cohesive groups. In terms of communications, data show that groups that exchange more technical or content-oriented communications perform more effectively than those who exchange less content-oriented communications (e.g., tension, frustration). Also, groups with more consistent communication patterns perform more effectively. Based on these findings, we have generated the following hypotheses:

H2: Group homogeneity on cognitive ability and background experience factors contribute to performance consistency for crews.

H3: Groups heterogeneous on personality characteristics will perform more consistently than groups homogeneous on these variables.

H4: Groups reporting higher cohesion will perform more consistently.

H5: Groups with more content-oriented (technical) communications will perform more consistently than groups exchanging nontechnical communications.

H6: Groups more consistent in their communications will be more consistent in their performance.

METHOD

The objective of this study was to identify factors that contribute to effective crew performance (mean level) and identify factors that contribute to within-crew performance variability. As reported previously, three general factors are the focus of this study. These include task characteristics; team member characteristics that involve abilities, background characteristics, and personality characteristics; and team characteristics and process variables that include group homogeneity and heterogeneity on abilities, background and personality characteristics, group cohesion, and communications patterns.

Data for the study were collected during week-long formal training programs conducted for nuclear power plant operators from seven utilities in Japan. This program included formal classroom training, as well as hands-on training exercises in which crews performed in a high-fidelity simulator to diagnose and correct various abnormal operations malfunctions. All crews followed the same schedule throughout the week of training.

Sample

One hundred twenty-six operators from seven Japanese nuclear power utilities participated in the study. At the home plant, operators held positions such as turbine operators, reactor operators, and senior reactor operators. All subjects were male, with an average age of 33 years and with nearly 5 years of control room operations experience (mean = 4.9 years) and an average of 3 years of experience in auxiliary operations positions (work conducted outside the control room).

Training Simulations

Hands-on training exercises took place within a high-fidelity control room simulator located at the Nuclear Training Center (NTC) in Tsuruga, Japan. The high-fidelity training simulator is designed to replicate the control room in terms of equipment and processes. Thus, operators were provided with plant condition information in the same or similar manner as in their actual home plant control room and were required to take the same actions, as in the actual control room, to correct plant abnormalities and malfunctions.

Simulated training events, or scenarios, were specifically developed for NTC training programs. Twenty-seven different scenarios were available for study. To ensure that a range of abnormal events were included in the current study, a team of experts consisting of engineers and control room supervisors evaluated each scenario on 10 dimensions. These dimensions included time margin (time required to perform required tasks); volume of tasks (total number of tasks that must be performed), volume of information (the maximum rate at which information is provided); frequency of monitoring tasks (frequency with which operators are required to monitor plant parameters); difficulty of diagnosis (complexity of inference required to determine the root cause of the event); difficulty of decision making (difficulty of selecting or planning the control tasks); complexity (complexity of the task given that procedures are not clearly defined or available); skill (skill required to manipulate controls); communication requirements (frequency of communications required among control room operators); and communications outside of the control room (the frequency of communications required outside of the control room). Using rating data from the team of experts, seven scenarios were selected to represent a range of conditions along these 10 dimensions. These seven scenarios include:

1. Feedwater Control Valve Failure (FWCVF)
2. Station Blackout (BO)
3. Steam Generator Tube Rupture (SGTR)
4. Turbine First Stage Pressure Sensor Failure (P1st)
5. Pressurizer Level Control Failure (PrzLC)
6. Feedwater Line Break (FWLB)
7. Loss of Coolant Accident–Pressurizer Gas Phase Break (LOCA).

Data Collection: Training Scenarios

Four video cameras were used to record operator actions and communications during each scenario. Fig. 12.2 shows the layout of the control room, placement of the cameras, and assigned areas of the control room operators. Crew members consisted of three control room operators, each playing a different role. The senior reactor operator (SRO) acted as the group leader and coordinated the efforts of the operators. The other two operators played the role of reactor operator (RO) or turbine operator (TO). Camera 1 was used to cover the left wing and the center portion of the main control board, while Camera 2 was used to cover the right wing and center portion. Camera 3 was used to cover electrical and control boards that were separated from the main control board. Camera 4 was used to provide an overview of the entire control room. All cameras were affixed to the top of the control boards. Each operator was asked to wear a wireless remote microphone during each scenario, so all communications could be captured.

Data Collection: Instruments and Procedures

Several different test, questionnaire, and performance assessment instruments were developed or selected for inclusion in this study. Descriptions of the data collection instruments and procedures used for performance

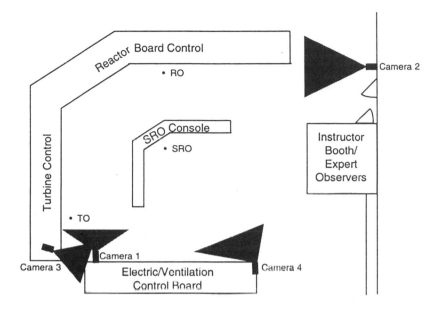

FIG. 12.2.   Simulator TV camera positions.

assessment, team member characteristics, and team characteristics and processes are provided here.

Performance Assessment.   Crew performance measures were developed by research staff working in conjunction with the NTC instructors. During the data collection, two expert raters observed crews as they performed in each training scenario. (See Fig. 12.2 for location of the expert observers during the training scenarios.) Following each training scenario, each rater independently evaluated the crew on three rating dimensions. Seven expert raters participated in the study. Across different pairs of raters, interrater reliability levels ranged from .62 to .97; the mean interrater reliability across all raters was .80.

Expert raters provided crew performance ratings on three dimensions: (a) team unity, (b) team performance, and (c) team spirit. For each performance dimension, raters were provided with guidelines for the types of behaviors to use to guide their ratings. These are provided in Table 12.1. Analysis of the crew ratings revealed that the performance dimensions were highly intercorrelated (mean = .81). For that reason, we also computed an overall crew rating defined as the mean of the three crew performance dimensions. Data for the overall rating were included in all subsequent analyses.

TABLE 12.1
Rater Guidance for Crew Performance Rating Scales

1. How well did the team work together during the scenario?
   - SRO provides adequate instruction and RO and TO listen and comprehend.
   - Recognize each crew members' technical expertise and are aware of what each crew member is doing
   - Each crew member understands his own role
   - Group atmosphere is positive

2. How well did the team perform during the scenario?
   - Follow and understand the scenario in each accident
   - Little leakage occurs during a pipe breakage accident
   - Pay attention to all details even in less critical accidents
   - Recover from an accident early and quickly

3. How much enthusiasm/team spirit did the team members display during the scenario? (average of three members)
   - Speaks loudly and clearly
   - Speaks frequently
   - Refers to written procedures and other materials frequently
   - Moves briskly about the control room

Team Member Characteristics. During the first part of the week of training, operators were asked to complete tests and questionnaires administered by NTC instructors.[2] These instruments included measures of cognitive abilities, personality, background and previous job experience. Selection of tests and questionnaires for inclusion in this study was a function of the abilities and skills required for effective control room performance and based upon results reported in similar types of research efforts (Dunnette et al., 1982). Criteria for including specific tests and questionnaires were: (a) those that had been used in Japan and for which normative data for Japanese samples were available, (b) ease of administration, (c) length of time required for administration, and (d) for tests not administered in Japan, test items that would require little verbal translation (e.g., figural and spatial test items). For those tests that required translation, a backtranslation procedure was used. That is, test instructions and test items were translated into Japanese by one expert, and translated back into English by another expert. Backtranslations were reviewed by research staff to ensure that they possessed the same meaning as the original.

Table 12.2 contains a list and description of the tests and questionnaires included in the study to measure team member characteristics. Note that for the current study and a pilot-study, operators' scores were compared with normative data from Japanese samples, where available, and U.S. samples.

---

[2]NTC staff were trained to administer these tests and questionnaires. Results from a pilot study indicated that administration procedures were carefully followed.

TABLE 12.2
Description of Team Member Characteristics Variables

Measure	Ability or Characteristic Assessed	Number of Items
Cognitive Ability Measures		
Bennett Mechanical Comprehension Test	Mechanical Aptitude	68
Employee Aptitude Survey (EAS) Numerical Ability	Number Ability	75
EAS Numerical Reasoning	Reasoning	20
EAS Space Visualization	Spatial Visualization	50
EAS Visual Pursuit	Spatial Scanning	30
Battelle Visual Scanning Test—High and Low	Attention (Perceptual Speed)	200
Raven's Progressive Matrices	General Intelligence	47
MMPI Personality Scales		
Scale 0	Potency—Tendency to seek and enjoy positions of influence and to be enthusiastic and energetic.	70
Scale 4	Adjustment—Tendency to maintain a calm, even mood and not become distraught by stressful situations.	50
Scale 7	Dependability—Tendency to be disciplined, organized, planful, honest, trustworthy, and accepting of authority.	48
MMPI Validity Scale	Validity—These items serve as a check on whether or not trainees are reading each item carefully. Referred to as the Lie Scale on the MMPI.	15
Ego Strength	Stability—Tendency for a strong sense of reality and feelings of personal adequacy.	68
Social Presence	Represents the tendency to be tactful and helpful in interpersonal situations.	24
Impulsiveness	Impulsive Behavior—Tendency to act without careful thinking.	21
Work Attitude	Represents one's interest in working hard and trying to do one's best.	37
Academic Achievement	Represents the tendency to strive for competence in one's work.	18
Background Information		
Background Questionnaire	Measures experience and other individual characteristics of operations including age, eyesight, height, grade level, current length and type of training, experience in training simulator, and type and amount of job experience.	

A comparison of means and standard deviations indicated that operators' scores were within the normative score range as reported in previous studies. No tests nor questionnaires were eliminated because of extreme or unusual means and standard deviations.

Because of the large number of variables collected and the relatively small sample size, scores on these measures were factor analyzed and factor scores were used in subsequent data analysis. These factors are defined in Table 12.3. Again, because of sample size, factor analyses were conducted at the broad characteristic level (i.e., cognitive variables were factor analyzed separately from the experience variables). Test and questionnaire data were factor analyzed using principal components with varimax rotation. Factor scores were computed by summing unit-weighted z-scores of variables identified as members of a particular factor.

Cognitive ability test score data revealed a four-factor solution that accounted for 75.4% of the variance. These factors are labeled Numerical Reasoning, Attention, Spatial Intelligence, and Spatial Ability. Factor analysis of personality scale scores produced a four-factor solution that accounted for 82.6% of the variance. These factors are labeled Dependability, Social Skills, Sense of Competence, and Validity. The validity factor, unlike the other personality factors, is composed of only one scale, the Lie scale from the MMPI. Experience and background data revealed a five-factor solution that accounted for 75.4% of the variance. These factors were labeled Vision, Maturity, Stature, Recency of Experience, and Job Experience.

Team Characteristics and Processes. This study contained two crew process measures described in Table 12.4. The first measure, Group Atmosphere, asked crew members to describe the general demeanor and cohesion of the crew that they worked with at NTC. The second instrument, Communications Patterns, was designed to obtain information about the specific communications among crew members during each scenario. Note that the communication items consist, in general, of two broad classes of communications. The first is factual informative statements or requests for information (e.g., suggestions, acknowledgment) and the second is statements unrelated to task performance (e.g., tension release, frustration, etc.).

Communications pattern data were obtained by asking operations experts to review the videotapes. As experts viewed these tapes, they coded each type of communication emitted by crew members.[3] Scores for each

---

[3]Communications patterns data were obtained from a group of operations experts (e.g., NTC instructors) who viewed each videotape and collectively categorized each communication uttered. Given the nature of this data collection process, the expert raters felt more confident providing ratings based on consensus, rather than independent communication rating assignments. For this reason, interrater reliability estimates were not calculated.

TABLE 12.3
Description of Team Member Characteristics Factors

Characteristic Factor Name	Factor Content	Factor Description
Cognitive Factors		
Numerical Reasoning	Numerical Reasoning (+) Numerical Ability (+)	*High:* Indicates that one can perform simple arithmetic operations and reason with numbers. *Low:* Indicates that one has a difficult time reasoning with numbers or performing simple arithmetic operations.
Attention	Visual Scanning High (+) Visual Scanning Low (+)	*High:* Indicates that one can concentrate to identify stimuli embedded in simple or complex material. *Low:* One tends to have a difficult time identifying stimuli embedded in simple or complex material.
Spatial Intelligence	Raven's Progressive Matrices (+) Bennett Mechanical (+)	*High:* Indicates that one can reason using complex figures and can identify operations of routine physics principles. *Low:* Indicates that one is unable to reason with complex figures and does not comprehend routine physics/mechanical principles.
Spatial Ability	Visual Pursuit (+) Space Visualization (+)	*High:* Indicates that one can quickly and accurately work through spatial problems. *Low:* One is unable to quickly and accurately scan through spatial displays or solve simple spatial problems.
Personality Factors		
Dependability	Work Attitude (+) Impulsiveness (+) Scale 4 (MMPI) (+) Scale 7 (MMPI) (+)	*High:* Indicates that the operator strives for competence, is efficient and thorough. *Low:* Indicates that one is disorganized, not a planner, reacts rather than plans ahead.

(Continued)

TABLE 12.3 (Continued)

Characteristic Factor Name	Factor Content	Factor Description
Social Skills	Social Presence (−) Scale 0 (+)	High: Tendency to be tactful and helpful in interpersonal situations and enjoy positions of influence. Low: Indicates that one is uncomfortable in interpersonal situations and avoids taking charge.
Sense of Competence	Ego Strength (+) Academic Achievement (+)	High: Tendency to report feeling highly competent and to strive for competence. Low: Tendency to feel less competent and less likely to strive for competence.
Validity	MMPI Validity Scale (+)	High: Tendency to carefully read information before responding. Low: Tendency to respond too quickly.
Experience Factors Vision	Eye Correction Right (+) Eye Correction Left (+)	High: More correction needed to adjust eyesight. Low: Less correction needed to adjust eyesight.
Maturity	Age (+) Start-Ups (+) Shut-Downs (+)	High: Indicates higher age and experience in starting and shuttling down reactor operations. Low: Indicates lower age and experience in starting and shutting down reactor operations.
Stature	Height (+)	High: Indicates one is tall. Low: Indicates one is short.
Recency of Experience	Number of Years Since Start-Up (+) Number of Years Since Shut-Down (+)	High: Indicates that it has been many years since participating in start-up or shut-down. Low: Indicates a short time since participating in these events.
Job Experience	Direct Experience (+) Auxiliary Experience (+) Education Levels (−)	High: Indicates that one has more work experience and lower formal education. Low: Indicates one has less work experience and more formal education.

TABLE 12.4
Description of Team Process Measures

Measure	Process Assessed	Number of Items
Group Atmosphere	Assesses group cohesiveness and stress experienced by working in the group	11
Communication Patterns	Assesses broad categories of communications for each member of the crew (SRO, RO, and TO) • Inquiry • Report • Information supply • Instruction for control actions • Suggestions • Acknowledgement • Tension release • Frustration • Talking to self • Non-Codable	10 categories for each crew member. Counts are totaled across all crew members and each scenario to produce ratio scores for each communication category (e.g., number of Inquiry Comments/Total Number of Communications)

communication variable represent, for a given crew, the proportion of communications emitted during a training scenario (e.g., Inquiry) relative to the total number of communications emitted during that scenario (e.g., number of Inquiry Communications/Total Number of Communications).

RESULTS

Task Characteristics

Before examining within-crew variability, it was necessary to demonstrate if performance variability across tasks (scenarios) was a function of the different task characteristics. Therefore, we conducted a repeated measures analysis of variance (ANOVA) consisting of two variables: scenario difficulty (7 levels) and crew (34 levels). Crew performance scores consisted of the overall crew rating for a given scenario computed as the mean value across the three crew dimensions. Results from this analysis indicated no significant differences for crew performance by scenario [$F = (6, 186)$ 1.25ns, $p > .05$]. That is, across all crews, performance did not increase or decrease as a function of varying task demands.

Because results from the ANOVA suggest that crew performance does not vary as a function of task demands, we examined the data in greater detail to determine if crews differ in terms of within-crew performance variability. Mean overall crew performance scores were plotted against within-crew performance variability scores (within-crew standard deviations) for each crew; these are presented in Fig. 12.3. From this figure, it is clear that crews obtaining high overall performance scores (mean rating = 4.50 and higher) obtain a wide range of within-crew performance variability scores (standard deviations range from .20 to 1.00). Crews performing at lower mean levels (lower than 4.50) obtain an even wider range of within-crew performance variability scores (standard deviations range from .20 to 1.60). Nevertheless, both high performing and low performing groups are observed to vary in their performance across the seven training scenarios.

We also examined the within-crew performance variability by treating the seven performance scores as items comprising a scale and computed coefficient alpha for 34 teams on this seven-item scale. This allows us to estimate the average amount of within-crew performance variability. The higher coefficient alpha, the less within-crew performance variability (internal consistency reliability across the "seven-item scale.") Coefficient alpha computed for all 34 teams was estimated at .88. An estimate of the true reliability is .94. In general terms, this result suggests that there is little within-crew variability across the seven training scenarios. Within the nuclear power plant arena, however, it is clear that even small performance deviations can result in costly errors, in terms of a situation that threatens the public or one that threatens costly equipment. Given the small amount of potential variance and the accompanying potential of costly errors, we determined that it was valuable to use a relaxed significance level (p-level) in evaluating correlations between independent and dependant variables. Because this is an exploratory study, we determined that it was important to consider all characteristic and process variables that may contribute to within-crew performance variability. Therefore, in reporting these data, significance testing alpha level was set at $p < .10$.

Results from the repeated measures ANOVA indicated that within-crew performance variability is not a direct function of mean overall performance. Therefore, we computed the correlations between characteristics factor and process scores and performance variables (mean and standard deviation) for the individual and crew characteristic factors and group process factors. Findings from these analyses are summarized here.

Relationships Between Team Member Characteristics and Overall Performance

Effects of team member characteristics on mean overall group performance and within-crew performance variability were examined. Results from these

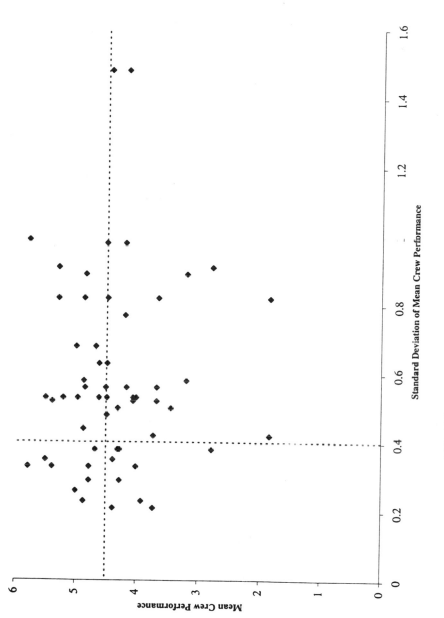

FIG. 12.3. Mean crew performance by performance variability.

analyses are presented in Table 12.5. Two team member characteristic factors correlate significantly with overall performance. Crews with high mean Validity factor scores $(-.36; p < .05)$ perform less effectively than groups scoring, on average, low on this factor. This finding suggests that crew members who carefully read each item (low Validity factor scores) obtain higher performance ratings than those who are less careful (high Validity factor scores). In addition, crews scoring high on Job Experience $(.44; p < .01)$ perform more effectively than crews with less job experience, on average. Thus, crews with more time on the job are more likely to perform better than crews with less time on the job.

Mean group characteristic factor scores were also correlated with within-crew performance variability scores (see Table 12.5). These data indicate that crews with more Job Experience $(-.34; p < .05)$ and with higher mean scores on the Attention factor $(-.28; p < .10)$ are *less* variable in their performance. Those crews with higher mean scores on the Maturity factor (older and with more actual experience in plant operations) and with a greater reported Sense of Competence $(.32; p < .10$ for both factors) are *more* variable in their performance than crews with lower scores on these factors. Taken together, these findings may suggest that crew members may overestimate their own abilities, and if so, they may perform less consistently in different training scenarios. These findings provide some support for Hypothesis 1, which predicted that higher scores on these experience and cognitive factors would lead to more consistent performance.

TABLE 12.5
Team Member Characteristics (Mean Level)

Characteristic (Crew Mean)	Crew Performance	
	Mean Overall Crew Performance	Standard Deviation of Mean Crew Performance
1. Numerical Reasoning	.20	−.02
2. Attention	.09	−.28[a]
3. Spatial Intelligence	.10	−.12
4. Spatial Ability	.10	.06
5. Dependability	.13	−.23
6. Social Skills	.08	−.04
7. Sense of Competence	−.16	.32[a]
8. Validity	−.36[b]	.20
9. Vision	−.20	.15
10. Maturity	.08	.32[a]
11. Recency of Experience	.09	−.07
12. Job Experience	.44[c]	−.34[b]

[a]$p < .10.$ [b]$p \le .05.$ [c]$p \le .01.$

Team Characteristics

This section considers characteristics of the group in terms of homogeneity and heterogeneity of the team member characteristics. In these analyses, standard deviations about the group mean on team member characteristic factors were correlated with overall crew performance and within-crew performance variability. Results from these analyses are presented in Table 12.6.

Data for mean overall crew performance indicate that only crew homogeneity on one characteristic factor correlates with overall mean performance. That is, crews homogeneous on Social Skills ($-.58$; $p < .01$) perform more effectively than crews heterogeneous on this factor. Concerning within-crew performance variability, two characteristics factors emerged as correlates. Crews homogeneous on Spatial Ability ($.35$; $p < .05$) and on Maturity ($.30$; $p < .10$) are more consistent in their performance than crews heterogeneous on these factors. This provides some support for Hypothesis 2, which predicted that crews homogeneous on cognitive ability factors and background experience factors would perform more consistently. No support was found for Hypothesis 3, which predicted that crews heterogeneous on personality variables would perform more consistently than crews homogenous on these variables.

The finding that teams homogeneous in Maturity are more consistent in their performance appears to conflict with results reported in Table 12.5. That is, crews with high average scores on the Maturity factor are *less* consistent in their performance (Table 12.5), whereas crews homogeneous

TABLE 12.6
Crew Member Characteristics (Standard Deviation of Mean)

Characteristic (Standard Deviation of Crew Mean)	Crew Performance	
	Mean Overall Crew Performance	Standard Deviation of Mean Crew Performance
1. Numerical Reasoning	$-.05$	.26
2. Attention	.01	$-.23$
3. Spatial Intelligence	$-.09$	.35[b]
4. Spatial Ability	.11	.23
5. Dependability	.10	$-.16$
6. Social Skills	$-.58$[c]	$-.17$
7. Sense of Competence	$-.14$	$-.14$
8. Validity	.01	.14
9. Vision	$-.22$	$-.01$
10. Maturity	.09	.30[a]
11. Recency of Experience	$-.11$	$-.11$
12. Job Experience	.14	$-.13$

[a]$p < .10$. [b]$p \leq .05$. [c]$p \leq .01$.

on the Maturity factor are *more* consistent in their performance (Table 12.6). In the case of crews with high average Maturity scores vs. crews with low average Maturity scores, conflicts may result from crew members in the assistant roles (RO and TO) taking actions without consulting the senior crew member (SRO). From the raters' perspective (discussed later in this chapter), it is inappropriate for assistants to circumvent the SRO. Therefore, these crews may obtain lower ratings than crews with lower Maturity factor scores. In the latter case, crews with similar levels of Maturity recognize the duties and responsibilities for crew members in different roles and perform within those roles. In crews with more variation on this factor, raters may once again observe crew members attempting to circumvent the senior crew member and thereby obtain lower ratings.

Team Processes

Team process variables include measures of cohesion and communications patterns. For both sets of variables, we examined the relationships between these process variables and mean overall performance and within-crew performance variability. Results from analyses using the group cohesion measure, Group Atmosphere, revealed no significant correlations between mean Group Atmosphere scores and overall performance or within-crew performance variability. No significant correlations were obtained in computing the relationship between within-crew variability on Group Atmosphere and overall performance or within-crew performance variability. For this study, then, group cohesion as defined by the Group Atmosphere scale did not contribute to performance or within-crew performance variability in any manner and Hypothesis 4 is rejected. Although this is discussed in greater detail in the following section, this finding may well be due to the limited time that crew members worked together in this study (1 week), thereby limiting cohesion among crew members.

Similar analyses were conducted using the Communications Pattern scores. Correlations computed between the mean crew communications patterns and overall performance and within-crew performance variability are reported in Table 12.7. According to this table, several types of communications appear related to mean overall performance. For example, crews providing relatively more Suggestions ($-.50$; $p < .01$) obtain lower mean overall performance ratings as compared to crews that provide fewer suggestions. Although discussed in more detail later, this finding indicates that providing suggestions during the training scenario was viewed as inappropriate by the expert raters. On the other hand, crews providing relatively more Acknowledgments ($.42$; $p < .05$) obtained higher mean overall performance ratings than crews providing fewer Acknowledgments.

These results also demonstrate that crews providing relatively more

TABLE 12.7
Communication Pattern Data (Crew Mean Score)

Communication Variable/Mean Ratio Score	Crew Performance	
	Mean Overall Crew Performance	Standard Deviation of Mean Crew Performance
Inquiry	−.29	−.18
Report	.27	.04
Information Supply	.21	.12
Instruction for Control Actions	.09	−.22
Suggestions	−.50[c]	−.05
Acknowledgement	.42[b]	−.24
Tension Release	−.08	.65[d]
Frustration	−.55[d]	.30[a]
Talking to Self	−.32[b]	−.18
Non-Codable	−.58[d]	.13

[a]$p < .10.$ [b]$p \le .05.$ [c]$p \le .01.$ [d]$p \le .001.$

non-technical communications are more likely to receive lower overall performance ratings. For example, crews providing relatively more Non-Codable ($-.58$; $p < .001$), Frustration ($-.55$; $p < .001$), and Talking to One's Self ($-.32$; $p < .10$) comments obtained lower ratings than crews providing a relatively smaller number of these comments.

These same non-technical communications also appear to be the major contributors to within-crew performance variability (Table 12.7). Crews emitting more Tension Release ($.65$; $p < .001$) and Frustration ($.30$; $p < .10$) comments are more variable in their performance across the seven scenarios. This supports Hypothesis 5, which predicts that groups exchanging more non-technical communications would perform less consistently.

Next, we examined crew consistency in communications. These variables were computed by estimating the consistency of a particular communication pattern variable for a crew across the seven scenarios. Thus, for each crew we computed the standard deviation of mean communication. These variables indicate the degree to which crews consistently used the same communication patterns from one scenario to the next. To distinguish these variables from within-crew performance variability, we refer to crew consistency (low SD) and crew inconsistency (high SD) in discussing the communication pattern variables. These data are presented in Table 12.8.

According to the data in Table 12.8, Hypothesis 6 is well supported in that crew consistency in many of the technical and nontechnical communications pattern variables lead to higher performance. That is, crews consistent in Inquiry ($-.33$; $p < .10$); Information Supply ($-.43$; $p < .01$); Instruction for Control Actions ($-.52$; $p < .001$); and Suggestions ($-.62$; $p < .001$) obtained higher overall performance scores. In addition,

TABLE 12.8
Communication Pattern Data (Crew SD Score)

Communication Variable (Standard Deviation of Mean Ratio Score)	Crew Performance	
	Mean Overall Crew Performance	Standard Deviation of Mean Crew Performance
Inquiry	$-.33^a$	$-.15$
Report	$-.24$	$.01$
Information Supply	$-.43^c$	$.06$
Instruction for Control Actions	$-.52^d$	$.06$
Suggestions	$-.62^d$	$.01$
Acknowledgement	$-.15$	$-.27$
Tension Release	$-.12$	$.45^c$
Frustration	$-.59^d$	$.27$
Talking to Self	$-.14$	$-.18$
Non-Codable	$-.61^d$	$.08$

[a]$p < .10.$ [b]$p \leq .05.$ [c]$p \leq .01.$ [d]$p \leq .001.$

crews consistent in providing comments related to Frustration ($-.59$; $p < .001$) and Non-Codable ($-.61$; $p < .001$) also obtained higher performance scores as compared to crews that are less consistent.

In terms of within-crew performance variability, only one communication consistency variable yielded a significant correlation. Crews more consistent in providing Tension Release comments across the seven training scenarios ($.45$; $p < .01$) were *less* variable in their performance across the seven scenarios. These data suggest that crew consistency or inconsistency in technical communications, in general, has little or no impact on within-crew performance variability. It may be that consistency in communications, regardless of the type of communication, makes for consistent performance because crews establish a pattern of communicating with one another and therefore focus less on new or varied communication patterns, but instead on the task at hand in each of the seven training scenarios. This conclusion would suggest that communications patterns develop early in the team formation process.

DISCUSSION

Research designed to investigate factors that influence individual or group performance variability is limited, even though many noted researchers have emphasized the need for such data to better understand performance. This chapter explored the factors that influence within-crew or within-team performance variability and included mean team performance in these analyses as a point of reference. This particular study includes subjects currently employed as nuclear power plant operators in Japan. Performance criteria consisted of expert ratings of crew performance in high-fidelity training scenarios. These scenarios were selected by operations engineers to ensure that they varied in terms of difficulty and complexity in diagnosing and correcting control room malfunctions.

This study examined the influence of task characteristics (defined by the seven different training scenarios), team member characteristics, and team characteristics and processes in predicting crew variability. Our discussion of the findings focuses on: (a) an interpretation of the findings; (b) the context in which independent and dependent variables were collected; and (c) the instrument used to assess crew/team performance, as compared to other devices recommended in the literature.

Interpretation of Findings

In general, we found moderate support for our hypotheses regarding within-crew performance variability. Three of the six hypotheses were supported, one received partial support, and two were rejected.

Results related to the influence of task difficulty (as defined in the seven training scenarios) indicate that in this study, any variation in task difficulty or complexity (as defined by operations experts), did not translate into systematic performance variability across crews. This finding permitted further exploration of the data to determine if team member or crew characteristics and process influence within-crew performance variability.

Results from this investigation indicate that some crew member characteristics and group processes may influence within-crew performance variability as predicted by Hypotheses 1, 2, 5, and 6. In terms of team member characteristics, crews with higher mean crew scores on Attention (ability to identify stimuli embedded in complex material) and with more Job Experience (higher tenure in both crew operations and auxiliary operations) are more consistent in their performance. These data also suggest that crew members may overestimate their abilities (Sense of Competence) and practical experience (Maturity) and, as a result, perform in a more variable manner. Crew characteristics representing crew variation (homogeneity or heterogeneity) on certain characteristics also lead to variability in performance. These include heterogeneity on Spatial Ability measures and on Maturity. Taken together, these findings suggest that crews that are highly perceptive, with similar spatial abilities, with extensive job experience, similar in age and actual operations experience, and with members who do not report feeling highly competent are more consistent in their performance. It is important to note that these factors focus only on within-crew performance variability and not on performance effectiveness.

Considering these team member and crew characteristics, it is somewhat surprising that we did not find more of the ability factors related to within-crew performance variability. Bass (1980) argued that abilities of teams (as measured, in part, by intelligence tests) influence team performance. If this is the case, then we might expect that crew variability in intelligence (Spatial Intelligence factor in this study) would influence the mean crew performance, and possibly, within-crew performance variability. As data from this study demonstrate, very few cognitive ability factors are significantly related to mean crew performance or within-crew performance variability. This may indicate that this sample of nuclear power plant operators from Japan is not comparable to the U.S. samples used in previous studies. We discuss later the issue of cultural differences in more depth.

Analysis of crew process data revealed that group cohesion (mean scores and group homogeneity–heterogeneity) scores, as measured in this study, did not contribute to mean crew performance nor to within-crew performance variability, causing the rejection of Hypothesis 4. McIntyre and Salas (1995) argued that there is little evidence to suggest there is one appropriate interaction style that would lead all highly effective (and consistent) groups to report high cohesiveness. As these researchers note, the level of cohesiveness reported by group members is a function of the situation or circumstances. Those surrounding the crews performing in this study are explored in terms of the context described in the following sections.

In contrast to group cohesion, results from this study indicate that communications patterns among crew members contribute to within-crew performance variability. In general, crews that more frequently provide nontechnical communications, such as tension release and frustration perform less consistently. In addition, crews that are less consistent (across training scenarios) in providing nontechnical communications, such as tension release are also more variable in their performance. In sum, it appears reasonable to conclude that the nontechnical communications are more likely to produce variable performance, especially in situations when performance in determined by raters.

It is also important to note that, in general, the relative type of communications that crews provide during operations contribute to performance effectiveness. Crews that communicate more nontechnical than technical comments are rated as less effective. In addition, crews that were less consistent in the types of communications provided across the seven scenarios were also rated as less effective. This conclusion applies to both technical and nontechnical communications. This finding is consistent with findings from other studies investigating communication patterns (Kanki, 1989; Kanki, Lozito, & Foushee, 1989). A final note concerning these communications patterns. The data collected simply represent the relative number of different types of communications. There was no attempt to track these communications in terms of who was speaking to whom, nor do we report which operator provided specific comments. Such a data collection and analysis procedure would have permitted more sophisticated analysis of the communications process among crew members and may have provided more insight about how crews communicate with each other, especially in a highly structured setting such as nuclear power plant operations.

Study Context

As shown in Fig. 12.1, the external conditions play a role in team performance and effectiveness. Because all team members had similar operations experience at their home plant and were performing in virtually the same context (training simulator), we did not include this element in the study design. It is, however, important to examine the context as it relates to the study findings. Critical features of the context involve nuclear power plant operations and in a different culture—Japan. These two features are addressed in turn.

Nuclear power plant operations crews can be defined as tactical decision-making teams (McIntyre & Salas, 1995). According to McIntyre and Salas, tactical decision-making teams are differentiated from slower paced, non-emergency decision-making teams using the following criteria: (a) requires decision making under time pressure and threat; and (b) the consequence for error is immediate and more severe than for the slower paced nondecision-making teams; and (c) are more likely to be an intact team, as opposed to a loosely knit team. Team members performing in this study were all highly experienced in performing in nuclear power plant control rooms (average years of experience 4.9 years) Thus, team members were very knowledgeable about the duties and responsibilities required of the roles they were asked to play in the training scenarios. One factor that reduced the realism of these training sessions concerns the role each member played. Even though crew members were knowledgeable about the duties and responsibilities of each role, they may have played a role different from their current home plant assignment. For this reason, performance for some crew members may not accurately reflect the actual duties and responsibilities they performed in their home plant. This difference in training versus home plant assignment very likely influenced individual crew member performance evaluations; it is unclear how this might affect crew performance evaluations.

Another aspect of nuclear power plant operations concerns the well-developed procedures used to guide crew performance. That is, operations requirements for all crew members have been strictly defined and designed to anticipate all types of operating and emergency conditions. Operating procedures also require specific types of communications. For example, when an alarm or enunciator sounds, someone in the crew must acknowledge this alarm by pointing to it or stating which alarm is sounding. The importance of this acknowledgement response can be seen in the communications results in that expert raters provided higher ratings to crews that provided more acknowledgment communications relative to other types of communications. Thus, the types of communications provided during a training scenario are prescribed to some degree. Such prescriptions influence raters' perceptions of effective and ineffective crew performance.

Cultural Context

As reported earlier, these data were collected in a nuclear training facility located in Japan. In designing the study and developing or selecting data collection instruments, we paid special attention to cultural factors that might influence the results. Concerning the independent variables, all results were compared to normative data available from Japanese samples or from U.S. samples. These comparisons revealed that mean scores for operators in this study generally conformed to the normative data. In some instances, however, the study sample scored higher than expected on some cognitive ability measures.[4] These higher than expected scores suggest that test scores for their sample of operators may be restricted in range. This may explain why we found very few of the cognitive abilities to influence group (and individual) performance.

A second feature of the cultural context concerns performance assessment. One of the most critical features of the study was to evaluate both individual and group performance. In working with NTC instructors, we learned that following each training session, operators were provided feedback on their performance as individuals and as a crew. This feedback, however, was not recorded or at least did not necessarily follow written guidelines. We constructed individual and group performance evaluation instruments using input from NTC instructors and operations experts. The important point here is that written (numerical) performance evaluations of crew and individual performance were uncommon in the training setting (and the home setting) even though NTC trainers and home plant supervisors provide feedback to the operations crews. Thus, NTC trainers and

---

[4]An example of test scores that were slightly higher than expected were found on the Advanced Ravens Progressive Matrices test. In this study, power plant operators obtained higher than expected scores for their job classification. In fact, operators' mean score is comparable to data obtained from a U.S. college sample. This finding suggests that the sample of operators may have been highly screened (only the best operators were selected for control room operations).

operations experts were not accustomed to assessing performance using evaluation instruments. We provided day-long training and follow-up training to ensure that these raters used consistent metrics for making their ratings.

A final comment about cultural differences concerns the policies and procedures guiding crew performance. As indicated previously, nuclear power plant operations are guided by well-defined policies and procedures. In addition, crew interactions are also well-defined. In this setting, the senior operator (SRO) is the leader and is responsible for making all decisions. The assistant operators (RO and TO) are there to support the SRO; generally these operators are discouraged from making suggestions for actions. As demonstrated in the data, expert raters gave lower scores to those crews in which suggestions were made. This represents a considerable difference in terms of the U.S. definition of team processes. In the United States, teams are encouraged to exchange ideas and suggestions. As a result, it is possible that findings from this study are limited to not only the nuclear control room operator occupation, but limited to the job as it is performed in Japan as well.

Crew Performance Measurement

This book focuses on theory and measurement of team performance. As a summary of the data reported in this study, we provide an assessment of crew performance measurement and our thinking about future studies that can incorporate theory with practice.

Evaluation of Crew Performance Measurement. Team performance and within-crew performance variability are complex constructs that impose measurement challenges. Understanding the constructs and designing valid measures of team performance are topics presented in this and many research articles and books. One such attempt at defining the rules for team performance measurement is provided by O'Neil, Baker, and Kaslauskas (1992). Rules provided by these authors are described here, along with an evaluation of the measures designed and administration context for the present study.

1. **Team performance assessment is measured in context.** In the present study, we measured crews performing in their natural environment—a simulated nuclear power plant control room. Simulator trainers and operational experts participated in the development of crew rating dimensions that corresponded to elements used to provide feedback to crews and crew members.

2. **Team performance assessment requires integrated, sensible tasks studied over adequate time periods.** The high-fidelity simulation of control room operations presented crews with realistic tasks. Furthermore, simulations were paced in such a manner as to depict realistic time demands for emergency operations.

3. **Team performance assessment should be reserved for procedural and problem solving tasks.** Specific training scenarios were selected to present crews with the challenge of adhering to routine procedures (e.g., acknowledging enunciators and alarms), yet at the same time, working together to diagnose and correct plant malfunctions.

4. **Do not trade validity for assessment and ease.** In this study, the training facility incurred additional costs to set up and operate video and audio equipment and provide expert raters to provide both process and performance data. These additional features helped to ensure that the demand on expert raters was reduced (e.g., raters provided performance effectiveness rating as they directly observed performance, and then provided communications patterns counts from videotapes).

5. **Specify the domain and scoring criteria using state-of-the-art approaches.** We addressed this requirement by first identifying operator performance rating dimensions from the literature. We then worked with NTC trainers and operations experts to construct crew performance rating dimensions used in this study.

6. **Invest in trained judges.** Expert raters were trained to use the crew rating dimensions using videotaped crew performance collected during previous research efforts. Raters then participated in a pilot study. We evaluated the interrater reliability data from this study and determined that additional training was needed. Raters participated in a second training session using videotaped performances of crews participating in the pilot study.

7. **Plan assessment procedures so as to minimize potential corruption.** Corruption, as used by the authors, refers to the potential for ratees to pander to the crew performance criteria without actually adjusting crew performance. In this study, crews were aware of the evaluation process but were not informed of the specific dimensions on which they would be rated.

In sum, we would argue that team performance measurement in the present study adheres to the requirements defined by O'Neil and his colleagues. The content of the team performance effectiveness and within-crew performance variability criteria, however, are examined below in relation to the teamwork construct.

Evaluation of Team Performance Construct.   As indicated earlier, team performance measurement procedures may conform to established guidelines, but the content of these measures may not conform to conventional wisdom. Therefore, we examine the team performance and performance variability construct used in this study with other examples of teamwork measures. As a conclusion, we identify areas for future research in the area of team performance assessment and identifying the sources of performance variability.

The team performance construct can be measured in many ways depending on the task performed and the definition of team performance (Cannon-Bowers, Tannenbaum, Salas, & Volpe, 1995). McIntyre and Salas (1995) identified four behavioral characteristics that define team performance for situations in which teamwork is essential to effective outcomes. These four characteristics include:

1. Performance monitoring—team members monitor one another's performance.
2. Feedback—team members provide feedback to and accept it from one another.
3. Closed-loop communication—teamwork involves effective communication among members that often involves closed-loop communication.
4. Backing up behaviors—implies a willingness, preparedness, and proclivity to back fellow members up during operations.

The reader is encouraged to compare the above teamwork behaviors with those included in the crew performance assessment instrument (Table 12.1). It is clear that these four critical teamwork behaviors are represented in rating Dimensions 1 and 3. The crew performance rating dimensions used in the present study also contain a dimension focusing on effective team performance (Dimension 2). Correlations among the three rating dimensions (average $r = .81$) suggest that expert raters very likely concentrated on taskwork outcomes, as opposed to teamwork outcomes. Thus, the performance instrument used in this study combined teamwork behaviors along with quality of team/crew performance. This confounds outcomes from teamwork and taskwork. Thus, factors identified as contributing to crew performance variability also confound teamwork and taskwork outcomes.

This conclusion points to the issue of defining the teamwork construct. Using guidance from McIntyre and Salas, a more precise measure of teamwork may have involved a combination of our crew performance dimensions (1) team unity and (3) team spirit, along with a more sophisticated procedure for collecting and analyzing communication patterns.

Defined in this manner, crew processes may be considered as both independent and dependent variables in understanding the construct teamwork. The challenge is to determine methods for measuring team processes as input and output in the teamwork framework. Based on data from the present study and from the literature, however, it may be more appropriate to consider a dynamic relationship between the independent and dependent variables included in the study. Figure 12.4 provides a graphic depiction of the potential relationships between team member and team characteristics, team process variables, and team performance effectiveness and within-crew performance variability. According to this figure, team member characteristics and team characteristics contribute to team process variables (teamwork), which in turn contributes to team performance effectiveness.

This exploratory study examined the potential for uncovering sources of within-crew performance variability. Even though we found support for some hypotheses, these findings highlight other questions for future research. For example, in this study, results suggest that there was very little within-crew performance variance. In this instance, does it make sense to pursue sources of performance variability? We would argue that the benefits of identifying sources of variability are strongly related to the outcomes from errors on the job. For those jobs that involve the potential for life and death decisions, performance variability is a critical construct. A second issue concerns the performance effectiveness variable used in this study. In other studies of crew performance, more objective measures of performance effectiveness are used (e.g., number of errors). If performance is measured in this manner, then conclusions about sources of performance variability may be very different from the findings reported here. Therefore, it is important to investigate other measures of performance effectiveness to identify sources of variability. Finally, drawing from the previous discussion and the model presented in Fig. 12.4, we recommend designing investigations of teamwork and team performance effectiveness that permit

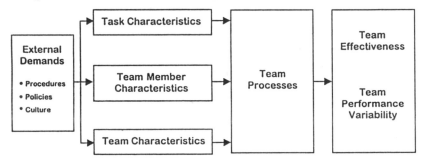

FIG. 12.4. Hypothesized relationships among team characteristics, processes, and performance variables.

a dynamic examination of the variables that contribute to team effectiveness and team performance variability.

REFERENCES

Argote, L. (1982). Input uncertainty and organizational coordination in hospital emergency units. *Administrative Science Quarterly, 27,* 420–434.

Barrick, M. R., & Mount, M. K. (1991). The big five personality dimensions and job performance: A meta-analysis. *Personnel Psychology, 44,* 1–26.

Bass, B. (1980). Team productivity and individual member competence. *Small Group Behavior, 11,* 431–504.

Bass, B., & Barrett, B. (1981). *People, work, and organizations.* Boston: Allyn & Bacon.

Borman, W. (1991). Job behavior, performance and effectiveness. In M. Dunnette & L. Hough (Eds.), *Handbook of industrial and organizational psychology* (Vol. 2, pp. 271–326). Palo Alto, CA: Consulting Psychologists Press.

Cannon-Bowers, J. A., Tannenbaum, S. I., Salas, E., & Volpe, C. E. (1995). Defining competencies and establishing team training requirements. In R. Guzzo & E. Salas (Eds.), *Team effectiveness and decision-making in organizations* (pp. 333–380). San Francisco, CA: Jossey-Bass.

Cooper, R., & Payne, R. (1972). Personality orientations and performance in soccer teams. *British Journal of Social and Clinical Psychology, 11,* 2–9.

Dickinson, T. (1969). The effects of work interaction and its interplay with task organization on team and member performance. (Doctoral dissertation, The Ohio State University). *Dissertation Abstracts International, 30* (4-B).

Dunnette, M. D., Bownas, D. B., & Bosshardt, M. J. (1981). *Prediction of inappropriate, unreliable, or aberrant job behavior in nuclear power plant settings.* Washington DC: The Edison Electric Institute.

Dunnette, M., Rosse, R., Houston, J., Hough, L., Toquam, J., Lammelein, S., King, K., Bosshardt, M., & Keyes, M. (1982). *Development and validation of an industry-wide electric power plant operator selection system.* (Tech. Rep). Minneapolis, MN: Personnel Decisions Research Institute.

Evans, C., & Dion, K. (1991). Group cohesion and performance: A meta-analysis. *Small Group Research, 22,* 175–186.

Fernandez, J. (1992). Soldier quality and job performance in team tasks. *Social Science Quarterly, 73,* 253–265.

Foushee, H., Lauber, J., Baetge, M., & Acomb, D. (1986). *Crew factors in flight operations: The operational significance of exposure to short-haul air transportation operations.* (NASA TM-88322). Mountain View, CA: NASA.

Foushee, H., & Manos, K. (1981). Information transfer within the cockpit: Problems in intracockpit communications. In C. Billings & E. Cheaney (Eds.), *Information transfer problems in the aviation system* (pp. 63–71). NASA TP-1875. Moffett Field, CA: NASA-Ames Research Center, September, (NTIS No. N81-31162)

Galbraith, J. (1977). *Organizational Design.* Reading, MA: Addison-Wesley.

Gertman, D. I., Haney, L. N., Jenkins, J. P., & Blackman, H. S. (1985). *Operational decision-making and action selection under psychological stress in nuclear power plants.* (NUREG/CR-4040/XAB) Washington, DC: U.S. Nuclear Regulatory Commission.

Ghiselli, E. (1956). Dimensional problems of criteria. *Journal of Applied Psychology, 40,* 1–4.

Glass, G., Willson, V., & Gottman, J. (1975). *Design and analysis of time series experiments.* Boulder, CO: Colorado Associated University Press.

Hanges, P., Schneider, B., & Niles, K. (1990). Stability of performance: An interactionist perspective. *Journal of Applied Psychology, 75,* 658–667.

Helmreich, R. L., Sawin, L. L., & Carsud, A. L. (1986). The honeymoon effect in job performance: Temporal increases in the predictive power of achievement motivation. *Journal of Applied Psychology, 71,* 185–188.

Helmreich, R., Wilhelm, J., Gregorich, S., & Chidester, T. (1990, June). Preliminary results from the evaluation of cockpit resource management training: Performance ratings of flightcrews. *Aviation, Space, and Environmental Medicine,* 576–579.

Hill, M. (1982). Group versus individual performance. Are N+1 heads better than 1? *Psychological Bulletin, 91,* 517–539.

Itoh, J., Yoshimura, S., Ohtsuka, T., & Matsuda, F. (1990). Cognitive task analysis of nuclear power plant operators for man-machine interface design. In *Proceedings of the Topical Meeting on Advances in Human Factors Research on Man Machine Interactions* (pp. 96–102). Nashville, TN: The American Nuclear Society.

Johnston, W. (1966). Transfer of team skills as a function of type of training. *Journal of Applied Psychology, 50,* 102–108.

Kanas, N. (1985). Psychosocial factors affecting simulated and actual space missions. *Aviation, Space, and Environmental Medicine,* August, 806–811.

Kane, J. (1986). Performance distribution assessment. In R. Berk (Ed.), *Performance assessment: Methods and applications* (pp. 237–273). Baltimore, MD: Johns Hopkins University Press.

Kanki, B. (1989, April). Communication variations and aircrew performance. *International Symposium on Aviation Psychology, Proceedings* (Vol. 1), Columbus, OH.

Kanki, B., Lozito, S., & Foushee, H. (1989). Communication indexes of crew coordination. *Aviation, Space, and Environmental Medicine, 60,* 56–60.

Keller, R. (1986). Predictors of the performance of project groups in R & D organizations. *Academy of Management Journal, 29,* 715–726.

Klein, M., & Christiansen, G. (1969). Group composition, group structure, and group effectiveness of basketball teams. In J. Loy & G. Kenyon (Eds.), *Sport, culture, and society* (pp. 397–408). New York: MacMillan.

Komaki, J., Collins, R., & Penn, P. (1982). The role of performance antecedents and consequences in work motivation. *Journal of Applied Psychology, 67,* 334–340.

Martens, R. (1970). Influence of participation motivation on success and satisfaction in team performance. *Research Quarterly, 41,* 510–518.

McBride, D. J. (1988). *An exploration of team information processing in a dynamic group task involving uncertainty* (AFIT/CI/NR 88–120) Wright Patterson Air Force Base, OH (NTIS No. AD A196 195/2/XAB).

McCain, L., & McCleary, R. (1979). The statistical analysis of the simple interrupted time-series quasi-experiment. In T. Cook & D. Campbell (Eds.), *Quasi-experimentation: Design and analysis issues for field settings* (pp. 233–293). Chicago: Rand McNally.

McIntyre, R. M., & Salas, E. (1995). Measuring and managing for team performance: Emerging principles form complex environments. In R. Guzzo & E. Salas (Eds.), *Team effectiveness and decision-making in organizations* (pp. 9–45). San Francisco, CA: Jossey-Bass.

Miesing, P., & Preble, J. (1985). Group processes and performance in a complex business simulation. *Small Group Behavior, 16,* 325–338.

Morris, C. (1966). Task effects on group interaction. *Journal of Personality and Social, Psychology, 5,* 545–554.

Naylor, J., & Briggs, G. (1965). Team training effectiveness under various conditions. *Journal of Applied Psychology, 49,* 223–229.

Nieva, V., Fleishman, E., & Reick, A. (1978). *Team dimensions: Their identity, their measurement, and their relationships* (Contract No. DAHC 19–78-C-0001). Washington, DC: Response Analysis Corporation.

O'Neil, H., Baker, E., and Kaslauskas, E. (1992). Assessment of team performance. In R. Swezey & E. Salas (Eds.), *Teams: Their training and performance* (pp. 153–175). Norwood, NJ: Ablex.

O'Reilly, C., Caldwell, D., & Barnett, D. (1989). Workgroup demography, social integration, and turnover. *Administrative Science Quarterly, 34*, 21–37.

Picano, J. (1991). *Psychological factors influencing performance and aviation safety. 1.* (AGARD-AG-324) Washington DC: National Aeronautics and Space Administration.

Pfeffer, J. (1983). Organizational demography. In L. Cummings & B. Staw (Eds.), *Research in organizational behavior*. Greenwich, CT: JAI Press.

Rouse, S. H., & Rouse, W. B. (1982). Cognitive styles as a correlate of human problem-solving performance in fault diagnosis tasks. *IEEE Transactions on Systems, Man, and Cybernetics, SMC-12* (5):649–652.

Ruffell-Smith, H. (1979, January). *A simulator study of the interaction of pilot workload with errors, vigilance, and decisions* (NASA TM-78482). Moffett Field, CA: NASA-Ames Research Center.

Schmidt, F., Hunter, J., & Caplan, J.R. (1981). Validity generalization results for jobs in the petroleum industry. *Journal of Applied Psychology, 66*:261–273.

Schneider, B. (1987). The people make the place. *Personnel Psychology, 40*, 437–452.

Sherif, M. (1966). *In common predicament: Social psychology of intergroup conflict and cooperation*. Boston: Houghton-Mifflin.

Stein, M. (1982). Creativity, groups, and management. In R. Guzzo (Ed.), *Improving group decision making in organizations* (pp. 127–155). New York: Academic Press.

Steiner, I., & Dodge, J. (1956). Interpersonal perception and role structure as determinants of group and individual efficiency. *Human Relations, 9*, 467–480.

Terborg, J., Castore, C., & DeNinno, J. (1976). A longitudinal field investigation of the impact of group composition on group performance and cohesion. *Journal of Personality and Social Psychology, 34*, 782–790.

Triandis, H., Hall, E., & Ewen, R. (1965). Member heterogeneity and dyadic creativity. *Human Relations, 18*, 33–55.

Tushman, M. (1977). Special boundary roles in the innovation process. *Administrative Science Quarterly, 22*, 587–605.

Tushman, M. (1979). Impacts of perceived environmental variability of patterns of work related communication. *Academy of Management Journal, 23*, 482–500.

Tziner, A., & Eden, D. (1985). Effects of crew composition on crew performance: Does the whole equal the sum of its parts? *Journal of Applied Psychology, 70*, 85–93.

Tziner, A., & Vardi, Y. (1983). Ability as a moderator between cohesiveness and tank crew's performance. *Journal of Occupational Behavior, 4*, 137–143.

Wagner, W., Pfeffer, J., & O'Reilly, C. (1984). Organizational demography and turnover in top management groups. *Administrative Science Quarterly, 29*, 74–92.

Wiersema, M. F., & Bird, A. (1993). Organizational demography in Japanese firms: Group heterogeneity, individual dissimilarity, and top management team turnover. *Academy of Management Journal, 36*(5), 966–1025.

Wood, R. (1986). Task complexity: Definition of the construct. *Organizational Behavior and Human Decision Processes, 37*, 60–82.

Wright, P. M., McMahan, G. C., Smart, D., & McCormick, E. J. (1995). *Team cognitive ability as a predictor of team performance*. Paper presented at the 10th annual meeting of the Society of Industrial and Organizational Psychologists, Orlando, FL.

Zenger, T., & Lawrence, B. (1989). Organizational demography: The differential effects of age and tenure distributions on technical communication. *Academy of Management Journal, 32*, 353–376.

13
The Measurement of Team Process Behaviors in the Cockpit: Lessons Learned

Ashley Prince
Michael T. Brannick
University of South Florida

Carolyn Prince
Eduardo Salas
Naval Air Warfare Center
Training Systems Division, Orlando

BACKGROUND

The word *teamwork* implies that what a team does in order to function as a team is not necessarily easy. Statistics citing failures in teamwork also tell us that it cannot be considered a natural process; teamwork does not just occur when two or more people come together to do a task. Defining the process that teams use to get their jobs done has been formidable. However, as more and more of the business of our daily lives becomes dependent on what teams do, the definition and measurement of their processes becomes increasingly important, no matter how difficult the task.

The finding that 60% of all aviation accidents are due to human error (Lauber, 1987) revealed a pressing need to explore the ways that aircrews function as teams. As Foushee (1984) noted, when an individual team member commits an error and the team does not catch that error and correct it, the error becomes a team error. This accident statistic has been made all the more compelling as a research issue because of the increasing population of air travelers and the reliance of much business in this country on aviation for the transport of goods and products. All are closely dependent on the skill and work processes of these crews. An even more important reason for focusing on the team functioning in aircrews is that, although the failure of any team may lead to decreased organizational effectiveness, the failure of a cockpit crew may lead to the loss of life.

Not only has a clear need for research in aircrew performance been established, but, within aviation, there is an opportunity afforded for study that is unusual for teams performing "real" work. Because cockpit crews need to practice and be tested in a safe environment, they routinely use simulators that are close replicas of the aircraft they fly. These simulators provide an excellent opportunity to observe crews as they work on tasks that are identical to those in their jobs. They also permit experimental manipulations and training interventions without concern about interference in ongoing work. The addition of videotaping capabilities to the simulators makes it possible for multiple observers to have access to an otherwise closed working situation.

Thus, the concern over human error, the recognition of the importance of the aircrew's work, and the opportunity for study has led to research in recent years focusing on the functioning and the measurement of team performance in cockpit crews. Under the auspices of the Federal Aviation Administration (FAA) and the National Aeronautics and Space Administration (NASA), a number of experiments with airline crews have been conducted. Research has begun also in the military services (Prince & Salas, 1993). The expectation is that the knowledge resulting from the research could lead to training that will increase efficiency, reduce errors, and decrease fatalities.

Teams whose work environment is an airplane's cockpit can differ appreciably in some of the tasks they perform. These differences may be due to their organization's charter, its climate and rules, the type of aircraft the team flies, or their assigned mission. A commercial airline crew is responsible for the safe and timely transport of passengers to their expected destination, yet a military aircrew is often tasked with assignments that require crews to do work that is in addition to flying the aircraft (e.g., electronic surveillance). As a result, the military crew may include some individuals who are more involved with the performance of these secondary tasks than with the conduct of flight. Still, all cockpit crews do have common tasks related to flying the aircraft (adhering to the physics of flight, giving safety a priority, attending to regulations, monitoring instruments), and all are similar in the team interactions they use to ensure the accomplishment of these tasks (Prince & Salas, in press). This justifies their treatment as a coherent group.

Already, attempts to study cockpit crews and to measure their processes are providing some valuable lessons on those processes and on measurement specific to these teams. Because some of the process skills that have been identified for cockpit crews are similar to those for other types of teams (Prince & Salas, 1989), we believe that these lessons will be relevant for the measurement of the process of other teams as well.

We begin this chapter with a brief overview of the research on developing measures for team processes in aviation teams. Next, three experiments in a progression of research that was planned to investigate team process measurement in aircrews are presented and their results discussed. Then, based on the research discussed here, we offer some lessons learned on the measurement of team process to help guide future research and application.

AVIATION TEAM RESEARCH OVERVIEW

It was the team effort of the two Wright brothers that was responsible for the very first manned flight. Despite the close relationship between teamwork and aviation from its beginning, an interest in measuring team processes and performance has come about only in recent aviation history. Thus, the research overview of aviation team performance measurement is somewhat brief. Despite the small number of research efforts, these accumulated results from early studies have provided a base for present measurement efforts.

Much of the research on aviation team processes has centered on ways to capture performance through analysis of crew member communications (Brannick, Roach, & Salas, 1994). This analysis has utilized the classificatory concept (Carnap, 1966/1995), by determining categories of communication. It then introduces quantification through the simple process of counting the incidents of each category within each team's total communications. One of the first such attempts was made by Williges, Johnston, and Briggs (1966) who used a simulated radar controlled aerial intercept task to analyze team communications as they related to team effectiveness. Audiotapes were made of the communications of 64 undergraduate males who performed the task in teams of two (32 teams). Each team's communications were analyzed by a 48-item classification scheme. The 48 items were distributed into five categories: identification, task irrelevant, declarative statement, tactical statement, and tactical command. Williges et al. (1966) found that communication among team members facilitated performance "only when a more efficient information channel (e.g., standard operating procedure) is not available" (p. 477).

Another experiment in which communication categories were analyzed was reported by Siegel and Federman (1973). They studied the communication content of helicopter teams performing in a simulated antisubmarine warfare environment by using a set of categories consisting of 28 items (e.g., provides information in response to request). Data from the team communications were factor-analyzed and four factors emerged: (a) probablistic structure (alternatives are considered); (b) evaluative interchange (interchange of ideas, proposals, and data); (c) hypothesis formulation (interpretation of past performance); and (d) leadership control (opinions of crew members are allowed to emerge). In a second scenario, using a different helicopter simulator, geographic location, and sample, Siegel and Federman (1973) rated the communication on the same 28 items and factor-analyzed the data. They found that three of the four communication factors were the same in the second mission; only hypothesis formulation did not emerge as a factor in the second study. Subsequently, Siegel and Federman developed a training program emphasizing the use of communication factors. When the program was administered and evaluated, results indicated no significant difference between the control group and the trained group but performance was affected in the correct direction.

In 1979, Ruffell-Smith, who was looking for information on stress effects, videotaped line-qualified, airline crewmembers in a realistic scenario that included some potentially disastrous problems. He reported an observed wide range of ways that the crews handled the requirements and problems of the flight. Some crews took longer to realize they had a problem than others and decisions that were made on what to do about the problem situations were not the same. Ruffell-Smith also observed dissimilarities in the ways the crews handled their situations; for example, some captains did most of the work, yet others delegated many of the tasks.

In order to analyze the differences between these crews at a greater level of detail, Foushee and Manos (1981) classified the communication content of the crews in Ruffell-Smith's (1979) research into specific categories. The categories included: (a) crewmember observations; (b) commands; (c) inquiries or requests for information; (d) response uncertainty; (e) agreement; (f) acknowledgments; and (g) pushes (repetitions of already stated commands or inquiries). These researchers found that crews demonstrated differences in communication pattern and content. They also discovered that frequency in number of commands, observations, inquiries, and acknowledgments increased during emergency periods. Foushee and Manos were able to relate frequency of communication with overall performance. (The overall performance had been rated separately by expert pilots.) Specifically, teams with high frequency communications received higher performance ratings than those teams with low frequency ratings.

In an attempt to investigate this same issue in a military environment, Oser, Prince, and Morgan (1990) used a modified version of the communication categories defined by Foushee and Manos (1981) to code the communications of 14 teams of military aviators flying a specially designed scenario in a full mission simulator. They were able to replicate Foushee and Manos' finding that communication content varies depending on the nature of the flight segment, but they were unable to find differences in the communication frequencies that related to crew performance.

While most researchers have looked at specific categories of information, some have been more interested in the potential patterns of communication that may reveal differences in the crews. Kanki, Lozito, and Foushee (1987) analyzed transcripts of 10 airline crews who had participated as subjects in an earlier experiment (Foushee, Lauber, Baetge, & Acomb, 1986). Using the operational performance of all the crews who participated in the original study, the crews were assigned to three different groups (e.g., low, high) based on the number of operational errors they had committed. Kanki et al. (1987) separated the five low-error crews (top performers) and the five high-error crews (bottom performers) from the larger group. They found that the low-error crews demonstrated patterns of communication similar to each other (e.g., more commands given by captains, type of response of copilot to captain's commands). High-error crews showed no consistency with each other. In further analysis, Kanki, Greaud, and Irwin (1989) included the middle range error crews and were not able to make a discrimination.

Prior to flight, many crews are required to meet together and share some information about the upcoming flight. This meeting provides an opportunity to begin team building activities. For this reason, Ginnett (1987) analyzed the pre-flight communications and crew interactions of nine airline captains and observed the subsequent performance of these captains with their crews in actual flight. Using Hackman's (1983) normative model approach to work group effectiveness, Ginnett hypothesized that early in the group process, it is important to develop boundaries, come to terms with the task, and develop norms for the group. Furthermore, Ginnett stated that the appointed leader most likely will take on this function. The captains who were asked to participate in Ginnett's research had been nominated by senior pilots (check airmen) who were familiar with the performance of a large number of pilots within their airline.

Five captains were selected for the research based on outstanding ability in managing the crew and four were selected who were known to have problems in working with crews. Ginnett observed the captains in the initial meetings as they briefed their crews. He noted that effective leaders developed boundaries, addressed the task, and developed norms of the group. Three of the four less effective leaders did not accomplish these tasks. During the flights that followed the briefs, Ginnett noted that the more effective captains were consistent in their leadership behaviors throughout; they provided a rationale for statements, stressed the importance of interactions, delegated tasks, established their own competence, listened, and engaged the crews in the process. Less effective captains showed no consistency in leadership behaviors.

Little research in this area has directly addressed the cognitive processes that may underlie crew interactions. One of the first researchers to do so was Orasanu (1990), who investigated the decision-making process of crews by analyzing crew communications from a cognitive perspective. She proposed four cognitive components which support decision making in natural environments: (a) situational assessment (interpreting situational cues to recognize when a problem exists; (b) meta-cognition (defining the problems and working out a plan to solve it; setting priorities); (c) shared mental models (articulating situation assessment and mental cognitive processes and shared understanding of specific elements); and (d) resource management (management of information, cognitive work, communication, scheduling coordination of actions).

Subsequently, Orasanu and Fischer (1991) analyzed data collected previously by Chidester, Kanki, Foushee, Dickinson, and Bowles (1990) and Foushee, Lauber, Baetge, and Acomb (1986) on air carrier crews. They concentrated on the five top-performing crews and the five lowest performing crews (performance was based on crew errors) in one data set and the four high and low performers in the second. Orasanu and Fischer found that high-performance crews demonstrated greater situation awareness, used low workload periods to make plans, and collected more relevant information when compared with the poorer performing crews.

Work done by Helmreich and his colleagues under the auspices of NASA represents a different approach to the measurement of crew processes by investigating links between crewmember attitudes and the functioning of effective teams (Helmreich & Foushee, 1993). The Cockpit Management Attitudes Questionnaire (CMAQ; Helmreich, 1984) was developed to capture crewmember attitudes and to relate them to the attitudes of crew members who had been identified as effective team members. By looking at aviators' CMAQ responses before team interaction training and responses made on the CMAQ after the training, Helmreich and Wilhelm (1991) were able to demonstrate that those who underwent training to improve teamwork changed their responses as a result of the training programs and this change was in a positive direction.

Helmreich and his associates have also developed 40 "behavioral markers" (e.g., "Avoids 'tunnel vision,' being aware of factors such as stress that can reduce vigilance"; Helmreich & Foushee, 1993, p. 27) to be used when observing crews in realistic simulations (Helmreich et al., 1991). These behavioral markers are classified into three interpersonal and cognitive task clusters (i.e., team formation and management tasks, communication processes and decision tasks, and situation awareness, workload management tasks; Helmreich & Foushee, 1993). The behavioral markers are used to make up a checklist (the Line/LOS checklist) that is used by an observer (usually an instructor pilot or check airman) to rate crews on their performance.

In related research, Clothier (1991) analyzed Line/LOS checklist scores that had been collected on crews at one airline for two different years. In the first year, trained crews had been through a team training program; before the ratings were made in the second year, the crews had attended a second, recurrent training program. She reported that checklist scores were higher for the crews in the second year than they had been in the first year. In addition, she compared the checklist data on 2,000 untrained crews with 1,000 trained crews in 1989, when the initial training was introduced, and found there was a significant increase in ratings for 12 of 14 performance areas for the trained crews. She interpreted these data as supporting the value of the team training programs.

Summary of Aviation Team Measurement Research

In describing the research on the measurement of aviation team processes, diversity is a useful word. While Williges et al. (1966) were interested in the categories of communication, Helmreich and his associates (1993) have focused on attitudes and behavioral markers, and Ginnett (1987) measured leadership actions. The size of the samples studied vary. Numbers of teams observed in each controlled experiment are generally small, ranging from 9 (Ginnett, 1987) to 32 (Williges et al., 1966). Kanki et al. (1987) and Orasanu (1990) looked closely at small numbers of crews that have been identified as top performers or the lowest performers by previous research and other researchers have looked at the full range of teams (e.g., Foushee & Manos, 1981; Oser, Prince, & Morgan, 1990; Ruffell-Smith, 1979). At the same time, Clothier (1991) analyzed data from an unusually large number of teams. Purposes of the research have differed as well.

Helmreich and Foushee (1993) described some of their research as designed to validate a training program, Ginnett (1987) and Orasanu (1990) to explore different theories, and Siegel and Federman (1973) to develop training. The researchers have used different populations, from experienced aviators studied online as they perform their duties (e.g., Ginnett, 1987) to undergraduate college students, who have been observed and their performances recorded in simulated aviation-like tasks (e.g., Williges et al., 1966). Different scenarios are used in all of the experiments that have been reported. Difficulty of the scenarios, including such considerations as workload levels has not been standardized. For some of the crews in Clothier's (1991) research, the scenario was a real flight, while the scenarios Orasanu and her colleagues have used in their research (see Orasanu, 1994) had been designed to be very demanding. Scenario difficulty could account for some researchers being able to discriminate among crews' performance (Foushee & Manos, 1981) while others were not able to do so (Oser et al., 1990). The research by Helmreich and his associates is unique in the aviation research we have presented, since they look at large numbers of teams within their organizational environment. Although this kind of research provides interesting results, it has a disadvantage in the lack of control (e.g., ensuring equivalence of scenarios or training of raters) available to the researcher who conducts an experiment.

In most cases, team communications have been analyzed, although the same categories have been used only rarely. For example, Williges et al. (1966) employed a 48-item classification scheme; Siegel and Federman (1973) had 28 items; Foushee and Manos (1981) recorded seven categories; and Kanki et al. (1987) looked for patterns of communication. Orasanu (1990) and Ginnett (1987) both analyzed communications, each from a different theoretical standpoint.

The diversity in the research has been due in part to the lack of a unifying theory and to a failure to reach agreement on the constructs that are important for measurement of aviation team process. Measuring different types of cockpit crews, with varying tasks and diverse measures has not allowed an efficient comparison of the outcomes of the experiments.

When we reviewed the work that had been done before developing our research plans, what appeared to be missing was a coherent group of experiments designed to build logically on one another. We believed this type of research required controlled experimentation so that variables that may have an impact on team performance could be investigated. We have completed three experiments in this series now, and each is detailed in the next section.

RELATED PROCESS MEASUREMENT EXPERIMENTS

The need for a reliable, valid rating instrument for cockpit team processes has become more pressing in recent years. Due to the need to increase the effectiveness of aircrew performance, aviation organizations have not waited for research to determine team processes and to design measurement instruments before developing training that is aimed at improving teamwork. Unfortunately, this training cannot be evaluated, nor can trainees receive meaningful feedback on their team performance until psychometrically sound measurement instruments are developed. This section highlights a systematic research effort to develop reliable, valid measurement of team process, tailored to the cockpit crew. It contains a description of the first three experiments in a series of planned research designed to investigate team process and its measurement. Each of these experiments measures two-person teams in simulated aviation tasks.

They progress from employing participants with no knowledge of aviation tasks, a scale based on earlier general team research (Morgan, Glickman, Woodard, Blaiwes, & Salas, 1986), and a general team task with an aviation "flavor," to the use of military pilots, a scale based on an aviation coordination demands analysis (Prince & Salas, 1993), and more realistic aviation scenarios. Each experiment was designed to explore one or more specific team process measurement questions and each built upon the preceding research. The lessons learned from the earlier research and these first three experiments have been extracted and are provided in the final section of this chapter.

Critical Team Performance Elements for Measurement

In the first of the three experiments in this research series, Brannick, Roach, and Salas (1994) investigated the critical elements that contribute to team performance and the impact of different sources of information on the quality of team process evaluations. Participants were 104 individuals who were unfamiliar with aviation tasks. They participated in two-person teams (52 teams). The task was presented using a software program (Falcon); (Louie, 1987) on a personal computer. This task, to shoot down enemy aircraft, was based on the capabilities of the software that represented air combat between friendly and enemy aircraft. Interdependency was built into the task by design to require team members' interaction (e.g., the enemy could not be destroyed unless the two team members were working together). Team members were trained on the equipment for 20 to 45 minutes to a predetermined level of competence and then "flew" the scenario for 30 minutes. Each team was audiotaped.

Team performance was evaluated on three levels (communication frequency, team process, and objective criteria) by three sources (on-site judges, off-site judges, and self-ratings). On-site observers also provided ratings of overall team effectiveness to use as a subjective outcome measure. Team members made self-ratings on their team process and overall team effectiveness.

Communication behaviors were grouped into four communication categories: questions asked; information volunteered; instructions/commands; and jokes/social comments. The team process variables used to evaluate team performance included technical coordination; interpersonal cooperation; team spirit; and the quality of giving and accepting suggestions. These variables were adapted from the previous general team scale developed by Morgan, Glickman, Woodard, Blaiwes, and Salas (1986) on a task that was not aviation-related. Objective outcome measures of team performance included the time it took to shoot down the enemy and the number of radar locks on target.

Multitrait–multimethod (MTMM) analyses were used to evaluate the effects of sources of information on the team process measures. Acceptable internal consistency measures were achieved for all three groups of observers (on-site, off-site, and self). Brannick et al. (1994) found that on-site observer team process ratings were predictive of overall self-evaluation and, to a lesser extent, self-evaluations predicted overall observer evaluations. Although communication frequency was not related to the overall subjective evaluative outcome ratings, it was a better predictor of the objective criteria than the process ratings. In general, it was concluded that observers and sources provided their own unique information and that neither could be substituted for one another.

Exploring Construct Validity in a Team Process Measurement Scale

Subsequent to the first experiment, research was conducted to develop an aviation-specific team process rating scale. This started with a literature review of team research and was followed by critical incident interviews conducted with over 200 military cockpit crew members. These interviews were used to identify team behaviors that are related to effective team performance. A survey instrument sent to a second sample of crew members confirmed the behaviors that had emerged from the interviews and provided ratings for criticality, frequency, and difficulty on each. Following this, a mishap analysis of 225 aviation mishaps was conducted to determine if the identified behaviors (or a lack thereof) were implicated as causes in mishaps (Hartel, Smith, & Prince, 1991). The final list of behaviors was classified into seven skill dimensions (using a card sort process) and then were used as the basis for the development of the scale. The seven dimensions were communication, leadership, assertiveness, situation awareness, mission analysis, adaptability, and decision making (see Table 13.1).

The second experiment in this series, Brannick, Prince, Prince, and Salas (1995) was designed to explore construct validity of the aviation team measurement scale that resulted from the coordination demands analysis. The experiment was planned to control for some of the possible threats to validity that were identified in the first experiment (i.e., videotapes were used by off-site raters and the raters' tasks were simplified). In addition, this experiment employed predictive, known groups; aviators flying realistic scenarios, and planning periods.

A tailored version of the behavioral rating form developed on the behaviors identified as important for aviation teams (Prince & Salas, 1993) was used to record and evaluate the behavior of the team members. The original form contained general behaviors that had been determined to be important for aircrew processes (see Table 13.2). In the revised form, specific, pre-defined behaviors that were part of the seven skill dimensions were identified and were put in order of expected occurrence in the scenario. These behaviors were determined by subject matter experts who provided expectations of what high performing crews should do. To promote discriminant validity, assignments of these behaviors to specific dimensions were made through a consensus meeting of the research team. A code book

TABLE 13.1
Common Terms for Aviation Team Process

	Leadership	Decision Making	Situation Awareness	Adaptability	Communication	Assertiveness	Mission Analysis (Planning)
Helmreich & Foushee (1993)	Leadership[b] Followership/ Task Concerns	Communication[a] & Decision Tasks	Situation[a] Awareness and Workload Management		Communication[a] & Decision Tasks	Advocacy &[b] Assertion	Preparation/[b] Planning/ Vigilance
United States Army Aviation Center (1992)	Flight Team[c] Leadership	Application of[c] Appropriate Decision Making	Maintenance of[c] Mission Situation Awareness		Decision &[c] actions communicate & acknowledge	Advocacy &[c] Assertion Practiced	Mission Planning[d] & Rehearsal

[a]Task cluster. [b]Task area. [c]Basic quality. [d]Objective.

TABLE 13.2
Specific Behaviors for Rating Team Situation Awareness

Mission Situational Awareness (U.S. Army Aviation Center, 1992)	Situation Awareness (Prince & Salas, 1993)
1. Routinely updates others on mission status and situation awareness elements' status	1. Demonstrates ongoing awareness of mission status
2. Anticipates the situation awareness needs of others	2. Provides information in advance
3. Verbalizes and acknowledges changes in the elements of situation awareness	3. Comments on deviations
4. Is aware of the physical and mental state of others	4. Demonstrates awareness of task performance of self and others
5. Alerts others to personal problems	5. Identifies problems/potential problems
6. Alerts others to the presence of obstacles	6. Verbalizes a course of action
7. Requests needed information	

that contained specific behavioral indices for each level of evaluation (based on a 1–5, *poor–excellent* rating scale) helped guide the raters in their evaluations. A subject matter expert (SME) rating scale was developed by an experienced military aviator. This scale was used to record technical performance of each team and to give each a score for that performance.

Participants in this study were 102 military pilots. Of these, 69 were members of an advanced undergraduate aviation training program and 33 were instructor pilots in the same program. The student pilots had already passed their solo flight, ensuring that they possessed sufficient knowledge of aircraft systems, navigation, and instrumentation and of the aircrew's roles to be able to perform the research task.

Microsoft Flight Simulator (Artwick, 1989) was used because its flexibility allowed the creation of realistic scenarios. A scenario facilitator assumed the roles of air traffic controller (ATC), other controlling agencies, and the "passengers" in the scenarios by following a detailed script. Audio and video equipment recorded the pilots' communications and simulator control.

Pilots "flew" in two person teams and participated in two scenarios, each scenario representing a complete mission or flight, from a pre-flight brief, through take-off, to landing. The scenarios were developed through a cooperative effort of pilots and researchers to ensure that events would require team process behaviors corresponding to each skill dimension, would be as realistic as possible, and would be at an appropriate level for the aviation experience of the participants. The same number of decision points was inserted in each scenario in an attempt to make the two scenarios equally demanding. A pilot test used three volunteer crews of experienced pilots who flew both scenarios and provided feedback on scenario realism, difficulty, and equivalence. Changes in the scenarios were made based on their suggestions.

The teams were first trained to "fly" the table-top simulator (this training required no more than 15 minutes) and then they received a mission brief that included the primary purpose of the mission. They were given the paperwork and materials necessary for the flight (e.g., maps, charts) and for approximately 10 minutes, they planned their strategy for the mission and assigned responsibilities. After training and pre-flight briefing, teams performed their first mission. Following this first flight, the team prepared for and flew the second mission.

All ratings were made off-site by watching videotapes. The raters had experience in observation of behaviors and training on the form to be used but had no aviation experience. MTMM analysis of data found evidence of convergent and discriminant validity (with a mean of .88 for Scenario A and .77 for Scenario B in the validity diagonal entries) between judges. In addition, the judges' mean ratings of the process variables were significantly correlated with the rating of team technical performance. Mean ratings for each dimension in each scenario were higher for teams of instructor pilots than teams of student pilots and were significantly higher in three of the dimensions in one scenario and four of the dimensions in the other scenario. The analysis treating scenario as method showed poor convergent validity (the mean of validity diagonal entries was .31), indicating that teams may not be consistent or reliable across two scenarios.

In this research, the scenarios were counterbalanced (half the subjects flew Scenario A first, the other half flew Scenario B first) and there was no evidence of improved performance in the second scenario for either group. Thus, it appeared that simply having the experience of flying in a scenario, using this system, was not sufficient for training to occur. Therefore, for the next experiment, feedback was introduced as a training manipulation to see if training on the process skills could be accomplished by practicing the skills and receiving feedback on them. This required ensuring that the rating form could be used online and that it could help the instructor provide useful feedback.

Measuring the Effect of Specific Experience on Team Process in an Inexperienced Team

This experiment was conducted with aviators who were in the early stages of their training. They had sufficient knowledge for the experimental task to be meaningful and for control and interpretation of cockpit instruments to be no challenge, but they had virtually no experience of flying and controlling the aircraft without an instructor backing them up. Fifty subjects flew with instructors in two scenarios, using the same equipment described in the second experiment in this series. Instructors were trained to maintain a particular role in both scenarios and were restricted by a script as to what they could say. These roles required the student pilots to back up the instructors while they flew and the instructors to turn over control of the aircraft to the student at one point. The scenario required the students to confer with air traffic controllers and the instructors in order to make decisions and plans after they had taken control of the airplane and to keep the instructors informed of these decisions and plans. Student interactions were observed and documented during the first scenario. Half the subjects received formal feedback from the instructor before starting the second scenario; the other half of the subjects received no formal feedback.

A rating form for this experiment was developed based on the skill behaviors identified by Prince and Salas (1993), and tailored to the specific events in the scenario. For example, the instructor was scripted to fly above his assigned altitude and when this happened, student communications were expected to bring this to the instructor's attention. Process behaviors were recorded by both instructor pilots and by researchers as the scenarios progressed and agreement was reached on the behaviors observed before feedback was given. Videotapes were made for further analyses after the experiment was completed.

Results indicated that all "crews" were rated higher on their process skills in their second scenario regardless of whether they had received formal feedback. (Scenarios were counterbalanced to control for possible differences in difficulty.) Close inspection of the scenarios revealed that all students were receiving feedback in the scenario itself as part of the natural unfolding of the flight, either from the instructor or from the task. Even when clear task feedback did not occur, it was apparent that the events that were inserted in the scenario to elicit process behaviors may have served as cues in themselves, preparing students for the next occurrence of a similar event. Student pilots who participated in the research were very competitive in the development of flight-related skills. Thus, for example, if the air traffic controller requested the crew to give him a report on some aspect of the environment, pilots were alerted to pay more attention to environmental factors, even if no feedback was given.

LESSONS LEARNED FOR MEASUREMENT RESEARCH WITH WORK TEAMS

We have organized some of the major findings based on both the literature and our experience in measuring team process in aircrews into five sections:

measurement techniques, stimulus design, sources of information, constructs to measure, and team training and feedback. A sixth category, special problems in reliability and validity, reports on issues and problems that remain to be resolved. Although the lessons are based on research with aircrews, we believe that many of the lessons have applicability to other types of teams.

Many of the lessons listed here appear obvious, yet they may be overlooked when planning research. They are presented as a guide for future research on team performance measures to help ensure that results may be interpretable and meaningful.

Measurement and Rating Techniques

1. Make the rater's task one that can be reasonably accomplished. If he or she is required to observe and rate multiple actions simultaneously, or to use a rating form that is not easy to use, information may be lost.

2. Videotape the participants so that the raters will be able to confirm information. If videotaping is not possible, have a dedicated individual during the experiment take notes of crew behaviors that are not verbal. Audiotapes lack important visual information on the task and the team actions. Videotaping does require several considerations. It can be expensive and difficult logistically when there are several team members. If a number of people are working together, placement of the camera creates a problem because placing the camera far enough away to view all team members will mean that facial expressions will be lost. If you have funds, consider multiple video cameras and sequencers to link them for simultaneous playback. It is very helpful to use lapel microphones and a stereo mixer so that team members can be assigned auditory locations (i.e., panned left, right, or somewhere in the middle) for playback. When the raters use stereo headphones, assign auditory locations to help raters identify who is speaking.

3. Judges can provide psychometrically sound evaluations from watching job simulations and documenting behaviors. Good interjudge agreement appears to be largely a function of training (we achieved it with several different formats and contents).

4. Ensure rater expertise with both the task and the rating requirements through selection or training. Raters who are not intimately familiar with a complex task may have difficulty making important discriminations, even when they use a rating form with specific behaviors that can be easily observed. For example, if the behavior is an action taken, such as, "Called captain's attention to aircraft emergency," naive raters may give the same rating to all crews who perform this behavior without regard for the timing of the action or other happenings. If behavior and timing cannot be

predetermined unambiguously, inexperienced raters will not know how to rate the action.

5. The purpose of the rating procedure and the level of experience of the judges will likely have an impact on whether the rating format should be in the form of a checklist or should allow for opportunistic ratings. Checklists are convenient to use and provide an excellent opportunity for high interrater reliability. Checklists are typically tied to events triggered by the scenario (e.g., "gear up by 500 feet"; "pulled out checklist in response to hydraulic pump warning light"). However, checklists can limit the behaviors to which the judges attend, with the result that important team process information arising from behaviors not detailed on the checklist may be ignored. Since aircrews operate in a dynamic environment and a variety of different behaviors can lead to the same outcome, an opportunistic rating scale may be recommended. In addition, in a team environment, much of the stimulus material for one member is the behavior of the other members. Such behavior is not scripted (unless some team members are confederates of the experimenter) and thus is much more difficult to put into a checklist. In essence, checklists usually are deficient measures, but in using a more opportunistic format to reduce deficiency, one may sacrifice reliability for opportunity. Of course, one may use both formats.

6. Measures of team processes are sensitive to team skill composition and are predictive of team outcomes as measured by an independent measure of task performance.

Stimulus Design

1. The research task should be selected for relevance to the participants. This helps ensure the motivation to perform the task may relate to the motivation of trained, professional team members.

2. A simulation should include all activities that may be relevant. For example, Foushee et al. (1986) found that aviation teams' performance is affected by time spent working together. Most aviation crews plan their flight and have the opportunity for team building that must otherwise be done in the task. Therefore, a simulation of the aviation task should include the planning period for those teams who customarily use one.

3. Tryouts should be used to calibrate scenarios; there is no substitute for pilot testing. Use teams that are at the same level of experience and knowledge as those who will participate in the research. We have found that, in a complex task, where skills and cognitive knowledge change with experience, it is difficult for more experienced team members to calibrate the difficulty level for less experienced team members. Even expert judges (including instructor pilots) have difficulty in estimating how successful

pilots in training will be when coping with problems that have not been included as part of the training curriculum.

4. Select multiple events for the scenario based on the skill(s) of interest. For example, if skill in interacting with air traffic control is to be assessed, there should be numerous interactions built into the scenario. This is crucial for reliable measures of skills.

Sources of Information

1. Sources of information (e.g., team member, observer) should not be substituted for one another without data demonstrating the equivalence of the sources.

2. The team member as a source of information has peculiar strengths and weaknesses. The use of team members is usually the most economical way to collect data (see the chapter by Hallam & Campbell). The work of Helmreich and colleagues (e.g., Helmreich & Foushee, 1993) has demonstrated that often it is the most feasible way to collect data on large numbers of teams. In addition, team members may have best access to information about effective functioning in the team. On the other hand, team member perceptions are subject to lack of objectivity and a possible self-serving or defensive bias.

Constructs to Measure

1. Evaluative and frequency measures are relatively independent sources of variance related to objective measures of team outcomes. Therefore, both should be considered in measuring team performance.

2. The level of measurement selected has important implications. Whether the rating procedure should emphasize individual performance or team performance depends on the purpose of the measure. For example, if one is training intact teams, it makes sense to provide feedback on the team's performance. However, if one is training individuals on team skills, feedback should center on the individual and his or her particular strengths and weaknesses. Emphasis on individual or team performance is also an important consideration depending on the research purpose (e.g., theory development and evaluation, team member selection).

3. Establish whether the measurement will be of outcome or process. When developing a checklist for team process, it is easy to confuse outcomes of team action with the processes. For example, if the checklist contains the statement, "Crew chose to go to their alternate," it does not describe the crew process, it just documents the outcome of the decision process. Statements that come closer to describing the process behaviors are

more specific and would include, "Discussed alternatives"; "Suggested divert fields"; "Asked co-pilot to check runway length."

4. The same scenario events may help provide measures of different constructs for different crews. For example, one crew that loses a radio may think through the problem and come to a proper diagnosis. Another team may have memorized a procedure for troubleshooting the problem. As a result, although the teams may solve the problem by using either memory or analysis, which are quite different mental processes, the more general point is that behaviors observed in response to real job situations are likely to be due to multiple abilities.

5. Behaviors that are sampled in response to job simulations may not have a simple factor structure, unless they are measured at a very high level analogous to g in intelligence tests. The measurement of the core constructs of teamwork are still at an early stage and can be compared with Binet's beginning work in developing intelligence tests. Because Binet had little in the way of theory to guide in the choice of items, he tried a large number of items and kept those that appeared to work. The situation with regard to measures of teamwork is somewhat better, because there are now some measures and theories. Unfortunately, the main problem has been sample size. There are no factor analyses of measures based on external observations of aircrews, although there are factor analyses of team member self-evaluations (see Gregorich, Helmreich, & Wilhelm, 1990). Similarly, significant differences have been found between the best and worst performing teams based on small samples, but there has been no cross-validation of such differences.

Team Training and Feedback

1. Aviators with low experience levels can improve their team process skills by flying a realistic scenario with a flight instructor who talks about the scenario events and who makes general comments.

2. Formal feedback at the end of a training scenario does not add to the performance of aviators in a second scenario if they have had the opportunity to receive feedback within the training scenario itself.

3. It can be difficult to assess team members on some skills because much of the stimulus for teamwork is other team members. An individual may have the ability to perform the task in a satisfactory manner, but because he or she is acting as a team member, the opportunity to perform that particular behavior is reduced. For example, it is impossible to show one's ability to correct the errors of other team members if they never make any.

4. Transfer of team training appears to increase with similarity of the new situation to the situation that was trained. That is, like events in two

different scenarios will likely result in a demonstration of transfer of training.

Special Problems in Reliability and Validity

1. Teams are not consistent or reliable in their process skills across scenarios. This can be due to a number of possible causes.

- Team members may be responding to task attributes in the scenarios that are not anticipated by the designers of the tasks.
- A short briefing before each scenario may not be sufficient for team building, so that initial accommodation of team members to one another may be taking place within the first task.
- Properties of a situation may have more effect on team behavior than stable team or individual differences.
- There may be a lack of rating opportunity to observe sufficient instances of behavior. The number of team process behaviors called for in each scenario may not be sufficient for a reliable assessment of that dimension. We found that the dimensions that had a larger number of behavioral examples and more opportunities for their demonstration in the scenarios also showed greater evidence of convergent and discriminant validity than those with fewer examples.
- The scenarios used may not be equivalent. One may be more difficult than the other, or specific behaviors called for within the scenario may be quite different, despite an appearance of similarity. For example, the decision-making behaviors required by one scenario may be quite different from those required by another scenario. Work that is relevant to the question of consistency of behavior was presented by Orasanu, Fisher, and Tarrel (1993) who found that decisions made in the cockpit vary in type and complexity. This suggests that optimal strategies for responding to these decision situations could also vary, and consistency of behaviors should not be expected to occur.

2. In designing a measure of team process, one must first consider the purpose the measure is intended to serve. For example, if the measure is intended to be used as a feedback tool, design considerations should focus on gathering the information in a way to provide meaningful feedback. Conversely, if the purpose of the measure is to assess the underlying constructs that contribute to team process, more attention should focus on the grouping of behaviors into the independent constructs.

3. The purpose of the measurement should determine the use of spectrum versus extreme groups analysis. Earlier research efforts have provided communication analyses of teams classified as either the "best or worst" teams in their group. This approach can be quite valuable for gaining insight into the behavioral differences between effective or less effective crews. However, if one's goal is to understand the underlying constructs of team process and their relationship to team outcomes, we need a spectrum approach in which the full range of team effectiveness is included. The extreme groups approach in aviation research has been used generally as hypothesis-generating research. Large numbers of variables are tested against a small number of crews. Even in the absence of Type I errors, the magnitude of effect is overstated with extreme groups.

4. The weighting of related behaviors into an overall dimension score should be considered because it is clear that some of team process behaviors have less impact on the performance of the team than others. Moreover, depending on the demands of the context, the same behavior can have a different impact on the team outcome. For example, a failure to make an assertive statement or to reply to a communication may be trivial in some situations and extremely important in others.

5. The timing of an action, not just the action itself, should be considered in a measure of team process. In a dynamic environment such as the one surrounding aircrews, simply accomplishing the tasks or demonstrating the process behaviors without timing considerations may not be sufficient. For example, if the crew decides not to take off after they have reached a certain speed in their take-off roll, they may cause considerable damage. The same decision, made seconds earlier, may be entirely reasonable. Similarly, a measure that assesses the pattern and sequencing of behaviors is recommended. As with the timing of the events, simply assessing the content of communication may not provide enough insight into the dynamic functioning of the crews. Likewise, if pattern and sequencing of communication is assessed alone without consideration of the quality of the communication content, information would likely be lost.

SUMMARY

The research on aviation team process measurement has not yet resulted in a rating scheme or measurement tool that has the necessary properties that make it reliable, valid, and useful. Each effort outlined here has given us some information that allows us to move ahead. Thus, the results of the research have been important in their contribution to the understanding that is required for team process measurement, particularly in measuring process as demonstrated by professionals who are working at tasks in naturalistic settings. Much of what has been learned in conducting this research is applicable to other work teams, particularly lessons that can improve experimental control and guide measurement considerations. The combination of applying the research lessons learned to a planned program of research holds the promise for developing and testing a tool for measurement that can be applied to aviation teams with confidence.

REFERENCES

Artwick, B. A. (1989). *Flight Simulator 4.0B* (computer program) Redmond, WA: Microsoft Corporation.

Brannick, M. T., Prince, A., Prince, C., & Salas, E. (1995). The measurement of team process. *Human Factors, 37,* 641–651.

Brannick, M. T., Roach, R., & Salas, E. (1994). Understanding team performance: A multimethod study. *Human Performance, 6,* 287–308.

Carnap, R. (1995). *An introduction to the philosophy of science* (M. Gardner, Ed.). Mineola, NY: Dover. (Original work published 1966)

Chidester, T. R., Kanki, B. G., Foushee, H. C., Dickinson, C. L., & Bowles, S. V. (1990). *Personality factors in flight operations: Vol. 1. Leadership characteristics and crew performance in a full-mission air transport simulation* (NASA Tech. Mem. No. 102259). Moffett Field, CA: NASA-Ames Reseach Center.

Clothier, C. C. (1991). Behavioral interactions across various aircraft types: Results of systematic observations of line operations and simulations. In R. S. Jensen & D. Neumeister (Eds.), *Proceedings of the sixth International Symposium on Aviation Psychology* (pp. 332–337). Columbus, OH: The Ohio State University.

Foushee, H. C. (1984). Dyads and triads at 35,000 feet. *American Psychologist, 39,* 885–893.

Foushee, H. C., Lauber, J. K., Baetge, M. M., & Acomb, D. B. (1986). *Crew factors in flight operations: III. The operational significance of exposure to short-haul air transport operations* (NASA Tech. Mem. No. 88322). Moffett Field, CA: National Aeronautics and Space Administration.

Foushee, H. C., & Manos, K.L. (1981). Information transfer within the cockpit: Problems in introcockpit communications. In C. E. Billings & E. S. Cheaney (Eds.), *Information transfer problems in the aviation system* (NASA Tech. Rep. No. 1875, pp. 63–71). Moffett Field, CA: NASA-Ames Research Center.

Ginnett, R. C. (1987). *First encounters of the close kind: The first meetings of airline flight crews.* Unpublished doctoral dissertation, Yale University, New Haven, CT.

Gregorich, S. E., Helmreich, R. L., & Wilhelm, J. A. (1990). The structure of cockpit management attitudes. *Journal of Applied Psychology, 75,* 682–690.

Hackman, J. R. (1983). *A normative model of work team effectiveness* (Tech. Rep. No. 2). New Haven, CT: Yale School of Organization and Management.

Hartel, C., Smith, K., & Prince, C. (1991). *Defining aircrew coordination: Searching mishaps for meaning.* Paper presented at the Sixth International Symposium on Aviation Psychology, Columbus, OH.

Helmreich, R. L. (1984). Cockpit management attitudes. *Human Factors, 26,* 583–589.

Helmreich, R. L., & Foushee, H. C. (1993). Why crew resource management? Empirical and theoretical bases of human factors training in America. In E. L. Wiener, B. G. Kanki, & R. L. Helmreich (Eds.), *Cockpit resource management* (pp. 3–41). San Diego, CA: Academic Press.

Helmreich, R. L., & Wilhelm, J. A. (1991). Outcomes of crew resource management training. *International Journal of Aviation Psychology, 1,* 287–300.

Helmreich, R. L., Wilhelm, J. A., Kelly, J. E., Taggart, W. R., & Butler, R. E. (1991). *Reinforcing and evaluating crew resource management. Evaluator/LOS instructor eference manual* (Technical Manual 90-2). Austin, TX: NASA/University of Texas at Austin.

Kanki, B. G., Greaud, V. A., & Irwin, C. M. (1989). Communication variations and aircrew performance. In R. S. Jensen (Ed.), *Proceedings of the fifth International Symposium on Aviation Psychology* (pp. 419–424). Columbus, OH: Ohio State University.

Kanki, B. G., Lozito, S., & Foushee, H. C. (1987). Communication indexes of crew coordination. In *Proceedings of the fourth International Symposium on Aviation Psychology* (pp. 406–412). Columbus, OH: The Ohio State University.

Lauber, J. K. (1987). Cockpit resource management: Background studies and rationale. In H. W. Orlady & H. C. Foushee (Eds.), *Cockpit resource management training: Proceedings of the NASA/MAC workshop* (NASA CP-2455; pp. 5–14). Moffett Field, CA: NASA-Ames Research Center.

Louie, G. (1987). *Falcon* (Computer program). Alameda, CA: Spectrum Holobyte.

Morgan, B. B., Jr., Glickman, A. S., Woodard, E. A., Blaiwes, A. S., & Salas, E. (1986). *Meausement of team behaviors in a Navy environment* (NTSC Tech. Rep. No. 86-014). Orlando, FL: Naval Training Systems Center.

Orasanu, J. M. (1990). *Shared and mental models and crew decision-making* (CSL Rep. No. 46). Princeton, NJ: Princeton University, Cognitive Science Laboratory.

Orasanu, J. M. (1994). Shared problem models and flight crew performance. In N. Johnston, N. McDonald, & R. Fuller (Eds.), *Aviation psychology in practice* (pp. 255–285). Hants, England: Avebury Technical.

Orasanu, J. M., & Fisher, U. (1991). Information transfer and shared mental models for decision making. In R. S. Jensen & D. Neumeister (Eds.), *Proceedings of the sixth International Symposium on Aviation Psychology* (pp. 272–277). Columbus, OH: The Ohio State Univesity.

Orasanu, J. M., Fisher, U., & Tarrel, R. J. (1993). A taxonomy of decision problems on the flight deck. In R. S. Jensen & D. Neumeister (Eds.), *Proceedings of the sixth International Symposium on Aviation Psychology* (pp. 226–232). Columbus, OH: The Ohio State University.

Oser, R. L., Prince, C., & Morgan, B. B., Jr. (1990). *Differences in aircrew communication content as a function of flight requirement: Implications for operational aircrew training.* Poster presented at the 34th annual meeting of the Human Factors Society, Orlando, FL.

Prince, C., & Salas, E. (1989). Aircrew performance: Coordination and skill development. In D. E. Daniel, E. Salas, & D. M. Kotick (Eds.), *Independent research and independent exploratory development (IR/IED) programs: Annual report for fiscal year 1988* (NTSC Tech. Rep. No. 89-009). Orlando, FL: Naval Training Systems Center.

Prince, C., & Salas, E. (1993). Training and research for teamwork in the military aircrew. In E. L. Wiener, B. G. Kanki, & R. L. Helmreich (Eds.), *Cockpit resource management* (pp. 337–366). Orlando, FL: Academic Press.

Prince, C., & Salas, E. (in press). Team processes and their training in aviation. In D. Garland, J. Wise, & D. Hopkin (Eds.), *Aviation human factors.* Mahwah, NJ: Lawrence Erlbaum Associates.

Ruffell-Smith, H. P. (1979). *A simulator study of the interaction of pilot workload with errors, vigilance, and decisions* (NASA TM-78482). Moffett Field, CA: NASA-Ames Research Center.

Siegel, A. I., & Federman, P. J. (1973). Communications content training as an ingredient in effective team performance. *Ergonomics, 16,* 403–416.

Williges, R. C., Johnston, W. A., & Briggs, G. E. (1966). Role of verbal communication in teamwork. *Journal of Applied Psychology, 50,* 473–478.

14 Performance Measurement Tools for Enhancing Team Decision-Making Training

Joan Hall Johnston
Kimberly A. Smith-Jentsch
Janis A. Cannon-Bowers
*Naval Air Warfare Center Training Systems Division,
Orlando, FL*

In today's work environment, high performance teams such as cockpit crews, firefighters, military command and control teams, and trauma surgical teams are routinely called on to perform complex and crucial tasks. Such teams must rely on effective *teamwork* and *taskwork* skills so that members can adapt to the changing and dynamic factors that drive high performance (e.g., rapidly evolving, ambiguous situations; complex, multicomponent decisions; information overload; auditory overload; command pressure; threat; adverse physical conditions; and swift interaction requirements; Orasanu & Salas, 1993). Taskwork skills consist of those skills necessary to complete individual aspects of team task demands.

Teamwork skills refer to those behaviors related to functioning as an effective team member. They consist of a set of team processes that support accurate exchange of information among members, effective flow of information to a single decision maker, and accurate decision making, all of which are required for successful team functioning. Although progress has been made in defining important teamwork competencies, in developing team training strategies (Salas & Cannon-Bowers, in press), and in developing performance assessment tools (Cannon-Bowers & Salas, this volume; Salas, Bowers, & Cannon-Bowers, 1995; Swezey & Salas, 1992; Zalesny, Salas, & Prince, 1995), recent reviews of the team training literature have repeatedly emphasized the need for more empirically-based principles and guidelines for team training (Cannon-Bowers, Tannenbaum, Salas, & Volpe, 1995; Orasanu & Salas, 1993). In particular, Cannon-Bowers and Salas (this volume) argue that a lack of validated, theoretically based performance assessment tools for team training is central to this requirement.

Cannon-Bowers and Salas (this volume) offered as a potential solution a "learning theory" approach to assessing individual and team performance processes and outcomes in training, a first step in building theoretically and empirically based team training strategies. They point out that training should be designed to incorporate multiple realistic task features and include an integrated performance measurement strategy designed to support the learning processes necessary to develop these complex skills. Essentially, they and others have made the case that to create the best environment for acquiring complex skills, training should be based on knowledge, skills, and attitudes (KSAs) identified through cognitive task analyses (see Orasanu & Salas, 1993). Furthermore, a crucial part of training should be the design of performance measures that will have a positive impact on changing task-related cognitive processes, psychomotor behavior, and teamwork skills (Salas & Cannon-Bowers, in press).

This chapter amplifies the points made by Cannon-Bowers and Salas. Specifically, we employ their conceptual framework as a means to organize, describe, and provide examples of an event-based strategy for building individual and team performance measures to support training. To do this, we begin by outlining a set of theoretical underpinnings (i.e., conceptual framework) for measuring team decision-making performance. Next, we explain our rationale for generating an event-based strategy for assessing teams that operate in high performance environments. In doing so, we describe the development of process and outcome measurement tools, and describe their application to a specific team training application. Finally, we discuss the implications of this approach for enhancing team decision-making performance, and summarize the major guidelines that can be drawn from this work.

CONCEPTUAL FRAMEWORK

Cannon-Bowers and Salas argue that performance measures for the purpose of training should be considered a special class of assessment tools whose intent is to provide descriptive, evaluative, and prescriptive information in support of the instructional process. The challenge of developing a team performance measurement system involves the development of *outcome* and *process* measures at both the *individual* and *team* levels. These measures need to be detailed enough to allow for identification of specific behaviors that can be linked empirically to important performance outcomes. Such a comprehensive system supports the diagnosis of deficiencies at the appropriate level (team vs. individual), and facilitates the accurate collection and evaluation of behavioral data, as well as the timely and coherent delivery of solution-oriented feedback. The following section begins with an examination of individual- and team-level outcomes and processes.

Linking Processes to Outcomes

Although outcome data can tell us which teams are successful and which are not, they do not tell us why, or how to train low performers to be more like high performers. Thus, outcome measures alone may not facilitate remedial training. Providing trainees with outcome data without the associated process information may actually hinder learning. As Cannon-Bowers and Salas (this volume) point out, teams often arrive at the correct decision through a flawed process, and/or by pure luck. In such cases, providing teams with outcome data alone will inadvertently reinforce processes that, over time and multiple situations, could result in incorrect decisions. Thus, the goal in decision making training in complex, dynamic environments should not be to train people to make the right decision in a given scenario, but to learn to make the decision right. This should result in more correct decisions over time and across a variety of situations (Cannon-Bowers & Salas, this volume). For example, preliminary data have indicated that a focus on process goals during practice sessions facilitates generalization of training over outcome goals (Kozlowski, Gully, Smith, Nason, & Brown, 1995).

Outcome measures are essential, however, for determining which processes are associated with the successful performance of a given type of team in a given type of situation. Recently, researchers have begun to theorize regarding the linkages between successful performance with team characteristics and required team competencies (Cannon-Bowers et al., 1995; Fleishman & Zaccaro, 1992; Gaddy & Wachtel, 1992; Zalesny et al., 1995). For example, Cannon-Bowers et al. (1995) developed a taxonomy of team competencies that are likely to be related to successful team performance based on whether or not the tasks performed by the team are stable or variable, and whether or not team membership is stable or variable. Other researchers have begun to identify unique situational conditions (e.g., high workload) that require strategies that may be ineffective if employed under different conditions (e.g., low stress; Serfaty & Entin, 1995).

In order to test such hypotheses, both outcome and process data are needed for different types of teams. Various processes can then be regressed on important team outcomes and beta weights can be compared. In this way, empirically based training objectives can be identified for different types of teams in different types of situations.

Discriminating Between Individual- and Team-Level Deficiencies

In addition to developing measures of process and outcome, identification of learning requirements and necessary developmental feedback is also dependent on a measurement system that can discriminate between individual- and team-level deficiencies. The nature of interdependent teams is such that they require individuals to perform some tasks that are specific to their particular position in the team, while sharing certain task responsibilities with other team members (Fleishman & Zaccaro, 1992). For example, in a surgical team, the anesthesiologist and the surgeon have certain nonoverlapping tasks and responsibilities that are linked to their training and expertise.

In addition, there are certain crucial tasks and responsibilities they share that contribute to managing patient care. Consequently, a breakdown in important processes may require remediation at either the team level, individual level, or both. For example, an incorrect team decision (team outcome) may be made because of a coordination breakdown between team members (team process), or because a single team member passed on incorrect information (individual process). Therefore, decisions made regarding which constructs should be measured at the team versus the individual level of analysis should be based, in part, on whether that process is the sole responsibility of an individual, or a responsibility that is shared by multiple team members.

Processes are best evaluated at the team level when associated actions can be accomplished by anyone on the team, and when fulfilling the action satisfies the requirement for the rest of the team. For example, it makes sense that compensatory processes such as providing backup and correcting errors are best evaluated at the team level. In this case, team-level feedback supports the instructional process, whereas individual-level feedback would not be useful. Once a team member has corrected an error, the opportunity and need to provide error correction no longer exists for the remaining team members. It would be unfair to give feedback on poor compensatory actions at the individual level because any team member could take responsibility for it. What really matters is that someone on the team corrects the error—it does not matter which team member does it. Unless the responsibility exists for a specific individual to demonstrate compensatory behaviors, team-level assessment is probably the appropriate level to measure them.

Validity, Diagnositicity, and Expediency

We have argued that the measurement of processes together with outcomes is crucial to diagnosing the underlying causes of successful versus unsuccessful team performance. In addition, we have suggested that assessment at both the individual and team level is necessary in order to pinpoint the locus of deficiency and to select appropriate remedial training activities. In addition, the effectiveness of performance assessment information for feedback and remediation is also dependent on the appropriateness of the metric selected to evaluate specific behaviors. For example, Cannon-Bowers and Salas identified a number of rating formats that can be used to evaluate team and individual processes and outcomes (e.g., behavior ratings, critical incidents, observation checklists).

An important factor in choosing an appropriate metric rests on the characteristics of the construct being measured. For example, a simple frequency count could be used to evaluate certain types of team errors. However, because the opportunity to correct team errors is generally not consistent across teams (or situations), frequency counts are not a valid measure of error correction. It would be more accurate to look at the percentage of times team errors were corrected (when they occur) so that (a) during feedback sessions, teams could use this information to establish goals for improvement in subsequent training sessions, and (b) instructors could assess training effectiveness by comparing percentages across trained teams.

In other cases, the quality of a response, or the severity of a particular type of error may need to be scaled using behavioral anchors. Therefore, the type of metric used to measure each team-related construct needs to be considered carefully so that the resulting evaluation is representative of each team or individual's true standing on some predetermined criterion or against comparative norms, and not an artifact or bias of the measurement tool (Bernardin & Beatty, 1984; Carroll & Schneier, 1983). This is also crucial to the instructional value of any feedback derived from performance assessments.

In addition to being valid indicators of effective and ineffective performance, assessments must be *diagnostic* in order to support the instructional process (Cannon-Bowers & Salas, this volume). For example, informing a team member that he or she needs to work on communication skills is not likely to be as effective as pointing out that the team member tends to clog the communication network with excess chatter, and to suggest that strict adherence to phraseology protocols can eliminate this problem. Thus, a performance measurement tool supports the instructional process to the extent that it provides information to trainees at the level of specific targeted behaviors. This information should include both what the trainee(s) did incorrectly, as well as what they should have, or could have done differently.

Besides being behaviorally specific, research has shown that in order to be useful, developmental feedback should be received close in time to the performance situation (Goldstein, 1991). Thus, team performance measurement tools will best support instruction when they allow trainers to observe and record behavioral data, evaluate performance, and organize a coherent debrief in an expedient manner.

In summary, the challenges of developing a team performance measurement system includes the development of individual and team process measures that allow for identification of specific behaviors that can be linked empirically to important performance outcomes. In the following section we describe an approach to exercise development in support of training Navy ship teams that facilitates the creation of this type of measurement system (Cannon-Bowers, Salas, & Grossman, 1991).

Event-Based Team Training and Assessment for Navy Teams

A common practice in Navy training is to provide simulation exercises that are conducted in a "freeplay" mode (Johnston et al., 1995). That is, the training has prespecified objectives at the start of the simulated exercise, but instructors are free to insert new training "events" into the training that do not have clearly specified objectives or performance expectations (we define an *event* here as a set of complex cues or occurrences that are characteristic of high performance situations). Consequently, feedback following exercises is less meaningful, and lacks specific goals for improving both individual and team performance. This is because analytical effort is required to determine which process and outcome measures are associated with particular events and how best to assess them. Inserting events "on the fly" does not allow prespecification of required/expected behavior and, hence, often does not provide a viable basis for feedback.

Instead, we propose that effective application of the measurement system described earlier requires that training events (with associated training objectives) be developed so that the various measurement tools can be systematically related to observed performance and to one another. We maintain that creating scenarios with multiple, prespecified training events allows for meaningful comparison of individual and team measures (Hall, Dwyer, Cannon-Bowers, Salas, & Volpe, 1993). Therefore, a training exercise is composed of a string of events that create an opportunity for the team to demonstrate proficiency on a series of specific, related objectives. Only when multiple measures are focused on the same predetermined scenario events can relationships between processes and outcomes be accurately examined.

Scenarios organized around predictable events also make it easier for assessors to observe, record, and evaluate performance normatively or against a stable criterion. In this way, comparisons across teams are more accurate, and the timeliness of performance feedback is enhanced. Finally, an event-based structure fosters the systematic manipulation of situational variables (e.g., workload; Hall et al., 1993). It allows one to examine differences in the efficacy of different performance strategies across various performance conditions. The information derived from this type of investigation is particularly useful for training teams that must frequently adapt to dynamically unfolding situations (e.g., air traffic controllers, surgical teams).

We have argued that an event-based approach to exercise development facilitates the development of a comprehensive performance measurement system that supports team training. The following section details the development of such a system that was designed to support team training for Naval ship teams.

EVENT-BASED PERFORMANCE MEASUREMENT FOR SHIPBOARD TEAMS

The performance measurement system that is described in this section was designed specifically to identify the team and individual processes that are linked to effective tactical decision making for Naval ship teams (Cannon-Bowers et al., 1991; Hall et al., 1993; Johnston et al., 1995). This system was also intended to support the identification of specific processes that break down under conditions of high workload and ambiguity, and the particular training strategies that are most effective under these conditions. Finally, the measurement tools developed as part of this comprehensive system are currently being adapted for use as feedback aids. The next sections describe 4 of these measures as well as preliminary efforts to use one of the tools to support team training for Navy ship teams. The development of this performance measurement system began with the creation of 4 event-based training exercises that are briefly described next.

Event-Based Scenario Development

Four event-based exercises were developed to evaluate the team coordination and decision-making skill of five-person combat information center teams (Johnston et al., 1995). The task is such that the five team members have specific responsibilities to carry out as an interdependent team. The four exercises were designed so that they could be presented on either a networked PC-based team simulator or embedded into consoles on board an actual ship.

The process followed in developing scenarios was as follows. First, subject matter experts created two 30-minute exercises, each with three events that were designed to stimulate a five-person team to coordinate their activities (Hall et al., 1993). Each event contained a tactical situation that required team members to coordinate and exchange information so that correct action could be taken. Second, 2 additional exercises were created by systematically adding pieces of information (workload) and conflicting information (ambiguity) to the events developed for the original two exercises. Next, both individual- and team-level process and outcome measures were developed to evaluate performance in the four exercises. Each of these measures focused on the key events in the four exercises; these are described next.

Development of Multiple Performance Measures

Cannon-Bowers and Salas describe a number of rating formats that can be used to evaluate various team and individual processes and outcomes. The development of the measures detailed below involved the matching of behaviors and outcomes to the appropriate metrics. An example of each type of measure follows.

   Team Outcomes.   Given the nature of the team task, the ultimate performance outcomes for anti-air combat information center teams are correct decisions to shoot hostile aircraft and not to shoot friendly aircraft. A number of subgoals or preliminary outcomes involve detection of potentially hostile contacts, evaluation of threats, assignment of weapons if necessary, and engagement of hostile contacts (Zachary, Zaklad, Hicinbothom, & Ryder, 1993).

   A performance measurement tool was developed to assess these team outcomes specifically for the four team training exercises of interest. Given the events embedded into these exercises, the correctness of team decisions regarding specific aircraft could be evaluated against a stable criterion. Figure 14.1 presents the Anti-Air Team Performance Index (ATPI), that utilizes a behaviorally anchored rating format. An instructor can use this tool to assess how well the task was performed by the team across each event. The first row identifies the scenario time associated with each aircraft of interest below it. The last row illustrates the ultimate team outcome (i.e., shoot/no shoot decision) that is rated on a scale from 0 to 3 using established criteria. Specific anchors make the diagnostic process consistent across instructors. Examination of performance outcomes across events allows the instructor to pinpoint the type of situations with which a team consistently has problems. Therefore, appropriate remedial activities can be targeted and completed.

   Individual Outcomes.   Certain preliminary (individual) outcomes that contribute to the team-level outcomes evaluated using the ATPI can be

SHOOT/ NO SHOOT

EVENT:	AT SCENARIO START	AT SCENARIO START	AT SCENARIO START	AT 10 MINUTES 30 SECONDS
TRACK NUMBER: CRAFT TYPE:	7026 COMMERCIAL HELICOPTER	7027 COMMERCIAL HELICOPTER	7030 MILITARY AIRCRAFT	7037 MILITARY AIRCRAFT
SHOOT / NO SHOOT	0 1 2 3	0 1 2 3	0 1 2 3	0 1 2 3

0	Fired missile at target; fired other weapons
1	Shot missile, but self-destructed it before contact
2	Initiated entire firing sequence and stop just short of release
3	Does not shoot at targets

FIG. 14.1. Team outcomes assessment tool.

linked to specific team positions. Examination of these individual level-outcomes (i.e., latencies and decision errors) can help instructors to identify the locus of a performance problem. Figure 14.2 illustrates an individual outcome measure, called the sequenced actions and latencies index (SALI; Johnston et al., 1995) that was developed for this purpose. The format we

AAWC FUNCTION   AIR WARFARE ASSESSMENT

EVENT:	AT SCENARIO START	AT SCENARIO START	AT SCENARIO START	AT 10 MINUTES 30 SECONDS
TRACK NUMBER: CRAFT TYPE:	7026 COMMERCIAL HELICOPTER	7027 COMMERCIAL HELICOPTER	7030 MILITARY AIRCRAFT	7037 MILITARY AIRCRAFT
THREAT EVALUATION	0 1 2 3	0 1 2 3	0 1 2 3	0 1 2 3

0	Did not report evaluation
1	Reported incorrect/delayed evaluation
2	Reported incorrect evaluation, but corrected it within 60 seconds
3	Reported correct evaluation within 60 seconds

FIG. 14.2. Individual outcomes assessment tool.

developed to evaluate individual-level outcomes is similar to that used to evaluate team-level outcomes described earlier.

Individual Processes. The five individual team members who make up the combat team each have specific process tasks and responsibilities that are related to their particular position in the team. For example, the Anti-Air Warfare Coordinator is responsible for coordination of the ship's air warfare resources, with a primary goal being to defend the ship. This includes monitoring critical computer-generated information and coordinating with other team members to eliminate conflicting information.

Examination of these individual taskwork processes can help to diagnose the root of individual performance outcome problems. Figure 14.3 illustrates the format used to evaluate such individual taskwork processes. This tool, called the behavior observation booklet (BOB; Hall et al., 1993; Johnston et al., 1995), is designed to display scenario events and related behaviors in a critical incidents format. Inspection of Figure 14.3 indicates that the first column requires the listing in chronological order of a brief description of all significant objective-based events, and the time at which they occur. This serves as a trigger to an instructor to note actions that take place during the events.

The next three columns divide task actions into their higher level task functions that have been determined prior to the exercise to be necessary to support the team task. Predetermined actions and functions must be identified by subject matter experts (SMEs), and noted for each event. During the training scenario, trainee actions are recorded in the second row by an instructor. At the end of the scenario, an instructor should have recorded enough information to compare to the expected actions in order to make a determination of how well the team member contributed to the team task during the scenario.

	FUNCTION	FUNCTION	FUNCTION
TIME XX:XX EVENT X	LIST EXPECTED ACTIONS WITHIN AN EXPECTED TIME FRAME	LIST EXPECTED ACTIONS WITHIN...	LIST EXPECTED ACTIONS WITHIN...
PERFORMANCE PROCESSES RECORDING	NOTE ACTUAL ACTIONS AND TIME PERFORMED	NOTE ACTUAL ACTIONS AND...	NOTE ACTUAL ACTIONS AND...

FIG. 14.3. Individual processes assessment tool.

Team Processes. After preliminary analysis of over 50 videotaped teams performing the four exercises noted earlier, SMEs identified a number of teamwork behaviors that appeared to differentiate between high performing and low performing teams. These behaviors have been grouped under four teamwork dimensions, labeled *team situation assessment*, *communication*, *supporting behavior*, and *team initiative/leadership*.

Situation assessment is defined as communication that promotes a team awareness of the surrounding environment, both internal and external to the team. This involves timely and accurate reporting of deviations and/or potential problems. *Communication* is defined as the clear and efficient exchange of relevant information. This requires using proper terminology, standard procedures for external communications, and an appropriate tone of voice. *Supporting behavior* is defined as monitoring the activities of other team members, taking action to correct errors, giving and receiving feedback in a nondefensive manner, and providing and seeking assistance or backup when needed. *Team initiative/leadership* is defined as providing needed guidance to other team members, helping team members focus their activities appropriately, anticipating tasks that should be performed, and providing instruction to other team members to enable them to perform or complete their tasks. Any team member can perform leadership functions.

A measure was developed to evaluate teams on these four teamwork dimensions as they deal with events in the four exercises (Smith-Jentsch, Payne, & Johnston, 1996). The Anti-Air Teamwork Observation Measure (ATOM) involves recording observations of specific behaviors associated with each of the four dimensions at the team level. Figure 14.4 shows a number of different types of metrics developed to assess teamwork behaviors at each exercise event.

Many of the negative behaviors (e.g., instances of improper phraseology, incomplete reports) can be evaluated via frequency counts. The need for

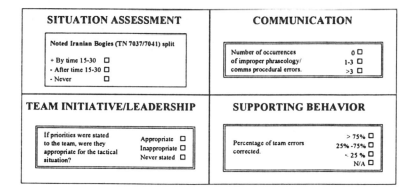

FIG. 14.4. ATOM target behavior ratings.

many behaviors under team situation assessment is predictable due to the vast quantities of information available and the rate at which it changes in a typical scenario. Therefore, the evaluation of those behaviors is tied specifically to predetermined deviations of which team members should have been aware at a particular time (e.g., when a team member needs to report that a commercial airliner and hostile aircraft have "split"). In addition, leadership behaviors such as stating team priorities are rated according to their accuracy for each particular event (i.e., appropriate, inappropriate, never stated). The opportunity and need to demonstrate certain supporting behaviors in the exercises, such as correcting another team member's error, cannot be controlled across teams. Therefore, percentages are used to evaluate the proportion of times these behaviors are exhibited in relation to the number of times they were needed. Finally, in addition to the evaluation of specific targeted behaviors under each dimension, the ATOM requires assessors to assign teams a qualitative rating (1–5) for each dimension using behaviorally anchored rating scales (see Fig. 14.5).

The ATOM worksheet, an online aid for instructors, provides raters with an exercise timeline, scenario information (e.g., ground truth), and space to record observations of relevant behaviors as they occur in the exercise. Once raters have recorded their observations using the worksheet, these observations are used to assign target behavior ratings and dimension-level ratings. In addition to being a data analysis tool, the format of the ATOM has been adapted to support the timely provision of developmental feedback to teams. The following section details the resulting tool (called the "On-Line ATOM & Debriefing Guide") as well as preliminary efforts to use it for shipboard research.

Performance Assessment and Feedback

As we have argued, performance measurement tools used for the purpose of training must provide assessments that offer teams specific diagnostic

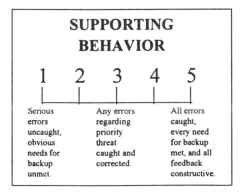

FIG. 14.5.   ATOM dimension ratings.

information about good and poor performance. Although the performance ratings allow one to empirically examine linkages between specific processes and outcomes, this quantitative information (i.e., numerical ratings) is not in a form that will necessarily facilitate learning. In other words, stating that a team used improper phraseology 3 times during an event is not likely to change team communications. In order for learning to occur, specific examples of phraseology errors need to be pointed out and correct alternatives discussed.

In order for a performance measurement tool to best support learning, it must employ a format that allows instructors to organize performance information quickly so that feedback can be delivered closely in time to performance. Feedback provided in a timely manner is easier for team members to understand and to use. Additionally, team members are better able to participate in diagnosing their own performance deficiencies when the training exercise is fresh in their minds.

During a team exercise, it is difficult for instructors to be aware of everything going on due to the complexity of the performance situation. A participative approach whereby the instructor enlists teams to contribute to the performance assessment and feedback processes is likely to result in more accurate diagnoses, as well as more productive solutions. Team members often notice problems, and potential problems, that instructors miss. Moreover, team member confusion and/or discomfort with a particular procedure does not always result in an overt error. Finally, specific process-oriented performance goals have been shown to facilitate learning and generalization. Thus, performance assessments will support greater learning when they focus the team on a limited number of specific goals for improvement on subsequent exercises.

The debriefing guide developed in conjunction with the ATOM incorporates each of these ideas (see Fig. 14.6). Instructors record examples of the specific targeted behaviors under each of the four teamwork areas described earlier using the ATOM worksheet. Next, salient examples of each of the behaviors are recorded in boxes within the ATOM debriefing guide. Finally, the teams' specific strengths, areas for improvement, and a specific goal are recorded under each of the four teamwork dimensions. Quantitative ratings from the original ATOM can also be obtained from both instructors and team members if time permits and if statistical analysis is desired. The instructor then uses the debriefing guide to lead team members in a discussion of their own teamwork processes.

Employing the debriefing guide serves several purposes in the feedback session. First, the debriefing guide sets the stage by introducing teams to the four dimensions of teamwork described earlier. Second, the three exercise events are summarized and the outcome of each is discussed. Third, positive and negative examples of specific behaviors associated with each of the four dimensions are discussed and relationships between these behaviors and

---

COMMUNICATION

SAY: Now I would like to talk to you about how your team's communication style may have influenced the team's performance at each of the critical events. Effective communication involves the clear and efficient exchange of relevant information. This requires using proper terminology, standard procedures for external communications, and an appropriate tone of voice.

ASK: Can you describe any instances where nonstandard phraseology was used? How did this/could this have led to confusion?

POINT OUT: According to my notes,

- IMPROPER PHRASEOLOGY

EVENT 1 _____

EVENT 2 _____

EVENT 3 _____

ASK: Can you describe any instances when there was excess chatter on the nets? How did this/could this have caused the team problems or made the team less efficient?

POINT OUT: According to my notes,

- EXCESS CHATTER

EVENT 1 _____

EVENT 2 _____

EVENT 3 _____

FIG. 14.6. Sample page from ATOM debriefing guide.

team outcomes are identified. Fourth, team members agree on strengths, areas for improvement, and specific goals to meet in the next exercise.

Preliminary data has indicated that teams who were debriefed using this methodology demonstrated improved performance on specific targeted behaviors under each of the four teamwork processes (Smith-Jentsch et al., 1996). Additionally, team members' ratings of their own teamwork processes became closer to instructor-assigned ratings over the course of four training exercises (Smith-Jentsch et al., 1996). These results suggest that the developmental feedback provided in the ATOM debriefing sessions improved the teams' ability to diagnose their own performance and to "self-correct."

SUMMARY AND CONCLUDING REMARKS

In this chapter we amplified the Cannon-Bowers and Salas concept of a *learning approach* to developing a set of individual and team process and outcome measures that support training. We described an event-based approach to training design that allows integrating and relating measures at the level of the individual and the team. To illustrate this concept, we presented examples of individual and team process and outcome assessment tools developed for high performance combat teams. We also described a performance feedback tool that was developed for the purpose enhancing shipboard team decision making.

These tools represent a first step toward the development of a strategy for integrating the assessment of complex performance processes and outcomes to enhance team learning during training. Further development requires research, and application to other team-based task domains. Currently, research is underway to validate the tools we developed, and the preliminary findings are encouraging (Smith-Jentsch et al., 1996). In addition, while there has been a relatively limited research focus with respect to the type of teams being studied (i.e., Navy teams), the data suggest that what we have learned here should be adapted to other team training domains. The following sections summarize the major guidelines we can offer for team performance measurement in training.

Guidelines for Team Performance Measurement in Training

Our theoretical and empirical data bases lead us to present the following guidelines:

1. Team performance measures must tap both individual- and team-level behavior so that appropriate diagnoses of performance deficiencies can be made.
2. Team performance measures must tap teamwork processes as well as outcomes since processes provide better diagnostic information.
3. The relationship between teamwork processes and outcomes must be made explicit as a basis to provide feedback.
4. The nature of the teamwork behavior being assessed must drive the specific measurement format (e.g., accuracy, frequency, quality, etc.).
5. Training events must be carefully crafted to elicit targeted behaviors.
6. Team and individual process and outcome measures must be specified in advance for each training event.

7. Event-specific performance measurement formats should provide a means to organize the observation of team performance.
8. Performance measurement scales should be formatted so that they are easy to use by instructors/assessors.
9. Performance measurement data collected during an exercise should form the basis of feedback to the team.
10. Self-correction in team members should be encouraged using observed and recorded performance data as a basis.

CONCLUSIONS

The team performance measurement tools described in this chapter represent the first step toward developing a comprehensive performance measurement system for team training. Future research should accomplish several goals. First, empirical validation of the concepts and formats presented here is needed. Second, the scales we described must be applied to a variety of high performance teams so that their generalizability can be assessed. Third, the use of event-based training (with associated measures and debriefing strategies) requires theoretical and empirical extension. Fourth, issues associated with the implementation of team performance measures (e.g., ease of use, user acceptance, expediency, etc.) must be investigated further. Taken together, these activities should lead to a set of theoretically and empirically rooted principles for assessing team performance during training.

REFERENCES

Bernardin, H. J., & Beatty, R. W. (1984). *Performance appraisal: Assessing human behavior at work*. Boston, MA: Kent.

Carroll, S. J., & Schneier, C. E. (1983). *Performance appraisal and review systems: The identification, measurement, and development of performance in organizations*. Glenview, IL: Scott, Foresman.

Cannon-Bowers, J. A., Salas, E., & Grossman, J. D. (1991). *Improving tactical decision making under stress: Research directions and applied implications*. Paper presented at the International Applied Military Psychology Symposium, Stockholm, Sweden.

Cannon-Bowers, J.A., Tannenbaum, S.I., Salas, E., & Volpe, C. E. (1995). Defining team competencies and establishing team training requirements. In R. Guzzo & E. Salas (Eds.), *Team effectiveness and decision making in organizations* (pp. 333–380). San Francisco, CA: Jossey-Bass.

Fleishman, E. A., & Zacarro, S. J. (1992). Toward a taxonomy of team performance functions. In R. W. Swezey & E. Salas (Eds.), *Teams: their training and performance* (pp. 31–56). Norwood, NJ: Ablex.

Gaddy, C. D., & Wachtel, J. A. (1992). Team skills training in nuclear power plant operations.

In R. W. Swezey & E. Salas (Eds.), *Teams: Their training and performance* (pp. 379–396). Norwood, NJ: Ablex.

Goldstein, I. L. (1991). Training in work organizations. In M. D. Dunnette & L. M. Hough (Eds.), *Handbook of industrial and organizational psychology* (pp. 507–619). Palo Alto, CA: Consulting Psychologists.

Hall, J. K., Dwyer, D. J., Cannon-Bowers, J. A., Salas, E., & Volpe, C. E. (1993). Toward assessing team tactical decision making under stress: The development of a methodology for structuring team training scenarios. *Proceedings of the 15th annual Interservice/Industry Training Systems Conference* (pp. 97–98). Washington, DC: National Security Industrial Association.

Johnston, J. H., Cannon-Bowers, J. A., & Jentsch, K. A. S. (1995). Event-based performance measurement system for shipboard command teams. *Proceedings of the first International Symposium on command and Control Research and Technology* (pp. 274–276). Washington, DC: The Center for Advanced Command and Technology.

Kozlowski, S. W. J., Gully, S. M., Smith, E. A., Nason, E. R., & Brown, K. G. (1995, May). Sequenced mastery training and advance organizers: Effects on learning, self-efficacy, performance, and generalization. In R. J. Klimoski (Chair), *Thinking and feeling while doing: Understanding the learner in the learning process.* Symposium conducted at the 10th annual Conference of the Society for Industrial and Organizational Psychology, Orlando, FL.

Orasanu, J., & Salas, E. (1993). Team decision making in complex environments. In G. Klein, J. Orasanu, R. Calderwood, & C. E. Zsambok (Eds.), *Decision making in action: Models and methods* (pp. 327–345). Norwood, NJ: Ablex.

Salas, E., Bowers, C. A., & Cannon-Bowers, J. A. (1995). Military team research: Ten years of progress. *Military Psychology, 7,* 55–75.

Salas, E., & Cannon-Bowers, J. A. (in press). Methods, tools and strategies for team training. In M. A. Quinones & A. Dutta (Eds.), *Training for 21st century technology: Applications of psychological research.* Washington, DC: APA Press.

Serfaty, D., & Entin, E. E. (1995, June). Shared mental models and adaptive team coordination. *Proceedings of the first International Symposium on Command and Control Research and Technology* (pp. 289–294). Washington, DC: The Center for Advanced Command and Technology.

Smith-Jentsch, K. A., Payne, S. C., & Johnston, J. H. (1996, April). *Guided team self-correction: A methodology for enhancing experiential team training.* Paper presented at the 11th annual conference of the Society for Industrial and Organizational Psychology, San Diego, CA.

Swezey, R. W., & Salas, E. (Eds.). (1992). *Teams: Their training and performance.* Norwood, NJ: Ablex.

Zachary, W. W., Zaklad, A. L., Hicinbothom, J. H., & Ryder, J. M., (1993). COGNET representation of tactical decision-making in Anti-Air Warfare. *Proceedings of the Human Factors and Ergonomics Society 37th Annual Meeting* (pp. 1112–1116). Santa Monica, CA: Human Factors and Ergonomics Society.

Zalesny, M. D., Salas, E., & Prince, C. (1995). Conceptual and measurement issues in coordination: Implications for team behavior and performance. In G. R. Ferris (Ed.), *Research in personnel and human resources management* (pp. 81–115). Greenwich, CT: JAI Press.

V REFLECTIONS

15

Principles for Measuring Teamwork: A Summary and Look Toward the Future

David P. Baker
University of Central Florida

Eduardo Salas
Naval Air Warfare Center Training Systems Division, Orlando

INTRODUCTION

Teams and, as a result, team performance measurement have received an increasing amount of attention since the 1980s (e.g., Driskell & Salas, 1991; Dyer, 1984; Foushee, 1984; Salas, Bowers, and Cannon-Bowers, 1995). There have been numerous articles on teams (see Dyer, 1984; Salas et al., 1995 for comprehensive reviews of the literature), and a number of books have been published that specifically address critical issues related to team performance (see for example, Guzzo & Salas, 1995; Swezey & Salas, 1992; Wiener, Kanki, & Helmreich, 1993). It goes without saying that teamwork has become a critical element of virtually almost all organizations.

For example, in the airline industry, team training is an integral part of pilot training (referred to as Crew Resource Management training), and in the future, team performance will be evaluated along with technical performance under the new Advanced Qualifications Program (AQP; Birnbach & Longridge, 1993). However, even with this increased emphasis on teams, we contend that there is still much to be learned about the measurement of team performance. This book documents a significant body of work that has been conducted in an attempt to understand the measurement process. It provides great insight with respect to both team performance measurement theory and outlines a number of applications and evaluations of team performance measures.

The goals of the present chapter are twofold. First, we review a series of principles for measuring team performance that we previously proposed (Baker & Salas, 1992). These principles raised a number of issues for

331

guiding research, so our intention is to assess the extent to which these questions have been addressed through the research presented here. Second, on the basis of our earlier principles and the chapters presented, we propose a series of updated principles for team performance measurement. We hope that these principles serve as a vehicle for constructing actual team performance measurement tools as well as guiding future research in this area.

TEAMS AND TEAM PERFORMANCE MEASUREMENT

We begin by documenting why team performance measurement research is important. First we define what a team is. We recognize that numerous definitions of a *team* have been proposed. We simply feel that it is important that readers have a common frame of reference for our discussion.

What Is a Team?

Throughout the chapters in this book, there has been a shared understanding of what defines a team and what the important characteristics of teamwork are. To summarize, teams consist of, at a minimum, two or more individuals. These individuals have specific role assignments, must perform specific tasks (i.e., taskwork), and must interact or coordinate (i.e., teamwork) to achieve a common goal or outcome (Dyer, 1984; Morgan, Glickman, Woodard, Blaiwes, & Salas, 1986; Salas, Dickinson, Converse, & Tannenbaum, 1992). In addition, teams make decisions (Orasanu & Salas, 1993), have specialized knowledge and skills (Cannon-Bowers, Tannenbaum, Salas, & Volpe, 1995), and often work under conditions of high workload (Bowers, Braun, & Morgan, chapter 5, this volume; Orasanu & Salas, 1993). Finally, teams can be distinguished from small groups (Brannick & Prince, chapter 1, this volume), because teams have unique requirements for coordination and task interdependency. Teamwork characteristically involves team members adjusting to each other either sequentially or simultaneously in order to achieve team goals (Dickinson & McIntyre, chapter 2, this volume).

As documented here, in the area of team research, it is safe to conclude that there is a shared understanding of the variables that define a team. This is important from the standpoint of team performance measurement because it sets boundaries on what constitutes a team (e.g., such as the interdependency among team members), and it defines variables with respect to team inputs, team processes, and team outcomes that should be accounted for in the measurement process. Essentially, it tells us what to measure when assessing team performance and presents a foundation on which to construct team performance measurement tools.

Why Is Measurement Important?

In chapter 1, Brannick and Prince note that capturing, defining, and measuring the interactions that are characteristic of teamwork are basic to our ability to understand the meaning of teamwork. In other words, team performance measurement research will contribute to our comprehension of the processes that define teamwork. Brannick, A. Prince, Salas, and C. Prince (1993a) outlined three reasons why team performance measurement is important. First, team theory cannot move beyond the conceptual stage without the development of psychometrically sound measurement tools. Measurement, in and of itself, will contribute to the building and validating of accurate models of teamwork. Second, without quantifiable indicators of team performance, it is hard to determine what constitutes good and poor teamwork. Such information is particularly important from the standpoint of providing performance feedback during team training (Cannon-Bowers & Salas, chapter 3, this volume). Last, measurement is vital in evaluating instructional approaches to training teams. Psychometrically sound and construct valid measures will provide an indication of the extent to which training is effective.

Although the importance of team performance measurement in understanding teamwork is well-established, there are still numerous questions as to how to assess team performance (Dyer, 1984). These questions can be organized under three global headings: what to measure, when to measure, and how to measure. With respect to what to measure, questions revolve around the appropriate unit of analysis (i.e., whether performance assessment should be made of individual team members, the team as a whole, or some combination of both), the critical skill dimensions and behaviors to assess, and the critical team knowledge structures to assess. With respect to when to measure, questions revolve around the rates at which teams mature and the appropriate time at which to capture team performance, as well as the extent to which multiple assessments need to be employed to ensure stability in the measurement process. With respect to how to measure, questions revolve around the format of the measurement device, the extent to which team performance can be objectively quantified, and the extent to which judges can accurately assess team performance.

In order to address some of these questions, we prescribed a series of six principles for guiding team performance measurement research (Baker & Salas, 1992). These principles were organized around theoretical, methodological, and psychometric issues that are important in team performance measurement and serve as a backdrop for summarizing the work presented in this book.

PRINCIPLES FOR TEAM PERFORMANCE MEASUREMENT: PROGRESS AND EMERGING PRINCIPLES

We felt that our six basic principles were important, because, as Dyer (1984) pointed out, team oriented research has been judged and will continue to be judged on the basis of the quality of the measurement techniques employed. Given that little research on team performance measurement had been conducted at that time, there was a great need for such work, and we felt that these principles in part set a foundation for structuring such investigations. In this section, we use these principles as an organizing framework to document relevant progress in the field of team performance measurement. Then, on the basis of these results, we update these principles to reflect current thinking in the field and to prescribe new avenues for future research.

Principle 1. For understanding teamwork, there is nothing more practical than a good theory (Baker & Salas, 1992).

This principle addresses the necessity for theory when conducting team performance measurement research. Specifically, we suggested that research was needed that established sound teamwork theories, and that measurement approaches should be based on this research. Understanding the knowledge, skills, and attitudes that define teamwork is critical to establishing a nomological net (Cronbach & Meehl, 1955) of the interrelationships of these variables that should be the basis for structuring measurement tools (Cannon-Bowers et al., 1995).

Progress

Early team theories attempted to establish underlying team processes and behaviors that impact team performance (Alexander & Cooperland, 1965; Boguslaw & Porter, 1962; Lanzetta & Roby, 1960; Morgan et al., 1986; Nieva, Fleishman, & Reick, 1978; Siskel & Flexman, 1962). These behaviors then were the basis for measurement tools.

More recently, theories of teamwork have evolved to include other variables (e.g., knowledge requirements, cognitive skills, etc.) in addition to team behavior (Cannon-Bowers & Salas, in press). In a comprehensive review of the team literature, Cannon-Bowers et al. (1995) defined teamwork to consist of a series of team competencies that can be distinguished from individual competencies. These researchers suggest that team competencies can be thought of as the requisite knowledge (i.e., principles and concepts underlying a team's task performance), skills (i.e., psychomotor and cognitive behaviors necessary to perform the team task correctly), and attitudes that result in effective team performance. Competencies can be generic or specific to a team or generic or specific to a task.

From the standpoint of team performance measurement, new theories about the cognitive requirements for teamwork present the most challenge. This research hypothesizes that team members develop and rely on shared knowledge structures (referred to as shared mental models) to enhance coordination and that these models are directly related to team performance (Cannon-Bowers et al., 1993; Converse, Cannon-Bowers, & Salas, 1991; Orasanu & Salas, 1993). According to Cannon-Bowers et al. (1993), shared mental models are organized bodies of knowledge that are shared across members of a team. They suggest that such models have the potential to affect teamwork at two levels. First, when communication channels are limited, shared mental models enable team members to anticipate other team member behaviors and information requirements (Converse et al., 1991). Second, shared mental models of a team task enable team members to perform team functions from a common frame of reference.

Recent work, presented in this volume, is directly related to our first principle. Of these chapters, Dickinson and McIntyre focus on team knowledge and attitudes, and Kraiger and Wenzel focus on team mental models.

With respect to team knowledge and attitudes, Dickinson and McIntyre hypothesize that not only does teamwork require the performance of critical team skills, but team members must also hold positive attitudes toward the team, receive rewards based on team goals, and possess knowledge of their own task and other team members' tasks. Effective team performance results from team members monitoring their own and other's performance, communicating with other team members, and providing feedback and back-up when needed. Therefore, team performance measures must not only focus on team behavior, but must also assess prevailing team attitudes as well as team knowledge requirements.

In terms of team cognitive skills, Kraiger and Wenzel suggest that team performance is directly related to the degree to which team members have a shared understanding of the team, the task, and the environment. These researchers document the importance of how team members acquire and represent this information (i.e., cognitive models) and how these models are shared among team members. As stated previously, the measurement of mental models and the degree to which these models are shared among team members presents one of the most challenging avenues for team performance research. These researchers advocate several strategies to pursue in this area that we discuss later.

Taken together, the research reviewed here suggests that considerable progress has been made regarding team performance theory development. Team performance theories have evolved beyond simply focusing on skills and behaviors and now account for specific knowledge requirements on the part of team members and the degree to which this knowledge is shared among team members (Cannon-Bowers & Salas, in press).

Emerging Principles

The Whole May Truly Be Greater Than the Sum of Its Parts.   To date, much of the research on teamwork has focused on specific attributes of teamwork as opposed to developing unified theories and measures of teamwork. As can be seen in the chapters in this book, some researchers focused on team behavioral skills (Komaki, chapter 11, this volume; A. Prince et al., chapter 13, this volume), some researchers focused on cognitive skills (Kraiger & Wenzel, chapter 4, this volume), and some researchers focused on team knowledge and attitudes (Dickinson & McIntyre, chapter 2, this volume). Unified theories of teamwork have been proposed (Cannon-Bowers & Salas, chapter 3, this volume; Cannon-Bowers et al., 1995; Salas et al., 1992), but unified measures of teamwork have not. Recent research suggests that such measures should attempt to assess the critical team knowledge, skill (both cognitive and behavioral), and attitude competencies (Cannon-Bowers & Salas, chapter 3, this volume). Such work is important because measuring a number of team process attributes simultaneously, in such a way that promotes understanding of the unique interactions among these variables, should provide great insight regarding the true nature and characteristics of team performance. In other words, it will only be through such research that valid models of team performance can be developed. With that in mind, we suggest the following principles:

Principle 1a: Full understanding of team performance requires behavioral, cognitive, and attitudinal-based measures.

Team Theory Has Taken Two Steps Forward, But Needs to Take One Step Back.   A review of the chapters in this book and the general literature on team performance measurement suggests that a great deal of theoretical work has been completed. There have been many discussions of the variables that define teamwork and what the appropriate strategies are for measuring these attributes. However, there continues to be, in our opinion, a void with respect to actual empirical research. Theorizing about teamwork has moved ahead at a rapid pace, but there has not been enough research that validates these theories. We hope now with the introduction of the new measurement tools in this book that team researchers will begin to conduct such studies. Whereas theories of teamwork are important for guiding the development of team process measures, it is equally important that empirical data exists to support these teamwork models. With that in mind, we suggest the following principle:

Principle 1b: The development of team performance measures must be guided, in part, by theory and, in part, by empirical research.

Principle 2: What you see may not be what you get (Baker & Salas, 1992).

Principle 2 highlights the *dynamic* nature of teamwork and the fact measurement approaches must account for this characteristic. Therefore, we argued that a single snapshot of a team's performance will likely be an insufficient measurement tool, especially if this snap shot is taken early in the team evolution and maturation process (Morgan et al., 1986; Morgan, Salas, & Glickman, 1994). This principle suggests that team performance needs to be sampled over a wide variety of occasions and conditions in order to get an accurate picture of a team.

Progress

Whereas there has been considerable theoretical progress regarding team performance, little research has focused on team development and its corresponding impact on the measurement of team performance. Early research in this area suggested that teams progressed through a linear sequence of developmental phases (Nadler & Berger, 1981). More recently, this thinking has evolved to suggest that teams develop through a variety of alternative paths (Morgan et al., 1994). For example, McGrath (1991) noted that teams may follow different paths to arrive at the same outcome. He suggested that teams engage in four modes of group activity (i.e., goal choice, means choice, policy choice, and goal attainment) with respect to three team functions (i.e., production, well-being, and member support). For each team function, teams always begin with goal choice and end with goal attainment; however, the mechanisms by which they arrive at goal attainment can vary significantly.

Morgan et al. (1994) provided a comprehensive framework for under-standing team development referred to as the Team Evolution and Maturation (TEAM) model. The TEAM model describes a series of developmental stages through which newly formed teams are hypothesized to evolve. These periods of development are considered to be relatively informal and overlapping. Sharp distinctions among phases are not possible due to the dynamic situations in which teams operate. To test the TEAM model, data were collected on Navy Command Information Center (CIC) teams going through training. The results suggested that team and task skills matured differentially and to some extent independently.

Most recently, McIntyre and Salas (1995) suggested that the most critical aspect of team development is the extent to which team members have worked together as a team. It is important to note that team experience is not synonymous with work experience or tenure, rather it involves team member experience in an intact team. These researchers point out that the fundamental aspects of teamwork (e.g., performance monitoring, feedback, closed-loop communication, backing-up behavior, team awareness, within-team interdependence) can vary within a team due to the extent of practice and training that has occurred. From the standpoint of team performance measurement, this implies that one-time measures of teamwork might result in different performance levels for different team skills, depending on the experience levels team members have with a given team. As experience increases for a given team, performance on these critical skills may change producing what appears to be unreliable results.

Research on team performance measurement needs to resolve such issues to ensure the integrity of measures that are employed. Unfortunately, little research presented here directly addressed the issue of team development and maturation, and how to account for the effects of these variables in team performance measurement. It will be recalled from our earlier work (Baker & Salas, 1992) that we called for performance measures that assessed teamwork at a variety of stages and in a variety of situations. The majority of the measures presented in this book still focused on a single snapshot of a team's behavior and do not account for team member experience. Therefore, questions can be raised regarding the extent to which teams have fully developed their teamwork capabilities in some of the empirical work presented here. In a positive light however, several chapters do note the potential effects of team development on the measurement process, and one other chapter notes how team performance measurement can contribute to team development.

With respect to the effects of team development on the measurement process, Bowers et al., in their investigation of team workload, pointed out that changes may occur in mutual team knowledge and communication behaviors as a result of team member experience. These researchers hypothesize that experience is likely to result in increased mutual knowledge among team members and a decrease in the requirements for communication. Fewer communication requirements among team members could result in decreased team workload; however, as Bowers et al. point out, empirical data do not exist to confirm this proposition. Similarly, Kraiger and Wenzel suggest that shared mental models will develop among team members over time, and therefore decrease the extent to which communication is required among members of a team.

Alternatively, with respect to the effects of team performance measurement on the team development process, Cannon-Bowers and Salas (chapter 3, this volume) delineate specific requirements for measuring team performance during training. These researchers suggest that team performance measures must support team training by providing a basis for remediation (i.e., the process by which performance deficiencies are used to design and structure subsequent instruction). These researchers go on to suggest that team performance measures in training must exist at both the team and individual levels; address processes and outcomes; describe, evaluate, and diagnose performance; and provide a basis for feedback and instructional strategy selection. In the context of this principle, this research suggests that team performance measures, appropriately designed for training, will facilitate the rate at which a team matures. In other words, effective team training, which employs accurate measurement and feedback mechanisms, may offset the extent to which team members require experience in an intact team to achieve maximum performance.

In summary, the research presented in this book provides some new insight regarding the effects of team development and maturation on the measurement process. However, while these issues are discussed at a theoretical level, no direct examination of how to account for team experience when assessing team performance was presented. We still believe that this presents a significant challenge for team performance measurement research.

Emerging Principles

Growing Up Is a Part of Life.   There is significant empirical evidence to support the notion that teams evolve and mature over time; teams grow up! (McIntyre & Salas, 1995; Morgan et al., 1986; Morgan et al., 1994). Team members and the team itself pass through different stages of development with respect to both taskwork and teamwork, and these stages may occur at different rates for different team members and teams. Therefore, research needs to determine whether or not different measures of team performance are effective at different stages of team development. Furthermore, measures might be developed to predict various stages of team development. Such measures would be valuable for providing feedback to team members regarding current team performance and, as a result, facilitating the team maturation process. With that in mind, we suggest the following principles:

Principle 2a: Measures must capture the dynamic nature of teamwork.

Principle 2b: Measures and measurement tools must reflect the maturation process of a team.

Teamwork: Team Members Have To Develop a Taste For It.   Empirical evidence also exists to suggest that team member experience will result in improved levels of team performance (McIntyre & Salas, 1995). In other words, team member experience with an intact team will moderate the level of team process observed and the extent to which mental models have developed among team members (Bowers et al., chapter 5, this volume; Cannon-Bowers & Salas, chapter 3, this volume; Kraiger & Wenzel, chapter 4, this volume). Under this principle then, we advocate that team process measures assess team member experience levels. Research on the this issue should determine the specific effects of team member experience on team process. Results of this research will be useful in more fully understanding team maturation and in determining the points at which it is appropriate to capture an accurate picture of the level of teamwork achieved by a team. With that in mind, we suggest the following principle:

Principle 2c: Measures must account for team member experience with a team.

Principle 3. There is no escaping observation (Baker & Salas, 1992).

This principle suggests that there is likely no practical way to escape the requirement for judges in the measurement process, especially when trying to capture team behavioral skills (e.g., team situation awareness, team leadership, etc.) as opposed to global team outcomes (e.g., the plane landed safely). We felt that measuring team behavior is perhaps the most challenging aspect of team performance measurement research. Therefore, we called for research in this area that explored the practical utility and reliability (i.e., from the standpoint of rater agreement) of various rating formats.

Progress

As noted in Principle 1, early team theories attempted to establish underlying team processes and behaviors that impact team performance, and these behaviors were the basis for measurement tools. Such tools typically require team experts to observe a team and then make judgments regarding that team's performance. These early conceptualizations of teamwork led us to conclude that observation is likely to be a critical part of the team performance measurement process, and we suggested that methodologies must be identified that result high levels of interrater agreement.

Recent theories of teamwork have evolved to include other variables (e.g., knowledge requirements, positive attitudes regarding teamwork, etc.) in addition to observable team behaviors. As noted previously, Cannon-Bowers et al. (1995) defined teamwork to consist of a series of team competencies. These include the requisite knowledge, skills, and attitudes that are necessary for effective team performance. Such models of teamwork suggest that the requirement for observation will diminish somewhat because team knowledge, cognitive skill, and attitude competencies cannot be readily observed. Therefore, to assess these team variables, new and innovative measurement methods will have to be employed.

The chapter by Kraiger and Wenzel (chapter 4, this volume) directly tackles the problem of measuring team member mental models. Initially, these researchers attempt to delineate clearly what the construct of a shared mental model is and then outline the corresponding requirements for measuring such a phenomenon. Kraiger and Wenzel suggest that measures for shared mental models should be able to assess: (a) how team members perceive, process, or react to external stimuli; (b) how team members organize or structure task relevant knowledge; (c) common attitudes or affect for task relevant behavior; and (d) shared expectations for that behavior.

Kraiger and Wenzel propose several methods for meeting the above challenges of assessing shared mental models in teams. These include: card sorting tasks, probed protocol analysis, and structural assessment. In general, the goals of these techniques are to elicit team member knowledge structures and then to compare the similarity of these knowledge structures across team members. Shared mental models are defined to exist when the resulting knowledge structures for team members are found to be similar in nature. Kraiger and Wenzel point out that several methods may be required to capture the shared mental model construct and that research needs to be conducted that tests these measures.

In summary, new developments in team theory (e.g., team competencies, shared mental models) will likely result in additional requirements to observing team member behavior in order to understand team performance. This research suggests that tools will need to be developed that provide detailed information about the cognitive processes of team members. Such information will not be readily accessible through observations of team member behavior, but require strategies that are outlined in chapter 4. This does not mean, however, that observation will not continue to be a part of the team performance measurement process. We still feel that observation will be a significant part of assessing and providing feedback regarding team behavioral skills. We only mean to point out that our thinking has evolved on this principle to indicate that observation is only likely to be one small component of measuring a team's performance.

Emerging Principles

Seeing Should Not Be a Necessary Requirement for Believing. The general consensus across the chapters in this book, and the literature on teams in general, suggests that teamwork is comprised of observable behaviors as well as critical team knowledge, attitudes, and cognitive skills. Therefore, measures that restrict themselves to observable team behavior are only capturing part of the picture. Team performance is far more complex and not simply represented by what team members do. To understand team performance, new measures that tap team member shared mental models and interpositional knowledge among team members must be developed and validated. This is critically important given that well developed mental models among team members may actually lead to decreases in observable team behaviors (Bowers et al., chapter 5, this volume). With that in mind, we suggest the following principles:

Principle 3a. Team performance is not simply represented by what team members do.

Principle 3b. Observation is critical for measuring and providing feedback regarding team behavioral skills.

Principle 3c. Measures that assess team member shared mental models and interpositional knowledge must be developed and validated.

Principle 4. Applications, applications, applications (Baker & Salas, 1992).

Principle 4 highlights the need for applications. We argued that team performance measures need to be developed, implemented, and evaluated for a wide variety of teams in a wide variety of settings to understand the measurement process better. We felt, and still feel, that this was one of most important principles, because data collected from these applications will be useful in guiding future measurement development and contribute to the development of teamwork theories.

Progress

In our article, we called for the development and application of team performance measures for a variety of teams in a variety of settings. At that time, most team performance measures had been developed and applied in tactical decision-making teams and aircrews; few measures had been developed and applied in other environments. We felt that this was a significant void in the field, because it was only through actual team performance measurement scale development and application that both theoretical and applied questions could be answered.

Now, as documented in the chapters in this book, great strides have been made from the standpoint of developing and applying team performance measures. The vast majority of the authors in this volume provide detailed information on how they went about developing a team performance measurement tool to address a need in a particular context. These applications span a variety of different teams and present a number of different formats for assessing team performance. These formats include behavioral checklists for measuring team skills and behaviors, surveys for assessing team member attitudes, and advanced computer simulations for assessing specific team processes such as team decision making.

With respect to behavioral checklists, several chapters in this book present research on such measures for assessing team skills and behaviors in aircrews. Chapter 7, by Dwyer, Fowlkes, Oser, and Lane, for example, describes a method of developing team performance measures that involves determining precisely what should be done during a team task and then developing a checklist on the basis of that information. Such a scripted checklist allows observers to record specific team behaviors, and this information can be used to render a judgment regarding overall team performance. Chapter 13, by A. Prince, C. Prince, Brannick, and Salas, reviews several different measurement scales that have been designed by the Navy to capture team behavior in aircrews. These scales vary in specificity from one end of the continuum, where a scale is scripted for a specific team task, to the other end of the continuum, where a scale can be applied to a variety of tasks.

With respect to survey methods, two of the chapters in this book present information on this approach. First, chapter 8, by Hallam and Campbell, describes the development of the Campbell–Hallam Team Development Survey. The purpose of this survey was to assess team-member perceptions of how their team is doing in order to provide feedback to team members to improve team performance. The survey was designed to be applied to a wide variety of teams, and the authors report reasonably strong psychometric evidence to support the use of this instrument. Chapter 9, by Mathieu and Day, also illustrates the use of a survey to measure team performance. These researchers developed a method to assess specific teamwork variables that were characteristic of within and between-departmental functions in a nuclear power plant setting.

With respect to computer simulations, chapter 6 by Hollenbeck et al. provides extensive information on a networked software program called TIDE^2. These researchers describe how this program can be used effectively to study team decision making and present preliminary data from two empirical investigations to support the use of this simulation.

Last, several other chapters outline and/or test specific strategies for assessing specific team attributes. For example, chapter 4, by Kraiger and Wenzel, describes techniques for assessing team member mental models, and chapter 5, by Bowers et al., describes measures for assessing team workload. These measures include properties of other measures described previously, but were designed to assess specific characteristics of teamwork.

On this basis of this research then, it is safe to conclude that significant strides have been made regarding the development and application of team performance measures. In addition, new measures are being applied in contexts outside of the military and aviation such as nuclear power plants (Toquam, MaCauly, Westra, Fujita, & Murphy, chapter 12, this volume) and theater teams (Komaki, chapter 11, this volume). Such efforts are consistent with the types of efforts we called for under this principle and should lend to significant gains in understanding the team performance measurement process.

Emerging Principles

Applications, Applications, Applications[2]. Even with all the excellent work that has been undertaken, we still feel that more team performance measures need to be developed, applied, and evaluated for different teams in different settings. In particular, we would like to re-emphasize that this principle calls for data to be collected on all new measures of team performance. To date, measures have been developed and applied, but far less data have been collected on the effectiveness of these techniques. These data are critical for understanding the psychometric properties of a measurement technique, as well as for building sound theories of team performance. With that in mind, we suggest the following principles:

> *Principle 4a. Team performance measures must be developed, implemented, and evaluated for a wide variety of teams in a wide variety of settings.*
>
> *Principle 4b. Psychometric data must be collected on all new measures of team performance.*

Applications, Applications, Applications[3]. Whereas there have been a significant number of team performance measures that have been developed to evaluate team behavioral skills, far fewer measures have been developed that assess other team competencies. Therefore, teamwork measures that assess team knowledge, attitude, and cognitive skill competencies need to be developed, applied, and evaluated. As called for under Principle 4b, data should be collected on these measures to determine their psychometric properties, as well as for constructing sound theories of team performance. With that in mind, we suggest one additional new principle:

> *Principle 4c. Measures that assess team knowledge, attitude, and skill competencies must be developed, applied, and evaluated.*

Principle 5. Judges and measures must be reliable (Baker & Salas, 1992).

Principle 5 highlighted the fact that team performance measures must be reliable. We emphasized that reliability includes internal consistency and temporal stability of the measurement tool as well as interjudge agreement. In addition, we noted the critical role reliability plays in determining the internal validity of team performance measurement scales.

Progress

In our earlier manuscript, although we pleaded for applications of team performance measures, we also noted that these measures needed to be reliable. Furthermore, we pointed out that reliability must take place at two levels. First, when team skills and behaviors are being observed by team experts and these experts make judgments regarding team performance, the reliability of these experts must be established. Second, with respect to the measurement tools themselves, the internal consistency of these measures and their component subscales must be determined as well as the temporal stability of variables that are being assessed.

There has been some research to suggest that judges can reliably assess team skills and behaviors. Brannick and his colleagues (Brannick et al., 1993a; Brannick, Roach, & Salas, 1993b; Dwyer et al., chapter 7, this volume; A. Prince et al., chapter 13, this volume) have conducted several investigations that have targeted the psychometric properties of team performance measures. In general, these investigations have shown that raters can achieve reasonable levels of agreement. For example, Brannick et al. (1993b) found on-site raters to achieve interrater reliabilities for various team process skills to range from a low of .57 (i.e., accepting suggestions) to a high of .81 (i.e., coordination), and Brannick et al. (1993a) found interrater reliabilities to range from a low of .78 (i.e., situation awareness) to a high of .93 (i.e., adaptability). Dwyer et al. (chapter 7, this volume) have reported some the highest levels of agreement with interrater reliabilities in excess of .90.

Alternatively, evidence for the internal consistency of team performance measurement tools has been less encouraging. Analyses of both the internal consistency of team process measures and the consistency of team behavior across different yet similar simulations has produced correlations that are low in magnitude. For example, Brannick et al. (1993a) found such correlations to range from a low of .02 (i.e., adaptability) to a high of .52 (i.e., communication) when examining the consistency of team process skills across two scenarios designed to be alternative forms of each other. These results indicate potential problems with the reliability of these measurement tools or the possibility that team performance in and of itself is unreliable. Given that the reliability data reported by Brannick and his colleagues is encouraging for the levels of interrater agreement that can be achieved and the research that has shown that teamwork evolves and matures over time, the latter proposition seems most likely.

Several chapters in the current book report additional data on the levels of interrater reliability that can be achieved with various team performance measures, though far less evidence is presented on the internal consistency of various measurement tools and the stability of various team skills. Regarding interrater reliability, Komaki (chapter 11, this volume) presents some preliminary data for her Theater Teamwork Effectiveness Measure (TTEM). Komaki suggests that any measure (i.e., team or individual) that requires judgment by an individual should demonstrate that independent raters agree on their recordings and obtain interrater reliability scores of 90% or better. However, as reported by Komaki, data collected on six theater productions by six expert raters has failed to meet this 90% agreement criterion for the TTEM. Disagreements seem to arise for particularly hard-to-define areas such as sound and light changes. For example, as Komaki notes, a director might request that the set lighting be increased and the lighting designer correspondingly increases the number of lumens. However, even the most experienced raters cannot discern such a change the next night when the team's performance is observed. Komaki reports that revisions to the TTEM continue to achieve this 90% agreement criterion.

The chapter by Toquam et al. also presents interrater reliability for their investigation of nuclear power plant teams. Here, seven expert raters provided team performance ratings on three dimensions; team unity, team spirit, and team performance. For each dimension, raters were provided with guidelines for the types of behaviors to use to guide their ratings. Analysis of the data showed, across different pairs of raters, that interrater reliability levels ranged from .62 to .97, with the mean reliability across all pairs of raters being .80.

Regarding internal consistency and stability team performance measures, Hallam and Campbell (chapter 8, this volume) present fairly comprehensive data for their Team Development Survey™ (TDS™). The TDS™ was designed to measure perceptions of team members and feed back this information to team members in a form they can use for identifying strengths and weaknesses. In other words, this survey was designed to assess how a team is doing and ways a team can improve its performance. Data on the reliability of this measure, collected from a wide variety of teams, has been encouraging. Hallam and Campbell report the scale scores of the TDS™ to have a median alpha of .69 and a median test–retest reliability of .80.

In summary, psychometric data are beginning to become available for measures that target team behavioral skills, but few data are available on measures that target team knowledge, attitude, and cognitive skill competencies. It appears that observers can, in fact, be trained to achieve high levels of agreement when evaluating team behaviors, but questions still remain regarding the internal consistency of team performance measures and the extent to which team performance in itself is reliable. Answers to these questions are vital precursors to understanding the requirements for valid team performance measurement. Generalizability analysis is a potentially powerful technique for pursuing such research (Mathieu & Day, chapter 9, this volume).

Emerging Principles

Judges, Measures, and Team Performance.   Here, we wish to modify our earlier principle so that it applies to team performance measures in a wider variety of contexts, especially when observation is not a requirement of the measurement process. We still feel in all team performance measurement research that information on the reliability of such measures should be collected. We simply wish to point out that reliability studies should be designed to reflect the specific characteristics of a measurement tool. Moreover, we advocate the researchers in this area look to techniques such as generalizability analysis (for an example of an application of this technique refer to Mathieu & Day, this volume) to understand the unique contributions of different variance components in the measurement process. With that in mind, we suggest the following principles:

Principle 5a. Reliability studies must reflect characteristics of the measurement tool.

Principle 5b. Team performance expert observers must demonstrate high levels of agreement (around 90%).

Principle 5c. Team performance measures must demonstrate internal consistency.

Past Performance May Not Be the Best Indicator of Future Performance. In addition to the reliability of team performance measurement tools, the reliability of team performance itself must be established. This may be difficult, because the team maturation literature suggests that team performance is not consistent over time and these changes are likely to vary across teams. Research in this area might initially focus on trying to distinguish those team skills that possess temporal stability from those that do not. With that in mind, we suggest the additional new principle:

Principle 5d. Measures must establish the reliability of team performance.

Principle 6. Validation for practice and theory (Baker & Salas, 1992).

This principle highlighted the fact that team performance measures must be valid. As noted earlier, validation is important for both applied and theoretical work in this area. From an applied standpoint, the development of valid team performance measures provides accurate information for the process of evaluating teamwork skills and conducting team training. From a theoretical standpoint, valid teamwork measures provide additional information on the knowledge, attitude, and skill competencies that underlie team process.

Progress

Few researchers have conducted extensive investigations into the validity of teamwork measures. Although the chapters in this book reflect extensive research from the standpoint of developing and applying actual measurement tools, little validation evidence is presented. However, we wish to temper this criticism somewhat by pointing out that we do recognize that team performance measures must be developed before actual validation research can be conducted. In addition, a number of the authors in this book point out the need for validating the measures they have reviewed or proposed and strategies for doing such research (see, e.g., for example Cannon-Bowers & Salas, chapter 3, this volume).

As with the research on reliability, Brannick and his colleagues have conducted the most significant research on the validity of team performance measures (Brannick et al., 1993a; Brannick et al., 1993b; A. Prince et al., chapter 13, this volume). To meet the psychometric requirements for valid team performance measurement, Brannick et al. (1993a) suggested that at a minimum, team process measures should: (a) be reliable in the sense that different judges should be interchangeable for one another, (b) be sensitive to differences in teams existing prior to task performance, and (c) be useful in predicting important team outcomes.

Brannick and his colleagues have attempted to address these issues by exploring both the reliability and construct validity of several team process measures. In general, these studies have demonstrated reasonable levels of interjudge agreement (refer to the research presented under Principle 5) and mixed results regarding construct validity. Investigations of construct validity have characteristically examined the extent to which team performance for a number of team process skills are consistent across alternate yet similar scenarios. Results of these studies have shown evidence of convergent and discriminant validity; however, method variance typically over-shadows these results.

Two chapters in this volume present preliminary data for the validity of various team performance measures. First, Hallam and Campbell (chapter 8, this volume) assessed the extent to which the TDS was related to three indications of the team's performance: an average independent observer performance rating, an average team-leader performance rating, and an average team member performance rating. Results of these analyses showed that the highest correlations between the three measures of performance and the TDS scores were for the Skills scale, Commitment scale, Innovation scale, and the Leadership scale. Correlations among these performance criteria ranged from a low of .36 to a high of .66 across these scales.

Second, Toquam et al. (chapter 12, this volume) examined the extent to which characteristics of the task, characteristics of crew members, and characteristics of crew processes influence crew performance variability in nuclear power plant operations. Team performance data were collected on operator teams from seven Japanese nuclear power utilities. Regarding the crew process data, analysis focused on communication within a team and its relationship to team performance variability on a simulated team task. The results showed that crews that were not proficient in sharing technical information throughout the team demonstrated higher levels of perfor-mance variability. In other words, teams with poor communication skills performed more poorly on a team task than crews with stronger team communication skills.

In summary, the research presented in this book outlines a significant body of work that develops and applies new team performance measure-ment tools, and these researchers are now beginning to examine both the construct- and criterion-related validity of these measures.

Emerging Principles

Content and Construct Validation.   Content and construct validation strategies will be particularly important for building team theories. Content validation strategies ensure that appropriate information is being sampled regarding specific team constructs (i.e., knowledge, skills, and attitudes), and construct validation strategies will provide empirical evidence to support the existence of those constructs. Collectively, this research should provide important information regarding team cognitive and behavioral skills, as well as the interrelationships of these skills. In other words, these studies will be vital for truly identifying the nomological net of variables that define team performance and determining how a team works most effectively. With that in mind, we suggest the following principles:

Principle 6a. The content and construct validity of team performance measures must be determined.

Principle 6b. Valid team performance measure must contribute to the development of valid team performance theories.

Criterion-Related Validation.   Criterion-related validation strategies are particularly important for understanding the extent to which team process is related to team outcomes. To date, most measurement research has focused on team constructs and, to a lesser extent, the relationship between team process and performance. Therefore, we suggest that criterion-related validation studies be undertaken that examine the extent to which team cognitive and behavioral skills are related to independent team performance criteria. Such research will make a valuable contribution in the area of team training, where evaluation and feedback are viewed as critical. However, this work should not exclude examining the underlying strategies by which teams utilize their coordination skills, because different coordination strategies may result in the same level of team performance, yet be variously efficient. For example, in certain cases stronger team members may compensate for weaker team members. In such cases, the level of performance achieved might be quite high but the efficiency by which such a team reaches this level of performance might be very low. With that in mind, we suggest the following principles:

Principle 6c. The criterion-related validity of team performance measures must be determined.

Principle 6d. Team performance measures must predict team outcomes.

Face Validation.   Last, team performance measures should possess face validity; they should look like they assess team performance. This issue is particularly important from the standpoint of team training and the degree to which trainees are receptive to feedback. Therefore, team performance measures should appear to be valid by targeting specific team skills that are derived from a thorough analysis of the team in question. With that in mind, we suggest the following principle:

Principle 6e. Team performance measures must look like they assess team performance.

LOOKING TOWARD THE FUTURE

In concluding, we suggest that the future of team performance measurement looks quite bright based on the significant body of research presented throughout the chapters in this book. Since we advocated our initial list of principles (Baker & Salas, 1992), team theory has advanced at a rapid pace; a number of new team performance measures have been developed and applied in a variety of contexts; and psychometric research has started to explore the properties of team performance measures, and continues to grow. This recent research was the foundation for an additional 20 principles that we presented in this chapter to guide future team performance measurement research. These emerging principles, as well as our original six principles, are presented in Table 15.1. With these new principles as the guiding framework, we see three major trends for the future of team performance measurement research over the next several years.

Unified Theories of Teamwork

First, we envision that future research on teams and team performance will see the development of unified theories of teamwork. Team theories will no longer be simply attitude-based, knowledge-based, or skill-based, but will account for all of these variables in a single model. In fact, some of this research has already begun. For example, Cannon-Bowers and her colleagues (Cannon-Bowers et al., 1995; Cannon-Bowers & Salas, chapter 3, this volume) defined *teamwork* to be a function of the environment in which the team operates and a set of critical team member attitude, knowledge, and skill competencies.

In this arena, we also envision that the future will bring more intricate theories of team member cognitive skills and the mechanisms by which team members develop shared mental models. Research on the cognitive aspects of teamwork and the measurement of these variables is really in the earliest phases and is likely to grow at a significant rate in the future (Kraiger & Wenzel, chapter 4, this volume).

New Measurement Development

Second, we envision that the future of team performance measurement will see continued growth in the area of developing team performance measurement tools. As we already pointed out under our original principles (i.e., Principle 4: Applications, Applications, Applications), this is one of the most critical areas, if team performance measurement research is going to continue to develop as a science. To date, the progress in this area has been outstanding and it appears that the future will see continued advancement in this area both with respect to measurement design and application. As noted throughout this chapter, this work is particularly important, because it is only through the application of team performance measures that

TABLE 15.1
Principles for Measuring Teamwork Skills

Original Principles	Emerging Principles
1. For understanding teamwork, there is nothing more practical than a good theory (Baker & Salas, 1992).	1a: Full understanding of team performance requires behavioral, cognitive, and attitudinal-based measures. 1b: The development of team performance measures must be guided, in part, by theory and, in part, by empirical research.
2. What you see may not be what you get (Baker & Salas, 1992).	2a: Measures must capture the dynamic nature of teamwork. 2b: Measures and measurement tools must reflect the maturation process of a team. 2c: Measures must account for team member experience with a team.
3. There is no escaping observation (Baker & Salas, 1992).	3a. Team performance is not simply represented by what team members do. 3b. Observation is critical for measuring and providing feedback regarding team behavioral skills. 3c. Measures that assess team member shared mental models and interpositional knowledge must be developed and validated.
4. Applications, applications, applications (Baker & Salas, 1992).	4a. Team performance measures must be developed, implemented, and evaluated for a wide variety of teams in a wide variety of settings. 4b. Psychometric data must be collected on all new measures of team performance. 4c. Measures that assess team knowledge, attitude, and skill competencies must be developed, applied, and evaluated.
5. Judges and measures must be reliable (Baker & Salas, 1992).	5a. Reliability studies must reflect characteristics of the measurement tool. 5b. Team performance expert observers must demonstrate high levels of agreement (around 90%). 5c. Team performance measures must demonstrate internal consistency. 5d. Measures must establish the reliability of team performance.
6. Validation for practice and theory (Baker & Salas, 1992).	6a. The content and construct validity of team performance measures must be determined. 6b. Valid team performance measure must contribute to the development of valid team performance theories. 6c. The criterion-related validity of team performance measures must be determined. 6d. Team performance measures must predict team outcomes. 6e. Team performance measures must look like they assess team performance.

validated theories of teamwork can develop. The future, then, is likely to bring new measures that contribute to building unified theories of teamwork and advancing our understanding of team member cognitive skills and shared mental models.

More Validation Research

Last, we envision that the future of team performance measurement research will bring more detailed investigations of the psychometric properties of team performance measures. This research will be a direct result of the development and application of new team performance measurement tools for a variety of teams in a variety of contexts. As more and more data become available through repeated applications, researchers will begin to examine the extent to which these measurement devices are reliable and valid. It is our hope that reliability studies will seek to partial out the variance that can be attributed to different components of the measurement process (e.g., observers, rating formats, etc.) and that validity studies will seek to establish the construct and criterion-related validities of team performance measures. The majority of chapters in this book note the importance of conducting psychometric studies and outline future plans for such investigations. Therefore, we believe that the next several years will see a significant growth in research in this area.

SUMMARY

As we concluded in our earlier manuscript, some strides have been made, but there is still much to be learned about the measurement of team performance. We hope that these revised principles present an up-to-date framework for conducting such research.

Furthermore, we hope that researchers capitalize on the massive amounts of diverse information on team performance measurement that has been presented throughout this book. We believe the future of team performance measurement to be bright, but there are still many lessons to be learned here and many questions have been raised that need to be answered.

REFERENCES

Alexander, L. T., & Cooperland, A. S. (1965). *System training research in team behavior* (TM-2581; DTIC No. AD620606). Santa Monica, CA: System Development Corporation.
Baker, D. P., & Salas, E. (1992). Principles for measuring teamwork skills. *Human Factors, 34,* 469–475.

Birnbach, R. A., & Longridge, T. M. (1993). The regulatory perspective. In E. L. Wiener, B. G. Kanki, & R. L. Helmreich (Eds.), *Cockpit resource management* (pp. 263–281). New York: Academic Press.

Boguslaw, R., & Porter, E. H. (1962). Team functions and training. In R. M. Gagne (Ed.), *Human performance and productivity* (pp. 387–416). New York: Holt, Rinehart, & Winston.

Brannick, M. T., Prince, A., Salas, E, & Prince, C. (1993a, April). *Impact of raters and events on team performance measurement*. Paper presented at the eighth annual conference of the Society for Industrial and Organizational Psychology, San Francisco, CA.

Brannick, M. T., Roach, R. M., & Salas, E. (1993b). Understanding team performance: A multimethod study. *Human Performance, 6*(4), 287–308.

Cannon-Bowers, J. A., & Salas, E. (in press). Teamwork competencies: The interaction of team member knowledge, skills, and attitudes. In H. F. O'Neil (Ed.), *Workforce readiness: Competence and assessment* Mahwah, NJ: Lawrence Erlbaum Associates.

Cannon-Bowers, J. A., Salas, E., & Converse, S. A. (1993). Shared mental models in expert team decision making. In N. J. Castellan, Jr. (Ed.), *Current issues in individual and group decision making* (pp. 221–246), Hillsdale, NJ: Lawrence Erlbaum Associates.

Cannon-Bowers, J. A., Tannenbaum, S. I., Salas, E., & Volpe, C. E. (1995). Defining competencies and establishing team training requirements. In R. Guzzo & E. Salas (Eds.), *Team effectiveness and decision making in organizations* (pp. 333–380). San Francisco: Jossey-Bass.

Converse, S. A., Cannon-Bowers, J. A., & Salas, E. (1991). Team member shared mental models: A theory and some methodological issues. *Proceedings of the Human Factors Society 35th Annual Meeting*, 1417–1421.

Cronbach, L. J., & Meehl, P. H. (1955). Construct validity of psychological tests. *Psychological Bulletin, 89,* 281–302.

Driskell, J. E., & Salas, E. (1991). Group decision making under stress. *Journal of Applied Psychology, 76,* 473–478.

Dyer, J. L. (1984). Team research and training: A state-of-the-art review. In F. A. Muckler (Ed.), *Human factors review* (pp. 285–323). Santa Monica, CA: Human Factors and Ergonomics Society.

Foushee, H. C. (1984). Dyads and tryads at 35,000 feet: Factors affecting group process and aircrew performance. *American Psychologist, 39*(8), 885–893.

Guzzo, R., & Salas, E. (1995). *Team effectiveness and decision making in organizations*. San Francisco: Jossey-Bass.

Lanzetta, J. T., & Roby, T. B. (1960). The relationship between certain group process variables and group problem-solving efficiency. *Journal of Social Psychology, 52,* 135–148.

McGrath, J. E. (1991). Time, interaction, and performance: A theory of groups. *Small Group Research, 21,* 147–174.

McIntyre, R. M., & Salas, E. (1995). Measuring and managing for team performance: Lessons from complex environments. In R. Guzzo & E. Salas (Eds.), *Team effectiveness and decision making in organizations* (pp. 149–203). San Francisco: Jossey-Bass.

Morgan, B. B., Glickman, A. S., Woodward, E. A., Blaiwes, A. S., & Salas, E., (1986). *Measurement of team behaviors in a Navy environment* (Tech. Rep. No. NTSC TR-86–014). Orlando, FL: Naval Training Systems Center.

Morgan, B. B., Salas, E., & Glickman, A. S. (1994). An analysis of team evolution and maturation. *The Journal of General Psychology, 120,* 277–291.

Nadler, L., & Berger, L. (1981). *A classification system for Navy teams* (final report). (DTIC No. AD A-105 400). Alexandria, VA: Mellonics Systems Development Division.

Nieva, V. F., Fleishman, E. A., & Reick, A. (1978). *Team dimensions: Their identity, their measurement, and relationships* (Final Tech. Rep., Contract DAH19–78-C-0001). Washington, DC: Advanced Resources Research Center.

Orasanu, J., & Salas, E. (1993). Team decision making in complex environments. In G. Klein, J. Orasanu, & R. Calderwood (Eds.), *Decision making in action: Models and methods* (pp. 327–345). Norwood, NJ: Ablex.

Salas, E., Bowers, C. A., & Cannon-Bowers, J. A. (1995). Military team research: 10 years of progress. *Military Psychology, 7*(2), 55–75.

Salas, E., Dickinson, T. L., Converse, S., & Tannenbaum, S. I., (1992). Toward an understanding of team performance and training. In R. W. Swezey & E. Salas (Eds.), *Teams their training and performance* (pp. 3–29). Norwood, NJ: Ablex.

Siskel, K., & Flexman, R. (1962). *Study of the effectiveness of a flight simulator for training complex aircrew skills.* Unpublished data, Bell Aeronautics Company.

Swezey, R. W., & Salas, E. (1992). *Teams their training and performance.* Norwood, NJ: Ablex.

Wiener, E. L., Kanki, B. G., & Helmreich, R. L. (1993). *Cockpit resource management.* New York: Academic Press.

Author Index

Subject Index